TAX JUSTICE AND TAX LAW

Most people would agree that tax systems ought to be 'just', and perhaps a great deal more just than they are at present. What is more difficult is to agree on what tax justice is.

This book considers a range of different approaches to, and ideas about the nature of tax justice and covers areas such as:

- imbalances in international tax arrangements that deprive developing countries of revenues from natural resources and allow wealthy taxpayers to use tax havens;
- protests against governments and large businesses;
- attempts to influence policy through more technical means such as the OECD's Base Erosion and Profits Shifting project;
- interpersonal matters, such as the ways in which tax systems disadvantage women and minorities;
- the application of wider philosophical or economic theories to tax systems.

The purpose of the book is not to iron out these underlying differences into a grand theory, but rather to gain a more precise understanding of how and why we disagree about tax justice. In doing so the editors are assisted by a stellar cast of contributors from four continents, with a wide variety of views and experiences but a common interest in this central question of how to agree and disagree about tax justice. This is, of course, not only an intellectual exercise but also a necessary precursor to achieving real-world change.

Tax Justice and Tax Law

Understanding Unfairness in Tax Systems

Edited by
Dominic de Cogan
and
Peter Harris

•HART•
OXFORD • LONDON • NEW YORK • NEW DELHI • SYDNEY

HART PUBLISHING

Bloomsbury Publishing Plc

Kemp House, Chawley Park, Cumnor Hill, Oxford, OX2 9PH, UK

1385 Broadway, New York, NY 10018, USA

29 Earlsfort Terrace, Dublin 2, Ireland

HART PUBLISHING, the Hart/Stag logo, BLOOMSBURY and the Diana logo are
trademarks of Bloomsbury Publishing Plc

First published in Great Britain 2020

First published in hardback, 2020
Paperback edition, 2022

Copyright © The Editor and Contributors severally 2020

The Editor and Contributors have asserted their right under the Copyright, Designs and
Patents Act 1988 to be identified as Authors of this work.

All rights reserved. No part of this publication may be reproduced or transmitted in any form or by
any means, electronic or mechanical, including photocopying, recording, or any information
storage or retrieval system, without prior permission in writing from the publishers.

While every care has been taken to ensure the accuracy of this work, no responsibility for loss or
damage occasioned to any person acting or refraining from action as a result of any statement in it
can be accepted by the authors, editors or publishers.

All UK Government legislation and other public sector information used in the work is Crown
Copyright ©. All House of Lords and House of Commons information used in the work is
Parliamentary Copyright ©. This information is reused under the terms of the Open Government
Licence v3.0 (http://www. nationalarchives.gov.uk/doc/open-government-licence/version/3) except
where otherwise stated.

All Eur-lex material used in the work is © European
Union, http://eur-lex.europa.eu/, 1998–2022.

A catalogue record for this book is available from the British Library.

Library of Congress Cataloging-in-Publication Data

Names: De Cogan, Dominic, editor. | Harris, Peter (Editor of Tax justice and tax law), editor.

Title: Tax justice and tax law : understanding unfairness in tax systems /
edited by Dominic de Cogan and Peter Harris.

Description: Oxford, UK ; New York, NY : Hart Publishing, an imprint of
Bloomsbury Publishing, 2020. | Includes bibliographical references and index.

Identifiers: LCCN 2020026409 (print) | LCCN 2020026410 (ebook) |
ISBN 9781509934997 (hardback) | ISBN 9781509935000 (ePDF) |
ISBN 9781509935017 (Epub)

Subjects: LCSH: Taxation—Law and legislation. | Tax administration
and procedure. | Fiscal policy.

Classification: LCC K4460 .T3844 2020 (print) | LCC K4460 (ebook) | DDC 343.04—dc23

LC record available at https://lccn.loc.gov/2020026409

LC ebook record available at https://lccn.loc.gov/2020026410

ISBN: HB: 978-1-50993-499-7
PB: 978-1-50994-552-8
ePDF: 978-1-50993-500-0
ePub: 978-1-50993-501-7

Typeset by Compuscript Ltd, Shannon

To find out more about our authors and books visit www.hartpublishing.co.uk. Here you will find
extracts, author information, details of forthcoming events and the option to sign up for our newsletters.

CONTENTS

About the Contributors .... *vii*

1. *Mapping Tax Justice Arguments* *1*
   Dominic de Cogan

PART I
CONCEPTIONS OF JUSTICE

2. *A Principle of 'Natural Justice': Sir William Petty's* Treatise of Taxes
   and Contributions *and the 'Royal Absolutist' Case for Excise* *17*
   Matthew Ward

3. *Balancing Conflicting Conceptions of Justice in Taxation* *35*
   Sonja Dusarduijn and Hans Gribnau

4. *(Un)Fairness as an Irritant to the Legal System: The Case of
   Two Legislatures and More Multinational Enterprises* *57*
   Emer Hunt

PART II
SOCIAL PROVISION

5. *Taxing for Social Justice or for Growth?* *81*
   Åsa Gunnarsson

6. *A Brief Theory of Taxation and Framework Public Goods* *101*
   Darien Shanske

PART III
CITIZENSHIP

7. *A Critical Analysis of How Formal and Informal Citizenships
   Influence Justice between Mobile Taxpayers* *117*
   Yvette Lind

vi *Contents*

8. *Immigration, Emigration, Fungible Labour and the Retreat from Progressive Taxation* *133*
   Henry Ordower

PART IV
INTERNATIONAL

9. *What May We Expect of a Theory of International Tax Justice?* *155*
   Dirk Broekhuijsen and Henk Vording

10. *Re-Imagining Tax Justice in a Globalised World* *169*
    Tsilly Dagan

11. *Between Legitimacy and Justice in International Tax Policy* *187*
    Ivan Ozai

PART V
JUSTICE AND PROCEDURES

12. *Tax Justice in the Post-BEPS Era: Enhanced Cooperation Among Tax Authorities and the Protection of Taxpayer Rights in the EU* *203*
    Christiana HJI Panayi and Katerina Perrou

13. *Tax Justice and Older People: An Examination Through the Lens of Critical Tax Theory* *221*
    Jane Frecknall-Hughes, Nashid Monir, Barbara Summers and Simon James

14. *Tax Tribunals and Justice for Litigants in Person* *241*
    Richard Thomas

15. *New Wave Technologies and Tax Justice* *261*
    Benjamin Walker

Index *281*

ABOUT THE CONTRIBUTORS

Dirk Broekhuijsen is Assistant Professor at the Institute for Tax Law and Economics of Leiden University and tax inspector at the Amsterdam Office of the Dutch Tax and Customs Administration.

Dominic de Cogan is Senior Lecturer in the Faculty of Law and Fellow of Christ's College, Cambridge.

Tsilly Dagan is Professor of Taxation Law at the Faculty of Law, Oxford University, Raoul Wallenberg Human Rights Professor of Law at Bar Ilan University and Fellow at Worcester College, Oxford.

Sonja Dusarduijn is Associate Professor at the Faculty of Law, Tilburg University.

Jane Frecknall-Hughes is Professor of Accounting and Taxation at Nottingham University Business School.

Hans Gribnau is Professor of Tax Law at Tilburg University and Leiden University.

Åsa Gunnarsson is Professor of Tax Law and Jurisprudence at Umeå University.

Peter Harris is Professor of Tax Law at the University of Cambridge.

Christiana HJI Panayi is Professor in Tax Law at Queen Mary, University of London.

Emer Hunt is Assistant Professor in the Sutherland School of Law, University College Dublin.

Simon James is Honorary Associate Professor in Economics, University of Exeter Business School.

Yvette Lind is Assistant Professor in Tax Law at CBS Law, Copenhagen Business School.

Nashid Rizwana Monir is Additional Commissioner of Taxes under the National Board of Revenue, Ministry of Finance, Government of the People's Republic of Bangladesh.

Henry Ordower is Professor of Law and past Co-Director of the Centre for International and Comparative Law at Saint Louis University School of Law.

Ivan Ozai is Tomlinson Fellow at the Faculty of Law at McGill University and a former tax court judge in Brazil.

viii   *About the Contributors*

Katerina Perrou is Assistant Lecturer at the University of Athens Law School and currently serves as Legal Counsel to the Governor of the Greek Independent Authority for Public Revenue.

Darien Shanske holds a J.D. from Stanford Law School, a Ph.D. from UC Berkeley in Rhetoric, an M.A. from McGill University in Philosophy, and a B.A. from Columbia University.

Barbara Summers is Professor of Human Judgment and Decision Making and Director of the Centre for Decision Research, Leeds University Business School.

Richard Thomas is a retired Judge (and previously member) of the First-tier Tribunal (Tax Chamber) and retired Assistant Director, HMRC.

Henk Vording is Professor of Tax Law at Leiden University.

Benjamin Walker is Senior Lecturer in the School of Accounting and Commercial Law at Victoria University of Wellington, New Zealand.

Matthew Ward is ECR Teaching and Access Fellow at the University of Oxford.

1

Mapping Tax Justice Arguments

DOMINIC DE COGAN

Tax justice debates are often framed in binary opposition between those who support lower taxes, a smaller state and greater self-sufficiency and those who support higher taxes and higher social spending. Whilst there is an element of truth to this caricature, the present volume reveals a much more complex patchwork of opinion in which it is possible to agree on some aspects of tax justice and disagree on others. This chapter presents an indicative map of these overlapping ideas whilst acknowledging that this is itself a contestable exercise in interpretation.

I. Introduction

What is tax justice? We can be sure that it is not the exclusive concern of academic theorists. It is something upon which almost everyone has a view, however inchoate. The wide currency of tax justice is useful to tax specialists as an entry point in discussing our work with others, but it is not an unmixed blessing. Tax justice can provoke strong emotions, yet it often seems that participants in 'debates' about it are in fact talking about very different things. This can lead to some quite confusing and superficial arguments, for instance between those who assert that 'corporations should pay their fair share' and those who assert that 'corporations already pay what the law requires'. These views themselves are of course far from superficial, but the assumptions underlying them need to be unpacked before there is the slightest chance of comparing like with like.

An obvious response to the indeterminacy of the term 'tax justice' is to devise and defend a definition and to use this as a starting point from which to interpret tax justice debates. This is a worthwhile endeavour and is carried out to varying degrees by all of the contributions to this volume. My colleagues explain themselves more fully than is possible in the limited space of this chapter, and accordingly it is not my aim here to summarise their arguments or indeed to defend my own conception of tax justice. The task of this chapter is the more limited one of sketching a map of the various approaches to tax justice that can be found in this volume.

This mapping task may at first sight appear to be value neutral, in the sense that it is irrelevant whether or not I agree with a particular view. My aim is to document the ways in which the contributors differ in their approach to tax justice, not to evaluate the decisions that they have made. All the same, even mapping the intellectual landscape involves some controversial decisions about which features of the debates to emphasise and which to downplay, or to be more specific, which difference of opinion to highlight as being particularly significant. My choices of issues to highlight are hardly hidden, forming as they do the subheadings of this chapter, yet they are inherently contestable. Indeed, they have already been contested by means of detailed and very helpful feedback on this chapter from many of the other contributors.

One point that is clear is that the common tendency to pigeonhole tax justice arguments into 'pro-tax' and 'anti-tax' camps has very little explanatory power in navigating the chapters of this volume. One of our contributors said in correspondence with me that 'the dichotomy of pro-tax and anti-tax is not so helpful, and I always think that it is biased'. For instance, one could in principle support higher taxes and more generous public expenditure yet oppose tax rules that failed to reflect a fair distribution of fiscal burdens, or which encouraged procedural unfairness. This highlights a critical point, which is that the contributions to this volume are best seen not as contributions to a binary argument, let alone expressions of a pre-existing agreement between authors. On the contrary, they showcase the sheer variety of overlapping opinions and emphases that are capable of being held on the topic of tax justice, with points of consensus complementing all of the disagreements. The strength of this volume, then, is its sheer diversity.

II. The Focus of Tax Justice Arguments

A. States and Taxpayers

A good starting point in navigating this diversity is in the distinction, suggested in conversation by Christiana HJI Panayi, between three different areas of focus. We might be concerned, first, with the relationship between one state and other states. An example of this is the discussion of the allocation of taxing powers and revenues *between states* that is often described as 'inter-nation equity'. Second, we might concentrate on the distribution of fiscal burdens *between taxpayers*. This might be extended to take into account cognate matters such as fiscal transfers and the distributional consequences of public expenditure. Third, our primary interest may be in the relationship *between states and taxpayers*, as may be seen in the debates concerning the rule of law, the protection of taxpayer rights and participatory democracy.

These areas of emphasis are helpful in highlighting the sheer range of topics that can be contemplated within the general description of 'tax justice' but are not equally easy to apply to the chapters of this volume. The *state-taxpayer* relationship is at the forefront of Richard Thomas's review of the treatment of litigants in person by the Tax Chamber of the First-tier Tribunal in the UK. The same might be said of Christiana HJI Panayi and Katerina Perrou's review of the protection of taxpayer rights within the EU, and of Tsilly Dagan's exploration of the tensions between revenue maximisation and the maintenance of a society of equals. Ivan Ozai focusses on *state-state* relations but argues powerfully that the achievement of fair distributive outcomes between states is a different question from the procedural representation of developing countries within organisations such as the OECD and that the two ought not to be conflated.

More difficult to categorise is Åsa Gunnarsson's argument in favour of a wider recognition of the role of tax in supporting social welfare goals. On the one hand, this raises obvious questions about the distribution of resources *between taxpayers* and *between taxpayers and the beneficiaries of public expenditure*. On the other hand, these matters are inextricable from Gunnarsson's explanation of social contract theory and more generally her understanding of *state-taxpayer* and *state-welfare* relationships. Similarly, the chapters of Henry Ordower and Yvette Lind show that questions of distributive justice quickly raise the further question 'distribution between whom'. This is brought into particularly sharp relief by the tax treatment of immigrants and expatriates, the extent to which tax treatments depend on citizenship and indeed what degrees of citizenship are relevant to tax law. A very different perspective on the same issues is offered by Matthew Ward, who looks at the role of taxation in constituting state-subject relations in respect of newly confiscated Catholic land in seventeenth-century Ireland and uses this history to contextualise the political theory of the time.

Even at this early stage, we have travelled a long distance from the simple binary notion of a debate between high-tax and low-tax commentators, or between large-state and small-state perspectives. Our authors have reached different decisions on what is important but in a way that suggests more a patchwork of opinion rather than a set-piece opposition between two monolithic approaches to justice. This sense of complexity and depth only increases as our journey approaches the next fork in the road.

B. National and Cosmopolitan

When thinking about tax justice, we might be most concerned with what happens within the borders of a given state. Alternatively, we might consider whether processes and outcomes are just, regardless of state boundaries. This has obvious relevance to distributive questions such as whether the justice of the tax/benefits position of a UK person ought to be compared only to other UK persons or to taxpayers and benefits recipients worldwide. It may also bear on the connected question of whether we view tax justice primarily as the responsibility of states or as an area of policy where close international coordination is indispensable. As

4 Dominic de Cogan

with many of the spectrums of opinion discussed in this chapter, it is easier to state the distinction between national and cosmopolitan approaches than to apply it to individual thinkers. However, a particularly clear statement of cosmopolitanism is made in the course of Dirk Broekhuijsen and Henk Vording's critical review of existing theories of international tax justice:

> Within Western countries, we have become familiar with raising 'justice' arguments with respect to modest, sometimes trivial, questions of tax legislation. When we look at justice on a worldwide scale, the issues are not at all trivial. They have to do with access to a decent life either in one's country of birth or in some better place of the world ...

It does not matter who you are or where you are. As a human, you deserve this access to a decent life, and tax has something to do with it. The complication is that, even if we hold that certain procedures and outcomes are deserved as humans rather than as citizens of a given state, national initiatives might still be the best (or only viable) means of providing these good things. There is something of this in the discussion of the taxation of older people by Jane Frecknall-Hughes, Nashid Monir, Barbara Summers and Simon James. Taxpayers within this category are likely to have certain common characteristics regardless of where they live, yet their actual experience is likely to depend on national choices as granular as the particular IT software used by each tax authority. In a different context but in similar vein, Gunnarsson notes that 'welfare programs are dependent on the fiscal culture of the nation state'. An even more extreme version of the same phenomenon is described by Ward, who shows that ideas about taxation may be directed to parochial and even sectional aims even if expressed in the most universal terms.

Many chapters in this book explore the interface between national and supranational approaches to taxation. As we have already seen, Ordower's and Lind's chapters look at the position of 'outsiders' in national tax systems, who may be described variously as 'immigrants' and 'expatriates'. The contributions of Dagan and of HJI Panayi and Perrou also act as correctives to a crude division between the national and the supranational. Dagan reminds us that in spite of economic globalisation and the mobility of some tax bases, there is still a widespread belief that a state ought 'to fulfil the collective will of its constituents as a society of equals in order to promote who they are as people ...'. Conversely, HJI Panayi and Perrou overturn the usual state-centred approach to the protection of taxpayer rights by showing that cross-border initiatives are not only compatible with such protection but may sometimes be essential.

C. Tax and Public Finance

A further divergence arises between those who focus narrowly on taxation and those who treat tax as an integral part of a wider collection of public finance problems. At least at first sight, some of the most familiar approaches to tax justice involve a radical abstraction of tax from its wider context. For example, when we think about the allocation of tax burdens according to 'ability to pay' or the need to exact an 'equal sacrifice' from the population, we tend to look first at the financial resources of taxpayers. We would accordingly expect the high earners and the wealthy to contribute more than those with more modest resources, either proportionately or on a progressive scale. We are less likely to think about the deservingness of individuals for welfare payments or other transfers from the state, or factors such as disability or structural disadvantage that can make it more difficult to earn income and require more of it to be spent on basic human needs. It is not that these matters are thought unimportant, but simply that the 'ability to pay' and 'equal sacrifice' frameworks allow them to be separated from the narrow question of how tax burdens ought to be distributed. The idea that similarly situated taxpayers should be treated similarly (horizontal equity) and dissimilarly situated taxpayers should be treated dissimilarly (vertical equity) is, if anything, even more consistent with this abstraction of tax from other questions.

In line with what John Snape and I have argued elsewhere,[1] this abstraction implies a certain view of the world whereby tax should either be insulated from wider political considerations altogether or treated as a predominantly technical matter with certain predefined outlets for political considerations (eg rate structures). Neither John nor I are comfortable with this view and we are joined by a number of contributors to the present volume. Perhaps the clearest expression of this discomfort is provided by Broekhuijsen and Vording, who argue that a narrow focus on tax burdens is an anachronistic survival from the eighteenth and nineteenth centuries when 'government activity was still limited to services of a "public good" nature' and in 'consequence, taxation was the main if not the only policy instrument that mattered to distribution'. In the twentieth century, by contrast, taxation became 'one of many government instruments', which meant that 'tax burden distribution lost its particular relevance to the positions of individual citizens'.

Lind offers a simple but powerful example of the considerations that become relevant once we abandon the attempt to analyse tax burdens in the abstract. She points out that rules that are formally neutral between potential taxpayers may be built upon a false assumption of gender neutrality in society more generally, '[r]esulting in the promotion of the male norm despite the system being formally gender neutral'. Frecknall-Hughes et al make the similar observation that a system of tax administration that assumes IT skills, reliable internet connections and good health may place the old at a systematic disadvantage. More generally, Gunnarsson argues that ideas about good taxation and welfare reflect 'fiscal culture', a point that is particularly and ironically obvious in Ward's relation of how 'natural law' was used in the seventeenth century to reinforce culturally embedded assumptions that now appear at best bizarre and at worst downright offensive.

---

[1] John Snape and Dominic de Cogan, 'Introduction: On the Significance of Revenue Cases' in John Snape and Dominic de Cogan (eds), *Landmark Cases in Revenue Law* (Oxford, Hart, 2019) 3.

6 Dominic de Cogan

III. Definitional Strictness

A temptation, at least for legal academics, is to insist that before speaking about tax justice we must achieve absolute clarity about how the term 'tax justice' is defined. There is an obvious merit in ensuring that participants in a debate agree what they are talking about before they then proceed to agree or disagree on the merits. However, it is also possible that something is lost by overemphasising definitional clarity. If, without deciding the matter for now, the object of our enquiry is an imprecise and fuzzy collection of ideas and feelings, then an overly precise attempt at definition may miss the entire point of what 'tax justice' is about. It is not a surprise, then, that our contributors take a range of attitudes towards definitional strictness. Without wishing to impose a straitjacket on colleagues who might see things in slightly different terms, it will be helpful to discuss these approaches in turn under the following headings: 'vernacular', 'philosophical tropes', 'relative justice' and 'absolute justice'.

At the least strict end of the spectrum is Emer Hunt's exploration of political rhetoric and its consequences for tax reform. It is not Hunt's primary concern whether political actors are using the language of tax justice correctly, but rather how they are using it, for what reasons and how it might have influenced legal change. Although she is most interested in what is said in legislative committees, for the obvious reason that they have a credible if sometimes indirect connection with what is actually legislated, we are all aware of even more informal ideas of tax justice. 'Big companies never pay their tax', 'the Tories hate the poor', 'the squeezed middle always loses out', 'why should hard-working people pay for the shirkers?' We do not need to agree with all or any of these sentiments in order to accept that they are worth studying and may sometimes have important real-world consequences.[2]

If Hunt's focus is on vernacular usage, several of our contributors take issue with the slightly more sophisticated but nevertheless irritating phenomenon of 'philosophical tropes'. This helpful term was used in the conference underlying this book to refer to the practice of adducing philosophers in support of views that one already holds, with the intention of adding additional weight to those views. The philosophical trope need not necessarily be representative of what the philosopher in question in fact wrote, and might not even be accurate. The point is that it is instrumentally helpful to the stating of an opinion. The clearest example of engagement with philosophical tropes in the present volume is Gunnarsson's dissection of what she terms the 'growth agenda' and in particular on the reliance on Adam Smith by commentators hoping to avoid the leakage of wider social and economic problems into tax policy. Irritation is expressed in a different direction by HJI Panayi

---

[2] I examine some of these consequences in the context of the taxation of the self-employed in Dominic de Cogan, 'CIR v National Federation of Self-Employed and Small Businesses (1981): All grievances converging on tax law' in Snape and de Cogan (n 1).

and Perrou, who warn a single-minded focus on avoidance and aggressive tax planning by multinationals tends to overshadow procedural propriety and risks turning tax justice into a mere 'slogan for the increase of the powers of tax authorities'.

Further along the scale of definitional strictness is the idea that it may be unnecessary, undesirable or even impossible to identify *perfect tax justice* but that it is nevertheless possible to say whether one situation is *more just than another*. This idea is most obviously associated with Amartya Sen, but recurs in various different forms throughout this volume. Broekhuijsen and Vording draw explicitly on Sen's elevation of pragmatic change over transcendental or 'other-wordly' conceptions of justice, but a similar approach is visible in Darien Shanske's idea of 'disgrace'. He argues that a refusal to fund certain public goods is not only bad but disgraceful, and that it is possible to identify and to alleviate disgrace without commitment to, or agreement on, any particular theory of justice. A 'relative justice' approach is also implied in the chapter of Sonja Dusarduijn and Hans Gribnau, who point out that the values underlying economic and legal approaches to tax justice do not always align. They also show, by reference to the 'Hillen incentive' in Netherlands tax law, that the political mechanisms used to reconcile and prioritise these values do not always work and may make things worse rather than better.

At the strictest extreme are those who believe that a theoretically robust definition of tax justice can be identified, even if it cannot necessarily be achieved in practice. At first sight, the most obvious example in this book is the identification of tax justice with natural law by seventeenth-century commentators, as discussed by Ward. However, even this turns out to have been intertwined with political compromise between the claims of Protestant landowners in newly acquired Irish land and the Crown's urgent need for revenues. Other authors in the volume have purchased clarity on the definition of tax justice by carefully confining the scope of their enquiry. For example, Benjamin Walker draws on well-known ideas of administrative justice in order to evaluate the risks and opportunities of increased use of technology by tax administrators. Not dissimilarly, Thomas appeals to a set of arguments that is familiar from the Leggatt Review of administrative tribunals in order to discuss whether the needs of litigants in person are being met by the modern tax tribunals. Perhaps the most categoric definition of justice in the entire volume is provided by Dusarduijn and Gribnau, who observe that:

> justice … regards the way in which benefits and burdens are distributed among men. Justice is *suum cuique*, to each his due. … The formula 'to each due' brings out the distributive character of justice. Principles of justice are therefore distributive principles.

This is helpful but operates at a very high level of abstraction, as becomes apparent when the authors characterise not only economic theory but also legal process values as – sometimes competing – concretisations of these 'distributive principles'.[3]

---

[3] The procedural approach of John Rawls likewise offers a useful framework for thinking about tax justice but is less conclusive on the necessary content of tax justice: see further Broekhuijsen and Vording, this volume.

8 *Dominic de Cogan*

Looking back at this whole section, it may be that what has been described is a series of techniques for dealing with the sheer elusiveness of tax justice: under-theorising, identifying opportunities for pragmatic improvements, restricting the scope of enquiry to certain relatively uncontroversial aspects of tax justice, or retreating to higher levels of abstraction. The suspicion must be that our search for a comprehensive, widely-agreed and relatively specific definition of tax justice has been inconclusive because there is no 'correct answer' to be found but only different layers of disagreement.

IV. The Content of Tax Justice

It is not by accident that I have left until relatively late in this chapter the most obvious question of all, that is, what our contributors believe are the substantive requirements of tax justice. This is partly because this is primarily their task rather than mine, but it also reflects a key argument of this chapter. That is that it is important not only *what* we think about tax justice but also *how we get there* and what assumptions and preoccupations we display along the route. Even when looking at substantive matters, though, there are a series of important decisions to be made about what to include within tax justice and why.

A. Procedures and Outcomes

The first of these decisions concerns whether we treat tax justice as a matter of outcomes or of procedures. Put simply, some commentators prefer to focus on the distribution question of how resources are best shared between governments and societies, and within societies, and others prefer to focus on the methods by which taxes are imposed and enforced. Yet the most passing acquaintance with John Rawls will remind us that these issues do not always come neatly divided. Rawls is of course primarily concerned with imagining a procedure by which we might imagine a just distribution of resources, but he refuses to follow the example of some libertarians who are willing to accept the results of procedures whatever they throw up. Instead, he complements his procedural theory with the 'maximin principle' whereby we should prefer distributive outcomes that improve the position of the least well-off in society.

A different type of cross-over between procedural and substantive approaches is to be found in the OECD's 'Inclusive Framework' on Base Erosion and Profits Shifting, which has increased the participation of non-members in the organisation's decision-making processes. As Ozai points out, this is a proceduralist approach which looks more to the fact of participation than to outcomes. It is clear from the OECD's publications that at least part of the motivation for the Inclusive Framework is substantive (eg to address the particularly heavy impact of BEPS on developing states) but Ozai argues persuasively that procedural legitimacy and distributive outcomes need to be considered carefully and that the former does not guarantee the latter.

If there are potential difficulties in using participation as a proxy for distributive justice, procedural approaches are on firmer ground when it comes to the relations between states and individuals. This is because, whether or not individuals have claims against states to any given distributive outcomes, we certainly expect to be treated with a minimum of respect and in a way that avoids unjustified discrimination and arbitrariness. In other words, what is often termed the 'rule of law' is important even if other things are also important. There is accordingly an approximate correlation between those commentators who focus on procedural justice and those who concentrate on state-citizen relations as discussed at the outset of this chapter.

B. Contextualisation

It was observed earlier in this chapter that there is a division between commentators who seek to examine taxation in the abstract and those who believe that tax justice is inextricable from wider questions of public finance, in particular public expenditure and welfare. Powerful examples of the latter tendency were found in the chapters of Lind, Frecknall-Hughes et al and Gunnarsson in the present volume. On closer inspection, however, this binary division turns out to be too crude. The question 'should taxation be abstracted from its wider context' does not conclude our analysis of tax justice but instead raises further questions. If answered negatively, we then need to ask what types of context are relevant and to what extent. These are matters of degree and judgement rather than binary classification.

In order to illustrate this, let us return to the idea that tax burdens ought to be distributed according to 'ability to pay'. As noted above, this is at least consistent with a radically abstract approach whereby tax liabilities are governed solely by financial income or wealth without any regard to other factors such as disabilities that make these resources more difficult to obtain or that increase non-discretionary expenditure. Few observers would wish to take such an austere approach to its logical conclusion, and indeed most real-world tax systems offer some special treatment for at least some classes of taxpayer (eg no income taxation of very low-earners, reliefs for childcare costs and so forth). In turn, it is possible for these treatments to be reconciled with the ability-to-pay principle, on the basis that a person with £X income and £Y childcare costs is less able to pay taxes than a person with £X income and no childcare costs. This flexibility in the ability-to-pay principle, which can be replicated in other conventional frameworks such as 'equal sacrifice', is nevertheless purchased at the expense of decreased certainty about what the principle requires in practical terms. Once again, we are returned to the question of which contextual factors are relevant.

10 Dominic de Cogan

There are compelling arguments for restraint in contextualisation. Whilst in theory it may seem worthwhile to include a wide range of personal characteristics in the determination of ability to pay, in practice this is likely to entail substantial complexity as well as heavy dependence on reliable access to detailed taxpayer information. Increased complexity is not necessarily to be disparaged,[4] but may have serious undesired consequences if it makes the law too difficult to understand, to administer, to comply with, or if it interferes too deeply with taxpayer privacy (eg with regard to the disclosure of medical conditions).

At the same time, too narrow an approach to contextualisation risks setting up arbitrary or ideologically charged assumptions about what is relevant to ability to pay, and treating any deviation from these assumptions as complexities that ought to be avoided. This point is brought out by Ordower, who uses notions of 'horizontal and vertical equity' in critical perspective, asking how these concepts ought to apply to immigrants whose inclusion on the scale of 'treating like cases alike' is precisely what is at issue. Gunnarsson states this line of critique more broadly, observing a tendency to use Adam Smith as a method of gatekeeping the tax field from certain extraneous influences. She explains that the continuing influence of Smith's principles of taxation, and in particular tax equity, demonstrate:

> the existence of inherent processes, in dogmatic legal scholarship, to delimit the influences of normativity from outside the law sphere. Therefore, when scholars move outside the box to discuss the basic normative foundations in the theoretical framework of tax law, they seem to need a strong footing in order to legitimise their perspectives.

This is deeply persuasive. The tax field contains a more or less universally recognised core of legal and economic principles, which can be examined without any special justification. Yet as soon as we either bring this core into question or simply decide to examine other questions such as social, political or historical context, a heavy justificatory burden lands on us to show that our work is valid and worthwhile. Indeed, whilst I would not presume to speak for John Tiley, one of the reasons why Peter Harris and I have continued the long-running *Studies in the History of Tax Law* series is to alleviate this burden and to provide a natural home for work that might otherwise be difficult to publish.

Perhaps the point that should be taken from Gunnarsson's insight is not that we should complain about having to justify ourselves but that a similar burden should be placed on 'core' scholarship. If academics cannot challenge widely accepted legal and economic principles, who else will? Once again, this point is put into sharp relief by Ward's chapter. The process of examining the cultural underpinnings of widely held intuitions about taxation in the seventeenth century unearths some ideas that seem deeply unattractive to twenty-first century eyes. Might the same be said of our own intuitions?

---

[4] See John Snape, *The Political Economy of Corporation Tax: Theory, Values and Law Reform* (Oxford, Hart, 2011) 175 ff.

C. Disciplinary Background

A possible contributing factor to differing views on the substantive requirements of tax justice is the disciplinary background of the observer, with philosophers, lawyers, economists, accountants, historians, political scientists, anthropologists, administrators and others perhaps likely to take different views. This may have something to do with the previous section, in that scholars who remain within the well-accepted 'core' of our disciplines may thereby develop a distinctively legal, or other, approach to justice in taxation. The problem with assessing these claims is that the present project was designed deliberately to downplay rather than emphasise disciplinary background. For a start, the selection process for the conference was extremely rigorous but did not treat academic disciplines as determinative despite the natural emphasis of the 'Centre for Tax Law' on tax law. The papers that were accepted, and a large number of those that with regret had to be turned down, had something distinctive and important to say, but this rarely if ever depended on the department in which the authors worked.

The CTL review panel was also motivated, in part, by our wish to include a variety of different perspectives rather than a room of people who already agreed with each other. It was therefore appreciated from the very outset that we would have to engage, if necessary in quite uncômfortable ways, with individuals whose entire worldview differed from our own. The outcome is that, even though each chapter bears the imprint of the professional background of its authors, I have not been able to trace any credible connection between these backgrounds and our substantive accounts of tax justice. This seems vaguely encouraging.

D. Political Positioning

A more credible explanation for the content of theories of tax justice is political positioning. At the very least, our political views seem to inflect the choices that we make when approaching questions of tax justice. For instance, without claiming any level of exactness, I would suggest that the following collection of views is approximately representative of right-of-centre opinion in the UK:

– the tax system is biased on the one side towards 'fat cats' and on the other side towards 'benefit scroungers', and against 'normal people';

– coercive powers in the tax administration are unacceptable and authoritarian, especially when directed against the aforementioned 'normal people';

– the distribution of tax revenues between states is less important, though the foreign aid budget is probably too high.

If a person holding these views were to think carefully about tax justice, the following further decisions on matters discussed within this chapter would be unsurprising:

12 Dominic de Cogan

- the courts provide the most convincing protection for taxpayers against state coercion, as per the influential right-wing legal theorist Albert Venn Dicey;[5]

- judicial control of tax administration need not impinge on the ability of democratically elected governments to enact their chosen tax policies into primary legislation, so long as the tax authorities apply this legislation in a faithful and procedurally fair manner;

- the distribution of fiscal burdens is primarily a matter for the normal democratic process and it is a mistake to pre-empt that process by over-theorising tax justice;

- in particular, it is legitimate for democratic representatives to adopt a sterner attitude towards welfare recipients (who take resources) than taxpayers (who provide resources).

In the same spirit of approximation, the following collection of views might be expected to command a reasonable level of acceptance amongst left-of-centre observers in the UK:

- tax systems ought to be biased towards the poor, vulnerable and underprivileged as part of a programme of correcting underlying biases within society;

- the procedural protection of taxpayers may well be important but is secondary to this redistributive imperative;

- national borders are not necessarily conclusive of redistribution and we should be aware of the claims of poor individuals and poor states outside the UK.

A person holding these views might reach the following further conclusions about the matters considered within the present chapter:

- following Murphy and Nagel,[6] taxpayers and welfare recipients are both reliant on state protection and are not analytically separate;

- whilst a legal and political system ought to protect individual rights, procedural nicety towards suspected tax avoiders should not automatically be prioritised over economic, social and cultural rights, such as the right to an adequate standard of living;[7]

- on the basis that certain distributive outcomes are thought desirable, tax justice needs to be defined with sufficient strictness to provide guidance on what those outcomes are.

I claim no particular validity for these sketches, and it is obvious that some on the political left might hold some of the views that I have labelled as right-of-centre, and

---

[5] See generally Albert Venn Dicey, *Introduction to the Study of the Law of the Constitution* 8th ed (Indianapolis: Liberty Fund, 1982).

[6] See generally Liam Murphy and Robert Nagel, *The Myth of Ownership: Taxes and Justice* (Oxford, OUP, 2002).

[7] See generally Philip Alston and Nikki Reisch (eds), *Tax, Inequality, and Human Rights* (Oxford: OUP, 2019).

vice versa. The point has only been to suggest that sets of ideas about tax justice may cohere, guided by the political ideologies of an observer, whether or not there is any strict logical connection between those ideas. Furthermore, and again encouragingly, we did not find a strict left-right divide amongst our contributors although some chapters are clearly inflected by political beliefs. To pick one of many possible examples, Shanske's highly emotive language of 'disgrace' expresses an urgent wish for increased social provision in the US, but he takes a strongly pragmatic attitude to the further question of precisely how improvements should be made and justified.

E. Shared Values

Instead of a clean left-right divide, what is to be found in this volume is a complex patchwork of views, in which political positioning is relevant to but not determinative of our accounts of tax justice. This may reflect the fact that despite differing on the 'forks in the road' discussed in the present chapter, we in fact agree on many things. Without claiming universal assent, most of us would agree that the distribution of tax burdens and government expenditure ought to be skewed in favour of the least fortunate; that a substantial level of state-provided services is defensible and desirable; that taxpayers should enjoy procedural protections under the rule of law; that claims of justice do not only arise within state boundaries; that tax avoidance can exacerbate the disadvantaged position of developing countries; that it is useful when calling for tax justice to have a defensible idea of what tax justice is beyond political slogans such as 'big companies are evil'; and that not all tax justice campaigns have met this seemingly basic standard. We do disagree on significant issues such as the proper focus of an enquiry into tax justice and the degree of priority to be given to taxpayer protections, but these cannot be slotted into a neat left-right axis.

The obvious conclusion to draw might, therefore, be that caricatured debates between pro-tax and anti-tax campaigners are *pointless* and ought to be discarded in favour of a more nuanced appreciation of where and how we diverge on questions of tax justice. For reasons that I discuss immediately below, and somewhat to my disappointment, I arrive at a slightly different conclusion. Nevertheless, on the basis of the contributions to this volume, we can certainly say that such caricatures are *inaccurate*. The idea that we had a room divided in two, with progressives on one side and conservatives on the other, or indeed that we were invariably progressive because of our academic background, is simply unrepresentative of our conference and of this book.

V. Conclusion: Campaigning

With this encouraging vision of shared values in mind, why do I not conclude that we should all drop partisan allegiances, understand our disagreements in a more

14 Dominic de Cogan

nuanced way and explore areas of agreement as well as divergence? After all, this chapter and this book may point the way to some quite surprising possibilities for co-operation between those of us who label ourselves quite differently on a political level. The problem is that this type of sophistication is simply not very useful for campaigning purposes. It is much easier to paint a Manichean picture of justice against obstruction, with all of those on the better side of the argument pulling together to overcome the obstruction.

At first sight, this may seem rather pessimistic or even sectarian, except that there may be some real substance to accusations of obstructionism. As I have argued in detail elsewhere,[8] the UK tax system has a deep strain of small 'c' conservatism and the same may be true of others. Moreover, there are good reasons of state-preservation for this conservatism. The failure to implement the reforms recommended by the Mirrlees Review is at the same time a refusal to improve the tax system and a refusal to put tens or hundreds of billions of pounds of tax revenues at risk without any real sense of whether they can ever be recovered.[9] The system is geared against change. In order to change anything, then, campaigners must struggle against a real inbuilt resistance, and in this context cannot possibly be blamed for a certain amount of caricature.

Perhaps the real tension, therefore, is between the reasons for *doing something* and *doing nothing*. In this sense, we really are unrepresentative as a group, on the basis that tax specialists who participate in a conference on tax justice must have at least some commitment to doing something; otherwise we would not have attended. A question that we really can contribute to, though, is whether we ought to prefer pragmatism or perfection, 'better' or 'best'. This is where things get really interesting, because in spite of our divergences on other matters, there is a strong emphasis throughout the book on the former. The subsequent chapters contain several spirited defences of pragmatism but nobody has mounted a full defence of perfection. This is, then, the message of the book: let's do better.

---

[8] Dominic de Cogan, 'Michael Oakeshott and the Conservative Disposition in Tax Law' in Monica Bhandari (ed), *Philosophical Foundations of Tax Law* (Oxford, OUP, 2017).

[9] Refer further to Dominic de Cogan, *Tax Law, State-building and the Constitution* (Oxford, Hart, 2020) 24–25.

PART I

Conceptions of Justice

2

A Principle of 'Natural Justice': Sir William Petty's *Treatise of Taxes and Contributions* and the 'Royal Absolutist' Case for Excise

MATTHEW WARD

This chapter traces the development of an argument for excise before the tax became a central feature of public finance in the British Isles. It finds a way into this argument through Sir William Petty's *Treatise of Taxes and Contributions* of 1662. The tendency to read the *Treatise* as a founding text of 'classical political economy' sterilises its argument for excise and the arguments for excise it inspired.[1] In seventeenth-century Britain, debates about the rights and forms of taxation were imbricated with debates in political and ethical theory. Excise greatly offended the political and ethical sensibilities of many in Britain, and before the 1640s arguments in its favour were seldom publicised. Petty's argument for excise depended on a concept of 'justice' defined in terms of natural law, which is one of the distinctive characteristics of what this chapter describes as the 'royal absolutist' case for excise. This argument developed on the ideological periphery of British politics and was facilitated on the geographical periphery of the British Isles. Irish politics formed a crucial context for the development of excise taxes and arguments in their favour. It is hoped that the case for excise identified in this chapter, connected as it is to natural jurisprudential theories of politics and ethics, will enrich the discussions of tax law and justice in this volume.

I. Introduction: Sir William Petty

Sir William Petty was born in 1623 into the family of a Hampshire clothier and died in London in 1687 a fellow of the Royal Society, a personal friend of the King

---

[1] F Amati and T Aspromourgos (eds), 'Petty Contra Hobbes: A Previously Untranslated Manuscript' (1985) 46 *Journal of the History of Ideas* 127, 127. See also T Aspromourgos, *On the Origins of Classical Economics: Distribution and Value from William Petty to Adam Smith* (London, Routledge, 1996) 2.

and a wealthy landowner.[2] His development of new ways of analysing political and economic problems also earned him the posthumous reputation as a founder of classical political economy and modern social science. It is easy to forget, then, that Petty lived much of his life on the geographical and intellectual peripheries of Britain, and that it was in these spaces that he developed the ideas for which he was later celebrated. Petty was one of the beneficiaries of the infamous Act of Settlement of 1652, which confiscated the land of Catholics involved in the rebellion of 1641 and the ensuing war. Catholic land was transferred to Protestants of English origin; and having undertaken the survey on which this transfer was based, Petty acquired 'sizeable estates' in five counties.[3] Petty's lands in Ireland, and the interest they gave him in the country's economy and politics, occupied him for the rest of his life. Ireland presented Petty with all sorts of problems. Land tenure was insecure and the institutions of law and government unstable. But these conditions also made for a roomier intellectual culture. In Ireland, Petty was free to enlist a wider range of what might be described as *avant-garde* intellectual resources to respond to the problems he faced. The *Treatise*, one of only a handful of Petty's works to be printed in his lifetime, is a case in point. Written in response to the politics of Irish land and finance in the early 1660s, its central argument, an argument for excise, belonged to a discourse on the *avant-garde* periphery of English royalism. Though the *Treatise* has matured into a canonical text of political economy, it started out life as a polemic in defence of an unpopular policy.

II. The *Treatise* in Context

When Charles Stuart was restored to the throne in May 1660, he faced two related problems which threatened the security of his Irish kingdom. He depended on the support of an army which had only reluctantly abandoned Henry Cromwell, the fourth son of Oliver, who had governed Ireland from 1655.[4] But to raise the taxes required to pay the army, Charles needed to reassure the Protestant proprietors in the Irish Parliament, of whom Petty was one, that their lands would be secure.[5] In 1661, Charles appointed the Duke of Ormond as his new Lord Lieutenant; and following his arrival in Ireland in July 1662, Ormond negotiated a new Act of Settlement

---

[2] T Barnard, 'Petty, Sir William (1623–1687)', *Oxford Dictionary of National Biography* (2004), available at www.oxforddnb.com.

[3] T Barnard, 'Sir William Petty as Kerry Ironmaster' (1982) 82C *Proceedings of the Royal Irish Academy* 1, 1.

[4] SJ Connolly, 'The defence of Protestant Ireland' in T Bartlett et al (ed), *A Military History of Ireland* (Cambridge, CUP, 1996) 232.

[5] In 1660, the Irish and Scottish administrations 'expected to spend roughly 90% of their total outgoings on their armies': W Ferguson, *Scottish-Irish Inter-Governmental Relations, 1600–1690* (PhD thesis, Cambridge University, 2014) 113. Petty was returned to the Irish Parliament for Enniscorthy and Inistioge: Barnard (n 2).

Sir William Petty's Treatise *and the 'Royal Absolutist' Case for Excise* 19

with Parliament.[6] In return, Parliament agreed to customs and excise duties on 'all … commodities, merchandizes and manufactures' and for the specific purpose of maintaining the 'army'.[7] It also adopted hearth money, a new levy of two shillings raised on every hearth or chimney.[8] The Act of Settlement was amended within months of its agreement and disputed throughout the Restoration, but the financial legislation was more successful.[9] Since customs, excise and hearth money were hereditary revenues, granted to 'his Majesty, his House and Successors yearly for ever',[10] they allowed successive monarchs to govern without Parliament until 1692.[11]

Petty published the *Treatise* in London in the summer of 1662, shortly before this legislation was passed.[12] At the time, the English Parliament was also negotiating a financial settlement for the Crown. Customs and excise levies were reinstated, though only on alcohol;[13] and hearth money was also adopted, though at a lower rate than in Ireland.[14] In the preface of the *Treatise*, however, Petty emphasised the Irish context of his intervention. Since Ireland depended on a 'great Army' to secure the country from 'future Rebellions', it 'should understand the nature and measure of Taxes and Contributions'.[15] In this respect, the *Treatise* might be read

---

[6] N Johnston, 'State formation in seventeenth-century Ireland: the Restoration financial settlement, 1660–62' (2016) 36 *Parliaments, Estates and Representation* 115, 131. See also C Dennehy, 'The Restoration Irish Parliament, 1661–6' in C Dennehy (ed), *Restoration Ireland, Always Settling and Never Settled* (Aldershot, Ashgate Publishing, 2008) 65.

[7] *The statutes at large, passed in the Parliaments held in Ireland* (Dublin, 1786–1804) 21 vols, II, 365–66.

[8] ibid, II, 504.

[9] Johnston (n 6) 135.

[10] 'Votes of the House of Commons of Ireland, for the grant to the King of two shillings yearly for ever …' Bodleian Library, Oxford [Bodl.], Carte 68, f 552r.

[11] I McGrath, *The Making of the Eighteenth-Century Irish Constitution: Government, Parliament and the Revenue, 1692–1714* (Dublin, Four Courts Press, 2000) 24.

[12] CH Hull (ed), *The Economic Writings of Sir William Petty* (Cambridge, CUP, 1899) 2 vols, I, 4. The *Treatise* may have been a pitch for office: T McCormick, *William Petty and the ambitions of political arithmetic* (Oxford, OUP, 2009) 135; D Coffman, *Excise Taxation and the Origins of Public Debt* (Basingstoke, Palgrave Macmillan, 2013) 198. The publication of the *Treatise* in London did not preclude a readership in Ireland. By 1660, a 'professional' trade in English books had been established in Dublin: R Gillespie, *Reading Ireland: Print, reading and social change in early modern Ireland* (Manchester, Manchester University Press, 2005) 79–83.

[13] Coffman concludes that 'a general excise was not realistic in England': *Excise* (n 12) 181–82; See also W Ashworth, *Customs and Excise: Trade, Production, and Consumption in England 1640–1845* (Oxford, OUP, 2003) 103–04; W Kennedy, *English Taxation: 1640–1799: an essay on policy and opinion* (London, G Bell & Sons, 1913) 55–56; P Seaward, *The Cavalier Parliament and the Reconstruction of the old Regime, 1661–1167* (Cambridge, CUP, 1988) 108–11. An excise on salt was proposed but rejected: E Hughes, *Studies in Administration and Finance, 1558–1825: with special reference the history of salt taxation in England* (Manchester, Manchester University Press, 1934) 136.

[14] M Braddick, *The Nerves of State: Taxation and the Financing of the English State, 1588–1714* (Manchester, Manchester University Press, 1996) 102.

[15] W Petty, *The Treatise of Taxes and Contributions*, in *The Economic Writings* (n 12) I, 5. The *Treatise* is seldom analysed in relation to Irish politics. This context is overlooked by those, already mentioned, who read the *Treatise* as a contribution to classical economics. McCormick, though more sensitive to its political context, concentrates on the extent to which it contributed to Petty's wider project of 'Universal Reformation': *Ambitions of Political Arithmetic* (n 12) 135–47. Others concentrate on the English context of the *Treatise* and integrate the *Treatise* into their stories of the development of the English fiscal state: Braddick (n 14) 114–15; Coffman (n 12) 197–99; Ashworth, (n 13) 55.

as a theoretical justification of the Crown's tax policy agenda, carefully timed for maximum political impact.

But the issue of land complicated Petty's attitude to Crown policy. The Act of Settlement did not simply reinstate the land titles of the new proprietors. Under the Act, a Catholic who had been acquitted of involvement in the rebellion was entitled to the immediate recovery of his lands, whether or not the Protestant occupant had been compensated.[16] This provision raised the possibility that Petty would be evicted from his lands, and he attempted to forestall it in the preface of the *Treatise*.[17] He imagined Ireland as a 'white paper' in which pre-existing claims of proprietorship had no bearing on the 'Settlement' that Ormond took 'in hand'.[18] Rather, the settlement was an 'opportunity, to pass into Positive Laws whatsoever is right reason and the Law of Nature'; and the law of nature accorded a conqueror a right to the property of the conquered.[19] Addressing the fundamental division in Irish Parliamentary politics, Petty attempted to reconcile the financial interests of the Crown and the property interests of the Protestant community. Natural law suggested a way of bridging these rival interests. It not only warranted the mass confiscation of Catholic land; it also justified the controversial excise and hearth money, described by Petty as an 'accumulative excise', on which Ireland's future security depended.[20]

III. Petty's Case for Excise

Petty considered a range of tax policies in the *Treatise* – customs, poll money, lotteries, benevolences, tythes and monopolies – but he concluded with an argument for excise. The 'perfect' form of excise was a tax on every commodity, calculated and levied 'just when it is ripe for Consumption'.[21] But since this was 'too laborious' a process, Petty settled for an 'accumulative excise': a single levy imposed on a 'Catalogue' of necessary commodities, which encompassed the labour and resources expended in turning the commodity into a consumable product.[22] Petty characterised the hearth money as an 'accumulative excise' and endorsed it as 'the easiest, and clearest, and fittest to ground a certain Revenue upon'.[23] But administrative efficiency and political convenience were not Petty's only 'Reasons for Excize'. Most importantly, the tax satisfied a principle of 'Natural

---

[16] JG Simms, 'The Restoration, 1660–85' in TW Moody (ed), *A New History of Ireland. III, Early Modern Ireland, 1534–1691* (Oxford, OUP, 2009) 422–24.

[17] The King to the Lords Justices of Ireland, 1st February 1662, Bodl, Carte 42, f 492r.

[18] Petty (n 15) 8.

[19] ibid 46. See also W Petty, 'An Answer to Twelve Queries' British Library, London [BL], Add MS 72883, f 60r.

[20] Petty (n 15) 94.

[21] ibid 91.

[22] ibid 92.

[23] ibid 94.

Sir William Petty's Treatise *and the 'Royal Absolutist' Case for Excise* 21

Justice' that 'men should contribute to the Publick Charge but according to the share and interest they have in the Publick Peace'.[24] A subject's 'share' in the public peace was proportionate to his 'Riches', rather than his 'Estates'; and since richness was simply the capacity to purchase commodities, his contributions should be aligned to his consumption.

This was an unusual characterisation of natural justice and an uncommon case for excise. As Petty acknowledged, excise had an 'odious' reputation in England.[25] An excise tax was first imposed by Parliament in 1643 and was levied throughout the Commonwealth. At first, it was justified as a temporary inconvenience, necessary to cover the expenses of war.[26] As complaints were raised that excise placed a disproportionate burden on the poor, this argument was embellished with claims that, insofar as the spendthrift paid more than the frugal, it was also equitable.[27] The exemptions from excise for certain commodities made it easier to argue in this moralistic vein that excise was a tax on luxury. But these arguments were of little use to Petty as he addressed the Irish situation in 1662. Though Cromwell had levied the excise 'indefinitely' following the dissolution of the Protectorate Parliament in 1655,[28] the Irish Parliament was the first to establish an excise on all domestic commodities as a hereditary grant.[29] This created the need for a case for excise as being just as well as necessary, and Petty found it in an older, 'royal absolutist' discourse about the rights and forms of taxation.

By the seventeenth century, indirect taxes on imported goods, or customs, had become a central feature of English public finance; but indirect taxes on domestic goods, or excise, were not imposed, and any attempts by the Crown to impose them faced widespread opposition. Although a case for excise was made by 'royal absolutists' in the early decades of the century, it was seldom publicised or printed. Elsewhere in Europe, excise taxes were adopted by governments and openly endorsed in print. In Holland, the financial backbone of the Dutch Republic, excise accounted for around 'two-thirds of all government revenues';[30] and Petty invoked the Dutch example in the *Treatise*.[31] An excise tax known as the 'alcavala' was also imposed in Hapsburg Spain and a case for indirect taxes developed around it. Nicole Reinhart has shown that in the moral-theological treatises of second scholasticism, the right of imposing emerged as 'the decisive category of sovereignty' and retained this position in Spanish 'Reason of State' discourse.[32]

---

[24] ibid 91.

[25] ibid 93. See also Braddick (n 14) 115.

[26] Coffman (n 12) 30.

[27] Anon, *Reasons and grounds for the necessitie, equalitie, and expediencie of an excise, to be granted upon the particulars contained herein* (Edinburgh, E Tyler, 1644) 3–4. Kennedy describes the general consensus that the poor should be exempt from indirect taxes: *English Taxation: 1640–1799* (n 13) 14.

[28] Coffman (n 12) 137.

[29] The excise on alcohol in England was not granted on a wholly hereditary basis: Ashworth (n 13) 16.

[30] M Prack, *The Dutch Republic in the Seventeenth* Century (Cambridge, CUP, 2005) 77.

[31] Petty (n 15) 59, 95.

[32] N Reinhardt, *Voices of Conscience: Royal Confessors and Political Counsel in seventeenth-century Spain and France* (Oxford, OUP, 2016) 123.

22 Matthew Ward

Francisco Suarez reclaimed civil and natural law as a combined basis for preroga-tive taxation in his *De Legibus* of 1612, and he refuted the claim, made by an earlier generation of scholastic thinkers, that taxes on consumption were unjust because they prejudiced the poor.[33]

The first sustained case for indirect taxes written in seventeenth-century England resembled Suarez's case in its use of civil and natural law. This was Sir John Davies's *Question concerning Impositions*, written in 1626 but not printed until 1656, which argued that customs could be imposed by royal prerogative and raised the possibility of taxes on domestic goods. An anonymous treatise, also from 1626, recommending an 'Excise' on the Dutch model remains unpublicised among state papers.[34] Following the failure of the 1625 and 1626 Parliaments to supply Charles I with adequate funds, the Privy Council established a 'commission' to consider the imposition of excise. Although the exposure of the scheme in 1628 caused consternation in Parliament, excise had become a viable policy option and was considered by the Crown throughout the 'personal rule'. It was in this context that Hobbes argued in *Elements of Law* that excise was demanded by natural law. Though widely circulated and copied upon its completion in 1640, the *Elements* was not printed in full until 1650 when a version of Hobbes's excise argument in *De Cive* was already available in print.[35] Taken together with a handful of other policy proposals, none of which were circulated beyond a small circle of Crown servants, they formed the 'royal absolutist' case for excise that Petty recovered in the *Treatise*.

IV. Sir John Davies and the 'Royal Absolutist' Tax Discourse

Sir John Davies was an English lawyer and crown servant who was despatched to Ireland in 1603 to serve as attorney general. He is best known to historians of polit-ical and legal thought as the exemplary expositor of the 'case for common law and custom'.[36] But the common law tradition and its practitioners were not as 'insular' as once imagined.[37] And since Ireland was a conquered country where the sover-eignty of the conqueror remained contested, the continental tradition of civil law,

---

[33] ibid 130.

[34] The National Archives [TNA], London, State Papers [SP] 26/43 I, ff 1-3v. In March 1622, Sir George Paul recommended a tax on 'necessary commodities' to the Duke of Buckingham but did not describe it as an 'excise': TNA, SP 14/128, f 92r. Both are discussed in FC Dietz, *English Public Finance, 1558-1641* (New York, American Historical Association, 1932) 194-95, 234.

[35] J Parkin, *Taming the Leviathan: the reception of the political and religious ideas of Thomas Hobbes in England, 1640-1700* (Cambridge, CUP, 2007) 20, 74-76.

[36] J Pocock, *The ancient constitution and the feudal law: a study of English historical thought in the seventeenth century* (Cambridge, CUP, 1957) 32.

[37] H Pawlisch, *Sir John Davies and the Conquest of Ireland: a study in legal imperialism* (Cambridge, CUP, 1985, 161.

Sir William Petty's Treatise and the 'Royal Absolutist' Case for Excise   23

which had more to say than common law about the attributes of sovereignty, was an indispensable fund of concepts for Davies.[38] He employed Jean Bodin's definition of sovereignty to explain the failure of England's conquest of Ireland.[39] And he also turned to civil law in a debate about the privileges of incorporated port towns in Ireland, a debate which raised questions about the rights and forms of taxation.

Since 1565, 'crown rights' had been transferred systemically to these towns as part of a 'successful campaign ... to expand English influence beyond the narrow boundaries of the English Pale'.[40] These rights included the 'control of all customs appointments and of customs revenue normally due to the crown'. By the turn of the century, the Crown wanted these powers restored, a shift in policy which was paralleled in Suarez's Spain where municipal taxes were increasingly regarded as 'dead wood that had to be cut away'.[41] In the *quo warranto* proceedings against the recalcitrant Waterford corporation, Davies cited the law of nations and the law merchant in support of the Crown's case.[42] He argued that whereas common law had little to say about customs, these branches of the civil law designated the levying of customs a prerogative right. Davies prevailed, and Irish customs revenue became 'a pillar of government finance' during James's reign.[43] English customs revenue also increased following the introduction of new, extra-parliamentary levies.[44] The Parliament of 1624 challenged the lawfulness of these levies;[45] and in 1625, following the accession of Charles I, Parliament broke with tradition by refusing the king the right to levy tonnage and poundage for the duration of his reign.[46] The following year, Davies wrote *The Question concerning Impositions*, in which he returned to the civil law tradition to establish a prerogative right to levy customs.

Davies dealt with the lawfulness of customs within the first six chapters of *The Question*: merchandise was a distinctive category of goods and levies on their exchange had a unique historical and legal basis. Since merchandise was 'transported' from one 'dominion' to another, it was governed not by English common law, which was 'Native and peculiar to our Nation only', but by the universal laws of

---

[38] ibid 161–65. See also G Burgess, *Politics of the Ancient Constitution: an introduction to English political thought, 1603-1643* (Basingstoke, Macmillan, 1992) 127–28; BP Levack, *The Civil Lawyers in England, 1603-1641, a political study* (Oxford, Clarendon Press, 1973), 144; and WN Osborough, *Studies in Legal History* (Dublin: Four Courts Press, 1999) 27–28.

[39] J Davies, *A Discoverie of the True Causes why Ireland was never entirely Subdued ...* (London, W Jaggard, 1612) 13–14; cf J Bodin, (JH Franklin ed and trans), *On Sovereignty: Four chapters from The Six Books of the Commonwealth* (Cambridge, CUP, 1992) Book I, ch 10.

[40] Pawlisch (n 37) 122–23.

[41] Reinhardt (n 32) 124.

[42] Pawlisch (n 37) 131. *Quo warranto*, 'by what warrant', was 'the 'judicial means' by which the 'King inspected and corrected those who misused corporate powers that derived from the King': P Halliday *Dismembering the Body Politic: Partisan Politics in England's Towns, 1650-1730* (Cambridge, CUP, 1998) 26.

[43] ibid 131.

[44] C Russell, *Parliaments and English Politics 1621-29* (Oxford, OUP, 1979) 60; Dietz (n 34) 177.

[45] Russell (n 44) 60.

[46] Dietz (n 34) 226.

24   *Matthew Ward*

nations and merchants.[47] Customs levies on merchandise were consistent with the 'common reason and equity' embodied in the law of nations; and they had been imposed by Kings according to this law before the development of positive laws.[48] The law of nations continued to govern merchandise through the law merchant, a 'branch' or 'part' of the law of nations; and it was according to the law merchant that present day Kings imposed customs levies.[49] The law merchant had been integrated into English law and its jurisdiction over merchandise was recognised by the common law. Whether or not 'Taxes and Tillages' on domestic goods required the consent of Parliament thus had no bearing, said Davies, on the King's prerogative right to levy customs.[50]

Had Davies concluded *The Question* there, however, it would have been a very different book. It would not have been as attractive to those who eventually printed it in 1656, when the Protectorate was scrambling to justify the imposition of excise by prerogative powers, nor would it have provoked as much debate among historians. But in Chapter Seven, Davies expanded his scope from the king's prerogative right to levy customs to 'the Kings Prerogatives in general', which he discussed with reference to the law of nature. Following the civil law authorities that he cited, Davies frequently spoke of the 'laws of nature and nations' as constituting a single corpus. In the opening passages of Chapter Seven, however, he distinguished the two in order to introduce his broader account of prerogative powers. 'By the Law of Nature all things were comon, and all persons equal, there was neither *Meum* nor *Tuum* [mine nor thine]'.[51] The law of nations 'brought in property'; and since the associated 'Contracts, Trade, and Traffiqye … could not be ministred without a King or Magistrate', it also 'took away the equality of persons'. The idea that the law of nations had introduced property and social stratification to an original state of common ownership and equality was well-established in the civil law tradition.[52] But it had been politicised by Hugo Grotius in *Mare Liberum*, his 1609 case for free trade and navigation, and there are reasons to believe that Davies was responding to Grotius's formulation.

Grotius followed the civil lawyers in distinguishing between 'proper' ownership and original common ownership but suggested that even proper ownership was developed under nature's instruction.[53] Nature instructed men to occupy and cultivate land to meet their physical needs; and when property was first established in law, the law imitated nature by recognising occupancy as the basis of propriety. Since the sea could not be occupied by men, it could not be owned; and

[47] J Davies, *The Question concerning impositions tonnage, poundage, prizage, custom, &c: fully stated and argued from reason, law, and policy: dedicated to King Hames in the latter end of his reign* (written 1626; London, 1656) 2.

[48] ibid 7.

[49] ibid 10.

[50] ibid 18.

[51] ibid 29.

[52] C Pierson, *Just Property: A History in the Latin West. Volume One: Wealth, Virtue, and the Law* (Oxford, OUP, 2013) 126.

[53] H Grotius, *The Free Sea (Hakluyt translation)* (ed D Armitage) (Indianapolis: Liberty Fund, 2004) ch 5.

Sir William Petty's Treatise *and the 'Royal Absolutist' Case for Excise*   25

since the territories of the state consisted in the property of its subjects, the state could not claim dominion of the sea. But another implication of Grotius's theory was that the acquisition and exchange of property, the substance of commutative justice, were governed by natural rather than positive law.[54] As Grotius clarified in *De jure belli ac pacis*, published in 1625, this reduced the need for state regulation of trade, which could and must be conducted freely according to natural law. 'Commerce' disseminated essential commodities to places where they would otherwise be unobtainable and no state had the right to hinder it by restricting the passage of merchants and 'Merchandize'.[55] States were entitled to impose customs duties on 'foreign Commodities' to 'recompense' for the costs of facilitating trade, but these duties could not be 'higher than the Reason for exacting requires; for on that depends the Justice of Customs and Taxes'.[56]

In the decade that followed the publication of *Mare Liberum*, the intensification of Anglo-Dutch rivalry encouraged James to reassert the Crown's historic claim to dominion of the sea.[57] Grotius needed to be repudiated, and John Selden and William Welwood attempted the task.[58] So too did Davies, albeit for reasons of domestic rather than international politics. The biographies of Davies and Grotius share some suggestive similarities. Davies had been taught civil law by Grotius's 'mentor' Paul Merula, a jurist at Leiden University;[59] and towards the end of the first decade of the seventeenth century, Davies also found himself grappling with the question of maritime dominion. In the case of the Bann fishery, Davies asserted the King's dominion of the seas to settle his right to a riverine fishery in Ulster.[60] Davies argued that the King's maritime dominions and the prerogative rights he exercised over them extended to tidal or 'navigable' rivers and the 'ports and havens' that adjoined them.[61] He repeated this claim in *The Question*, following his shift of focus in Chapter Seven to 'the Kings Prerogatives in general'.

Chapter Seven's formulation of the laws of nature and nations undermined Grotius's accounts of property and trade. Davies implied that property and Kings were established concomitantly, and he went on to describe the King as the 'Fountain' of both 'distributive' and 'commutative' justice.[62] To fulfil these

---

[54] R Tuck, *The Rights of War and Peace: Political Thought and the International Order from Grotius to Kant* (Oxford, OUP, 1999) 88–89; Pierson (n 52) 165–70.

[55] H Grotius, *The Rights of War and Peace* (ed Jean Barbeyrac) (Indianapolis, Liberty Fund, 2005) 3 vols, II, 443–44.

[56] ibid, II, 445.

[57] Tuck (n 54) 114.

[58] For Selden see Tuck (n 54) 113–20; for Welwood see TW Fulton, *The sovereignty of the sea: an historical account of the claims of England to the dominion of the British seas ...* (Edinburgh, W. Blackwood, 1911) 352–58.

[59] H Pawlisch, 'Sir John Davies, the Ancient Constitution and Civil Law' (1980) 23 *Historical* Journal 689, 695. For Grotius and Merula, see WSM Knight, 'The Infancy and Youth of Hugo Grotius' (1921) 7 *Transactions of the Grotius Society* 5, 12.

[60] Pawlisch (n 37) ch 5.

[61] J Davies, *A report of cases and matters in law, resolved and adjudged in the King's courts in Ireland ...* (1615; English trans: Dublin, printed for Sarah Cotter, 1762) 152–53.

[62] Davies, *The Question* (n 47) 76–77.

26 Matthew Ward

functions, the King was awarded an 'absolute and unlimited power' by the law of nations, and Davies made special mention of the powers of 'stoping and imbarring' trade and collecting 'Tributes and Customes'.[63] The initial chapters of *The Question* had implied that of the King's fiscal powers, only the power levy customs had survived the course of time; and Glen Burgess is satisfied that Davies left domestic property under the jurisdiction of the common law.[64] But subsequent chapters suggested otherwise.[65] Not only did Davies's interpretation of the King's *dominus maris* extend the King's prerogative power to levy customs deep into the territorial domain of the common law. Davies also argued that the king had the right to impose a number of other taxes but had voluntarily decided not to exercise it. The 'King of *England*', said Davies, 'hath and ever had as absolute Prerogative ... to lay Impositions' as 'any other King, Prince, or State in the world'.[66] This included impositions on domestic goods, or excise taxes, and Davies gave the example of the Spanish '*Alcavala*'.[67]

In the later chapters of *The Question*, then, Davies demonstrated how natural law, configured in a certain way, could be used to think afresh about the rights and forms of taxation. An account of natural law that rendered property and commercial society dependent on the distributive and commutative functions of the state, simplified the criteria by which a tax was adjudged to be necessary and just. Above all, it warranted the imposition of indirect taxes on imported and domestic goods. But the problem with *The Question*, at least for subsequent supporters of excise, was that Davies had tried to balance natural and civil law with the common law, and the common law imposed constitutional and geographical limitations on the use of prerogative powers. As we have seen, this tension manifested in the structure of *The Question* and muddied Davies's position on excise. But if Davies's ambivalence towards excise reflected the views of other Crown servants, in time these views would change. As the financial condition of the Crown deteriorated further, excise began to be discussed as a viable policy option.

V. Thomas Hobbes and the 'Royal Absolutist' Case for Excise

In the early years of his reign, Charles I faced a 'near crisis' in his finances: a combined consequence of his expensive military ambitions and the refusal of

---

[63] ibid, 30, 85.

[64] Burgess (n 38) 147.

[65] JP Sommerville cites these chapters to refute Burgess's interpretation of *The Question*: *Royalists and Patriots: Politics and Ideology in England, 1603–1640*, 2nd edn (Harlow, Pearson Education, 1999) 248–49. See also O Haivry, *John Selden and the Western Political Tradition* (Cambridge, CUP, 2017) 152–56.

[66] Davies, *The Question* (n 47) 148.

[67] ibid 156.

Sir William Petty's Treatise *and the 'Royal Absolutist' Case for Excise*   27

Parliament to grant him sufficient subsidies or the permanent right to levy tonnage and poundage.[68] Following the dissolution of Parliament in 1626, Charles appealed directly to the taxpayer to supply him with 'benevolences', an ill-conceived policy which was soon supplanted by the 'Forced Loan'.[69] The Crown may have thought that loans would be more constitutionally acceptable than an extra-Parliamentary tax. But since those who refused to pay the loans were often imprisoned without due process and removed forcibly from London, the policy provoked angry opposition nonetheless.[70] In 1628, Parliament listed the 'Forced Loan' alongside 'arbitrary imprisonment' in its Petition of Right, to which Charles acceded in June.[71] Charles then began to consider his other policy options; and in February 1628, he issued an abortive writ for Ship Money, the infamous tax to which he would resort in the 1630s.[72] But he also considered levying an excise tax, and his establishment of a secret 'excise commission' provoked an impassioned but often overlooked debate in the Parliament of 1628.[73]

In June 1628, just as the King was preparing to accept the Petition of Right, rumours of an excise commission spread throughout Parliament. Following the establishment of a Commons committee to investigate the rumours, Sir Edward Coke revealed the contents of the commission to a joint session.[74] The word 'excise' did not appear in the commission, but there was enough evidence, said Coke, to 'give us leave to fear that excises and whatever is comprehended in it was intended'.[75] Parliament's response to the commission stands as the most comprehensive record of public opposition to excise in Caroline England. Reflecting on whether to pursue an inquiry into the commission, Sir John Elliot remarked that 'If there were no more in this than the violation of our liberties we might sit still, but let us look to it as not only to that that infringes our liberties, but as to that that annihilates the state and government'.[76] Another Member considered the excise so 'Obnoxious to the commonwealth' that men would be justified to resist it 'even by force'.[77] The association of excise with continental absolutism and standing armies might explain the severity of Parliament's response. Nathaniel Rich presented excise and the threat of a Spanish-sponsored Catholic uprising in Ireland as two

---

[68] K Sharpe, *The Personal Rule of Charles I* (New Haven, Yale University Press, 1992), for the Crown's finances, 105; for war finance under Charles, 9–23.

[69] R Cust, *The Forced Loan and English Politics: 1626–1628* (Oxford, Clarendon Press, 1987) 2–3.

[70] ibid 58–62. See also LJ Reeve, *Charles I and the Road to Personal Rule* (Cambridge, CUP, 1989) 14–15.

[71] Russell (n 44) 344.

[72] Sharpe (n 68) 14–15.

[73] The commission is mentioned briefly in Russell (n 44) 338, Hughes (n 13) 116–17, and Coffman (n 12) 27.

[74] MF Keeler et al (eds), *Commons Debates 1628, Volume IV: 28 May-26 June 1628* (New Haven, Yale University Press, 1978) 241.

[75] ibid 296.

[76] ibid 200.

[77] ibid 191. Sir Robert Cotton was concerned that excise would provoke violence from the 'heedlesse multitude': *The danger wherein the kingdome now standeth, & the remedie* (London: s.n., 1628) 9.

28   *Matthew Ward*

components of a broader threat to English 'religion' and 'commonwealth';[78] and another Member discussed the excise in relation to the recent arrival in London of a garrison of German horses, which, he deduced, 'were for no other end but to make good those impositions'.[79] Parliament's actions were commensurate to its rhetoric: it demanded that the King disband the commission and imprisoned an Exchequer official as a token of revenge.[80]

The secretive inception of the commission obscures the arguments for excise employed by the Crown; but the statement that the Duke of Buckingham was forced to deliver to Parliament on behalf of the Crown hints at some of them and the sources on which they were based.[81] Buckingham's argument was slippery. On the one hand, he conceded that the right of the 'people' to 'consent' to taxes; on the other, he deferred to the King to determine when this right had been violated. Though Buckingham denied that the Crown was preparing to impose an excise, he took the opportunity to remind Parliament of the ubiquity of the policy in mainland Europe. He gave the Spanish 'alcabala' as an example and cited Suarez and Juan de Mariana as his sources. In the context of the 1628 Parliament, this was a provocative move. The previous year, in *Religion and Alegiance*, Roger Maynwaring had maintained the justice of taxing subjects according to their consumption of commodities;[82] and his supporting references to Suarez were cited against him by John Pym in a successful campaign in Parliament to have his book burned.[83] Having developed mainly in private counsels, the 'royal absolutist' tax discourse had now become public and was informing the development of Crown policy.

The 1628 Parliament did not deter the Crown from continuing to levy tonnage and poundage without Parliamentary sanction, or from considering the imposition of other indirect taxes.[84] Excises on victuals and alcohol were considered by the Crown on several occasions in the early 1630s. In 1632, an 'excise' on ale and beer was proposed, which was the first recorded instance of the Crown using the word to describe a proposed levy;[85] and the Lord High Treasurer William Juxon imposed a similar duty on wines in 1638.[86] The Crown's tax policy was particularly radical in Ireland. From 1632, Lord Deputy Wentworth forced successive subsidy grants through Parliament and attempted ambitious reforms to the collection of customs.[87] Despite these developments, however, more conventional policy

---

[78] *Commons Debates 1628, Volume IV* (n 74) 147, 169.

[79] ibid 191.

[80] MF Keeler et al (eds), *Lord Proceedings 1628, Volume V* (New Haven: Yale University Press, 1978) 647–49, *Commons Debates 1628, Volume IV* (n 74) 420.

[81] *Lord Proceedings 1628, Volume V* (n 80) 648–49.

[82] R Maynwaring, *Religion and Alegiance* (London, R Badger, 1627) 2 vols, II, 45.

[83] *Commons Debates 1628, Volume IV* (n 74) 108–09.

[84] Sharpe (n 68) 105.

[85] J Bruce (ed), *Calendar of State Papers Domestic Series, Charles I. 1631–1633* (London, Longman, Green Longman, & Roberts, 1862), 506, cited in Hughes (n 13), 117 n 455.

[86] Dietz (n 34) 283, 286.

[87] A Clarke, 'The Government of Wentworth, 1632–40' in TW Moody (ed), *A New History of Ireland. III, Early Modern Ireland, 1534–1691* (Oxford: OUP, 2009) 4, 243–69.

Sir William Petty's Treatise *and the 'Royal Absolutist' Case for Excise* 29

options continued to compete for the King's attention. He levied Ship Money from the mid-1630s and considered re-establishing the royal demesne or 'fisc'.[88]

Hobbes's *Elements* of 1640 constituted, among other things, an intervention in these debates about state finance. As in *The Question*, the discussion of tax policy in *Elements* was preceded by a claim about the development of private property from an original condition in which there was neither 'meum' nor 'tuum'.[89] Without the equivocation exhibited by Davies, Hobbes maintained that all claims of 'propriety' depended on the prior establishment of sovereign power, and this included propriety over one's person and money.[90] The sovereign thus had the right to tax his subjects to cover the costs of maintaining the public peace: the reason for his institution. Since every subject had an equal share in this peace, however, the 'law of nature' required that 'the Burthens and Charges of the Common Wealth' were also shared equally.[91] Hobbes concluded that the 'most equal' and undemanding way of 'dividing the burden of the publick charge', was for 'every man' to 'contribute according to what he spendeth', and he therefore endorsed a tax on every purchase that subjects made for 'their own provision'.

In his *De Cive* of 1642, Hobbes refined his case for excise and argued it more carefully. He repeated the claim that 'sovereigns are obliged by natural law to impose the burdens of the commonwealth equally upon the subjects'.[92] He also claimed that doing so would propitiate reluctant taxpayers, for it was unequal rather than heavy taxes that really vexed them. But he then proceeded to clarify that 'Equality' in relation to taxes 'does not mean monetary equality, but equality of burden, i.e. proportionate equality between burdens and benefits. For although all men equally enjoy peace, the benefits of peace are not equal for all'.[93] A flat-rate levy like poll-money, though an equal tax, was therefore unacceptable to Hobbes because it did not account for the inequality of 'benefits'. Of the two ways of measuring the 'benefits' that a subject accrued from the commonwealth, the value of his property or the size of his expenditure, the latter was the more equitable.[94] Taxing what subjects already possessed disproportionately favoured those who were prone to 'extravagant living' and had wasted all they had owned. Taxing expenditure on the other hand, accounted more accurately for the possessions that a subject had enjoyed 'by virtue of the commonwealth'. Hobbes rehearsed these

---

[88] For Ship Money see C Russell, *The Fall of the British Monarchies 1637–1642* (Oxford, OUP, 1991) ch 1. For the 'fisc' see J Bruce (ed), *Calendar of State Papers, Domestic Series, of the Reign of Charles I, 1635* (London: Longman, Green, Longman, Roberts, & Green, 1865) 515. See also GL Harris, 'Medieval Doctrines in the Debates on Supply, 1610-1629' in K Sharpe (ed), *Faction and parliament: essays on early Stuart history* (Oxford, Clarendon Press, 1978) 90.

[89] T Hobbes (ed M Rook), *Elements of Law*, in *The English Works of Thomas Hobbes* (Charlottesville: InteLex, 1995) 108.

[90] ibid 138–40; 170.

[91] ibid 181.

[92] T Hobbes, eds R Tuck et al, *On the Citizen*, 3rd edn (Cambridge, CUP, 2018) 147.

[93] ibid 147–48.

[94] ibid 148.

30 Matthew Ward

arguments in his *Leviathan* of 1651 alongside a swipe at the idea of re-establishing the royal demesne.[95]

Hobbes was personally involved in the fiscal politics of Caroline England. He had assisted the Cavendish family in collecting the 'Forced Loan' in Derbyshire, and his association with the 'heavy-handed approach of the Cavendishes' to the collection of Ship Money seems to have scuppered his chances of a Parliamentary seat in 1640.[96] It has been suggested by Johan Sommerville and Noah Dauber that Hobbes's support for excise is evidence of his 'sensitivity' to the unpopularity of Ship Money and particularly the complaint that Ship Money rates were calculated unfairly.[97] Dauber cites Hobbes's support for excise in *Elements* as supporting evidence for the claim that Hobbes was 'for a more participatory state', one equipped with mechanisms for adjusting policy in response to public opinion.[98] Considered in relation to the debates about taxation reconstructed in this chapter, however, these readings seem to soften Hobbes's argument for excise. They overlook the equivalent unpopularity of excise, the events of 1628 that solidified its reputation, and the subsequent incongruity of the claim that it was in accordance with natural law.

For this claim to be palatable, one must have already digested Hobbes's prior claims about natural law and its role in the creation of civil society: namely, that civil society was constituted by a covenant, under which men transferred their natural right to a sovereign in agreement with the first law of nature ('to seek peace').[99] In *Elements*, Hobbes discussed tax in relation to 'the law of nature' in general, but in *De Cive* he referred specifically to '*Aequitas*', 'fairness' or 'equity'; and an examination of Hobbes's concept of equity quickly leads us back to the first principles of his political theory.[100] Having been used as a synonym for 'distributive justice' in *Elements*, equity retained this meaning *De Cive* and *Leviathan*.[101] Equity was the observance in practice of the law of equality which instructed men to treat one another as natural equals.[102] Whoever was entrusted to 'distribute *Right*' or arbitrate disputes should be 'fair to both sides'. But since equity and equality were constitutive of 'Justice', the third law of nature, which consisted in fidelity to

---

[95] T Hobbes, *Leviathan* (ed R Tuck), 2nd edn (Cambridge, CUP, 1991), for excise, 238–39; for the demesne, 172–73.

[96] N Dauber, *State and Commonwealth: The Theory of the State in Early Modern England, 1549–1640* (Princeton, Princeton University Press, 2016) 201.

[97] JP Sommerville, *Thomas Hobbes: Political Ideas in Historical Context* (Basingstoke, Macmillan, 1992) 100; Dauber (n 96) 222.

[98] Dauber (n 96) 222. Having made his case for excise as an equitable tax, Hobbes argued for a 'free and open way for the presenting of grievances to … the sovereign authority': Hobbes, *Elements* (n 89) 182. This passage forms the basis of the Dauber's claim, which seems to conflate the ventilation of a grievance with a more positive act of political participation.

[99] Hobbes, *Elements* (n 89) 75; Hobbes, *On the Citizen* (n 92) 34; Hobbes, *Leviathan* (n 95) 92.

[100] T Sorell, 'Law and equity in Hobbes' (2016) 19 *Critical Review of International Social and Political Philosophy* 35.

[101] Hobbes, *Elements* (n 89) 88; Hobbes, *On the Citizen* (n 92) 50; Hobbes, *Leviathan* (n 95) 108.

[102] Hobbes, *On the Citizen* (n 92) 50.

Sir William Petty's Treatise *and the 'Royal Absolutist' Case for Excise*   31

the original covenant that established civil society, their meaning was determined by the principles and requirements of this covenant.[103] Natural equality must be 'admitted', said *Leviathan*, so that men would agree to 'enter into conditions of Peace'.[104] Hobbes collapsed equity into justice and justice into self-preservation and the abnegation of natural right.[105] An equitable policy was one that observed men's equality as members of civil society; that is, as participants in a covenant which secured their common and equal protection.

Hobbes's case for excise as an equitable and equal tax was thus remarkably *in*sensitive to contemporary political and ethical sensibilities, for his natural law theory reconfigured these concepts and distorted their conventional meaning. The connection between tax and armies in Hobbes's theory, the connection that had so concerned opponents of excise in the Parliament of 1628, underlines this point. Since an equitable policy was one that satisfied the principles of the covenant, and subjects entered into the covenant to preserve their lives from violent death, excise was all the more equitable for its capacity to sustain a permanent military force. *De Cive* argued that the maintenance of such a force was one of the 'essential' duties of the sovereign. To guarantee its security from external threats, a state should be '*forearmed*', and this meant that 'money for war must be accumulated in time of peace'.[106] Taxes were simply 'the wages of those who keep watch under arms'. *Leviathan* repeated this description of taxes but also coined a definition of war which reinforced the necessity of a permanent military force and a regular tax to sustain it. War, said Hobbes, 'consisteth not in actuall fighting; but in the known disposition thereto', and he identified interstate relations as an example of such a condition.[107] He thereby elided the distinction between wartime and peacetime that Parliamentarians had drawn to dispute the need for prerogative or regular taxation.[108]

Hobbes had an unorthodox political theory; but he also had a strategy to propagate this theory and this involved seducing his readers 'with familiar or attractive positions'.[109] It is important to be aware of this when we consider his case for excise. The case fell out of an account of natural law which suggested a wholly new formula for thinking about the rights and forms of taxation. Davies had also used natural law to challenge contemporary ways of thinking about tax, but his account of natural law coexisted uneasily with his account of positive law which tended to more conventional conclusions. There was no such tension in Hobbes's account.

---

[103] Hobbes, *Leviathan* (n 95) 100–01.
[104] ibid 107.
[105] Sorell (n 100) 35.
[106] Hobbes, *On the Citizen* (n 92) 146.
[107] Hobbes, *Leviathan* (n 95) 88–90.
[108] The main issues at stake in the Ship Money case were whether the tax was necessary to secure the safety of the realm and whom had the right to make that judgement: P Miller, *Defining the Common Good: Empire, Religion and Philosophy in Eighteenth-Century Britain* (Cambridge, CUP, 2004) 13.
[109] J Parkin, 'The Reception of Hobbes's *Leviathan*' in P Springborg (ed), *Cambridge Companion to Hobbes's Leviathan* (Cambridge, CUP, 2007) 444.

32   Matthew Ward

Tax could be discussed exclusively in terms of natural law for natural and positive law 'contain each other, and are of equall extent'.[110] The first and second laws of nature instructed men to 'seek peace' and to do so by way of a covenant; and the remainder, including the laws of justice and equity, guided subjects and sovereigns alike as to how to maintain this covenant. This account of natural law empowered the sovereign to impose regular taxes and instructed him to tax the consumption of commodities. Hobbes thus allowed the Crown a right and form of taxation that it increasingly sought but was repeatedly denied.

VI. The *Treatise* Revisited

By the time Parliament imposed the excise in 1643, a case for indirect taxes had already been developed by civil and natural lawyers on the *avant-garde* periphery of English royalism. In *Elements*, Hobbes had produced the only thoroughly theorised case for excise in Caroline England. Though the King imposed an excise in 1644, the tax soon became associated with the Parliamentary and Protectorate regimes. In the late 1640s royalists even attempted to exploit popular opposition to the excise by denouncing it for its effects on the poor.[111] The case for the Parliamentary and Commonwealth excise taxes shared little with the 'royal absolutist' case, however, and it is telling that the latter only re-emerged when Cromwell levied the tax 'indefinitely' by prerogative powers.

Perhaps the only exception was Henry Parker's *The Standard of Equality*, published under the alias Philo-Dicæus in 1647, as provincial opposition to the Parliamentary excise swelled into violent unrest.[112] Responding to the preferences of his gentry patrons in the Long Parliament,[113] Parker deployed several novel arguments in favour of excise. The most striking was his suggestion that excise justified property requirements for election to Parliament: the heavier burden borne by the gentry qualified their claims to privileged status.[114] The endorsement of excise along with a cluster of proposals to 'inspirit' trade and technological development also betokened a newer genre of English excise argument, developed in the Interregnum.[115] But arguing ambitiously and, in this context, unusually, for the establishment of excise on a permanent basis, brought Parker into contact with the older, royal absolutist case for excise.[116] Excise, he argued, satisfied the

---

[110] Hobbes, *Leviathan* (n 95) 185.

[111] Coffman (n 12) 54.

[112] M Braddick, 'Popular Politics and Public Policy: The Excise Riot at Smithfield in February 1647 and its Aftermath' (1991) 34 *The Historical Journal* 597, 597–626.

[113] Burgess (n 38) 187.

[114] Philo-Dicæus, *The Standard of equality. In Subsidiary taxes & payments* (London: D.H., 1647) 35–36, (unpaginated: references to numbered points).

[115] ibid 30.

[116] It is possible that Parker had read Hobbes's case for excise. For his connection with Hobbes see Parkin (n 35) 27–32.

Sir William Petty's Treatise *and the 'Royal Absolutist' Case for Excise* 33

principle that 'all Persons whatsoever, partaking of protection in the State, should share likewise equally in their payments, thereunto, according to their several proportions'.[117] And this, he said, was 'a rule of such undeniable Justice, that Nature it self might seeme to have dictated it'. Parliament did not have the time to test Parker's dubious prediction that the intrinsic equality of excise would eventually subdue the 'riots' that its imposition had provoked.[118] The policy was altered in response to the opposition,[119] and the case for its 'Natural Justice' did not recur in print until Petty published the *Treatise* in 1662 as a contribution to debates about Irish land and finance.

As we have seen, Ireland had facilitated the development of the 'royal absolutist' tax discourse under the early Stuart monarchy. Its partial conquest and the associated problems of government meant that the need for prerogative and indirect taxation was especially urgent. The same circumstances, however, afforded the Crown the freedom to experiment with a wider range of tax policies and with a wider range of legal arguments to defend them. In the early 1660s, Ireland was recently re-conquered and presented the Crown once again with both the necessity and the opportunity to pursue a radical tax policy agenda. The Irish Parliament cooperated with the Crown in return for a favourable land settlement for Protestant landowners and in order to fund an army to uphold that settlement. To address this political situation Petty needed a formula for thinking about taxation that justified indirect taxes, particularly excise, and for the purposes of maintaining an army; and this was to be found only in 'royal absolutist' discussions of tax.

It was not Petty's style to engage directly with other literature: the format of the *Treatise*, with its clipped prose and dense statistics, did not accommodate that sort of engagement. His engagement with 'royal absolutist' discourse can be established with some certainty, however. Petty acknowledged the royalist lineage of the political language he employed in the *Treatise*: he elaborated his conception of 'Sovereignty' in a coded rebuke of regicides and defence of Stuart authority.[120] We also know that the key contributors to the discourse were characters in his mental world: as well as being personally acquainted with Hobbes and sympathetic to his work,[121] he also read Davies and Suarez.[122] The formulation of Petty's case for excise, however, suggests that he was 'thinking with' Hobbes specifically.[123] Petty's argument for the justice of excise, like Hobbes's, involved an account of the origins and purpose of political society. A few years earlier, Petty had thought with Hobbes about this subject in a paper on 'systems of government'. Though the

---

[117] Philo-Dicæus (n 114) 7.

[118] ibid 27.

[119] Braddick (n 112) 625.

[120] Petty (n 15) 23.

[121] Q Skinner, 'Thomas Hobbes and His Disciples in France and England' (1966) 8 *Comparative Studies in Society and History* 153, 155; 160–163.

[122] For Suarez see Sir W Petty to R Southwell, September 1685, *The Petty-Southwell Correspondence, 1676-1687* (London: Routledge, 1997) 158–59. For Davies see W Petty, *The Political Anatomy of Ireland*, in *The Economic Writings* (n 12), I, 155.

[123] M Ward, '*Thinking with Hobbes*': *Political thought in Ireland, 1660-1730* (DPhil thesis, Oxford University) ch 1.

34 Matthew Ward

paper critiqued Hobbes's case for monarchy, it incorporated Hobbes's idea that all political societies originated with a 'transfer' of 'power' from 'the people';[124] and he returned to this idea in the *Treatise*. Tax was the medium by which a 'multitude of men' communicated their collective power to the sovereign to secure their 'Government and Protection'.[125] This established the sovereign's right to impose taxes; and Petty asserted this right with reference to 'Ship-Money'.[126] But it also determined the form that taxation should take. Since taxes were the price that subjects paid for 'Publick Peace', they should 'contribute to the Publick Charge but according to the share and interest' they had in this peace, and this was proportionate to their general consumption.[127]

It seems that Petty's argument for excise was picked up by the policymakers in Ireland that he wrote to influence: the Irish Parliament's 1662 'Act for the settling of the Excise' justified the tax as the 'most equal and indifferent levy that can be made and layed upon the people'.[128] In England, where the political nation remained roundly opposed to a general excise, this crisp justification of the tax appealed to its proponents. A 1663 pamphlet described excise as 'equal and indifferent',[129] as did Sir Joseph Williamson, the secretary of state.[130] Of all of Petty's projects, the *Treatise* was the most successful in his lifetime, a period marked by successive crises in the Crown's finances. In 1671, months before the 'Stop of the Exchequer', Petty was invited by the Crown to submit a proposal for a tax on 'all Persons and Things'.[131] And in the late 1670s, when the Crown was struggling to meet the costs of its bellicose foreign policy, associates of the dukes of Ormond and York engineered the publication of a third edition of the *Treatise* and developed its argument for excise in print.[132] In all, four editions of the *Treatise* were published before Petty's death in 1687. The contemporary reception of the text underlines its polemical character: it was used to argue for the justice of a profoundly unpopular policy. This argument was contingent upon a highly contested concept of justice, defined in relation to a specific account of the origin and purpose of political society. The *Treatise* was eventually canonised as 'classical political economy', and taxes on domestic consumption became central features of public finance. The justice of these taxes is still debated, but political theory is not, perhaps, as prominent a category in the debate as it used to be. Further investigation of the historical relationship between political theory and forms of taxation may broaden our understanding of how the taxes we have inherited were first conceived as being just.

---

[124] Amati and Aspromourgos (n 1) 130. Cf Hobbes, *On the Citizen* (n 92) 73.
[125] Petty (n 15) 18, 38.
[126] ibid 34.
[127] ibid 91.
[128] *Statutes passed in Ireland* (n 7) II, 365.
[129] Anon, *Considerations touching the Excise of Native and Foreign Commodities* ... (1663, London) 2. The pamphlet is dated by Coffman: *Excise* (n 12) 196.
[130] ibid 196–97.
[131] W Petty, 'Proposal for a proportionate taxation made by order of Charles II' BL, Add MS 72865, f 24r.
[132] Ward (n 123) ch 3.

3

Balancing Conflicting Conceptions of Justice in Taxation

SONJA DUSARDUIJN AND HANS GRIBNAU

This chapter elaborates on different conceptions of justice. Economic justice aims at correcting market outcomes to warrant a fair distribution of resources, whereas tax justice focuses on the fair distribution of the tax burden. Both elements of distributive justice have their own 'domain-specific' principles. These principles may collide. Hence, balancing both elements of distributive justice is necessary.

However, a balance also has to be sought between economic justice and legal justice and its core principles, such as legal equality, legal certainty and proportionality. Legal justice and economic justice pose diverging demands which the legislature should carefully balance. However, hasty parliamentary decisions and political decisiveness often seem to prevail over respect for legal values and principles, such as legal certainty and equality. This has been explained with an example of Dutch tax legislation: the (rapid) evolvement of an instrumental incentive in the tax regulation for homeownership.

Tax regulations therefore require a more careful political reflection on the fundamental tension between the focus on ends which are external to the law and legal principles. Moreover, the use of tax legislation for external ends should also be balanced with tax law's internal values and principles of tax fairness – foremost the ability-to-pay principle.

I. Introduction

Taxes are an important means to generate revenues for the provision of public goods, such as defence, health care, public education, infrastructure and social security. Governments pursue some of these public goods for the sake of economic justice. This can be done by the use of various policy instruments such as command and control regulation, permits and subsidies. However, taxes are also used as a policy instrument in their own right to enhance economic justice, for example to redistribute resources and to promote employment. In this way, policy goals are put in tax legislation and become part of the tax system, that is, a complex body of legal rules. However, both the tax system and the legal system aim for particular kinds of justice, tax justice and legal justice respectively.

Thus, various conceptions of justice are involved in taxation: economic justice, tax justice and legal justice. Economic justice aims for a fair distribution of economic burdens and benefits. Tax justice refers to a fair distribution of the tax burden. Economic justice and tax justice are thus both forms of distributive justice. Legal justice regards the justice of the legal system and should therefore respect principles of legal justice. Hence, tax laws should meet certain legal justice requirements. We will elaborate on the principles of legal (formal) equality, legal certainty and transparency – some of the main principles of legal justice. Importantly, the different kinds of justice – economic justice, tax justice and legal justice – may conflict.

The use of tax law to enhance economic justice often does not respect legal principles. For one thing, government's policies often change as well as the instruments employed to achieve these goals, resulting in a lack of both constancy and consistency of the law. Moreover, legislation often comes about hastily without ample deliberation and based on political compromise, often resulting in lack of clarity. Furthermore, the overuse of the law to achieve disparate policy goals and objectives has resulted in the excessive complexity of tax law – at the expense of, for example, certainty, equality and transparency. In practice, it seems that the legislature often implements policy goals aiming at economic justice without respecting the nature of tax law itself and its fundamental legal values and principles.

In order to get a better understanding of these conflicting values we will analyse a provision in Dutch tax law. This provision shows a conflict between, on the one hand, tax provisions which aim to enhance economic justice by using the tax system and, on the other hand, principles of tax justice (which itself is a form of economic justice inherent to the tax system) and the principles of legal justice.

This chapter is structured as follows. In the next section we will present a brief analysis of the various conceptions of justice employed: economic justice, tax justice and legal justice. Then, we will analyse a tax provision, which exemplifies the conflict between the aim of enhancement of economic justice by using the tax system, on the one hand, and various principles of legal justice, on the other. We will analyse the (rapid) evolution of an instrumental incentive in the tax regulations for homeownership. The successive changes were partly driven by economic justice considerations, namely mitigating or even preventing large financial risks for homeowners. The last section will wrap up the argument in a conclusion.

With regard to methodology, this chapter combines a political and legal philosophical approach of social, economic, tax and legal justice with an in-depth analysis of a Dutch tax provision applying different conceptions of justice.

II. Conceptions of Justice

A. Concept and Conceptions of Justice

Here, it is useful to distinguish between concepts and conceptions as an analytical tool. Political debates revolve around various conceptions of concepts such as justice.

> The 'concept' is the general structure, or perhaps the grammar, of a term ... A 'conception' is the particular specification of that 'concept', obtained by filling out some kind of detail.[1]

People can have different conceptions of concepts such as justice and they often argue with others about which particular conception is the better one.[2] Different conceptions thus account for different uses and meanings of a concept, on the general structure of which there is agreement. In short, the essentially contested concept of justice is understood through different conceptions of justice. The concept of justice is a kind of common ground for disagreement and argument about the force and scope of justice, and about what justice entails in particular cases.

Concepts such as economic justice, tax justice and legal justice form part of the broader concept of justice in general. We therefore start with the concept of justice, which relates to the way in which benefits and burdens are distributed among men. Justice is *suum cuique*: to each his due.

> The just state of affairs is that in which each individual has exactly those benefits and burdens which are due to him by virtue of his personal characteristics and circumstances.[3]

The formula 'to each his due' brings out the distributive character of justice. Principles of justice are therefore distributive principles.

B. Economic Justice

Economic justice aims for a fair distribution of economic burdens and benefits. Indeed, a large part of the benefits and burdens distributed in society are economic in nature. Economic theory should therefore take into account normative issues, such as distributive justice.[4] There should be a minimum guarantee of justice available in an economy in order to be perceived as legitimate. Consequently, in

---

[1] A Swift, *Political Philosophy* (Cambridge/Malden, Polity, 2001) 11.

[2] R Dworkin, *Taking Rights Seriously* (Duckworth, London, 1978) 134–36. Cf S Guest, *Ronald Dworkin* (Edinburgh University Press, Edinburgh, 1992) 34–37.

[3] D Miller, *Social Justice* (Oxford, Clarendon Press, 1976) 20. A possible distributive principle, for example, is that everyone should retain what he currently possesses.

[4] J Roemer, *Theories of Distributive Justice* (Cambridge MA, Harvard University Press, 1996) 3.

38   Sonja Dusarduijn and Hans Gribnau

economics giving each person his or her due regards the 'distribution of commodities, income, and wealth'.[5] Mill has argued that 'in the most advanced [countries], what is needed from an economic perspective is a better distribution', rather than increased production.[6] It therefore does not suffice to know whether a society is rich in economic terms, but it also necessary to know 'how its resources are distributed'.[7]

The enhancement of distributive justice in the economic sphere in order to diminish unequal distribution of goods implies interference with individual liberty. Freedom, free choice or liberty is at the core of economics, because people are assumed to enter freely into the market. Economic actors' behaviour that is exclusively rooted in the pursuit of freedom may however have negative, unfair effects for others – requiring correction.[8] Freedom may thus create large inequalities, which will not voluntarily be accepted by the least well off in society, and therefore not perceived as legitimate. Hence, the outcomes of free market exchange should conform to certain standards of (substantive) justice.[9] Indeed, problems of economic distribution 'cannot be resolved without considerations of justice and equity'.[10] Thus, today's economics would do well to recognise that values belonging to the domain of justice are (also) economic values rather than 'depicting them as non-economic, but as social or political'.[11] Consequently, in economics justice relates to distribution according to particular principles applicable to the design of economic institutions.[12] A theory of economic justice may advocate to diminish inequality in the distribution of goods and resources and allowing for redistribution thereof. Kolm mentions various items and stages of the economic and social process that could be the object of equality: productive resources like credit, technology, and human capital; income, consumption, goods, capacities, basic needs and opportunity.[13]

---

[5] S-C Kolm, *Justice and Equity* (Cambridge MA, The MIT Press, 1997) 45–46. Cf E Anderson, 'Equality' in D Estlund (ed), *The Oxford Handbook of Political Philosophy* (Oxford, OUP, 2012) 40–57 who advocates a relational rather than a distributive conception of equality.

[6] JS Mill, *Principles of Political Economy with Some of Their Applications to Social Philosophy* [1848] (Indianapolis, Liberty Fund, 2006), Book IV, 6:2, 755. Cf N Barry, *Welfare* (Buckingham, Open University Press, 1990) 31–32.

[7] CR Sunstein, *Free Markets and Social Justice* (Oxford, OUP, 1997) 6.

[8] For example, exploitation of workers, unequal distribution of gains from international trade by the more powerful trading partner, unequal opportunities for entrepreneurs with fewer resources, discrimination against women, ethnic groups and disabled persons, and environmental degradation; see I van Staveren, *The Values of Economics. An Aristotelian Perspective* (Abingdon/London, Routledge, 2001) 32.

[9] J Rawls, *A Theory of Justice* (Oxford, OUP, 1999) 178.

[10] S-C Kolm (n 5) 46. He subsequently argues that the efficiency criterion ('Pareto optimality') is insufficient.

[11] Van Staveren (n 8) 35.

[12] The concept of economic justice is closely related to what in political philosophy is often called 'social justice' (usually seen as a matter of distributive justice). The latter concept regards the distribution of benefits and burdens in society. 'Issues of social justice, in the broadest sense, arise when decisions affect the distribution of benefits and burdens between individuals or groups.' M Clayton and A Williams, 'Introduction' in M Clayton and A Williams (eds), *Social Justice* (Malden/Oxford/Carlton, Blackwell Publishing, 2004) 1.

[13] S-C Kolm, *Modern Theories of Justice* (Cambridge MA, The MIT Press, 1996) 10, 66–67; Van Staveren (n 8) 33.

Although many political economists endorse the concept of economic justice, there is no agreement on the use and content of this concept. The lack of consensus with regard to the exact objects of (in)equality and distribution make economic justice an essentially contested concept. Roughly speaking, Konow, who studies people's fairness values, argues that economic justice requires that a fair allocation of, for instance, income should vary in proportion to the relevant variables a person can influence (eg work effort), not according to those variables which he cannot reasonably affect (eg the presence of a physical handicap).[14] This is in line with redistributive theories, as shown above. The ultimate purpose of economic justice is to create an opportunity for each person to create a sufficient material foundation upon which to have a dignified, productive and creative life. Economic justice thus can be seen as economic fairness.[15] Literature shows numerous lively debates about how people should be compensated for their part in economic cooperation. Discussions about the best basis from a fairness perspective for this differential compensation, however interesting, transcend the scope of this contribution.[16]

To conclude, for the purposes of this chapter, distributive justice encompasses economic justice, which is about the distribution of all kinds of economic benefits and burdens between individuals or groups. We will now deal with economic justice applied to taxation, that is, tax justice which aims at a fair distribution of the benefits of a society through taxation.

C. Tax Justice

Tax justice can be conceptualised as a particular form of economic justice. It aims for a fair distribution of the tax burden over the members of society. Every (corporate) citizen has to pay his fair share. A fair distribution of the tax burden may even call for redistributive measures in order to diminish inequality in the distribution of resources.[17] In this way, the tax system itself is used to enhance redistributive justice, that is, a particular conception of economic justice.

The requirement of tax justice – a fair distribution of the tax burden – finds its expression pre-eminently in the ability-to-pay principle.

The ability-to-pay principle may be conceptualised as an operationalisation of the principle of equality, which justifies the distribution of the tax burden in proportion to income, according to Lang. To our minds, this calls for a proportional tax structure. However, according to Lang the ability-to-pay principle

---

[14] J Konow, 'A positive theory of economic fairness' (1996) 31 *Journal of Economic Behaviour & Organization* 14.

[15] This term is used by authors such as Konow (n 14).

[16] Cf Konow (n 14) for a short overview.

[17] C Webber and A Wildavsky, *A History of Taxation and Expenditure in the Western World* (New York, Simon and Schuster, 1986) 347 ff.

should be conceptualised as an instrument of solidarity and redistributive justice, as done in the welfare state. The latter conceptualisation calls for a progressive rate structure.[18] In this sense, Tipke characterises this ability-to-pay principle as the fundamental distributive tax principle of the social welfare state.[19] Tipke further shows how this moral principle is widely recognised in both constitutional law and tax law of many countries as the fundamental tax principle.[20]

The ability-to-pay principle is of course a very abstract principle and as such not directly applicable – like all principles.[21] It must therefore be operationalised into specific terms, mid-level principles, rules, provisions and a concrete tax object.

An operationalisation is the requirement that costs should be taken into when assessing someone's ability to pay. The deduction of income-acquiring costs follows from the tax principle that only net income offers an ability to pay and can thus be taxed. This requirement of tax justice is at stake in the provision we deal with.

D. Legal Justice

Next to economic justice as a species of social justice and its relative tax justice we distinguish legal justice. Legal justice regards the justice of the legal system, and because taxation should be levied by law (principle of legality), tax laws should meet certain legal justice requirements. The legal system aims to realise the value of legal justice.[22]

According to a legal conception of justice, the legal system has its own internal values and legal principles serve legal justice, which may set limitations on the use of taxes as a policy instrument serving the external value of social-economic justice. The legal system should conform to rule of law requirements in order to avoid arbitrary interference with citizens' liberty. The rule of law requires (government) power to be exercised according to the law and to govern via laws, that is,

---

[18] Eg J Lang, 'The influence of tax principles on the taxation of income from capital' in P Essers and A Rijkers (eds), *The Notion of Income from Capital* (Amsterdam, IBFD, 2005) 9–12. He argues that the ability-to-pay principle conceptualised as an operationalisation of the principle of equality makes it a purely legal principle. However, it could be argued that the principle of formal equality, treating all citizens formally alike, as a purely legal principle, calls for a head tax (poll tax). Moreover, a proportional rate already entails some kind of a redistribution.

[19] K Tipke, *Die Steuerrechtsordnung. Band I: Wissenschaftsorganisatorische, systematische und grundrechtlich-rechtsstaatliche Grundlagen* (2, völlig überarbeitete Auflage) (Köln, Verlag Dr. Otto Schmidt, 2000) 484.

[20] ibid 488–91. See also L Wijtvliet, *Tax Tectonics. Well-being and Wealth Inequality in relation to a Shift in the Tax Mix from Direct to Indirect Taxes* (Ph-D thesis) (Tilburg, Tilburg School of Economics and Management, 2018) 195 ff.

[21] H Gribnau, 'Not Argued From But Prayed to. Who's Afraid of Legal Principles?' (2014) 12(1) *eJournal of Tax Research*, 185; available at http://papers.ssrn.com/sol3/papers.cfm?abstract_id=2461247.

[22] ibid.

through promulgation of general and abstract norms.[23] Tax laws should promote certainty and equality with regard to the interference with taxpayers' liberty.

Fuller explains the fundamental nature of legal certainty. To our minds, his theory can be extended to encompass other legal values such as equality and proportionality. For Fuller, law properly so called, is not a one-way exercise of authority, that is, government imposing itself upon a subject, but depends upon interaction between lawgiver and citizen. The state's position of superior power ultimately rests on a tacit and relatively stable reciprocity.[24] For law to provide a basis for 'reciprocal (not to mention mutually respectful) interaction between lawgiver and legal subject' law has to comply with certain desiderata.[25] This reciprocity rests, Krygier says, on a 'more deontological, moral claim', since it is based on what Fuller calls 'the view of man implicit in the internal morality of law', that is, a view of man as a (potentially) responsible agent. 'Every departure from the principles of the laws' inner morality is an affront to man's dignity as a responsible agent.'[26] This view implies that the legislature's responsibility to persons is embodied by the principles that constitute the internal morality of law.[27]

Fuller's point of departure therefore is that 'every exercise of the law-making function is accompanied by certain tacit assumptions, or implicit expectations, about the kind of product that will emerge from the legislature's efforts and the form he will give to that product'. Consequently, the content of legislation and 'the lawmaking process is itself subject to implicit laws'.[28] Fuller's desiderata constitute the 'internal morality of law' – the morality that makes law possible. Serious violations of these 'canons' threaten a statute with ineffectiveness and seriously impede its acceptance as a law.[29] Again, we go beyond Fuller's theory by advocating not to restrict the internal morality of law to legal certainty but to encompass also other fundamental legal values such as equality and proportionality. We are therefore not dealing simply with the lawmaking process but also the outcomes produced by the legal system (itself closely connected to the political system).

---

[23] JLM Gribnau, 'Equality, Legal Certainty and Tax Legislation in the Netherlands. Fundamental Legal Principles as Checks on Legislative Power: A Case Study' (2013) 9(2) *Utrecht Law Review* 52.

[24] LL Fuller, *The Morality of Law* [1964] (New Haven, Yale University Press, 1977) 61.

[25] M Krygier, 'Rule of Law' in M Rosenfeld and A Sajó (eds), *The Oxford Handbook of Comparative Constitutional Law* (Oxford, Oxford University Press, 2012) 238.

[26] Fuller (n 24) 162–63.

[27] See K Rundle, *Forms Liberate: Reclaiming the Jurisprudence of Lon L Fuller* (Oxford: Hart Publishing, 2012) 100: this 'is a responsibility to collaborate with the legal subjects in the creation and maintenance of law'.

[28] LL Fuller, *The Anatomy of Law* [1968] (Westport: Greenwood Press, 1976) 60–61. See also GJ Postema, 'Implicit Law' in WJ Witteveen and W van der Burg (eds), *Rediscovering Fuller: Essays on Implicit and Institutional Design* (Amsterdam: Amsterdam University Press, 1999) 255–75.

[29] See WJ Witteveen, 'Laws of Lawmaking' in Witteveen and Van der Burg (n 28) 312–45.

E. Principles of Legal Justice

i. Legal Equality

The principle that like cases should be treated equally, and unalike cases proportionally different, is the classical notion of formal justice. Aristotle famously argued: 'Injustice arises when equals are treated unequally and also when unequals are treated equally.'[30] Equality is a vital part of the ideal of the democratic state under the rule of law. The principle of equality is therefore enshrined in constitutional documents and international treaties, for example in Article 26 of the International Covenant on Civil and Political Rights and Article 14 of the European Convention on Human Rights. In matters of taxation, Article 14 has to be read in conjunction with Article 1 of Protocol No 1 to the Convention.

To say that two persons or cases are the same in a certain respect is to presuppose a rule – a prescribed standard for treating them – that both fully satisfy. A rule is a general prescription for conduct or action in order to achieve a goal. The goal to be achieved constitutes the justification (rationale) of the rule.[31] Equality, therefore, is a logical consequence of an established rule. Rules, such as tax laws, discriminate because they are based on classifications. Public policies are laid down in laws, and this is not possible without such discrimination. These kinds of discriminations, therefore, need to be rational. In this way such discriminations, exceptions to the general assumption of equal treatment, will be justified. The democratically legitimised legislature thus has the important task of determining 'rational' (reasonable) classifications in (tax) law.[32] A prima facie violation of this requirement of reasonable classification occurs when a classification is 'under-inclusive': the legislative classification does not include all those who are similarly situated with respect to the purpose, that is, justification of the law. Under-inclusive classifications violate the principle of equality.[33] The same goes if rules are (deliberately) formulated too broadly, that is, over-inclusively. The legislative classification encompasses a state of affairs as a result of which more persons and cases meet the provision's conditions than justified by the purpose of the provision.[34] Examples

---

[30] Aristotle, *The Nicomachean Ethics* (ed D Ross) (Oxford, OUP, 1984) V 1131a–1131b.

[31] F Schauer, *Playing by the Rules: A Philosophical Examination of Rule-Based Decision-Making in Law and in Life* (Oxford, Clarendon Press 1991), 27. P Westen, 'The Empty Idea of Equality' (1982) 95 *Harvard Law Review* 548 argues: 'Before such a rule is established no standard of comparison exists.' As shown below, the application of this formal standard of comparison may yield outcomes other than those that would be indicated by direct application of the underlying rationale or justification.

[32] The legislature has to define a class by designating 'a quality or characteristic or trait or relation, or any combination of these, the possession of which, by an individual, determines his membership in or inclusion within the class'; J Tussman and J ten Broek, 'The Equal Protection of the Laws' (1949) 27(3) *California Law Review* 344.

[33] This concerns the principle of equality in its shape of the principle of consistency or non-contradiction; JLM Gribnau, 'Equality, Consistency, and Impartiality in Tax Legislation' in JLM Gribnau (ed), *Legal Protection against Discriminatory Tax Legislation* (The Hague, Kluwer Law International, 2003) 30; available at http://papers.ssrn.com/sol3/papers.cfm?abstract_id=2464179.

[34] JLM Gribnau, 'Separation of Powers in Taxation: The Quest for Balance in the Netherlands' in AP Dourado (ed), *Separation of Powers in Tax Law* (Amsterdam, IBFD, 2010) 56.

of over-inclusive tax rules violating the principle of equality are anti-avoidance rules to prevent tax evasion or abuse or undesirable use of tax legislation that are too broadly formulated. The tax legislation may also contain incentives for taxpayers who do not need them. This kind of over-inclusiveness (tax privileges) also violates the principle of equality.

ii. Legal Certainty

Legal certainty, a legal value rooted in the rule of law, allows individuals to regulate their behaviour and to be able to reasonably foresee the legal consequences of those acts. As just shown, Fuller appeals to the legislature to respect the 'internal morality of law' and comply with its desiderata – legal certainty being a crucial one. Legal certainty can be seen as a concept with various aspects as its (sub) principles.[35] Consequently, legal certainty may be promoted in several ways and is therefore not a monolith.

Fuller distinguished several desiderata, including generality, promulgation, non-retroactivity, non-contradiction and constancy. These various aspects of legal certainty may put forward competing demands. The various principles which make up legal certainty often provide arguments which point in divergent directions. This accounts for the fact that good lawmaking is a 'principled' balancing act: competing principles ought to be balanced time and again. Here we will elaborate on the aspects of clarity and constancy, because these will be of particular importance in this chapter.

Fuller argues that the clarity of laws is essential to control and direct human conduct. Laws should be clear and understandable. Montesquieu already argued that 'the style of the laws should be simple' for it 'is essential for the words of the law to awaken the same ideas in all men'.[36] Fuller maintains that clarity of laws may sometimes be achieved by incorporating into the law common sense standards 'which have grown up in the ordinary outside legislative halls'.[37] Clarity of the law is not to be reduced to a limited quantity of rules. In some situations, having a detailed set of rules could make things simpler and add to clarity, 'if it clears up grey areas in the tax law'.[38] Legislatures can craft laws with different levels of specificity to guide human behaviour, incorporating detailed rules or more general standards in the laws they write. Precision increases predictability. However, regulation through precise, specific rules does not always deliver optimal legal certainty. A prolix code of very specific rules has its drawback: it can be so difficult 'to apply

---

[35] See Fuller's 'principles of legality'; Fuller (n 24) 33–94 and H Gribnau, 'Legal Certainty: A Matter of Principle' in H Gribnau and M Pauwels (eds), *Retroactivity of Tax Legislation* (Amsterdam, IBFD, 2013), available at http://papers.ssrn.com/sol3/papers.cfm?abstract_id=2447386.

[36] Montesquieu, *The Spirit of Laws* [1748] (AM Cohler, BC Miller and H Stone eds) (Cambridge, CUP, 1998), XXIX, 16, 612–13.

[37] See Fuller (n 24) 64.

[38] J Slemrod and J Bakija, *Taxing Ourselves: A Citizen's Guide to the Debate over Taxes*, 4th ed (Cambridge MA, The MIT Press, 2008) 159.

44 Sonja Dusarduijn and Hans Gribnau

that it produces lack of coordination and inefficient decision-making that determinate rules are supposed to remedy.[39] The possibility and necessity of clearly stated laws also depends on the nature of the issue the law deals with. Lack of clarity may be inevitable with regard to very complex matters, which affect only a minority of taxpayers. Some tax law is extremely complex, and so, however clearly the propositions about it are expressed, users, taxpayers and officials alike, 'may still take some time to understand how it works.'[40]

Another requirement with regard to legislation holds that laws should not be changed too frequently. Frequent changes make it harder for people to gear their activities to the law. Constancy of the law – temporal consistency – offers the taxpayers a reliable legal basis for their future actions. Consequently, the (tax) legislature should take into account possible future taxpayers' actions in order to enhance temporal generality or consistency of the tax laws.[41] This demand for the constancy of the law directly serves the predictability of legislation and the legislature's reliability. However, tax provisions nowadays often look like disposables, resulting in unstable and unreliable tax legislation.[42] This lack of stability due to remedial legislation and new policy initiatives undermines the effort to achieve simplicity and diverts resources.[43]

iii. Transparency

Complexity generally goes at the expense of transparency; people will not be able to understand how elaborate technical details relate to the aim and logic of a regulation – including the underlying principles. This is true, of course, for non-expert taxpayers, but often even tax professionals cannot see the wood for the trees. Increasingly, many parts of the tax system are only transparent to those have specialised in study of the regulations involved. Facets of transparency are availability, publicity, accessibility, attainability and intelligibility.[44] Transparency is thus instrumental to a clear view of reality. 'Transparency ideally just produces a reflection of the way things really are.'[45]

Transparency of procedures, rules and information enhances accountability and may encourage trust. It is therefore a building block of fairness and integrity of

---

[39] L Alexander and E Sherwin, *The Rule of Rules. Morality, Rules and the Dilemmas of Law* (Durham/London, Duke University Press, 2001) 31.

[40] H Rogers, 'Drafting Legislation at the Tax Law Rewrite Project' in C Stefanou and H Xanthaki (eds), *Drafting Legislation A Modern Approach* (Aldershot, Ashgate, 2008) 80–81.

[41] See, eg, G Kirchhof, *Die Allgemeinheit des Gesetzes* (Tübingen, Mohr Siebeck, 2000) 3. See also A von Arnauld, *Rechtssicherheit. Perspektivische Annäherungen an eine idée directrice des Rechts* (Tübingen, Mohr Siebeck, 2006) 273ff.

[42] Cf Kirchhof (n 41) 546.

[43] A Sawyer, 'New Zealand's Tax Rewrite Programme – In Pursuit of the (Elusive) Goal of Simplicity' (2007) 103(4) *British Tax Review* 424.

[44] Cf J Hey, 'The Notion and Concept of Tax Transparency' in B Yavaşlar and J Hey (eds), *Tax Transparency. EATLP Annual Congress Zürich 2018* (Amsterdam, IBFD, 2019) 5–6.

[45] GC Bowker and SL Starr, *Sorting Things Out* (Cambridge MA, MIT Press, 1999) 312.

the (international) tax system. Tax transparency enables taxpayers to understand and to evaluate, to a certain extent, the fairness of tax system. The rationality of the tax system adds to its transparency.[46] The tax system is of course embedded in a body of political practices with their own inherent, often seemingly irrational, logic.[47] Nonetheless, the system of tax rules should be characterised by a certain degree of rationality with sufficient respect for tax justice principles. However, the legislature adding a rule to an already very complex system of rules with numerous very technical and detailed rules may violate (directly or indirectly) an underlying tax principle. The new rule thus causes a lack of principled consistency. An example, we will deal with is the violation of the basic rule of PITA 2001 to tax all sources of income. This rule is itself an operationalisation of the underlying ability-to-pay principle.

Transparency is also relevant for the layman. Very detailed, complex and technical tax systems are less intelligible for laymen and consequently distort their perception with regard to the justice thereof. Indeed, citizens must also be capable to identify with the system of tax laws, that is, believe that tax legislation reflects their own principles. Law therefore must also be intelligible for the members of society in order to enhance a sense of justice. A tax system that is perceived to be unjust will lead to an erosion of trust.[48]

F. On Balance

Economic justice aims for a fair distribution of economic benefits and burdens. Tax justice aims for a fair distribution of the tax burden. Economic justice and tax justice are thus both forms of social, that is, distributive justice. Legal justice regards the justice of the legal system. The legal system aims to realise the value of legal justice. Hence, tax laws should meet certain legal justice requirements.

These different concepts of justice show that justice is definitely not a monolith. Consequently, various concepts and conceptions of justice may compete with one another. In the same vein the values and principles they entail are often not harmoniously reconcilable. Moreover, various conceptions of justice are not monoliths either. The values and principles which serve a particular conception of justice may therefore collide. This boils down to Berlin's value pluralism, which affirms the reality of a deep conflict between ultimate human values that reason cannot resolve. Berlin argues that conflicts of values are an intrinsic element of human life

---

[46] K Tipke, 'Steuerrecht als Wissenschaft' in K Tipke (ed), *Gestaltung der Rechtsordnung. Festschrift für Joachim Lang* (Köln, Verlag Dr. Otto Schmidt, 2010) 26–30.

[47] Cf J Snape, *The Political Economy of Corporation Tax: Theory, Values and Law Reform* (Oxford, Hart Publishing, 2019).

[48] See SMH Dusarduijn, *De rechtsfictie in de inkomstenbelasting. De fiscale kleur van het alsof* (dissertation Tilburg) (Enschede, Gildeprint, 2015) 211–13 where the plea for this clarity is based upon Bentham's view.

46 *Sonja Dusarduijn and Hans Gribnau*

since 'not all good things are compatible, still less all the ideals of mankind'.[49] It is therefore often necessary to strike a compromise between different interpretations of concepts and the values and principles involved. The claims of various conceptions of justice and the ensuing values have be weighed against the claims of other conceptions and values which principles command our respect.

Radbruch's legal philosophy sheds light on the relation between fundamental legal values (to his mind: legal equality, purposiveness and legal certainty).[50] Each of these values exerts a pull in a particular direction, but undesirable overconcentration is kept in check by the countervailing forces of the other values. In practice, these conceptions of justice and their components must be constantly weighed and balanced, for there is no hierarchy between these fundamental legal values. This accounts for their 'non-conclusiveness', which they have in common with principles. 'Non-conclusiveness' is a crucial feature of values, as no legal value may be made absolute. According to Dworkin, the same goes for legal principles.[51]

Hence, lawmaking requires balancing diverging conceptions of justice, each with their own values, principles and rules. Different components of justice must be constantly weighed and balanced. Practice shows that tax legislation is not always the result of careful balancing diverging conceptions of justice and their particular requirements.

The following section will analyse an example of a conflict between the aim of enhancing economic justice by using the tax system and the principles of legal justice. First, it will deal with the (rapid) developments of an instrumental incentive in the tax regulations for homeownership.

III. The Hillen Incentive

A. Introduction

The overarching element in this example is the notional rental income of owner-occupied houses, which is an imputed income in Dutch tax law.[52] The tax law regulation for owner-occupied houses affects a massive number of taxpayers[53] but is extremely complex. The background of this legislation is the argument that ownership of the home saves rent. Although this saved rent is usually offset by mortgage interest charges and maintenance costs to be paid by homeowners, there

---

[49] I Berlin, 'Two Concepts of Liberty' in I Berlin, *Liberty* (H Hardy ed) (Oxford, OUP, 2002) 213. Cf J Gray, *Isaiah Berlin: An Interpretation of His Thought* (Princeton, Princeton University Press 2013).

[50] G Radbruch, 'Legal Philosophy' in *The Legal Philosophies of Lask, Radbruch and Dabin* (Cambridge MA, Harvard University Press, 1950) 117–22.

[51] Dworkin (n 2). For this 'non-conclusive character', see HLA Hart, 'Postscript' in HLA Hart, *The Concept of Law*, 3rd ed (Oxford, OUP, 2012) 261.

[52] Article 3.112 PITA 2001, the so-called 'eigenwoningforfait'.

[53] About 70% of Dutch households live in an owner-occupied house.

Balancing Conflicting Conceptions of Justice in Taxation   47

still is a striking economic difference between homeowners and tenants. After all, periodic rental payments can only be regarded as consumable, while homeowners have the possibility of building equity as their investment can grow. Considering the owner-occupied house as a taxable source of income can thus be seen as an element of economic justice, that is, redistribution from homeowners to less well-off tenants. Furthermore, taxing the income of owner-occupied houses can also be seen as a form of tax justice considering the difference in the ability to pay between homeowners and tenants. However, this is merely an assumed ability to pay as homeownership does not lead to a real increase in actual purchasing power; it only reflects possible increases in the future after having sold the house.[54] In that respect the levy on the assumed income from the owner-occupied house provides tension with the principle of the ability to pay.[55] Nevertheless, the Dutch legislature has qualified the owner-occupied house as a source of income. Consequently, the costs for this house, legally limited to the mortgage interest paid, can be deducted from this notional rental income.[56] The deduction of these income-acquiring costs follows from the tax principle that only the net income offers an ability to pay and can thus be taxed.

A logical consequence of the system thus chosen is that the absence of deductible costs will provide a higher taxable income. That is where the Hillen incentive enters, which is the popular name for article 3.123a Personal Income Tax Act (PITA) 2001. This provision offers an incentive for owners-occupiers with low or no mortgage debt, and therefore little or no deductible costs.[57] If the sum of the notional rental income and the interest cost would result in a positive amount, the Hillen incentive then ensures that the taxable sum of the notional rental income and any remaining interest cost is nil. This provision has two aims: its intention is not only to provide an allowance to (senior) taxpayers who have low income and who have fully repaid their mortgage debts, but also to follow the policy of the government to reduce privately incurred debts (see section III.C). Both aims are elements of economic justice.

However, this provision is an infringement of tax justice as it is a breach of the ability-to-pay principle: the income from a designated source of income is excluded from taxation. Moreover, the Hillen incentive also conflicts with legal justice as this provision is in fact a privilege representing a favourable deduction for a specific group. Not only is this incentive in tax law unmistakably at odds with

---

[54] Although houses tend to increase in value, they are also illiquid assets. The homeowner might not be able to sell if the housing market is down. Even if the market is up, there are significant transaction costs when selling. Both elements reflect nuances of the assumed ability-to-pay character of an owner-occupied house.

[55] AC Rijkers, 'Hebban olla vogala nestas' in K Braun et al (eds), *40 jaar Cursus Belastingrecht. Tribuut aan Leno Sillevis en Nico de Vries* (Deventer, Kluwer, 2010) 196.

[56] Even if these costs are higher than the income, which usually is the case as the notional income has been set at a fairly low amount.

[57] Although not every home acquisition debt is covered by a mortgage clause, the majority are. These debts will be referred to in this chapter as mortgage debts.

the principle of equality, tension with the principle of certainty is also present as this provision is an example of rapidly changing law. After all, the provision born in 2005 was terminated in 2019. Expectations raised in the past, to which taxpayers' choices and decisions with a long-term financial impact have been geared, were violated once this incentive was abolished. In addition, the lifecycle of this provision shows lack of clarity related to the concept of notional rental income itself. The resulting lack of insight in this system eventually led to an ill-considered extension of the transitional period grounded in public pressure and social sentiments, as will be discussed later on.

The complex issues related to the Hillen legislation thus show a remarkable resemblance to a Russian Matryoshka doll: when looking into one issue, a new one pops up.[58] In that respect, the successive changes in the Hillen incentive can be depicted as a series of collisions with various, divergent legal principles.[59]

B. Core of the Regime: Taxation of Owner-Occupied Houses in the Netherlands

To understand the implications of the Hillen incentive, it is necessary to consider its birthplace: the provisions in the PITA 2001 about homeownership, which are a patchwork of complicated legal measures and various transitional exceptions.[60]

Although one might doubt the income-generating character of the use of a house by its owner,[61] the Dutch legislature presumes this home to be a source of income, which consequently becomes taxable. Citizens owning a main residence therefore must annually report the (presumed) benefits of the own use of this home. This income is set at the economic rental value of this house, which is the notional rental income. This deemed income supposedly represents the balance of

---

[58] These nesting dolls are a set of dolls of decreasing size that fit inside each other.

[59] In both functions these principles interact with the trust of citizens and therefore with their compliance to contribute to society. See S Muehlbacher and E Kirchler, 'Tax Compliance by Trust and Power of Authorities' (2010) 24(4) *International Economic Journal* 607.

[60] See MEA Haffner, 'Dutch Personal Income Tax Reform 2001: An Exceptional Position for Owner-Occupied Housing' (2002) 17 *Housing Studies* 521. Other countries have made other policy choices with respect to owner-occupied houses. See for instance the comparative analysis of the fiscal and distributional consequences of including or excluding homeowners'' imputed rent in their taxable income by F Figari et al, 'Taxing Home Ownership: Distributional Effects of Including Net Imputed Rent in Taxable Income', *IZA Discussion Paper Series* no 6493 (April 2012); available at https://papers.ssrn.com/sol3/papers.cfm?abstract_id=2047279. An interesting comparison is Schedule A in UK income tax, which applied to notional rental income until the 1960s; see J Tiley, 'Aspects of Schedule A' in J Tiley (ed), *Studies in the History of Tax Law* (Oxford/Portland, Hart Publishing 2004) 81.

[61] The idea behind taxation on the enjoyment of an owner-occupied house is different from that from other actual sources of income. After all, there is no actual (economic) transaction between two or more parties, no other subject provides a means of satisfaction to the taxpayer. On the other hand, homeownership could qualify as a 'benefit in kind' that directly arises from the legal relationship to the source, the home. Nevertheless, no real means become available when someone provides a service to themselves. Rijkers thus disputes the source character of an own home: see Rijkers (n 55).

the revenue (enjoyment of the house itself) and general expenses (such as insurance premiums and regular maintenance costs) related to the personal use of this house.[62] This balance is assessed using statutory tables which are highly efficient. The use of this fixed rate levy not only offers a practical solution for the problems of concretising the benefits of own use of property, but also guarantees an efficient implementation of tax rules by the tax administration. This legal fiction does, however, treat unequal situations as though they were equal. In this case, the possible conflict with the equality principle was justified as the courts grant the legislature a (very) wide margin of appreciation with respect to tax legislation.[63] But even then, a fixed rate levy is intended to approximate as closely as possible to the empirical reality of taxpayer. The statutory tables used for owner-occupied houses do not meet that criterion of tax justice. For instance, in 2019 the notional rental income of an owner-occupied house with a value within the (large) bandwidth of €75,000 to € 1,080,00 is set at 0.65% of this value.[64] This percentage is far too small to be able to approximate the intended net rental value of the home.[65] This is not in line with the aim of the legislature to tax owner-occupiers as if they were renting the property to themselves at the price that they would charge as owner-lessor to third parties.

In general, no expenses other than mortgage interest may be deducted from the notional rental income.[66] Financing the purchase or renovation of an owner-occupied house therefore yields a tax deduction. The opportunity to deduct the costs of interest is often presented as an element of economic justice (aiming at the promotion of affordable housing). This view shows a lack of understanding of the logic of owner-occupied house regulation. The opportunity to deduct interest costs is after all a straightforward consequence of the legislature's choice to qualify owner-occupied houses as a source of income. Deduction of interest costs thus can

---

[62] It only applies to the main residence. Second homes and other immovable property are qualified as box 3 income, which represents a kind of wealth tax. Thus, no cost deduction is allowed.

[63] Supreme Court (HR) 29 June 2007, ECLI:NL:HR:2007:BA8050 (concerning the maximum in the rental value table). This wide margin refers to European Court of Human Rights (ECtHR) 22 June 1999, ECLI:NL:XX:1999:AV1935, (*Della Ciaja*). However, as the aim of each fixed rate levy is to correspond with the empirical reality of taxpayers as much as possible, the legislature thus should review its numerical compositions periodically. The notional rental income does not meet up to this requirement for maintaining trust from citizens. See Dusarduijn (n 48) 201–08.

[64] For more expensive houses the taxable notional rental income is higher: €7,020 plus 2.35% of the value of this property exceeding €1,080,000 (2019). This partly redistributive element – an element of economic justice – is referred to as 'the villa limit'. As our focus is on the Hillen incentive we will not further analyse this exception to the general regulation regarding the rental value of an owner-occupied house.

[65] CB Bavinck, 'Voorstel voor overheveling van de eigen woning naar box 3' (2006) 135 *Weekblad Fiscaal Recht* 879. Bavinck states that the tax advantages for homeowners are mainly based on this low value. The difference between a realistic rental value and the actual notional rental value is described in the literature as the 'rental value benefit'. This advantage is considerable. Caminada calculated that the real net rental value of owner-occupied houses only counts for one-third of the tax return of its owner. See K Caminada, 'Aftrekpost eigen woning: wie profiteert in welke mate? Ontwikkeling, omvang en verdeling van de hypotheekrenteaftrek en de bijtelling fiscale huurwaarde', *Department of Economics Research Memorandum 99.02* (Leiden, 1999), and section III.C, 'The first alteration: an instrumental incentive'.

[66] Other expenses are supposed to be included in the notional rental income.

50   *Sonja Dusarduijn and Hans Gribnau*

only be justified because the associated benefits are taxed.[67] Considering the low amount of the notional rental income the balanced total of this income and the related interest costs is negative in most cases. However, if homeowners finance their houses with their own resources, the presence of their debt-free houses inevitably results in a positive taxable amount (the notional rental income). The same situation occurs once house owners have repaid the entire mortgage debt. These consequences fully correspond with the choice of the legislature to allocate an income character to owner-occupied houses: in the absence of costs, the taxable income is the gross income (in this case, the notional rental income). Although this might seem self-evident, the logic in this operationalisation of tax fairness is not clear for homeowners. Apparently, this also applies to Member of Parliament Hillen and other politicians.

Homeowners do not experience their homeownership as an actual income, so the legal assumption collides with their views on taxation. Although taxing homeownership in the income tax is in accordance with economic justice and to a certain extent also with tax justice, in the view of homeowners this correspondence is clearly absent. This gap between the theoretical justice and the experienced fairness shows a lack of clarity in the legislation which conflicts with legal justice. In addition, very few people understand or are able to indicate how the notional interest income is composed or what underlying principles are taken into consideration.[68] That increases the intuitive thought of unfairness. In fact, most homeowners consider the opportunity to deduct interest costs as their inalienable right. The notional rental income is only considered to be an unwelcome and almost annoying decrease of that right. This converse approach shows the lack of clarity and transparency of the legal system for homeowners (and some politicians).

C. The First Alteration: An Instrumental Incentive

The lack of clarity regarding this issue increased when the Hillen incentive emerged in PITA 2001.[69] This incentive was introduced by a bill presented by Member of Parliament Hillen. His assumption was that in the absence of interest costs the remaining positive notional rental income would obstruct (further) repayment of mortgage debts. Hence an incentive would be necessary. By providing this incentive, the legislature not only provided an allowance for certain homeowners, but also aimed to influence the repayment behaviour of homeowners.[70]

---

[67] The interest paid on qualifying mortgage debts can be deducted during a period of 30 years. This maximum period has applied since 1 January 2001.

[68] RM Freudenthal, *In de ban van de vervlakking; een inkomstenbelastingsprookje in drie delen* (Amersfoort, SDU Publishers, 2004) 31.

[69] Article 3.123a PITA 2001, since 1 January 2005.

[70] Parliamentary Papers I, 2003/04, no 29 209, B, 1–2: '[It] is intended as a repayment incentive for homeowners with only a minor home debt. In addition, the government is convinced that the proposed measure also entails a (albeit smaller) incentive for repayment for the other homeowners.'

Balancing Conflicting Conceptions of Justice in Taxation   51

The second element focuses on economic justice in the sense of preventing large financial risks for homeowners, which is an element of the debt reduction policy of Dutch government. To this extent, the encouragement of debt repayment brought about by the Hillen incentive can be justified.

However, the justice of the first element is doubtful. In the political arena, the provision was presented as an arrangement for senior citizens with small pensions and fully redeemed mortgage debts. It not only seems sympathetic to grant these low income, less wealthy seniors this advantage, but it would also satisfy the need for the redistributive element of economic justice. However, the incentive is granted to homeowners of all ages and incomes, and thus includes taxpayers who could easily bear the tax on the notional rental income. It even turns out that especially wealthy and high-income elderly people can use this provision and are thus exempt from taxation of their own home. With regard to economic justice this is over-inclusive.[71]

Moreover, as the Hillen incentive ensures that the taxable net benefit from a owner-occupied house is fully neutralised, the deduction is in fact an (instrumental) exemption from the notional rental income.[72] The provision thus conflicts with tax justice in two ways. It not only denies the designated income source character of owner-occupied houses in the income tax system itself, but also interferes with the ability-to-pay principle as the presence of an owner-occupied house (though being an assumed source of income) is no longer included in the levy.[73] This is a violation of the basic rule – itself an operationalisation of the underlying principle of ability to pay – to impute income of owner-occupied houses.

The question then rises whether an objective and reasonable justification is available for the unequal treatment of homeowners with and owners without mortgage debts. However, in 2008 the Supreme Court ruled that the legislature had not exceeded its broad discretion with the introduction of the Hillen incentive.[74] This judgment did not come as a surprise: the Dutch Supreme Court traditionally

---

[71] In the year 2016 almost 22% of the 4.3 million households with owner-occupied houses used the Hillen incentive. The average capital of these households was over €93,000, which is remarkably higher than the average capital of other households, which is € 45,000. In addition, households using this provision appear to have a higher annual income than households which do not apply for this provision. That effect is visible in almost every age category. See the analysis of the Central Bureau of Statistics (CBS), available at https://www.cbs.nl/nl-nl/nieuws/2018/05/vooral-vermogende-ouderen-vrijgesteld-van-woningforfait. The structural loss of revenue caused by the Hillen deduction is €250 million per year. Parliamentary Papers II, 2003/04, no 29 209, 3, 2.

[72] Since the year 2014 a redistribution tool has been added to the tax regime in box 1. Homeowners who enjoy or might have enjoyed an interest deduction in the fourth tax bracket (52%) are confronted with a slowly increasing addition of fictitious income. This extra income is intended to gradually reduce the effective percentage of interest deduction to ultimately 30% (see article 2.10, para 2 and article 2.10a PITA 2001). The fiscal compensation of the Hillen incentive is therefore no longer complete.

[73] Moreover, the Hillen deduction exacerbates the unequal treatment of the capital invested in owner-occupied houses and other assets. See RP van den Dool, *Belastingheffing over kapitaalinkomen bij natuurlijke personen. Een onderzoek naar de mogelijkheden tot het invoeren van een vermogensaanwasbelasting* (Deventer, Kluwer, 2009) ch 2. We will not discuss this element in this chapter.

[74] HR, 8 August 2008, ECLI:NL:HR:2008:BD9390, para 3.3. No official translation.

52 Sonja Dusarduijn and Hans Gribnau

permits the legislature a (very) broad discretion (that is, a wide margin of appreciation).[75] In this case the wish to encourage repayment of mortgage debts was assessed as a sufficient justification for unequal treatment of comparable homeowners. The fact that the legislature was granted this wide margin of appreciation cannot, however, cover up the fact that the Hillen incentive is also an obviously infringement of the equality principle, and thus, the internal morality of law.

D. The Second Alteration: Abolition of the Incentive

Intensification of the debt reduction policy has led to new regulation for homeowners: a mortgage debt contracted after 1 January 2013 must contain a repayment obligation (at least on an annuity base) and must be fully repaid in 30 years.[76] These legal measures oblige every homeowner to repay all mortgage debts occurring after this date. Repayment of these debts therefore no longer depends on the encouragement given by the Hillen incentive; it now is a matter of rule. This should have led to an abolition of the Hillen incentive, which as a specific incentive has become superfluous.[77] That legislative change would have created a good balance between the principle of legal certainty for existing situations and the principle of equality for other positions. For the first group of homeowners, a transitional arrangement would have guaranteed the predictability of law, protecting this group from arbitrary state interference with not only their plans but also with their need for certainty.[78] Allowing the incentive to be (temporarily) continued for this group would have been more in line with the principle of certainty. Despite this, the legislature failed to abolish the Hillen incentive in 2013, although the 'old' justification for the unequal treatment between homeowners had become blurred.[79]

The incentive was kept alive until a new coalition agreement (setting out the policy plans of the newly formed cabinet) was made public in October 2017. This agreement held a remarkable provision, indicating that 'in light of the repayment obligation' the Hillen incentive would be phased out over 20 years.[80] This announcement of the gradual decrease of the deduction provided by the Hillen incentive almost stirred a riot, especially among wealthy senior citizens.[81] This resistance against the so-called 'repayment fine'[82] was loud and fierce, as seen on the website 'Stop the Repayment Fine':

---

[75] The Dutch Supreme Court follows the ECtHR in this respect; see eg ECtHR 22 June 1999, ECLI:NL:XX:1999:AV1935, (*Della Ciaja*).

[76] *Parliamentary Papers II*, 2012/13, no 33 405, 3, 1–3. For these repayment requirements see article 3.119a ff PITA 2001. We abstract from the transitional law in this respect.

[77] In view of the need for predictability, this abolition should ideally have taken place with a transitional provision for homeowners with mortgage debts incurred before 2013.

[78] Gribnau (n 21).

[79] Dusarduijn (48) 211–13.

[80] Coalition Agreement 2017–2021, *Confidence in the Future*, Owner-occupied housing market, 35.

[81] The unified protest was and is still being led by the political 50 Plus Party.

[82] This description is a clever way of framing the argument.

First, people are encouraged for years by the government to repay as much as possible. When they have done so, you [the government] present them the bill. That feels like a knife in the back![83]

The objections that resonate in this anger closely relate to an important possible consequence of a lack of legal certainty: the perceived (un)reliability of the government. Since the proposal for abolition of the provision was part of the Coalition agreement in October 2017 and, as such, is not part of the proposals for tax changes traditionally presented by the Dutch government on '*Prinsjesdag*' (third Tuesday in September), one could also speak of 'pressure-cooker-legislation'. However, due to the very long transitional period, the bringing into effect of the abolition itself shows no hastiness at all.[84] So the public upheaval was much ado about nothing.

E. The Third Alteration: Lobbyists and Tribal Fury

At first sight, this resistance seems to focus on the lack of trustworthy legislation – the idea that the confidence generated by the legislature has been violated. This implies a neglect of the principle of certainty. However, this resistance is actually aimed at the income character of owner-occupied houses. After all, it is the taxation of the notional rental income itself that causes the fury. On the one hand this underlines the opportunistic character of this resistance: during the years where deduction of interest costs – in fact costs of the source – could take place, the income character never led to disputes. On the other hand, it clearly shows that the legal tax system and its own logic itself is not clear to citizens (which accounts for a lack of transparency). The presence of a source of income – whether actual of presumed – should lead to taxation as it represents an ability to pay. This ability is even greater in the absence of source costs such as interest.

Nevertheless, the uproar shows that the legislature obviously has not succeeded in its attempts to clarify the logic of the system of tax regulation regarding home-ownership. Meanwhile, the emotional pleas of senior homeowners have led to an even longer transition period of 30 years, although most senior taxpayers can easily afford the tax payment.[85] Tax legislation in the Netherlands will thus, up to and including 2048, accommodate a tax incentive that not only conflicts with the legislature's fundamental choice to qualify the owner-occupied house as a source

---

[83] See https://www.50pluspartij.nl/actueel/2199-aflosboete-referendum-afschaffen-wet-hillen. This quotation was taken from the website of the '50Plus Party', a political party in the Netherlands that advocates pensioners' interests.

[84] See JE van den Berge, 'Hillen uitgefaseerd' (2018) 87(1) *Maandblad Belastingbeschouwingen* 9.

[85] During this period the advantages of the Hillen incentive will gradually diminish to nil. In this period the deduction of the Hillen incentive will only be abolished in equal annual steps of 3 percentage points. Concretely: the Hillen incentive will amount to up to 962/3% of the difference between the notional rent value and the interest costs in 2019, in the year 2020 this would be 931/3% and so on. The devil thus is in the detail. Van den Berge (n 84) wonders: 'Who now expects this phasing out will actually take place in thirty years?'

54 Sonja Dusarduijn and Hans Gribnau

of income, but is also in conflict with the equal and neutral treatment of citizens. Besides that, this incentive contains a substantial windfall gain because a large part of the homeowners would have shown the pursued repayment behaviour without this tax incentive. This is either based on the current repayment obligation for mortgage debts or based on their own wish to be debt free. An incentive for those groups is not needed; it is in fact over-inclusive, that is, a tax privilege. Finally, the facility itself and its long-term transitional arrangement is rooted in the pressure applied by lobbyists, who are citizens with the means and the resources to influence the policymakers. This successful pressure is at odds with the trust of other, non-lobbying citizens. That adverse effect on both economic and legal justice is even greater now that, contrary to claims of the opponents of abolition of the Hillen incentive, the advantages of the Hillen incentive turn out to apply to (mostly elderly) homeowners with high income and a wealth far above average.[86] Even though the generous transitional arrangement meets the principle of legal certainty, the facility itself carries considerable tension with both the principles of equality and neutrality, and may look like unjust privilege for wealthy individuals.

F. The Alterations Briefly Evaluated

This description of the multiple faces of the Hillen incentive show that incentives can lead to infringements of the principles of tax justice. Moreover, the longer these infringements exist, the more the favoured citizens will rely on the expectation that they will not be abolished. This is feeding a false expectation. As tax law ultimately strives to achieve the realisation of values such as a fair distribution of collective burdens, recognition of those values by members of society is needed to maintain their trust in government. Taking citizens seriously is therefore important. However, sometimes citizens must accept that changes in tax legislation can be at odds with their own individual interests. The rating and acceptance of those changes not only require a clear view on the facts; they also require a relationship of trust between citizens and the legislature. The example of the Hillen incentive clearly shows that this relationship is unsteady. This too has provided pressure groups such as the 50 Plus Party an opportunity to successfully enforce an arrangement based on incorrect sentiments and twisted facts. The public may favour these enforced changes, but legal principles may set boundaries to the claims of representative politics and negate certain legislative choices. The legislature should pursue its objectives within the boundaries set by fundamental principles, which represent fundamental moral values. Legislative omnipotence is not the rule

---

[86] As the analysis of the CBS clearly shows, see n 71 above. Besides that, the disadvantage of abolition of the instrument is not excessive. For owner-occupied houses worth €300,000 (the modal value), the future notional rental income (0.6%) amounts to €1,800 per year. Converted at a future rate of 37%, this means a levy of ultimately only €665 per year. This levy will only slowly add up to this amount in 30 years.

of law. Positive law should respect fundamental legal principles constituting its normative core.[87]

In our opinion the rise and fall of the Hillen incentive is not an example of rapidly changing law; rather, it shows an overly slow repair of a blurred incentive and the proven lack of proper explanation of the need for change. Changing circumstances can and often even must lead to changing legislation. However, the legislative procedure in the Netherlands should ensure a careful weighing of interests when amending the law.[88] Being able to counterbalance one-sided lobbyism is an important element of a reliable, trustworthy government. Above all, this accumulation of trust issues related to this provision show the desperate need for transparency, the motivation of both choice for and design of not only rules themselves but also of incentives as an exemption to those rules. After all, if the criteria for their existence are no longer met, both lose their justification.

IV. Conclusion

This chapter has elaborated on different conceptions of justice. Justice thus has many faces. Economic justice aims at correcting market outcomes to warrant a fair distribution of resources, whereas tax justice focuses on the fair distribution of the tax burden. Both elements of distributive justice have their own 'domain-specific' principles. Important tax principles as the ability to pay might then collide with redistributive principles of economic justice, especially when instrumental incentives enter the tax law. Balancing diverging principles of distributive justice thus is necessary.

However, a balance also has to be sought between economic justice and legal justice and its core principles, such as legal equality, legal certainty and proportionality. In short, legal justice and economic justice pose diverging demands. When using tax law to enhance economic justice, the legislature should therefore carefully balance these two different conceptions of justice. However, hasty parliamentary decisions and political decisiveness often seem to prevail over respect for legal values and principles. This results in short-lived tax laws designed to promote economic justice which, however, exist at the expense of legal certainty. These laws may also impair the equality principle, leading to over- or under-inclusive regulations. Here, we touch on the core of the imbalances in the existing tax system, leading to a collision with these important legal values and principles. This has been explained with an example of Dutch tax legislation: the (rapid) evolvement of an instrumental incentive in the tax regulation for homeownership. This example

---

[87] Ideally, changing the law is a process of better realising substantive values already present in the legal order; P Kahn, *The Reign of Law: Marbury v Madison and the Construction of America* (New Haven, Yale University Press, 1997) 62.

[88] *Parliamentary Papers II*, 2017/18, 34 819, no 8, 6.

has been analysed to illustrate the conflict between policies which aim to enhance economic justice by using the tax system and, on the other hand, principle[s] of tax justice (an expression of distributive justice inherent to the tax system) and the two core aspects of legal justice (legal equality and legal certainty).

This example does not only show that instrumental incentives in tax law almost naturally collide with the legal principle of equality, but also display a striking imbalance with legal certainty. After all, a basic requirement in any legal order is that the law is clear and accessible. This also goes for tax law; its rules should be clear and comprehensible for taxpayers. This gateway to trust in taxation implies that tax laws must be understandable for those who are subject to these laws. The example shows that this important aspect of legal certainty is not met. The Hillen incentive violates the requirement that costs should be taken into account when assessing someone's ability to pay. Moreover, the Hillen incentive consti- tutes a clear violation of the basic rule of PITA 2001 to tax all sources of income; itself an operationalisation of the underlying tax fairness principle of ability to pay. This violation shows that the foundations and implications of the tax system for owner-occupied homes are unknown and unclear for both homeowners and politicians. Furthermore, a rapid succession of both far-reaching and smaller legis- lative changes in the provision make it difficult to warrant not only accessibility of but also consistency in tax law. Too little focus on both aspects increases the risk of poor quality, thus less trustworthy laws, as shown in the short history of the Hillen incentive and in the alterations of the general tax credit. This accumulation of changes is at odds with legal certainty due to the reduced stability of the law. The government does not show itself as a reliable, trustworthy partner because it does not give citizens the confidence that they can attune their behaviour to a stable law.

To conclude: tax regulations should be based on a more careful reflection on the fundamental tension between the ends which are external to the law on the one hand and the internal legal values, such as legal certainty, equality and propor- tionality, on the other hand. Moreover, the use of tax legislation for external ends, such as economic justice, should also be balanced with the tax laws' internal values and principles of tax fairness – foremost, the ability-to-pay principle. A more care- ful approach by the tax legislature is needed to balance conflicting conceptions of justice, in order to ensure that all aspects of justice are taken seriously.

4

(Un)Fairness as an Irritant to the Legal System: The Case of Two Legislatures and More Multinational Enterprises

EMER HUNT

In 2012 and 2013 politicians and multinational enterprises discussed (un)fair tax during legislative hearings in the United Kingdom and the United States. During these hearings, various multinational enterprises sought to compel recognition of their fairness because they obey the law but were confronted with accusations of unfairness and aggression because they only obey the law. The aftermath of these hearings saw enforcement of state aid by the European Commission directed at the tax practices of certain member states and various legislative initiatives in the area of international tax. These were described as being motivated by, or achieving, fairness. The chapter deliberately does not dissect what was meant by fair, either during the legislative hearings or in its aftermath. Instead it takes the Anti-Tax Avoidance Directive (ATAD), which refers to fairness, and theorises that this is an illustration of how the legal system assimilates environmental irritations. At the same time, ATAD seeks to reconcile the maintenance of member state sovereignty in the area of tax with the impetus towards fair taxation in the international arena.

I. Introduction

'You are a company that says you "do no evil". And I think that you do do evil, in that you use smoke and mirrors to avoid paying tax.'

Margaret Hodge MP, Chair of the House of Commons Committee of Public Accounts to Google, 16 May 2013

Over the past several years, the architecture of the international tax system has been marked by a to-ing and fro-ing of allegations of unfairness: politicians casti-gated Apple, Google, Starbucks and Amazon, each of which appeared before

58 *Emer Hunt*

either the UK Public Accounts Committee (PAC) or the US Senate Permanent Subcommittee on Investigations (Senate PSI).[1] For their part, the multinational enterprises also enrolled fairness, either countering these allegations with their own assertion of unfair treatment by politicians or describing their own activities as fair. In the aftermath of these legislative hearings, and without drawing a causal link, there have been highly substantive regulatory and legal moves directed at the tax practices of member states and multinational enterprises. These moves took the form of state aid enforcement actions by the European Commission against Ireland, the Netherlands and Luxembourg to countermand tax rulings given by them to Apple, Starbucks and Amazon, respectively. Other moves were made by the G20, which mandated the Base Erosion and Profit Shifting (BEPS) project to address tax avoidance. Legislative moves to combat tax avoidance were initiated by the European Union, specifically because tax avoidance can 'undermine fair burden-sharing between taxpayers (in particular between companies and private citizens) and fair competition for businesses'.[2] All these moves were described by the G20, the OECD and the European Commission as being motivated by fairness.[3] The payment of tax is thereby linked to fairness.[4] This chapter chronicles these

---

[1] See, in the USA, Senate, *Offshore Profit Shifting and the U.S. Tax Code – Part 1 (Microsoft & Hewlett-Packard)* (US Senate Permanent Subcommittee on Investigations 2012), available at www.gov info.gov/content/pkg/CHRG-112shrg76071/pdf/CHRG-112shrg76071.pdf (accessed 7 January 2020) (hereafter Senate PSI Microsoft and HP) and Senate, *Offshore Profit Shifting and the U.S. Tax Code – Part 2 (Apple Inc.)* (US Senate Permanent Subcommittee on Investigations 2013), available at www.gov info.gov/content/pkg/CHRG-113shrg81657/pdf/CHRG-113shrg81657.pdf (accessed 7 January 2020) (hereafter Senate PSI Apple). See, in the UK, the House of Commons Committee of Public Accounts (PAC) PAC, *Hearings of November 2012 with Starbucks, Google and Amazon* (London, The Stationery Office, 2012), available at https://publications.parliament.uk/pa/cm201213/cmselect/cmpubacc/716/7 16.pdf (accessed 7 January 2020) (hereafter PAC 2012 hearings), PAC, *Hearings of 16 May 2013 with Google and HMRC* (London, The Stationery Office, 2013), available at https://publications.parliament. uk/pa/cm201314/cmselect/cmpubacc/112/112.pdf (accessed 7 January 2020) (hereafter PAC 2013 hearings).

[2] European Commission, 'Tax Transparency Package', available at https://ec.europa.eu/taxation_ customs/business/company-tax/tax-transparency-package_en#tax_rulings (accessed 7 January 2020).

[3] ibid. See press releases of G20: G20, 'Leaders' Declaration', St Petersburg, 6 September 2013, available at www.g20.utoronto.ca/2013/2013-0906-declaration.html (accessed 7 January 2020); G20, 'Leaders' Communiqué', Brisbane, 15–16 November 2014, available at www.g20.utoronto.ca/2014/ 2014-1116-communique.html (accessed 7 January 2020); G20, 'Leaders' Communiqué', Antalya, 16 November 2015, available at www.g20.utoronto.ca/2015/151116-communique.html (accessed 7 January 2020); G20, 'Leaders' Communiqué', Hangzhou, 5 September 2016, available at www.g20. utoronto.ca/2016/160905-communique.html (accessed 7 January 2020). See press release of the OECD on launching BEPS in July 2013; OECD, 'Closing tax gaps – OECD launches Action Plan on Base Erosion and Profit Shifting', 17 July 2013, available at www.oecd.org/tax/beps/closing-tax-gaps-oecd-launches-action-plan-on-base-erosion-and-profit-shifting.htm (accessed 7 January 2020).

[4] See, generally, T Pogge and K Mehta, *Global Tax Fairness* (Oxford, OUP, 2016); T Dagan, 'International tax and global justice' (2017) 18 *Theoretical Inquiries in Law* 1. This chapter is not dealing with fairness as a procedural or administrative matter, or fairness as a component of encouraging taxpayer compliance with the law. Fairness, and the perception of fairness, have been studied within the context of taxpayer compliance. See, eg, V Braithwaite, 'Responsive Regulation and Taxation: Introduction' (2007) 29 *Law & Policy* 3 and J Farrar et al, 'Tax Fairness: Conceptual Foundations and Empirical Measurement' (2018) *Journal of Business Ethics* 1. For fairness within an administrative sphere, see D de Cogan, 'A Changing Role for the Administrative Law of Taxation' (2015) 24 *Social & Legal Studies* 251.

references to fairness, and traces them to the references to fairness contained in the preamble to 2016 European Council Directive on anti-tax avoidance (ATAD).[5]

No real attempt is made to unpick the varying meanings of fairness. This is too gigantic a task to be undertaken on what is, after all, the slender evidence of multi-party expressions of fairness in legislative hearings and in press releases accompanying enforcement action or legislative initiatives. Instead the spread of fairness is traced, until it ends up in ATAD. This process of irritation of the legal system has been described before. Teubner, describing the 'good faith' doctrine as a European irritant to the common law legal system of contract, mused on how this doctrine would be reconstructed within its new home in the common law system.[6] He sees the embedding of a foreign concept within a legal system as a product of certain external pressures from culture and society. This is what Luhmann labels the environmental pressures which irritate the legal system into action.[7] Both view the legal system as bombarded by external pressures, but synthesising these pressures with its own idiosyncratic mechanism of self-production. Both the legal side and the social side take a distinct evolutionary path: 'due to their close structural coupling they permanently perturb each other and provoke change on the other side'.[8] This chapter does not assert a full structural coupling between the political system and its discussion of fairness, and the references to fairness which appear in ATAD. Indeed such a structural coupling would imply a clarity as to the intended meaning of fairness which its use in a number of different contexts might not sustain. Instead there is a tentative coupling between the environmental noise on fairness and ATAD, perhaps reflected in its location in the Preamble to ATAD. This is the process which is examined here.

II. The Hearings in the US Senate PSI And UK PAC

The legislative hearings were quite dramatic. They were televised, broadcast, discussed and debated.[9] The politicians accused the multinational organisations of

---

[5] Council Directive (EU) 2016/1164 of 12 July 2016 laying down rules against tax avoidance practices that directly affect the functioning of the internal market, [2016] OJ L 193/1. Council Directive (EU) 2018/822 of 25 May 2018 amending Directive 2011/16/EU as regards mandatory automatic exchange of information in the field of taxation in relation to reportable cross-border arrangements [2018] OJ L 139/1 refers to the creation of an environment of fair taxation.

[6] G Teubner, 'Legal Irritants: Good Faith in British Law or How Unifying Law Ends Up in New Divergencies' (1998) 61 MLR 11.

[7] N Luhmann, K A Ziegert and F Kastner, *Law as a Social System* (Oxford, Oxford University Press, 2004).

[8] Teubner (n 6) 28.

[9] See, eg, J Politi, 'Apple chief Tim Cook defends tax practices and denies avoidance', *Financial Times*, 21 May 2013, available at www.ft.com/content/c1a2383a-c228-11e2-ab66-00144feab7de (accessed 8 January 2020) and ND Schwartz and BX Chen 'Disarming Senators, Apple Chief Eases Tax Tensions', New York Times, 21 May 2013, available at www.nytimes.com/2013/05/22/technology/ceo-denies-that-apple-is-avoiding-taxes.html (accessed 8 January 2020).

60   Emer Hunt

being aggressive and of pursuing questionable and dubious tax practices. The hearings were important and all the more powerful because of the contemporaneity of the attack on both sides of the Atlantic, the compulsion on the multinational enterprises to appear, the high status of the questioners, the information made available by the multinational enterprises, and the media attention given to the parliamentary hearings.[10] Testimony before the PAC has been described as high in trustworthiness, which 'does not mean that the assertions made are necessarily true, that descriptions provided are necessarily plausible – it simply means that there are good reasons to assume that we are actually getting their public view on things'.[11] All of these points converge to make it worthwhile studying what is happening when politicians and multinational enterprises speak about fairness and tax.

Between September 2012 and May 2013 Apple, Microsoft and Hewlett-Packard appeared before the Senate PSI and Starbucks, Google and Amazon appeared before the PAC.[12] The hearings are prefaced by gratitude on the part of the politicians to the multinational enterprises for having turned up: the Chair of the PAC greets Starbucks, Google and Amazon:

> Margaret Hodge MP: 'Can I thank you all for agreeing to come and give evidence to this Committee this afternoon?'[13]

The shared spirit of inquiry lasted only as long as evasive answers were not given: the answers of an Amazon executive who was accused of being evasive were dismissed:

> Margaret Hodge MP: '... we will expect a serious person to appear before us. We will order them, and do that as soon as we can after recess, probably on a Thursday morning.'[14]

A similar welcome, but displaying really quite profound admiration, was on display in the Senate PSI:

> Senator McCain: 'I think it is important that all of us make it very clear the admiration that we hold for Apple. The incredible changes that Apple has caused in our lives and the spread of information and the capabilities to share information and knowledge throughout the world have been phenomenal.'[15]

---

[10] R Pelizzo, R Stapenhurst, V Sahgal et al, 'What Makes Public Accounts Committees Work? A Comparative Analysis' (2006) 34 *Politics & Policy* 774. For an interesting examination of the rhetorical framings of tax professionals appearing before the legislative hearings, see S Addison and F Mueller, 'The dark side of professions: the big four and tax avoidance' (2015) 28 *Accounting, Auditing & Accountability Journal* 1263 and, in relation to the Enron investigation, RJ Craig and JH Amernic, 'Enron discourse: the rhetoric of a resilient capitalism' (2004) 15 *Critical Perspectives on Accounting* 813. For a study of the Australian Senate investigation into tax avoidance, see B McCredie and K Sadiq, 'CSR and tax: a study in the transition from an "aggregate" to "real entity" view of corporations' (2019) *Pacific Accounting Review* (in press).

[11] PAC, *Tax avoidance: The Role Of Large Accountancy Firms* (London, The Stationery Office, 2013). For a study of this PAC hearing, see Addison and Mueller (n 10) 1269.

[12] See references in n 1 above.

[13] PAC 2012 hearings (n 1) Ev 21.

[14] PAC 2012 hearings (n 1) Ev 37.

[15] Senate PSI Apple (n 1) 8.

And later, bidding farewell to Apple:

> Senator McCain: '... we congratulate you on all of your successes and that of Apple, and as we said earlier, you have managed to change the world, which is an incredible legacy for Apple and all of the men and women who serve it.'[16]

Even Senator Levin, who questioned Apple most persistently about moving the 'crown jewels of a company, to a tax haven' – Ireland – concluded warmly:

> I want to again thank you, all of you, and I want to commend your company for the great work that you produce.[17]

No doubt the multinational enterprises were acutely aware that there is, in the UK, an obligation to attend, and failure to attend will be viewed as 'disobedience' to the House of Commons.[18] Similarly in the US, there is a legal obligation to appear before the Senate PSI and testimony before the Senate PSI is sworn to be the truth, the whole truth and nothing but the truth.[19]

Nonetheless, this stance expresses a spirit of inquiry, where the ostensible point of the legislative hearings can be summed up in the PAC Chair's introduction of the purpose of the hearings to Starbucks, Amazon and Google as being:

> Margaret Hodge MP: '... to try to understand why you don't pay the corporation tax that it appears, on the facts, is due.'[20]

This is an interesting formulation, possibly tendentious, as it calls into contention certain facts which appear to, but might not, sustain a liability to tax. Margaret Hodge subsequently indicated that immorality, rather than illegality, was the accusation being made.[21]

In the Senate PSI, Senator Levin set out the contrary objectives of the politicians and the multinational enterprises:

> Apple executives want the public to focus on the U.S. taxes the company has paid, but the real issue is the billions in taxes that it has not paid, thanks to offshore tax strategies whose purpose is tax avoidance, pure and simple.[22]

The characterisation of the behaviour of the multinational enterprises in both the Senate PSI and PAC hearings divorces a legal tax liability from what we might label a social or moral obligation to pay tax.[23] It sets the tone for a proliferation of

---

[16] Senate PSI Apple (n 1) 43.

[17] Senate PSI Apple (n 1) 64.

[18] TE May, P Simon, D Miller et al, *Erskine May's Treatise on the Law, Privileges, Proceedings and Usage of Parliament* (LexisNexis 2011) 820.

[19] Senate Rules of Procedure for 113th Congress, available at www.hsgac.senate.gov (accessed 7 January 2020).

[20] PAC 2012 hearings (n 1) Ev 21.

[21] PAC 2012 hearings (n 1) Ev 40.

[22] Senate PSI Apple (n 1) 7.

[23] See, eg, H Gribnau, 'Corporate Social Responsibility and Tax Planning' (2015) 24 *Social & Legal Studies* 225, P Sikka, 'Smoke and mirrors: Corporate social responsibility and tax avoidance' (2010) 34 *Accounting Forum* 153.

62   Emer Hunt

moral communication, each participant vying with the others to persuade all.[24] For present purposes, it must be noted that each of the multinational enterprises was at pains to specify that it was a compliant taxpayer and had done nothing illegal. In Tim Cook's testimony to the Senate PSI, he stated:

> Apple: 'We pay all the taxes we owe, every single dollar.'[25]

In the PAC hearings, each of Amazon, Google and Starbucks noted that they were compliant taxpayers:

> Amazon: 'We set up our business across Europe for the benefit of our tens of millions of customers and sellers across Europe. We pay all applicable taxes in all jurisdictions.'[26]
>
> Google: 'We run the business in a robust way. We think we do it in a way that is appropriate. It is certainly legal. We pay all the tax we are required to.'[27]
>
> Starbucks: 'We are an extremely high taxpayer. We clearly are not aggressively looking to avoid tax, or looking to avoid tax on any structure anywhere.'[28]

There was no sustained attempt to refute the legality of what had been done.[29] Indeed the spirit of inquiry resulted in there being no follow up to an observation of an expert witness before the Senate PSI in the following exchange:

> Expert: 'Could I make one comment just to be sure the record is correct? In my testimony – and I want to be crystal clear – I said I take no position on the legal correctness or strength of any tax position taken by Apple. I do not want that construed as saying what they have done is also fine. I have no idea. And that was not the point of the hearing ...'
>
> Senator Levin: 'Thank you. I think you have put it very clearly. There is no effort to vilify anybody. We are trying to shine a spotlight on the practices of a big company ...'[30]

Senator Paul articulated this acceptance of the legality of the tax practices. In the same extract, he also indicated that Apple was being treated unfairly:

> 'So if you want to chase [Apple] out, bring them here and vilify them. It is exactly the wrong thing to do. We should be giving them an award today. We should be congratulating them on being a great American company and hiring people and not vilifying them for obeying the law. I mean, they are obeying the law. No one is accusing them of breaking the law.'[31]

---

[24] V Valentinov, 'The ethics of functional differentiation: reclaiming morality in Niklas Luhmann's social systems theory' (2019) 155 *Journal of Business Ethics* 105.

[25] Senate PSI Apple (n 1) 37.

[26] PAC 2012 hearings (n 1) Ev 47.

[27] PAC 2012 hearings (n 1) Ev 43.

[28] PAC 2012 hearings (n 1) Ev 24.

[29] A challenge to the legality of what is done by multinational enterprises is clearer in PAC legislative hearings relating to professional tax advisers, see PAC, *Tax avoidance: the role of large accountancy firms*, Ev 4 (London, The Stationery Office, 2013), available at https://publications.parliament.uk/pa/cm201213/cmselect/cmpubacc/870/870.pdf (accessed 8 January 2020). See also Addison and Mueller (n 10).

[30] Senate PSI Apple (n 1) 33.

[31] Senate PSI Apple (n 1) 32.

III. The Debate Over Fair Taxation: US Senate PSI and UK PAC

The discussion in the Senate PSI and UK PAC is often characterised by all parties laying claim to fairness. Take this exchange between Margaret Hodge, MP and the Google executive:

> Margaret Hodge MP: 'So you are minimising your tax even though it is unfair to British taxpayers.'
>
> Google: 'It is not unfair to British taxpayers. We pay all the tax you require us to pay in the UK. We paid £6 million of tax last year—'
>
> Margaret Hodge MP: 'We are not accusing you of being illegal; we are accusing you of being immoral.'[32]

With this exchange, unfairness is equated to immorality by the legislators but, from Google's point of view, its discharge of legal tax liability cannot be suffused with unfairness. A similar assertion of fairness, but also a tacit admission that aggressive tax avoidance is incompatible with fairness, is to be found in Starbuck's statement:

> I assure you that we have every intention to be a fair taxpayer everywhere we are. We are never aggressive in avoiding taxes by any means.[33]

There is also an emphasis on the perception of fairness, rather than its content, and whether the problem with the tax practices of the multinational enterprises is that they breach a necessary perception of fairness. Examine this exchange in the Senate PSI with Tim Cook, CEO of Apple:

> Senator McCain: 'Can you understand there is a perception of unfair advantage here, Mr. Cook?'
>
> Apple: 'Sir, I see this as a very complex topic that – I am glad that we are having the discussion, but, honestly speaking, I do not see it as being unfair. I am not an unfair person. That is not who we are as a company or who I am as an individual. And so I would not preside over that, honestly. I do not see it in that way.'[34]

Mr Cook, speaking both on behalf of Apple and personally, cannot conceive of the company's behaviour or his own behaviour as unfair. However, he implicitly accepts that the tax system could be viewed as unfair insofar as he calls for a 'dramatic simplification' of the tax code and adds:

> Apple: 'We make this recommendation with our eyes wide open, fully recognizing that this would likely result in an increase in Apple's U.S. taxes. But we strongly believe that such comprehensive reform would be fair to all taxpayers, would keep America globally competitive, and would promote U.S. economic growth.'[35]

---

[32] PAC 2012 hearings (n 1) Ev 40.
[33] PAC 2012 hearings (n 1) Ev 31.
[34] Senate PSI Apple (n 1) 45.
[35] Senate PSI Apple (n 1) 38.

64   Emer Hunt

Perceptions of fairness and ethical behaviour can also be discerned from the questions about the likely consumer response to tax issues.[36]

> Ian Swales MP: 'Do any of you have any discussions internally about issues such as consumer power and the value of your brand, and how that could be influenced by the ethical behaviour or perceptions of your company? How do you factor that into the sort of discussion we have had this afternoon?'

> Google: 'Everybody who uses any Google service has a choice. All of our services are free to consumers, so we work extremely hard to try to ensure those services work well and that those consumers feel a level of trust in us. We talked earlier about the statement, "Don't be evil." For us, that means that when we give you websearch results we try to give you the best and most neutral results we can. That is how we operate.'[37]

There is a suggestion that the aftermath of the global financial crisis and the attendant difficulties of states in raising revenue are part of the motivation for fairness.

> Margaret Hodge MP: 'It is the UK where we seek the taxes in these troubling times, and we want everybody to give their fair share – all in it together.'[38]

This is also evident in the Senate PSI hearings, where Senator Levin observed:

> [Congress] are major contributors to the problems that I have outlined, so we have to do better, particularly facing a fiscal disaster, but even if we were not, it is just simply not fair to your average taxpayer that pays his taxes to see these kind of loopholes that are both used and created where they do not exist, and then companies getting away with it.[39]

The discourse over fairness could have taken an earlier starting point. There was a plethora of newspaper investigations: *Wall Street Journal* in 2005,[40] *Reuters*, the *New York Times*, *The Times* and the *Guardian* in 2012,[41] together with reports

---

[36] See, eg, I Hardeck and R Hertl, 'Consumer reactions to corporate tax strategies: Effects on corporate reputation and purchasing behavior' (2014) 123 *Journal of Business Ethics* 309.

[37] PAC 2012 hearings (n 1) Ev 48.

[38] PAC 2012 hearings (n 1) Ev 31.

[39] Senate PSI 2012 (n 1) 76.

[40] G R Simpson, 'Irish Subsidiary Lets Microsoft Slash Taxes in U.S. and Europe', *Wall Street Journal*, 7 November 2005, available at www.wsj.com/articles/SB113132761685289706 (accessed 7 January 2020).

[41] T Bergin, 'How Starbucks avoids UK taxes', *Reuters*, 15 October 2012, available at https://uk.reuters.com/article/us-britain-starbucks-tax/special-report-how-starbucks-avoids-uk-taxes-idUKBRE89E0EX20121015 (accessed 7 January 2020); C Duhigg and D Kocieniewski, 'How Apple Sidesteps Billions in Taxes', *New York Times*, 28 April 2012, available at www.nytimes.com/2012/04/29/business/apples-tax-strategy-aims-at-low-tax-states-and-nations.html?_r=0 (accessed 7 January 2020)); A Mostrous, 'Times Investigation: the Tax Avoiders', *The Times*, 19 June 2012, available at https://www.thetimes.co.uk/article/times-investigation-the-tax-avoiders-0rkt3fhwtrn (accessed 13 May 2020); L Prieg, 'Forget plumbers. Forget shaming individuals. Tax avoidance is systemic', *Guardian*, June 2012, available at https://www.theguardian.com/commentisfree/2012/jul/24/forget-cash-in-hand-tax-avoidance-systemic (accessed 13 May 2020).

from non-governmental organisations such as Christian Aid,[42] Oxfam[43] or the OECD report on harmful tax competition,[44] each or all of which could well be posited to have propelled the discussion of international tax up the social agenda. Equally, events such as the austere aftermath of the Global Financial Crisis, the Occupy movement, and the publication of the LuxLeaks database of confidential tax rulings between Luxembourg and actual or putative Luxembourger taxpayers have also developed the salience of international tax as a policy issue.[45] Yet what renders the legislative hearings worthy of study is that a cohort of multinational enterprises gave public testimony about their views of tax, including their obligations as taxpayers, and explicitly maintained that their behaviour was fair in the face of allegations of unfairness by politicians.

What can be seen from these extracts is that fairness is a contested battlefield: both politicians and multinational enterprises claim to be fair and each, either implicitly or explicitly, sees the other's insistence on a certain approach to tax as unfair. In the Senate and the PAC, multinational enterprises sought to compel recognition of their fairness because they obey the law, but were confronted with accusations of unfairness and aggression because they only obey the law.

IV. Changes in the International Tax Landscape

Much of the debate within the legislative hearings could be described as mere rhetoric although analyses of rhetoric emphasise the persuasive role of language in structuring social action.[46] This chapter is not concerned with quantifying any influence of the legislative hearings in effecting subsequent changes in practice or law. What should be noted, nonetheless, is the litany of concrete legal changes in this area which happened after the Senate PSI and PAC hearings. These initiatives in the area of international tax have a dual aspect.

---

[42] Christian Aid, 'The shirts off their backs: How tax policies fleece the poor', September 2005, available at https://www.christianaid.org.uk/resources/about-us/shirts-their-backs-2005 (accessed 7 January 2020); Christian Aid, 'Death and taxes: The true toll of tax dodging', May 2008, available at https://www.christianaid.org.uk/resources/about-us/death-and-taxes-true-toll-tax-dodging (accessed 7 January 2020); Christian Aid, 'False profits: robbing the poor to keep the rich tax-free', March 2009, available at https://www.christianaid.org.uk/resources/about-us/false-profits-robbing-poor-keep-rich-tax-free (accessed 7 January 2020).

[43] Oxfam, 'Tax havens: Releasing the hidden billions for poverty eradication', briefing paper, 1 June 2000, available at https://policy-practice.oxfam.org.uk/publications/tax-havens-releasing-the-hidden-billions-for-poverty-eradication-114611 (accessed 7 January 2020).

[44] OECD, *Harmful Tax Competition Emerging Global Issue* (Paris, OECD, 1998).

[45] S Dallyn, 'An examination of the political salience of corporate tax avoidance: A case study of the Tax Justice Network' (2017) 41 *Accounting Forum* 336; L Oats and G Morris, 'Tax avoidance, power and politics' in N Hashimzade and Y Epifantseva (eds), *The Routledge Companion to Tax Avoidance Research* (Routledge, 2018).

[46] Addison and Mueller (n 10); R Suddaby and R Greenwood, 'Rhetorical Strategies of Legitimacy' (2005) 50 *Administrative Science Quarterly* 35; and Craig and Amernic (n 10).

66   *Emer Hunt*

First, the European Commission used state aid provisions to challenge the tax rulings given by certain member states to three of the multinational enterprises which appeared before the legislative hearings.[47]

Secondly, there have been a number of legislative initiatives. Under the auspices of a G20 mandate, the OECD has pursued the BEPS project, which has sought to ensure that jurisdictions collaborate to terminate tax avoidance strategies.[48] The European Commission has announced an Action Plan for fair and effective corporate taxation within the EU.[49]

V. Tax Rulings: State Aid Enforcement

In June 2013, the European Commission sent requests for information to certain member states, Ireland, Luxembourg and the Netherlands, about tax rulings.[50] Three of the multinational enterprises which had appeared before the Senate PSI or the PAC – Apple, Amazon and Starbucks – were the subject of enforcement actions. Certainly, Apple's characterisation of its relationship with Ireland during the Senate PSI could have signalled state aid to be a fruitful approach:

> Apple: '… so as a part of recruiting us, the Irish Government did give us a tax incentive agreement to enter there, and since then we have built up a sizable operation there, nearly 4,000 people.'[51]

Each of Ireland, the Netherlands and Luxembourg was found by the European Commission to have provided illegal state aid to, respectively, Apple, Starbucks and Amazon.[52] The decisions of the European Commission were appealed by the member states and the multinational enterprises. The General Court annulled the decision of the Commission in the case of Netherlands – Starbucks, and other appeals are pending.[53]

---

[47] Commission Decision (EU) 2017/1283 of 30 August 2016 on State aid SA.38373 (2014/C) (ex 2014/NN) (ex 2014/CP) implemented by Ireland to Apple: [2017] OJ L187/1; Commission Decision (EU) 2018/859 of 4 October 2017 on State aid SA.38944 (2014/C) (ex 2014/NN) implemented by Luxembourg to Amazon: [2018] OJ L 153/1; Commission Decision (EU) 2017/502 of 21 October 2015 on State aid SA.38374 (2014/C ex 2014/NN) implemented by the Netherlands to Starbucks: [2017] OJ L 83/38.

[48] See www.oecd.org/tax/beps/ (accessed 7 January 2020). On BEPS, see generally, Y Brauner, 'What the BEPS' (2014) 16 *Florida Tax Review* 55 and A Christians, 'BEPS and the new international tax order' (2016) *BYU Law Review* 1603.

[49] See European Commission, 'Commission presents Action Plan for Fair and Efficient Corporate Taxation in the EU', press release, 17 June 2015, available at http://europa.eu/rapid/press-release_IP-15-5188_en.htm (accessed 7 January 2020).

[50] Regarding the Commission's work in this area, see https://ec.europa.eu/competition/state_aid/tax_rulings/index_en.html (accessed 7 January 2020).

[51] Senate PSI 2013 (n 1) 46.

[52] See n 47 above.

[53] Joined Cases T-760/15 and T-636/16, *The Netherlands and Starbucks Corp/Starbucks Manufacturing Emea BV v Commission*, EU:T:2019:669.

(Un)Fairness as an Irritant to the Legal System 67

The recourse to state aid law to challenge the grant of tax rulings by member states to taxpayers was novel, although the state aid rules have been part of the law of the European Union since 1957.[54] This novelty, in itself, caused allegations of unfairness. In August 2016 the US Treasury issued a white paper on the state aid enforcement actions taken by the European Commission, citing a letter from US Congress to the US Treasury Secretary, in which was stated:

> [The] United States has a stake in these cases and has serious concerns about their fairness and potential impact on the U.S. fisc.[55]

This could be taken as a reference to procedural fairness, and the white paper disputes the European Commission's enforcement actions on the basis of lack of predictability.[56] A more expansive concept of fairness, encompassing a substantive fairness, can be read into the closing sentence of the white paper:

> The U.S. Treasury Department remains ready and willing to continue to collaborate with the Commission on the important work of ensuring that the international tax system is fair, efficient, and predictable.[57]

While the decisions of the European Commission in these cases had recourse only to state aid law, the accompanying press releases referred to fair taxes,[58] as did conference speeches given by Commissioner Vestager.[59] Referring to the

---

[54] LL Gormsen, *European State Aid and Tax Rulings* (Cheltenham, Edward Elgar Publishing, 2019).

[55] US Treasury, 'The European Commission's Recent State Aid Investigations of Transfer Pricing Rulings', U.S. Department of the Treasury White Paper, August 24, 2016, 4, available at www.treasury.gov/resource-center/tax-policy/treaties/Documents/White-Paper-State-Aid.pdf (accessed 7 January 2020).

[56] ibid 5. Appeals to the European court by Ireland and Apple also dispute the decision of the European Commission on the basis of lack of legal certainty and retroactivity. See Case T-892/16 *Apple Sales International and Apple Operations Europe v Commission* and Case T-778/16 *Ireland v Commission* [2017] OJ C 53/39.

[57] US Treasury (n 55) 25.

[58] European Commission, 'State aid: Ireland gave illegal tax benefits to Apple worth up to €13 billion', press release, 30 August 2016, available at https://ec.europa.eu/commission/presscorner/detail/en/IP_16_2923 (accessed 7 January 2020); European Commission, 'Commission decides selective tax advantages for Fiat in Luxembourg and Starbucks in the Netherlands are illegal under EU state aid rules', press release, 21 October 2015, available at https://ec.europa.eu/commission/presscorner/detail/en/IP_15_5880 (accessed 7 January 2020), European Commission, 'State aid: Commission finds Luxembourg gave illegal tax benefits to Amazon worth around €250 million', press release, 4 October 2017, available at https://ec.europa.eu/commission/presscorner/detail/en/IP_17_3701 (accessed 7 January 2020).

[59] See, eg, speeches by Commissioner Vestager: M Vestager, 'Independence Is Non-negotiable', Chatham House Competition Policy Conference, London, 18 June 2015, available at https://wayback.archive-it.org/12090/20191129202709/https://ec.europa.eu/commission/commissioners/2014-2019/vestager/announcements/independence-non-negotiable_en (accessed 8 January 2020) and M Vestager, 'Working together for fairer taxation', The Tax Dialogue, Copenhagen, 2 September 2016, available at https://wayback.archive-it.org/12090/20191129212646/https://ec.europa.eu/commission/commissioners/2014-2019/vestager/announcements/working-together-fairer-taxation_en (accessed 8 January 2020).

68   Emer Hunt

Luxembourg – Amazon case, Joaquin Almunia, Commissioner for Competition, stated:

> It is only fair that subsidiaries of multinational companies pay their share of taxes and do not receive preferential treatment which could amount to hidden subsidies.[60]

Algirdas Šemeta, Commissioner for Taxation, had a nuanced message, indicating that fair tax competition – presumably by member states – was required but, at the same time, tax rules had to abide by fair play:

> Fair tax competition is fundamental for a healthy Single Market and our common economic prosperity. As we work together to restore growth and competitiveness, it is essential to tackle the harmful tax practices which erode the tax bases of EU Member States. Fair play in taxation must be the rule.[61]

In relation to the Netherlands – Starbucks, Commissioner Margrethe Vestager, who succeeded Commissioner Almunia in charge of competition policy, also cited fairness:

> Tax rulings that artificially reduce a company's tax burden are not in line with EU state aid rules. They are illegal. I hope that, with today's decisions, this message will be heard by Member State governments and companies alike. All companies, big or small, multi-national or not, should pay their fair share of tax.[62]

The state aid decisions of the Commission in the cases of Ireland, the Netherlands and Luxembourg did not quantify the tax foregone by reference to principles of fairness. Each of the three cases is a detailed and reasoned analysis of tax rulings based on the application of Article 107 of the Treaty on the Functioning of the European Union (TFEU). In summary, the legal argument revolved around the selectivity of treatment of the multinational enterprise through the grant of a tax ruling.[63]

Nonetheless, Commission press releases announcing infringement findings all refer to the requirement for fairness in the legislative agenda. The press release in October 2017 about the Luxembourg – Amazon case can serve as an example of the almost identical language used in each of the press releases:

> This Commission has pursued a far-reaching strategy towards fair taxation and greater transparency and we have recently seen major progress.

---

[60] European Commission, 'State aid: Commission investigates transfer pricing arrangements on corporate taxation of Amazon in Luxembourg', press release, 7 October 2014, available at https://ec.europa.eu/commission/presscorner/detail/en/IP_14_1105 (accessed 7 January 2020).

[61] ibid.

[62] European Commission, 'Commission decides selective tax advantages for Fiat in Luxembourg and Starbucks in the Netherlands are illegal under EU state aid rules', press release, 21 October 2015, available at http://europa.eu/rapid/press-release_IP-15-5880_en.htm (accessed 7 January 2020).

[63] Joined Cases (n 53). See, generally, Gormsen (n 54).

Later in the press release, it is stated:

> ... the Commission launched a new EU agenda to ensure that the digital economy is taxed in a fair and growth-friendly way.[64]

In this way, the Commission in its press releases presents legislative change and state aid actions as two facets of a wider agenda of, to quote the title of one of Commissioner's Vestager's speeches, 'Why Fair Taxation Matters'[65]

VI. Fairness Initiatives: Hard and Soft Law Changes

Nor was Vestager's a lone voice: other politicians referred to fairness as requiring changes in the international tax system, but also called for unified action through the G20.[66] The G20 mandated the OECD to develop soft law instruments, known as the BEPS project, which have been influential in effecting change at a jurisdictional level.[67] The BEPS project explicitly invokes the concept of fairness in advocating or prescribing change in the international tax architecture: the OECD in 2013 put the BEPS project within the context of 'a tense situation in which citizens have become more sensitive to tax fairness issues';[68] the G20, in endorsing the OECD BEPS project in 2013, referred to tax avoidance undermining people's trust in the fairness of the tax system[69] and, in 2014, stated:

> We are taking actions to ensure the fairness of the international tax system and to secure countries' revenue bases. Profits should be taxed where economic activities deriving the profits are performed and where value is created.[70]

In March 2015, the European Commission announced the Tax Transparency Package, where automatic exchange of information in relation to tax rulings was introduced to counter tax avoidance which 'undermines fair burden-sharing among taxpayers and fair competition between businesses'.[71] This was followed

---

[64] It is reported that Luxembourg gave illegal tax benefits to Amazon worth around €250 million; European Commission, 'State aid: Commission finds Luxembourg gave illegal tax benefits to Amazon worth around €250 million', press release, 4 October 2017, available at https://ec.europa.eu/commission/presscorner/detail/en/IP_17_3701 (accessed 7 January 2020).

[65] Vestager, 'Why Fair Taxation Matters', Copenhagen Business School, Denmark, 9 September 2016, available at https://wayback.archive-it.org/12090/20200221215712/https://ec.europa.eu/commission/commissioners/2014-2019/vestager/announcements/why-fair-taxation-matters_en.

[66] G Osborne, P Moscovici and W Schäuble, 'We are determined that multinationals will not avoid tax', *Financial Times*, 16 February 2013, available at www.ft.com/content/6b12990e-76bc-11e2-ac9 1-00144feabdc0 (accessed 7 January 2020).

[67] A Christians and SE Shay, 'Assessing BEPS: Origins, Standards, and Responses' (2017) 102A *Cahiers de Droit Fiscal International* 17.

[68] OECD, *Action Plan on Base Erosion and Profit Shifting* (Paris, OECD Publishing, 2013), 8.

[69] G20, St Petersburg (n 3).

[70] G20, Brisbane (n 3).

[71] European Commission, 'Combatting corporate tax avoidance: Commission presents Tax Transparency Package', press release, 18 March 2015, available at https://ec.europa.eu/commission/presscorner/detail/en/IP_15_4610 (accessed 7 January 2020).

in June 2015 by an Action Plan for fair and effective corporate taxation within the EU.[72] In January 2016 the anti-tax avoidance package, entitled 'Fair Taxation', was announced, and included ATAD.[73] In June 2016, ATAD was adopted by the European Council and its measures were to be implemented by member states by 1 January 2019.

The segregation in terminology between the state aid decisions (no quantification of tax foregone by reference to fairness) and their accompanying press releases (references to fairness) was clear: the European Commission's commentary on its own decisions ascribed motivations of fairness to measures which did not themselves refer to fairness. In contrast to this approach, ATAD, a legal instrument, refers to fairness. Admittedly, it is in the preamble to ATAD, which provides a context for the directive, rather than in its body.

> Preamble (1) to ATAD: 'The current political priorities in international taxation highlight the need for ensuring that tax is paid where profits and value are generated. It is thus imperative to restore trust in the fairness of tax systems and allow governments to effectively exercise their tax sovereignty.'

This is an echo of the emphasis placed on the perception of fairness by Senator McCain, where a distinction was drawn between the perception and, by implication, the substance of fairness.[74] It is an argument that the tax system will have legitimacy in the eyes of the public only when it is perceived as fair.[75] The use of the word 'restore' implies that trust has been lost in the fairness of tax systems. This is conceptually similar to the directive dealing with the mandatory automatic exchange of tax information, which refers to the *creation* of an environment of fair taxation.[76]

The ATAD does not ignore the substance of fairness, and indeed explains the function of the ATAD in terms of fairness:

> Preamble (1) to ATAD: 'In response to the need for fairer taxation, the Commission … sets out an action plan for fair and efficient corporate taxation in the European Union.'

> Preamble (2) to ATAD: 'It is essential for the good functioning of the internal market that, as a minimum, Member States implement their commitments under BEPS and more broadly, take action to discourage tax avoidance practices and ensure fair and effective taxation in the Union in a sufficiently coherent and coordinated fashion.'

---

[72] European Commission, 'Action Plan on Corporate Taxation', 17 June 2015, available at https://ec.europa.eu/taxation_customs/business/company-tax/action-plan-corporate-taxation_en (accessed 7 January 2020).

[73] European Commission, 'Fair Taxation: Commission presents new measures against corporate tax avoidance', press release, 28 January 2016, available at http://europa.eu/rapid/press-release_IP-16-159_en.htm (accessed 7 January 2020.

[74] See above at n 34.

[75] R Lanis and G Richardson, 'Corporate social responsibility and tax aggressiveness: a test of legitimacy theory' (2012) 26 *Accounting, Auditing & Accountability Journal* 75.

[76] See above at n 5.

The references to fairness in ATAD cover both the perception and the substance of fairness. Both efficiency and effectiveness are paired with fair taxation, which is limited to corporate taxation in one place but applied more generally to tax in Preamble (2). The ATAD is a wide-ranging directive, with substantial legal effect. Positioning it as having the function of achieving fair taxation while, at the same time, allowing member states to exercise their tax sovereignty, adds an inchoate ingredient to its interpretation.

VII. Fairness: An Irritation of the Legal System by the Political System

There are many possibilities as to how these references to fairness could be examined.[77] We could attempt a deconstruction of what each individual in the legislative hearings, praying in aid fairness to bolster their argument or position their rhetoric, means by fairness. Is it the same fairness that appears through the state aid enforcement commentary, the G20, OECD and European Commission press releases and, ultimately, fetches up in ATAD? We could then assess these constructions of fairness by reference to a theoretical stance on fairness, probably by recourse to Rawls' theory of justice and the governance of the 'basis structure' of society if we were to bargain under fair conditions.[78] The G20 call for fairness 'involves the idea of fair terms of cooperation: these are terms that each participant may reasonably accept, provided that everyone else likewise accepts them'.[79] Such an approach would be especially interesting because Rawls developed his theory primarily in relation to a territorial state, which is intimately connected with tax-raising powers.[80] Territory matters: tax law was traditionally predicated on the existence of territorial lines.[81] This was not disputed by the European Commission in the Ireland – Apple state aid case[82] and the US objected to the state aid enforcement because of its effect on the US fisc.[83]

---

[77] See, eg, Gribnau (n 23); Pogge and Mehta (n 4); P Dietsch, *Catching Capital: The Ethics of Tax Competition* (Oxford, OUP, 2015).

[78] J Rawls, *A Theory of Justice* (Harvard, Harvard University Press, 2009).

[79] J Rawls, 'Justice as Fairness: Political not Metaphysical' (1985) 14 *Philosophy & Public Affairs* 223, 232. See above at n 66, where Osborne, Moscovici and Schäuble address the need for cooperation in very similar terms.

[80] For a discussion on territoriality in international tax law, see RS Avi-Yonah, 'International tax as international law' (2004) 57 *Tax Law Review* 483 and W Schön, 'Persons and territories: on the international allocation of taxing rights' [2010] *British Tax Review* 554.

[81] This was expressed in 1889 by Lord Herschell in the judgment of the UK House of Lords in *Colquhoun v Brooks* (1889) 2 TC 490, 499: 'The Income Tax Acts, however, themselves impose a territorial limit, either that from which the taxable income is derived must be situate in the United Kingdom or the person whose income is to be taxed must be resident there.'

[82] Commission Decision, *Ireland to Apple* (n 47) [195].

[83] US Treasury (n 55).

72   Emer Hunt

The very premise of the legislative hearings in the UK and the US was based on national tax considerations: the orientation was towards avoidance of national taxes, without considering other jurisdictions:

> Senator McCain: 'For years, Apple has opted to forgo fully contributing to the U.S. Treasury and to American society by shifting profits and circumventing U.S. taxes.'[84]

In the PAC, issues of fairness are presented in a UK context:

> Jackie Doyle-Price MP: 'We in Britain are very concerned about fair play, and one of the reasons why we have embraced Starbucks is because of your emphasis on fair trade and your emphasis on ethics.'[85]

Indeed, the foreignness of Google, Starbucks and Amazon is noted by the PAC:

> Margaret Hodge MP: 'Our particular interest, of course, is that now that so much of UK business is carried out by global entities, corporation tax, and the way in which tax is collected, is hugely important. All three of you are American-based companies, which is also of particular interest.'[86]

The call for mutually advantageous co-operation, which is the basis of the actions of the G20 in calling for a global solution,[87] could be analysed as a search for Rawlsian-inspired justice in an international arena. This co-operative territoriality might be consistent with identifying the international arena as a 'basic structure'. Beitz's reasoning on matters of international co-operation appears relevant, where he argues '... the parties to the original position cannot be assumed to know that they are members of a particular national society, choosing principles of justice primarily for that society. The veil of ignorance must extend to all matters of national citizenship, and the principles chosen will therefore apply globally'.[88] Into this mix could be put Hart's view on mutual restrictions, where he wrote 'in the case of mutual restrictions we are in fact saying that this claim to interfere with another's freedom is justified because it is fair: and it is fair because only so will there be an equal distribution of restrictions and so of freedom among this group of men'.[89] Add to this the peculiarities of the European Union as a (sometimes reluctant) exercise in sharing tax sovereignty: the appeal to fairness is linked, in Preamble (1) of ATAD to allowing member states effectively to exercise their tax sovereignty. An effective exercise of tax sovereignty by some may be incompatible

---

[84] Senate PSI Apple (n 1) 8.

[85] PAC 2012 hearings (n 1) Ev 31.

[86] PAC 2012 hearings (n 1) Ev 21.

[87] See, eg, the G20 endorsement of tackling tax avoidance, and promoting tax transparency and automatic exchange of information in September 2013, G20, St Petersburg (n 3). For an examination of a global solution, see T Rixen, 'Tax competition and inequality: the case for global tax governance' (2011) 17 *Global Governance* 447.

[88] CR Beitz, 'Bounded morality: justice and the state in world politics' (1979) 33 *International Organization* 405.

[89] HLA Hart, 'Are there any natural rights?' (1955) 64 *The Philosophical Review* 175.

with fairness for others.[90] The competing narratives of tax sovereignty and fair taxation are played out in the Preamble to ATAD.[91]

But these diffuse calls to fairness are too meagre an offering on which to substantiate a theory of fairness. To do so would elevate the random references to fairness in the legislative hearings and in the press releases accompanying the enforcement action under EU state aid rules and various hard and soft law initiatives. The calls for fairness, or allegations of unfairness, throughout the legislative hearings are visceral responses to conflict, not forensic analyses of what is fair: the word is simply used as a shorthand for a type of moral disapproval by politicians, or by the multinational enterprises as an assertion of ethical behaviour on the basis of complying with the law.[92] Von Groddeck sees the communication of moral or social values by corporates as allied with increasing complexity and uncertainty.[93] There is not enough detail in the legislative hearings to discern what is meant by fairness in a global world; there is only a loud cry of unfairness and general dissatisfaction with the tax practices of multinational enterprises, or with the actions of the European Commission, and a more muted, but nonetheless discernible assertion of fairness by multinational enterprises because they obey the law in every jurisdiction in which they do business.

VIII. Fair within ATAD

One reference to fairness is qualitatively different, at least to a lawyer. This is the incorporation of the concept of fairness in ATAD. This moves fairness from the expression of social or moral values within the political system to a component of a legal instrument within the legal system. Each system construes meaning quite differently from other systems, and a construction of meaning from the environment of the legal system may be heard as 'order from noise',[94] or may not be heard but, if heard, will be given an alien construction by the legal system.[95] Fairness moving into the legal system will have resonances within the legal system, but in a way that is crafted by the legal system in its inimitable way.

But, first, can references to fair taxation in the preamble to ATAD be seen as outside noise entering the legal system? Is it an irritant or just a formulation of

---

[90] Dietsch (n 77).

[91] CM Radaelli, 'Harmful Tax Competition in the EU: Policy Narratives and Advocacy Coalitions' (1999) 37 *Journal of Common Market Studies* 661.

[92] Valentinov (n 24).

[93] V von Groddeck, 'Rethinking the Role of Value Communication in Business Corporations from a Sociological Perspective – Why Organisations Need Value-Based Semantics to Cope with Societal and Organisational Fuzziness' (2011) 100 *Journal of Business Ethics* 69.

[94] Luhmann, Ziegert and Kastner (n 7) 80.

[95] G Teubner, 'Social Order from Legislative Noise? Autopoietic Closure as a Problem for Legal Regulation', in G Teubner and A Febbrajo (eds), *State, Law, and Economy as Autopoietic Systems: Regulation and Autonomy in a New Perspective* (Giuffrè, 1992).

74 Emer Hunt

what is already inherent within EU law? There are a few references to fairness in the TFEU, most notably in relation to fair competition, ensuring a fair standard of living for the agricultural community and fairness towards non-EU citizens.[96] None of these references is relevant to tax matters. Previous directives in the area of tax co-operation incorporate references to fairness[97] although other tax directives do not.[98]

From a common law point of view, there are indeed many references to fairness in administrative law and from a procedural point of view, tax authorities must treat taxpayers fairly.[99] This, however, is some way short of ensuring that trust is restored in the fairness of the tax system, and that member states must ensure fair and effective taxation in the Union, both of which are to be found in the Preamble to ATAD.

This emphasis on fairness is particularly challenging in the context of a common law interpretation of tax, which has traditionally been an area of positivist legal reasoning, where interpretation was ostensibly divorced from a normative bias. Given the positivist, autopoietic nature of the legal system,[100] extraneous matters do not intrude into this distinction: 'the corporation tax that it appears, on the facts, is due'[101] is levied by the legal system on the basis of positive law, rather than equity, morality or fairness.[102] Indeed this positivist stance is acquiesced to by the politicians in the legislative hearings, with an acceptance that the political system can change the law:

> Senator McCain: 'So the moral of the story, at least in my view, is that Apple has violated the spirit of the law, if not the letter of the law, and I agree that a great deal of responsibility lies with Congress.'[103]

---

[96] See Preamble to the TFEU, Articles 39(1)(b), 67(2), 79(1) and 80 TFEU and Article 3(5) of the Treaty on European Union.

[97] See, eg, references to fair taxation in Council Directive (EEC) 77/799 of 19 December 1977 concerning mutual assistance by the competent authorities of the member states in the field of direct taxation [1977] OJ L 336/15, and Council Directive (EU) 2018/822 of 25 May 2018 amending Directive 2011/16/EU as regards mandatory automatic exchange of information in the field of taxation in relation to reportable cross-border arrangements [2018] OJ L 139/1.

[98] See, eg, Council Directive (EU) 2015/2376 of 8 December 2015 amending Directive 2011/16/EU as regards mandatory automatic exchange of information in the field of taxation [2015] OJ L 332/1, Council Directive 2003/123/EC of 22 December 2003 amending Directive 90/435/EEC on the common system of taxation applicable in the case of parent companies and subsidiaries of different Member States [2004] OJ L 007/41 and Council Directive 2003/49/EC of 3 June 2003 on a common system of taxation applicable to interest and royalty payments made between associated companies of different Member States [2003] OJ L 157/49.

[99] See, eg, de Cogan (n 4). For a recent consideration by the UK courts of an obligation of fairness on the part of the tax authorities, see S Daly, 'R. (Hely-Hutchinson) v HMRC: Fairness in Tax Law and Revenue Guidance' [2016] *British Tax Review* 18.

[100] G Teubner, *Autopoietic Law – A New Approach to Law and Society*, vol 8 (Walter de Gruyter, 1987).

[101] See text above at n 20.

[102] S Picciotto, 'Constructing compliance: Game playing, tax law, and the regulatory state' (2007) 29 *Law & Policy* 11 and A Christians, 'Sovereignty, taxation and social contract' (2009) 18 *Minnesota Journal of International Law* 99.

[103] Senate PSI Apple (n 1) 30.

Senator Paul: '... [nobody] has said that Apple broke any laws. So they are brought before this Committee and harangued and bullied because they tried to minimize their tax burden legally.'[104]

Apple also asserted a positivist approach, although it went further by saying that both the spirit and letter of the law were observed:

We not only comply with the laws, but we comply with the spirit of the laws. We do not depend on tax gimmicks.[105]

Google, appearing before the PAC, also indicated a positivist approach to tax law compliance:

The tax we pay in the UK is a function of the activity that people do in the UK that is in line with UK law, and the way we operate around the world is in line with the law in every jurisdiction in which Google operates.[106]

The Chair of the PAC, Margaret Hodge, accepted that tax avoidance was within the law, saying to Google:

You are avoiding tax – within the law.[107]

Both Amazon and Starbucks also asserted a positivist stance to tax compliance, but Starbucks went further and also claimed a (subjective) ethical position:

Amazon: 'If Governments decide to change these rules, we will see how we continue to comply with all corporate laws.'[108]

Starbucks: 'We sincerely believe that we are doing everything to an ethical standard – not just the legal standard, but exactly what we should be doing.'[109]

Thus the chronological sequence from 2013 to 2016 above sustains an interpretation of the spread of fairness from the political sphere to the legal sphere. It was contested within the political system. There was no consistency as to who was fair and who unfair. Fairness was then adopted within the ATAD as a context in which the directive is to be interpreted. It is a challenge to the traditionally positivist approach to the interpretation of tax law to ascribe meaning and consequence to something as nebulous as fairness.[110]

This casts the references to fairness within the legislative hearings as an irritation to the legal system. Teubner examined the importation of the continental

---

[104] Senate PSI Apple (n 1) 31.

[105] Senate PSI Apple (n 1) 37. In response to the description of tax gimmicks, the expert witness before the Senate PSI, J Richard Harvey, stated: 'I about fell off my chair when I read that because, when I think about tax gimmicks, certainly some of the techniques that Apple uses could, in general usage of the word, be considered "gimmicks".'

[106] PAC 2012 hearings (n 1) Ev 40.

[107] PAC 2012 hearings (n 1) Ev 42.

[108] PAC 2012 hearings (n 1) Ev 50.

[109] ibid.

[110] J Freedman, 'Defining taxpayer responsibility: in support of a general anti-avoidance principle' [2004] *British Tax Review* 332 and Picciotto (n 102).

76   Emer Hunt

principle of 'good faith' into the common law through an EU Directive on Unfair Terms in Consumer Contracts.[111] He saw this as an 'outside noise which creates wild perturbations in the interplay of discourses within these arrangements and forces them to reconstruct internally not only their own rules but to reconstruct from scratch the alien element itself'.[112] Thus the question becomes what evolutionary changes might be effected in the legal systems of member states through the conflictual importation of an outside noise: namely fairness.

IX. Fair within the Preamble:
What is its Effect?

Ultimately, the ATAD will be subject to interpretation by the courts.[113] The moot question, which is ultimately for resolution by the courts of the European Union, is the extent to which references to fairness in the Preamble to ATAD will inform its interpretation.

There are precedents for examining the purpose of directives in the light of their preamble. In the case of *Henke*, the Court of Justice of the European Union (ECJ) looked at the purpose of the directive, which in that case concerned the safeguarding of the rights of employees on transfer of undertakings and businesses.[114] The ECJ declined to give the directive a relevance which extended to the transfer of functions from a municipal authority to another administrative body.

More detailed are the related cases of *Sturgeon*,[115] and *Nelson*,[116] in which there was a challenge to a prior interpretation of Regulation 261/2004 where the ECJ had referred to its purpose as expressed in the preamble. These cases related to whether air passengers should be entitled to compensation for delayed flights, or merely for cancelled flights. The teleological approach to interpretation is evident from the mission statement by the court: '… it is necessary, in interpreting a provision of Community law, to consider not only its wording, but also the context in which it occurs and the objectives pursued by the rules of which it is a part'.[117] Given that it was apparent from the preamble that the regulation was designed to give a high level of protection to air passengers, the ECJ held in favour of delayed aircraft passenger being entitled to compensation. The ECJ was invited, in the

---

[111] Teubner (n 6).

[112] ibid 12.

[113] For an overview of the principles of interpretation adopted by the European courts, see K Lenaerts and J Gutiérrez-Fons, 'To say what the law of the EU is: methods of interpretation and the European Court of Justice' (2013) 20 *Columbia Journal of European Law* 3.

[114] Case C-298/94 *Henke v Gemeinde Schierke and Verwaltungsgemeinschaft Brocken* EU:C:1996:382.

[115] Joined Cases C-402/07 *Sturgeon v Condor Flugdienst GmbH* and C-432/07 *Böck and Lepuschitz v Air France SA* EU:C:2009:716.

[116] Joined Cases C-581/10 *Nelson v Deutsche Lufthansa AG* and C-629/10 *TUI Travel plc v Civil Aviation Authority* EU:C:2012:657.

[117] ibid para 71.

later case of *Nelson*, to find that the court in *Sturgeon* had exceeded its jurisdiction. Again the ECJ referred to preamble to the Regulation to support the view that passengers suffering long delays or cancellations are in an equivalent position of inconvenience. The relevant part of the preamble records that 'the number of passengers denied boarding against their will remains too high, as does that affected by cancellations without prior warning and that affected by long delays'.[118] While there is no doubt that cancelled and late flights are annoying, this recital seems either anodyne or lacking in specificity. How high is too high? How much tax is fair?

X. Conclusion

It is as yet unknown what effect the purpose of ATAD will have on its interpretation. In ATAD the legal system can be observed as having metabolised moral dicta relating to unfairness, and internalised them. Certain facets of fairness have been indicated throughout the legislative hearings: unfairness as immorality and unfairness as exemplified by unfair tax competition by jurisdictions. This is contrasted with the necessity for having multinational enterprises pay their fair share of tax, with a strong emphasis on an obligation to a particular jurisdiction. These issues are differently described by participants in the legislative hearings, and are given different weight, and their application may be disputed. Ultimately, however, these are descriptions of normative stances or behaviours, which can be gathered under a large umbrella: morality of tax practices of both states and multinational enterprises. These are encapsulated in the references to fairness in ATAD, where they await the attention of the courts.

[118] ibid para 9.

PART II

Social Provision

PART II

Social Norms

5

Taxing for Social Justice or for Growth?

ÅSA GUNNARSSON

For several decades now, tax policy debate has been strongly influenced by a discourse that builds on what seems to be the conflicting interest between taxing for growth and taxing for social justice. The conflict implies a trade-off between efficiency and equity. The dominant internal tax policy trend has been increasingly influenced by the optimal tax theory, postulating that tax neutrality principles and horizontal equity should be guiding for the ultimate goal of taxing for growth. Consequently, the social justice dimension of tax law reforms has become a relatively underdeveloped competence in both tax policy debate and research. The neglect of welfare obligations has created non-sustainable structural problems. This chapter attempts to contextualise the problem from the perspectives of tax fairness principles and social contract models. Based on the European situation, one conclusion is that a constructive road-map for future tax reforms is a comprehensive tax base reform.

I. Introduction

The aim of this chapter is to deliver a thought-provoking view on what consequences the tax policy hegemony of taxing for growth policies have had on tax sustainability gaps regarding inequalities. Empirical, comparative facts are mainly related on the European situation, based on a research project on fair and sustainable taxation.[1] Some analyses will also be underpinned by Swedish examples on law reforms.

Since the beginning of the 1980s, the dominant trend in international tax policy has been the increasing influence of the optimal tax theory. A neoliberal economic rationale with a 'taxing for growth' paradigm through fiscal efficiency has been implemented worldwide, resulting in an international tax reform pattern which focused on introducing efficiency-oriented income tax policies. Supporters

---

[1] The European Union's Horizon 2020 research and innovation programme 2014–2020 FairTax 649439.

82 *Åsa Gunnarsson*

of this rationale postulate that tax neutrality should be a guiding principle for the ultimate goal of taxing for growth.[2] By concentrating only on avoiding excess burdens of tax law on the economy, other tax objectives and principles have been downgraded; in particular, this is the case for the tax fairness perspectives related to redistributive aspects on taxation.

The institutionalisation of going for growth through fiscal efficiency tax policy has, on a global scale, influenced the whole tax community.[3] Consequently, the social justice dimension of tax law has become a quite underdeveloped competence in both tax policy debate and research. Inspired by a simple message about bad and good tax systems, borrowed from an animated fairy tale, in this chapter I return to my early research on the historical context of tax fairness principles to give a perspective on how views on good and bad tax systems have changed over time.[4]

The neoliberal rationalities of the 'taxing for economic growth – there is no other way' concept will be explained, and criticised from the perspective of a critical tax policy framework anchored in social contract analysis.[5] My view is that fiscal cultures grow out of the style of national governance, institutional and economic frameworks, levels of tax compliance, and differing concepts of welfare obligations. This approach to tax law and policy research is far from common, but rather surprisingly it is partly supported by OECD's New Approach to Economic Challenges (NAEC). When reflecting on lessons learnt from the 2007 international crisis, NAEC recommends the adoption of longer-term perspectives on the institutional setting on how economies are shaped by history, social norms and political choices.[6]

My ambition in this chapter is to show how welfare programs are dependent on the fiscal culture of the nation state. The evolution of tax fairness is explained against the backdrop of an early idea of voluntarism and exchange in taxation, followed by the need for a tax fairness concept adjusted to the societal context of industrialisation and the development of welfare states. Ability to pay became a principal representative for the ethical and social relation between the state and citizens, justifying both vertical and horizontal equity. Efforts were also made to carve out what could be argued as an egalitarian tax culture, from the position of collecting revenue for a comprehensive welfare state. After 'the Great Recession' more radical perspectives on redistribution and tax equity emerged, which considered the relevance of the early welfare state approach as a model to design tax

---

[2] M Schmelzer, *The Hegemony of Growth: The OECD and the Making of the OECD Growth Paradigm* (Cambridge, CUP, 2016); C Sandford, *Successful Tax Reform: Lessons from an Analysis of Tax Reform in Six Countries* (Bath, Fiscal Publications, 1993).

[3] S Steinmo, 'The Evolution of Policy Ideas: Tax Policy in the 20th Century' (2003) 5 *British Journal of Politics and International Relations* 206.

[4] Å Gunnarsson, *Skatterättvisa* (Tax Equity) (Uppsala, Iustus Förlag, 1995).

[5] Å Gunnarsson, 'The Making of a Critical Tax Policy Framework' in R Banakar, K Dahlstrand and L Ryberg Welander (eds), *Festskrift till Håkan Hydén* (Lund, Juristförlaget i Lund, 2018).

[6] OECD, *Final NAEC Synthesis, New Approaches to Economic Challenges* (Paris, OECD, 2015).

policies to achieve a fairer distribution of wealth and incomes. The escalating humanitarian crisis in Greece, which drew much media attention during summer 2015, also gave an insight into the scale of the problem of how structural adjustment programmes, fiscal austerity and reduction in taxation restrict the space for possible proposals on new tax reforms with a social justice profile. The chapter ends with reflections on how future tax reforms ought to be based on a multidimensional concept of tax policies to achieve fair and sustainable tax bases.

II. The Good and the Bad

'The good and the bad' approach used in this chapter is taken from a video titled 'Tax the Rich: An animated fairy tale', narrated by the American actor Ed Asner,[7] and originally created by the California Federation of Teachers. As all fairy tales, the message of this video is simple. There are good and bad tax systems and policies. Good ones are based on an egalitarian fiscal culture, which recognise social justice as the solidarity between citizens and between citizens and the welfare state. Each tax citizen pays taxes based on ability to pay, in order to contribute to the funding of social security for all citizens and the common good. In the fairy tale, the policy-makers destroy the good tax system. They start by criticising the loopholes of the tax code as unfair, but most of all, inefficient for the economy. This opens up for a turn to a new-old policy direction, promoting the argument that there is no way to stimulate economic growth apart from cutting income taxes. Tax equity becomes equivalent to what is good for economic growth. When social justice no longer plays a part in tax policy concern, the welfare state erodes. The income gap becomes extremely large, poverty increases, and the rich don't pay any income tax at all. This does not bother the tax policy-makers in the fairy tale, who stand united behind the message: taxing for economic growth is the only option.

For me, the story highlights some important aspects of the relation between tax policy-making and tax scholarship. It points at a fundamental shift in the common view shared by both scholars and politicians on the basics for a good tax system. During the first stages of welfare reforms, tax systems were designed and legitimated under solidarity principles to fulfil welfare or social state ideals on social justice. Tax laws were used as a tool to carry out social reforms, most commonly in the field of family support. Vertical equity was the central objective of tax policy. From the 1980s these ideals of tax fairness changed and were replaced by non-intervention and neutral tax policies to level the field for economic growth. Horizontal tax equity became the dominant objective for tax policy.[8] Much of the development from 1980 onwards shows that tax policy-makers seem to have

---

[7] Video originally created by the California Federation of Teachers, available at http://www.mrctv. org/videos/ed-asner-narrates-tax-rich-animated-fairy-tale.

[8] Steinmo (n 3).

84 *Åsa Gunnarsson*

captured many tax scholars under a hegemonic ideology. Policy-makers and scholars have joined under the same paradigm – that there are no other strategies and objectives for tax reforms than *going for growth* through fiscal efficiency – which have driven out all types of social justice considerations. This has resulted in even more narrow theoretical perspectives and an obvious resistance to applying critical and crosscutting approaches in tax studies.[9]

III. The Early Doctrine of Tax Fairness

On a global scale, much contemporary tax law research still defines its theoretical base against the first set of tax principles formulated by Adam Smith in the eighteenth century, in which he sets out guidelines on what should constitute a good tax system in a liberal political economy.[10] Even though these canons were written in the context of a society totally different from our own, they are still influential because they present a normative statement about the justification of the tax burden in the relation between the state and its citizens, of which the first canon is the tax equity principle. I think that this proves the existence of an underlying recognition in tax-law research that principles on tax justice are vitally important for democracy, government and political discourse. But it also proves the existence of inherent processes, in dogmatic legal scholarship, delimiting the influences of normativity from outside the law sphere. Therefore, when scholars move outside the box to discuss the basic normative foundations in the theoretical framework of tax law, they seem to desire a strong footing in order to legitimise their perspectives. Hiding behind the scholar defined as 'the father of modern economy' may be regarded as a safe zone. Another view may be that the feeling of uncertainty experienced in an academic position outside the traditional framework may be grounded in an underdeveloped tax doctrine on tax justice, and the general problem of theoretical limitations when it concerns the dogmatic position.[11]

After Smith, liberalism and utilitarianism have produced tax theories based on the idea of a voluntary exchange and an individualistic view of the relation of the individual to the state. A characteristic of liberalism is that the similarity of taxation to a voluntary exchange transaction is taken as a basis for an equitable distribution of a tax burden given as a function of fiscal concerns. An equitable exchange between state and individual is expected. A fair distribution of a tax is

---

[9] See, eg, K Brooks, Å Gunnarsson, L Philipps and M Wersig (eds), *Challenging Gender Inequality in Tax Policy Making: Comparative Perspectives* (Oxford, Hart Publishing, 2011); AC Infanti, 'A Tax Crit Identity Crisis? Or Tax Expenditure Analysis, Deconstruction, and the Rethinking of a Collective Identity' (2005) 26 *Whittier Law Review* 707.

[10] D Boucoyannis 'The Equalizing Hand: Why Adam Smith Thought the Market Should Produce Wealth Without Steep Inequality' (2013) 11(4) *Perspectives on Politics* 1051; A Smith and JR McCulloch, *An Inquiry into the Nature and Causes of the Wealth of Nations* (Edinburgh, A and C Black and W Tait, 1838).

[11] Gunnarsson, *Festskrift* (n 5).

regarded as the equitable exchange between the tax paid by the individual taxpayer and the public performance of the state. Two Swedish scholars, Knut Wicksell and Lars Lindahl, became widely recognised for their view that a decisive factor in the willingness of the individual taxpayer to pay, when weighing private against public consumption, is that the marginal tax for each individual citizen must not exceed that citizen's marginal benefit from government expenditure, estimated in money terms. The equitable exchange theory was given concrete form in the so-called Lindahl solution, which defines the willingness to pay for public services and goods in a way similar to market pricing.[12] If decision-making costs are ignored, such a solution might be achieved politically by direct application of the full contractarian requirement of unanimous agreement. In practice, however, the information required to implement the Lindahl solution is not available, and bargaining without any costs cannot generate it. A tax fairness principle, called the benefit principle, was developed on the basis of this theoretical thinking, but it has not played a directly significant role in the development of the modern income tax system in the twentieth century.[13] In a later formulation, the benefit approach concentrates on the efficiency aspects, which is what Musgrave calls the 'allocation branch' of budgetary policy.[14]

The fact that the benefit theory has not been influential on income tax laws does not mean that it is entirely irrelevant. The conflict over how far the tax system should reflect the taxpayer's ability to pay and how much it should regard the benefits the taxpayer receives is always there.[15] The benefit principle, therefore, remains useful in cases where public services provide specific benefits to identifiable groups or even to specific individuals. The emphasis on the 'user-pays' is obvious. The sharp separation of allocation and distribution in the benefit tax tradition is also reinforced by modern public choice theorist analysis of majority voting models.[16]

IV. Ability to Pay Principle as both Horizontal and Vertical Equity

In contrast to the benefit principle, the ability to pay principle originally emerged from the philosophical idea of the state as a social organism built on a mutual

---

[12] K Wicksell, *Ein neues Prinzip der gerechten Besteuerung* (Jena, 1896), translated and reprinted in RA Musgrave and AT Peacock (eds), *Classics in the Theory of Public Finance* (St Martin's Press, 1967); E Lindahl, *Die Gerechtigkeit der Besteuerung: eine Analyse der Steuerprinzipien auf Grundlage der Grenznutzentheorie* (Lund, Lund University, 1919).

[13] Gunnarsson, *Skatterättvisa* (n 4) 96–97, 99–104; Å Gunnarsson, 'Equity Trends in Taxation' in G Lindencrona, SO Lodin, and B Wiman (eds), *Liber Amicorum to Prof Em Leif Mutén* Series on International Taxation (Kluwer Law International, 1999).

[14] JG Head, 'Tax-Fairness Principles: A Conceptual, Historical, and Practical Review' in AM Maslove (ed), *Fairness in Taxation: Exploring the Principles* (Toronto, Buffalo, London, University of Toronto Press, 1993).

[15] Gunnarsson, *Skatterättvisa* (n 4) 277; Gunnarsson, 'Equity Trends' (n 13).

[16] Head (n 14).

86   Åsa Gunnarsson

dependency between state and individual, and it has been afforded a position of strong general validity. It is regarded as the best expression of the ethical idea of distributive equity in tax law, particularly in the definition of income. There are two theoretical interpretations of the theory of ability to pay. One is an equality-oriented interpretation, implying horizontal equality of treatment. The other interpretation is based on an egalitarian fiscal tax policy with the aim of levelling incomes and wealth, implying vertical equality.[17]

Regardless of the approach chosen, the measurement of the individual taxpaying capacity should be equal to the amount or degree of private needs satisfaction that the taxpaying citizen can achieve. This position of needs satisfaction can, in turn, be measured in two different ways. One is to compute the satisfaction of needs from the origin side; the other makes the calculation on the usage side. The measurement of the individual's capacity to pay can, accordingly, comprise different acquisitions of means or resources, such as cash income, yield, benefits and wealth. The taxpaying capacity can also be measured by consumption of goods and services. Moreover, restrictions on the personal satisfaction of needs, relevant to the ability to pay tax, must be considered. In tax theory, it is generally accepted that income is, in practice, the best indicator of what represents a person's opportunities for private needs satisfaction, leading to the conclusion that the individual is the preferred unit for measuring observed income.[18] In contrast, using the marital unit increases the potential for errors, as the unit's true ability to pay will in part depend upon the correlation between the primary earner's capacity to earn and the number of hours the secondary earner works.[19]

The theoretical income concept of Haig-Simons, defining income as the net accretion of a spending-unit's power to consume over a certain period of time without distinctions as to source or use, has given substance to the ability to pay principle. This interpretation favours a so-called global or comprehensive personal income tax base, consolidating all incomes from separate sources to one aggregated sum that is taxed at a single income tax rate. A contrasting structure is the schedular/dual income tax schedule, under which each source of income is subject to separate treatment for rate and base. Differentiated tax on different tax objects means that the calculation of tax is removed both from the tax subject and from a unitary assessment of the ability to pay tax. This is in conflict with the core of the principle of ability to pay, namely, a subject-related ability to perform. The whole idea of a direct income tax as the dominating tax form rests on this fundamental

---

[17] Å Gunnarsson, 'An Egalitarian Fiscal Culture Favors Gender Equality – the Swedish Example' in JM Lorenzo Villaverde, H Petersen and I Lund-Andersen (eds), *Contemporary Gender Relations and Changes in Legal Cultures* (Copenhagen, Djøf Forlag, 2013).

[18] Gunnarsson, *Skatterättvisa* (n 4), 115–24; MJ Boskin, 'Factor Supply and Relationship among Choice of Tax Base, Tax Rates and the Unit of Account in the Design of an Optimal Tax System' in HJ Aaron and MJ Boskin (eds), *The Economics of Taxation* (Washington, The Brookings Institution, 1980).

[19] P Apps, 'Tax Reform and the Tax Unit' (1984) 1 *Australian Tax Forum* 472 and J Grbich, 'The Tax Unit Debate: Notes on the Critical Resources of a Feminist Revenue Law Scholarship' (1990–91) 4 *Canadian Journal of Women and the Law* 512.

assumption. The real effect of the schedular income tax system is to leave the subject-related principle of equal treatment of taxpayers with equal tax capacity, and instead focus on the equal treatment of equal income.[20]

The vertical, welfare state interpretation of the ability to pay principle has been used as an objective for progressive income taxation and for taxes on wealth. Regarding progressive income tax scales, the theoretical justification has been rather weak. One attempt is to apply the theory of sacrifice and the marginal utility of income on the ability principle, presuming that the subjective utility decreases for every utility unit acquired. Even if the hypothesis justifies a progressive income tax rate profile, the approach does not fit well with the interventionistic function of social welfare programs, as sacrifice theory is a utilitarian concept based on subjective elements and does not serve redistributive purposes.[21]

Wealth taxes presuppose that the possession of wealth confers advantages over and above the pecuniary income derived from that wealth. It has been argued that funded income provides greater economic security – power to take advantages of any economic opportunities, control over economic resources and status – than pecuniary income. The conclusion to be drawn is that the benefits of wealth are to some extent independent from income and net wealth need to be taxed in order to achieve horizontal equity. The strongest argument against this is embedded in the Haig-Simons concept of income. The perfect income tax base includes all accumulation in wealth, realised as well as unrealised. From this standpoint net wealth can only represent an independent measurement of ability to pay, if the income and consumption tax bases are narrow, and/or if some kind of accessions tax does not exist. This allows for the presumption that net wealth to some extent conveys unused economic capacity. If the fund theory is not accepted, other tax policy value judgements need to be added. Such a value is the redistribution of wealth for which a wealth tax could be a powerful instrument.[22]

V. Tax Principles in the Context of Social Justice in Welfare State Economies

The power to tax is an important part of democracy and the legitimacy of governments. A welfare state needs a sustainable and fair tax base, and the way the tax system is structured has a strong influence on economic and social attitudes and the behaviour of the citizens, which feeds the demands for tax equity. The manifestation of distributive principles through law is based on the dominant

---

[20] Gunnarsson, *Skatterättvisa* (n 4) 114–24; Gunnarsson, 'Equity Trends' (n 13); Head (n 14).

[21] Gunnarsson, 'Equity Trends' (n 13).

[22] Gunnarsson, *Skatterättvisa* (n 4), 280–28; S James and C Nobes, *The Economics of Taxation. Principles, Policy and Practice* (Harlow, Prentice Hall, 1996/97) 218–24.

88   *Åsa Gunnarsson*

political conception of social justice.[23] The interventionist, egalitarian function of the welfare state is most strongly reflected in the social policy tax theory, based on the objective to use taxation for equalisation through redistribution of economic resources through progressive taxation. Social policy tax theory is coherent with welfare state objectives on social justice, justified by the solidarity principle.[24] On an aggregated level, social justice in welfare economies is a basic political issue for all welfare states and relates to a fair and just link between social burdens and benefits.[25]

A weak spot, however, is that the egalitarian fiscal tax policy lacks a tax law doctrine about social justice that captures the relations between rights and obligations in a welfare state. Budget policies and substantive regulations regarding social spending and taxation, are obviously intertwined in welfare state policies.[26] One very basic example of this is how the income concept constructed by tax law in many jurisdictions is transplanted into regulations on social transfers. Another example is the use of tax law to carry out social reforms, most commonly in the field of family support. However, in tax research as well as in tax policy discourses, very little, if any, attention has been given to this social dimension of tax law for many decades now.[27]

Social justice is not a neutral concept. It expresses and reproduces assumptions of normality about the self and society. Tax laws are reflections of these assumptions, but the underlying politics, values and modes of life shaping the assumptions are removed. It is taken for granted that the separation between values and politics on the one side and law on the other side, produces neutral and fair principles for distributing legitimate needs.[28] That is why a platform for an impartial perspective is needed when discussing tax fairness, tax equity principles and tax justice. Constitutions of welfare states are theoretical often described as 'social contracts', wherein the state negotiates and distributes resources and agency between capital and labour. The notion of the 'social contract' implies that there exists a relation between the tax subject and the state.[29] Impartiality is an essential feature in the quasi-constitutional setting of thinking in contracts with the aim to elaborate on the nature of the relationship between the state and its citizen. Social contract

---

[23] Å Gunnarsson, 'Challenging the Benchmark in Tax Law Theories and Policies from a Gender Perspective – The Swedish Case' in K Brooks, Å Gunnarsson, L Philipps and M Wersig (eds), *Challenging Gender Inequality in Tax Policy Making: Comparative Perspectives* (Oxford, Hart Publishing, 2011).

[24] Gunnarsson, *Skatterättvisa* (n 4) 115–34.

[25] Head (n 14); N Lacey, *Unspeakable Subjects. Feminist Essays in Legal and Social Theory* (Oxford, Hart Publishing, 1998) 50–52; C Young, *Women, Tax and Social Programs. The Gendered Impact of Funding Social Programs through the Tax System* (Ottawa, Status of Women Canada, 2000).

[26] B Haskel, 'Paying for the Welfare State: Creating Political Durability' (1987) 59(2) *Scandinavian Studies, Rethinking the Welfare State* 221–53; O Sjöberg, 'Paying for Social Rights' (199) 28(2) *Journal of Social Policy* 275.

[27] D Sainsbury, 'Taxation, Family Responsibilities and Employment' in D Sainsbury (ed), *Gender and Welfare States Regimes* (Oxford, OUP, 1999).

[28] Lacey (n 25) 229–230.

[29] Gunnarsson, *Festskrift* (n 5).

theory has a long tradition, which basically provides an idealistic, original idea on justice captured in a contract.[30]

For me, the social contract model serves to target the historical phases of large-scale, institutional processes that explain welfare state regulations on how to distribute resources and agency between capital and labour. In fact, the birth of the modern fiscal state, its underlying fiscal structure and the concept of citizenship emerged in the early twentieth century and laid the foundation of the welfare state. Keynesian economic management of advanced capitalist economies and social justice principles, controlled tax reforms.[31] The ambition of defining and comparing welfare state typologies have, in my view, also contributed to classify different social contract models for welfare state regimes. The typologies of three welfare state concepts, developed by Esping-Andersen, shows that social justice is a basic political issue for every welfare state, which incorporates both democratic issues and the interest of social stability in welfare capitalism. The three typologies are:

– liberal regimes, characterised by modest, means-tested benefits targeted at low-income groups, and market solutions of social problems;

– conservative regimes, shaped by traditional family values leading to family-based support, encouraging non-working wives and motherhood; and

– social democratic regimes, promoting an universal social support system, which implies decommodifying welfare services to reduce market-based economic inequalities, integrating welfare and emancipation objectives.[32]

But in the same way as tax law doctrine lacks a social dimension, the competencies of tax law scholarship have not been a part of the classification of different types of welfare state models in welfare state research. As a consequence, questions concerning the nature of the tax system in relation to important expenditure programs or central welfare state commitments have been quite neglected in welfare state research. That is why a cluster analyse developed by Wagschal of a four-family taxonomy, partly based on the Esping-Andersen concept, are of particular interest in the modelling of welfare states. Exemplified by the EU Member States, the four families of taxation are:

– the English-speaking family (UK), with relatively low levels of taxation and a predominance of the ability to pay principle;

– the Continental family (Austria, Belgium, France, Germany, the Netherlands), based on the Bismarck tradition of social security financing, relying heavily on social contributions;

– the Nordic family (Denmark, Finland, Sweden), showing the highest levels of taxation and relatively low social contributions; and

---

[30] J Rawls, *A Theory of Justice: Revised Edition* (Harvard University Press, 1971).
[31] Steinmo (n 3).
[32] G Esping-Andersen, *The Three Worlds of Welfare Capitalism* (Cambridge, Princeton University Press, 1990).

90 Åsa Gunnarsson

– a peripheral or residual cluster, including a Southern (or Mediterranean) family (Italy, Portugal, Spain, Greece) as well as Ireland, with medium levels of taxation and no clear predominance of one of the two fundamental taxation principles.

Conservative and liberal parties are dominant in the English-speaking family of taxation, while Christian democratic and social democratic parties strongly shape the Continental and the Southern family. The Nordic family is primarily influenced by social democratic parties. As always, these types of classifications simplify complex issues, and new families of taxation can always be added.[33]

The two sets of classifications show the need for a more comprehensive theoretical perspective to encompass both the income and the expenditure sides of the public budget. If not, we end up with a fragmented picture of the fundaments of the historical layers that characterise different typologies of welfare regimes and tax systems. Another problem is also that these classifications do not include a gender dimension. As a consequence, much of these mainstream frameworks for tax systems to fund various forms of social security schemes do not consider the correlations and rationalities for female labour supply and totally neglect the issues of care work.[34]

VI. Neutrality Principles for Economic Growth

Neutrality principles, both formal and substantial, have shaped tax laws. The ambition here is, however, not to discuss competitive neutrality or neutrality as equality of treatment. Instead, the context is the special interpretation of what constitutes tax neutrality as a part of optimal taxation, which has guided the international trend in redesigning national budgets and tax systems. The ideology benchmarks neutral and non-distorting tax regulations as fiscal taxation. Fundaments of the tax ideology behind the tax reform formula are not new. It is built on an economic philosophy, convincingly presented by Friedrich Hayek in 1956, according to which economic intervention creates excess burdens or welfare

---

[33] U Wagschal, 'Families of Taxation: Convergence or Divergence', presented at the 43rd ECPR Joint Session in Warsaw (29 March–2 April 2015), available at https://ecpr.eu/Filestore/Paper Proposal/644825b7-bc80-4458-8f03-1e107bf76eaf.pdf; M Fink, J Janová, D Nerudová, J Pavel, M Schratzenstaller, F Sindermann and M Spielauer, 'Policy Recommendations on the Gender Effects of Changes in Tax Bases, Rates, and Units. Results of Microsimulation Analyses for Six Selected EU Member States' (2019) *FairTax Working Papers Series*, no 24.

[34] J Lewis, 'Gender and the Development of Welfare Regimes' (1992) 2(3) *Journal of European Social Policy* 159; D Sainsbury 'Taxation, Family Responsibilities and employment' in D Sainsbury (ed), *Gendering Welfare States* (London, Sage, 1994); Å Gunnarsson, *Tracing the Women-Friendly Welfare State: Gendered Politics of Everyday Life in Sweden* (Göteborg, Makadam Förlag, 2013); S Saxonberg, 'From Defamilialization to Degenderization: Toward a New Welfare Typology' (2013) 47(1) *Social Policy Administration* 26.

losses, which can be restricting for economic growth.[35] And Harvey Peck gave the following definition of fiscal taxation as early as 1936:

> Taxation for fiscal purposes means taxation for the purpose of raising revenue to defray government expenditures, while taxation for non-fiscal purposes is taxation not to provide revenue to carry on a given program of public expenditures but to produce directly certain economic or social effects irrespective of whether revenue is actually raised or not.[36]

Neutral taxation benchmarks taxes that distort the economic efficiency of market processes as little as possible, implying a trade-off between efficiency and equity. Tax rules that deviate from this benchmark on fiscal taxation are defined as tax expenditures. By making a distinction between fiscal and non-fiscal taxation, a normative standard for a good tax system is constituted. The neoliberal aspect of the ideology of fiscal taxation, preserving distributional neutrality and status quo, is that it does not provide any incentive for social justice. Hereby, a line between fiscal purposes and social justice has been drawn, meaning that tax regulations with redistributive intentions are seen as political interventions in the market economy.[37]

The 'going for growth' mantra and the ideology of fiscal taxation, also received very powerful support when the Organisation for Economic Cooperation and Development (OECD) began publishing the *Going for Growth* series in 2005, with the aim of promoting sustainable economic growth for the well-being of the OECD citizens. The institutionalisation of going for growth through fiscal efficiency tax policies have, on a global scale, influenced the whole tax community. Many scholars and policy-makers have pointed out the homogeneity of the main features of these reforms. They are:

- broader labour incomes tax bases but low progressivity;
- capital and corporations taxed moderately or not at all;
- uniform tax rates applied on the consumption of goods and services;
- introduction of in-work tax subsidies;
- a shift from direct taxes to indirect taxes.[38]

---

[35] FA Hayek, 'Progressive Taxation Reconsidered' in M Sennholz (ed), *On Freedom and Free Enterprise. Essays in Honour of Ludwig von Mises* (Princeton, Nostrands Company, 1956) 265.

[36] HW Peck, 'The Use of the Taxing Power for Non-Fiscal Purposes' (1936) 183 *Annals of the American Academy of Political and Social Sciences* 'Government Finance in the Modern Economy' 57.

[37] Å Gunnarsson, 'The Use of Taxation for Non-fiscal Purposes' in J Bolander (ed), *The non-fiscal purposes of* taxation (Yearbook for Nordic tax research, Copenhagen, DJÖF, 2009); Gunnarsson, *Tracing* (n 34).

[38] Sandford (n 2); K Messere (ed), *The Tax System in Industrialized Countries* (Oxford, OUP, 1998); P Birch Sørensen, *Swedish Tax Policy: Recent Trends and Future Challenges* (Stockholm, Swedish Ministry of Finance, 2010); B Brys, M Stephen and J Owens, 'Tax Reform Trends in OECD Countries' *OECD Taxation Working Papers*, No 1 (OECD Publishing, 2011); Å Gunnarsson, M Schratzenstaller and U Spangenberg, *Gender equality and taxation in the European Union'* (Research paper for European Parliament's Committee on Women's Rights and Gender Equality and commissioned, overseen and published by the Policy Department for Citizen's Rights and Constitutional Affairs, 2017).

VII. The Tax Base Issue

A basic element in the neutrality principle developing under the influence of taxing for growth and optimal tax theory, was the tax base issue. The policy justified uniform taxation in conjunction with the goal of ensuring that taxation should only fulfil a neutral fiscal purpose. Subjecting all types of income and consumption, irrespective of source, to income tax was aimed to fulfil the principle of distributional neutrality and a broader income tax base.[39] For instance, the Swedish tax reform of 1991 expanded the income tax base by almost one per cent. However, this broadening of the income tax base was not sufficient to cover the tax revenue losses caused by cuts to income tax rates. The remaining revenue losses from the income tax reform were covered by increases in indirect taxes, in particular VAT but also social security contributions.[40] In this respect, Sweden followed the path-specific restructuring of tax bases by making a relatively large shift from direct to indirect taxation.[41]

Tax policy regarding capital income and economic growth perspective has been a particularly debated topic. Some of the literature on optimal tax, which had an initial high impact, argued that capital incomes should not be taxed at all, because capital taxation distorts saving behaviour, which risks reducing capital formation and capital investments.[42] A zero rate is also preferable under the 'race to the bottom' hypothesis on tax competition between jurisdictions regarding the mobile capital income tax base. The hypothesis is that a capital tax rate cut in one country tends to attract an immediate inflow of capital, thereby reducing the tax base of other countries. It has been assumed that these countries would respond to the shrinking tax base and to declining tax revenues by lowering their capital tax rate to competitive levels. In equilibrium, tax rates on mobile capital would approach zero in all countries.[43]

Yet another angle for study of optimal tax theory is the argument in favour of taxation of capital gains. It has been stated that capital income might be taxed for redistributive reasons, ie in order to redistribute more income than is possible with the labour-income tax alone. This is not merely an ideological position. Rather, it has been noted that some capital income could be labour income in disguise as some individuals generate substantial higher returns to savings, stock market

---

[39] Å Gunnarsson and M Eriksson, 'Discussion Paper on Tax Policy and Tax Principles in Sweden, 1902–2016' *FairTax Working Paper Series* no 08 (2017).

[40] P Birch Sørensen, 'Dual Income Taxes: A Nordic Tax System' in I Claus, N Gemmell, M Harding and D White (eds), *Tax Reform in Open Economies* (Cheltenham, Edward Elgar, 2010) 78.

[41] Sandford (n 2); Brys et al (n 38).

[42] C Chamley, 'Optimal Taxation of Capital Income in General Equilibrium with Infinite Lives' (1986) 54(3) *Econometrica* 607; KL Judd, 'Redistributive Taxation in a Simple Perfect Foresight Model' (1985) 28(1) *Journal of Public Economics* 59, AB Atkinson and JE Stiglitz, 'The Design of Tax Structure: Direct versus Indirect Taxation' (1976) 6(1–2) *Journal of Public Economics* 55.

[43] T Plümper, VE Troeger and H Winner 2009, 'Why is There No Race to the Bottom in Capital Taxation?' (2009) 53(3) *International Studies Quarterly* 761.

investments, entrepreneurial efforts and other investments, and therefore capital income is to some extent a return to labour supply, work effort, human capital or investment ability. Taxing capital income is then desirable in order to redistribute resources from individuals with a high earning ability to individuals with a low earning ability.[44]

VIII. The Nordic Dual Income Tax Paradox

Another outflow of tax neutrality in fiscal taxation, also grounded in the neutrality principle of horizontal equity defined as uniform tax treatment of all types of income, is the Nordic innovation of a dual income tax. It is quite contradictory construction in relation to the neutrality principle, as the terminology of dual indicates a departure from the Schantz-Haig-Simons global income concept, by separating the income tax base into two parts. One tax income for labour and transfer income and one for capital income.[45]

The introduction of this particular form of schedular income took place in Sweden through Swedish tax reform from 1991. It did not give rise to much controversy, which can be explained by the design of a more uniform taxation regime covering different sources of income from capital, like private homes, capital gains and most forms of investment income.[46] Considering the magnitude of the change – shifting from a progressive comprehensive income tax, taxing all sources of income of individuals in line with the ability to pay principle, to a schedular system based on a principle of horizontal equity – this was quite a radical departure from the ideology guiding the development of modern tax systems. In particular, the Nordic dual income model, even in its original design, created a tax wedge between capital and earned income by combining a progressive tax on earned income with a low flat-rate tax on capital income. The intention was that the difference in formal tax rates would be solved by the effect of inflation and that a vast majority of taxpayers would be liable only for the flat-rate local municipality tax on approximately the same level as the capital income tax.[47]

In reality, the dual income tax reform created incentives for unequal tax treatment of equal levels of incomes. The Swedish experience is that since the introduction of a dual income tax in 1991, the uniformity of the capital income tax

---

[44] B Jacobs, 'From Optimal Tax Theory to Applied Tax Policy' (2013) 69(3) *FinanzArchiv* 338, 362; J Banks and PA Diamond, 'The Base for Direct Taxation' in JA Mirrlees (chair), *The Mirrlees Review. Dimensions of Tax Design* (Oxford, OUP, 2010) 548.

[45] Gunnarsson, *Skatterättvisa* (n 4); J Owens, 'Fundamental Tax Reform: The Experience of OECD Countries', *Background Paper* no 47, Tax Foundation, Washington DC (2005); OECD, 'Fundamental Reform of Personal Income Tax', *Tax Policy Studies* no 13; Birch Sørensen, 'Dual Income Taxes' (n 40).

[46] K Andersson and L Mutén, 'Sweden' in K Messere (ed), *The Tax System in Industrialized Countries* (Oxford, OUP, 1998); SO Lodin, *The Making of Tax Law: The Development of Swedish Taxation* (Uppsala, Iustus Förlag, 2011).

[47] Gunnarsson (n 13, 1999); Birch Sørensen, *Swedish Tax Policy* (n 38).

base has gradually been eroded through several reforms. In particular, the 2006 reduction in the capital tax on dividends from shares in close companies from 30 per cent to 20 per cent was a clear deviation from guiding principles and policies. The reform led to an increase in the tax wedge between capital and labour income, and most importantly, opened up incentives for income shifting. The tax cut in combination with a simplification of the income splitting system for close companies, the so-called 3:12 regulations, fuelled the possibility for active owners with a majority of votes to tax a part of their profit as dividends under the scheme of as capital income tax instead of wages under the tax scheme of labour income. Empirical evidence shows an obvious change in behaviour on both individual and company level after the 2006 reform. One of them is the increase of dividend income by over 80 per cent in close companies. High-income active owners benefited most from the income shifting, and it also seemed to have been contraproductive in relation to the objective behind the 3:12 rules, which was to equalise risks between labour-intensive and capital-intensive family businesses and also to stimulate entrepreneurship.[48] The latest *Long-Term Survey of the Swedish Economy*, published in December 2019, confirms the increase in capital incomes, contributing to a widening of the income inequality gap, and that this development is partly related to the incentives for income shifting in the 3:12 rules.[49]

IX. Structural Adjustment Programmes, Fiscal Austerity, Neoliberal Tax Policy and Detaxation

Economic Adjustment Programmes (EAPs) were introduced in the Eurozone in the wake of the financial crisis by the 'Troika' consisting of the IMF, European Central Bank and European Commission. These programmes have been used as policy instruments connected to those conditional bailout loans granted by the Troika to governments that cannot fund their budgets from domestic resources or international debt markets.[50] In the case of Greece,[51] the EU institutions and the European leaders imposed an austerity policy that created an unsustainable debt burden on the Greek state and its citizens, and which was heavily criticised

---

[48] A Alstadsæter and J Martin, *Income Shifting in Sweden: An empirical evaluation of the 3:12 rules* (Report to the Expert Group on Public Economics 2012(4), Stockholm, Ministry of Finance, 2012); A Hilling, N Sandell and A Wilhelmsson (2017), 'The Planning in Partner-owned Cloe Corporations' (2017) 1(1) *Nordic Tax Journal* 108; SO Lodin and P Englund, *Yes box! En ESO-rapport om en ny modell för kapital- och bostadsbeskattning* (Rapport till Expertgruppen för studier i offentlig ekonomi 2017:4, Stockholm, Regeringskansliet, Finansdepartementet, 2017).

[49] *Huvudbetänkande av Långtidsutredningen* SOU 2019:65 (Stockholm, Norstedts Juridik, 2019).

[50] SL Greer, 'Structural adjustment comes to Europe: Lessons for the Eurozone from the conditionality debates' (2014) 14 *Global Social Policy* 51.

[51] *The Economic Adjustment Programme for Greece* (European Economy, Brussels, Occasional Papers No 6, Brussels European Commission, 2010).

by many actors, not least influential scholars.[52] Austerity is a form of voluntary deflation with the policy of cutting public spending and introducing privatisation to restore competitiveness in order to promote growth.[53] An important part is also fiscal austerity, which promotes the increase of certain types of taxes, and also argues that taxes should not be used for social investments in the reproductive part of the economy or in maintenance of the welfare state regimes. Fiscal austerity policies saw a renaissance in the aftermath of the global economic crisis in 2008 when governments raised taxes in the attempt to reduce structural deficits in the public budget. Austerity policies are one important element in the structural adjustment programs traditionally imposed on developing nations by IMF and the World Bank to ensure debt repayment and economic restructuring when they lend money to poor economies in debt. These programs have been heavily criticised for increasing poverty instead of reducing it.[54]

That the same structural adjustment policies have been implemented in the Eurozone, prompted me to look back and re-evaluate my post-doctoral research regarding New Zealand in the 1990s.[55] New Zealand was the first non-third world country to introduce in 1984 what at that time was defined as a pure neo-liberal model of structural adjustment. The fiscal policy agenda shifted from tax fairness principles on ability to pay and redistributive profiles, to efficiency and neoliberal norms. Jane Kelsey claims that this policy agenda of fiscal restraints on the state budget eroded the central government's defence of the objectives of a comprehensive welfare base. It became obvious that the title of Kelsey's book, *The New Zealand experiment: A world model for structural adjustment?*[56] anticipated a development that few tax experts had discussed, let alone criticised, as neoliberal tax policies in western welfare economies have seldom been contextualised as part of structural adjustment programs. Kelsey should be given a lot of credit for pinpointing the larger scale of the so-called New Zealand experiment as early as the 1990s. I claim that the integration of fiscal austerity with structural adjustment programs is a world model for dismantling the welfare state, but has also become a backlash against gender equality. It is against this wider societal and historical context that the neoliberalist tax policy discourses should be debated.

A concept about structural detaxation developed by Kathleen Lahey points out systematic tax changes that are similar to the fiscal austerity structural adjustment policies. The concept aims to capture systemic removal or reductions of tax rates and tax bases, leading losses of revenue that are non-transparent and have only

---

[52] *Resolution of Feminist Economists gathering at the IAFFE conference in Berlin, July 16–18, 2015*; T Picketty JD Sachs, H Flassbeck, D Rodrik and S Wren-Lewiset, 'Austerity Has Failed: An Open Letter From Thomas Piketty to Angela Merkel' (*The Nation*, 7 July 2015, available at http://www.thenation.com/article/austerity-has-failed-an-open-letter-from-thomas-piketty-to-angela-merkel.

[53] M Blyth, *Austerity: The History of a Dangerous Idea* (Oxford, OUP, 2013).

[54] Greer (n 50).

[55] Gunnarsson (n 13, 1999).

[56] J Kelsey, *The New Zealand experiment: A world model for structural adjustment?* (Auckland, Auckland University Press, with Bridget Williams Books, 1997).

96 *Åsa Gunnarsson*

vague justification. The incentives for tax reforms are often passive as the policy goals are non-specific – formulated in general terms such as enhancing growth or stimulating economic activity. Lahey has, based on the Canadian experience, shown how structural detaxation have become gender regressive as the cuts in tax bases and rates have been allocated to income levels and assets that a very low population of women share with men.[57]

From a Swedish perspective a similar development can be seen. After the 1991 tax reform, a systematic deviation from the tax principles governing broad-based income, consumption and wealth/property taxes was noticed. Sweden has been renowned for open and political transparent law reform processes, in which preparatory works performed by Government Committees have played a central role for achieving justification and sustainability. Opposite to this position, an increasing invisibility of tax politics has developed, resulting in diffuse policy goals not corresponding with tax principles. Observers of the welfare state and the public sector have come to a growing insight about the structural effects of the new order of tax policy over recent decades. In the main, this new order of tax policy contains lower tax on capital, corporate profits, tax credits for domestic and maintenance work, working tax credit and the abolishing of all wealth taxes. As a consequence, the tax-to-GDP ratio dropped from 50.4 per cent in 1990 to 43.3 per cent in 2015. This process of reducing or abolishing taxes has been in play without any apparent consideration to the long-term stability of the tax system. The *Commission on Tax Base Mobility*, the *Commission on Unified VAT* and the *Property Tax Commission*, all from around 2005, represent the last notable major political effort to advance the tax system after the 1991 tax reform. We have defined this development as the death of tax reform design. It is a consciously provocative statement in order to pinpoint the consequences of abandoning a tax-principle based governance of tax reforms that has traditionally characterised Swedish tax policy.[58]

X. Conclusions: Fair and Sustainable Tax System from a European Perspective

Even though the fairy tale about the good and the bad tax system mediates a simplified message, it pinpoints a basic ethical precondition for taxes in a welfare state. In theory, the recognition of citizens' social rights and the protection against social risks ought to correlate with the obligatory common responsibility to generate the public funding needed to pay for them. In that way, the obligation of the citizen is based on the legitimate demand that they support certain social needs. By detaching tax law from the politics of welfare state law and from a social dimension, tax

---

[57] KA Lahey, 'Uncovering Women in Taxation: The Gender Impact of Detaxation, Tax Expenditures, and Joint Tax/Benefit Units' (2015) 52(2) *Osgoode Hall Law Journal* 427.
[58] Gunnarsson and Eriksson (n 39).

law research seems to be stuck in denial regarding political realities. One central part of fiscal systems has always been potentially decisive for redistributive policies, and tax reforms have very often been used as vehicles to promote social and equality policies. Tax fairness is also an important precondition for fiscal sustainability.

Studies on the development of European national tax systems reveal that the introduction of modern taxes on income, wealth and consumption was based on solid tax principles and objectives. Even though economic and political priorities have undermined and challenged the interpretation and implementation of these fundamental principles, many important national tax reforms indicate that a 'good', well-designed tax system should be constituted in tax principles and based upon problem-focused outcomes to achieve sustainable and fair tax systems. Both the legal and economic doctrine have showed that a systematically coherent and democratically valid tax policy framework based on values, aims and principles is necessary to obtain fairness and sustainability. On the European level, the tax policy framework should be based on the European Treaties as well as international commitments that the EU and its Member States have undertaken, such as the most recent ratification of the Paris agreements and the Social Development Goals. Officially, the most pressing demands of European citizens currently are economic stability and social justice. Tax principles and the design of tax policies need to recognise that these two objectives are intertwined. Tax research as well as numerous public reports confirm that such a comprehensive approach to tax policy, integrating social justice and welfare objectives in a concept of fair and sustainable taxation will, for many reasons, be a difficult task. Trade-offs between growth enhancing and social or equality objectives have blurred the principles and outcomes of tax systems. One has to recognise the complexity of the sustainability concept. What makes sustainability so important is what makes it so difficult. Sustainability is not only about economic growth – it is also about a number of other different goals. Of course, the difficulty is that achieving one sustainable objective may threaten the other.[59] It is important to return to the Brundtland Report, from 1987, stating that future development of the planet would be considered sustainable if the present generation were able to satisfy its own needs, without compromising the ability of future generations to do so as well.[60]

The tax policy paradigm, based on optimal tax theory, promoting neutrality of taxation under a one-sided growth-oriented GDP-based approach as the central indicator of welfare, has influenced the EU Commission's tax policy statements over the last decades and created tax sustainability gaps. This one-dimensional 'tax for growth' policy paradigm has to be questioned, as it neglects many general

---

[59] U Spangenberg, A Mumford and S Daly, 'Navigating taxation towards sustainability. Contradictions between social, gender, environmental, and economic ambitions, obligations and governance capacities in European law' *FairTax Working Paper Series* no 16 (2018); Gunnarsson and Eriksson (n 39); Steinmo (n 3).

[60] L Seghezzo, 'The Five Dimensions of Sustainability' (2009) 18(4) *Environmental Politics* 539, citing World Commission on Environment and Development, *Our common future* (Oxford, OUP, 1987).

98   *Åsa Gunnarsson*

obligations of society for human well-being and central indicators of welfare. This has created the following non-sustainable structural problems:

- a prevailing focus on economic growth;
- an absence of tax measures that tackle inequalities in income and wealth;
- high and increasing weight of labour taxes;
- a lack of EU-level environmental taxation;
- decreasing importance of corrective Pigouvian taxes at Member State level, particularly of environmental taxes;
- intense tax competition including profit shifting;
- tax compliance issues and tax fraud;
- decreasing progressivity of tax systems;
- unused potential to use taxation at the EU level to promote sustainable growth and development in Europe;
- persisting intragenerational inequalities and lack of coordinated life course approaches in tax and social policies;
- persisting socio-economic inequalities between men and women and lack of gender equality insights in national tax policies.

Based on the key-challenges addressed for reaching smart, sustainable and inclusive growth, five dimensions of tax policies for sustainable tax systems in EU Member States should be considered: social, economic, environmental, institutional/cultural and equality.[61]

A basic problem is that even though the tax fairness and sustainability gaps are recognised on an EU policy level there is a lack of both effective legal mechanisms and policy guidelines to promote social justice in the field of taxation on Member State level. To increase taxes with an overall regressive impact, such as indirect taxes on consumption in combination with a reduced progressive profile on income taxation and a limited share of wealth-based taxes, will obviously lead to a loss of redistributive power. The risk for a long-term increase in income inequality is a societal challenge, pointed out by many experts.[62]

Connecting this assessment on tax sustainability to the re-emerging tax equality and tax equity policy trends, shows that that sustainability and fairness are interconnected issues in the design of the tax system. From a welfare state perspective, tax sustainability has a strong social pretext as social welfare obligations are distributed over the public budget, so when social justice is excluded as guiding

---

[61] A Mumford and Å Gunnarsson, 'Sustainability in EU Tax Law' (2019) 54(2) *Intereconomics. Review of European Economic Policy* 134.

[62] M Schratzenstaller et al, 'EU Taxes as genuine own resources to finance the EU budget. Pros cons and sustainability-oriented criteria to evaluate potential tax candidates' (2016) *FairTax Working Paper* no 3.

principle for tax policies, the revenue side of public budgets becomes detached from social programmes aiming at a more equal distribution of post-tax incomes. Another aspect of the dilemma is that, irrespective of the lack of directly addressed social dimensions in tax reforms, each welfare state has, from a tax base perspective, to identify a sustainable mix of tax bases in order to meet legitimacy demands that always in a way or another includes political aspects of social justice, equity or equality.

A policy striving towards greater tax fairness can improve the degree of sustainability within the tax system. Taxation has many sources, and the same source is often used as a tax base for several taxes, as in the case of labour income. It can be taxed by a multiplicity of taxes. At the production level, labour can be the source of assessing payroll taxes designated to cover social security contributions. At the household level, labour is the source for direct income tax, and when the income is used it is a possible source of indirect taxes, of which general consumption taxes constitute a major tax base in many EU countries. A comprehensive tax base approach to national tax systems has to consider this complexity. One-sided tax policies only promoting growth-oriented regulations have been argued to be the efficient way to economic sustainability. However, today the literature presents research that questions this policy paradigm. A one-sided taxing for growth paradigm can in the end undermine economic sustainability, as there seems to be a correlation between taxing for growth and economic-efficiency driven reforms during the last decades and the increase of income inequality.

Consequently, a comprehensive tax base reform addressing the five dimensions of sustainability has to consider:

- the non-progressive and high direct and indirect tax burden on labour income;
- the lack of progressive contributions from capital and wealth-related taxes;
- the need to agree on a common, supra-national, sustainable solution for the corporate tax base; and
- the potential to further implement Pigouvian taxes in European tax systems to internalise externalities as a complement to other tax bases.

6

A Brief Theory of Taxation and Framework Public Goods

DARIEN SHANSKE

The literature on the question of how best to distribute the burden of taxation is technical and vast. However, in order for there to be a tax burden to distribute, there must first be a relatively stable social order that establishes, among other things, property rights. But the establishing of property rights is not costless; some revenue must have already been collected. How does one evaluate the distributive implications of a system of revenue collection that is a precondition for distributive questions? The dominant response to this question is to move beyond it by noting that, as a matter of fact, *we* are no longer in this liminal position and so we can sensibly discuss how best to distribute the tax burden.

In this short chapter I argue for two basic points: First, as to the funding of the set of basic goods that make distributive questions possible, which I call 'framework' goods, there is a strong argument that we should relax our demands for use of the 'best' tax system. Second, there are likely more scenarios in which this insight about the financing of framework goods applies than one might think. Put simply, if we think a developing country would be well-justified in using a sub-optimal set of taxes to provide framework goods, and I think that we should, then it should also follow that a developed country would be well-justified in using a sub-optimal set of taxes to provide near-framework goods.

I. Introduction

'[I]t is disgraceful that so prosperous a nation cannot guarantee even a decent minimum of medical care to all those over whom it exercises dominion.'

Ronald Dworkin[1]

I find applying the lessons of moral philosophy to the theory of taxation to be hard. Yet I think many current questions relating to taxation and public finance

---

[1] R Dworkin, *Sovereign Virtue* (Cambridge MA, Harvard University Press, 2000) 318.

102 *Darien Shanske*

in the contemporary United States are relatively easy. Leaving aside that I am just idiosyncratic (and of course I am), I want to consider why this might be so. After all, based on the passage above, Ronald Dworkin seemed to share a similar intuition. Note that the sentence above comes from the end of a chapter on health care and justice. Within the chapter (and his book), Dworkin wrestles with hard questions of rationing medical care and applies his abstract rubric involving how much insurance individuals might buy hypothetically. There is much to be said for Dworkin's rubric, but it is hard to see why a society that uses some other rubric, or applies his rubric differently as to health care, has committed a disgraceful act.

There is only a disgrace, it seems to me, if there are morally significant public goods to be provided and that they can be provided for a low – morally much less significant – price. But can we say any more about this? Which goods are we talking about exactly and when exactly is the price so compelling that not purchasing the good is disgraceful? I will sketch out an approach to thinking about these questions in this chapter.

The argument I will develop in this chapter aims to fill a relative lacuna in the taxation literature as concerns public goods. It is common ground, usually, that governments ought to finance public goods, but the details matter greatly, including the question of who should be doing the financing. But distribution of the burden only comes into play once there is a situation in which individuals have relatively stable property rights to begin with. Thus the provision of some set of public goods – let us call them framework goods – has at least a certain kind of priority over the question of how they ought to be paid for. For instance, Rawls, roughly following Wicksell, thinks that one principle of taxation (proportionate taxation) is appropriate 'to raise the revenues that justice requires'.[2] Rawls thinks that the benefit principle is appropriate beyond that.[3] One might disagree with Rawls and instead argue that we should always use our one best theory of taxation to finance all public goods. After all, if we don't use our best tool, then we will need to fix the distortions created by the clumsier tools and then use further clumsy tools to fix those mistakes and so on.[4]

---

[2] J Rawls, *A Theory of Justice* (Cambridge MA, Harvard University Press, 1971) 278. Rawls does not believe that proportionate taxation as to these primary goods is essential and is quite pragmatic as to what mix of taxes could be appropriate: ibid at 279. Rawls might be wrong in terms of his own philosophy in preferring proportionate taxation at all. D Elkins, 'Consumption Taxation in Rawls' Theory of Justice' (2019) 29 *Cornell Journal of Law and Public Policy*, forthcoming. What is important for my purposes is that, at least in the abstract, Rawls argues that a different principle of taxation can apply as to financing some core goods and this principle apparently persists even when the public goods required by the difference principle have been provided.

[3] Rawls (n 2) 283. And Rawls believes that progressive taxes, eg inheritance taxes, are appropriate for other goals, such as 'to preserve the justice of the basic structure with respect to the first principle of justice and fair equality of opportunity'. Ibid at 279.

[4] At a high level of abstraction, I take this to be Kaplow's argument for use of the income tax over narrow excise taxes. See L Kaplow, *The Theory of Taxation and Public Economics* (Princeton, Princeton University Press, 2008) 183–85, 190–92.

A *Brief Theory of Taxation and Framework Public Goods* 103

This might all seem quite abstract and getting pretty far from an actually disgraceful situation. After all, we live in an economy with relatively stable property rights and thus there is no reason not to finance all public goods, including the framework goods, using the best tax system possible. We can envision this process by analogy with Wittgenstein's ladder;[5] however we financed ourselves to a functional society, now that we are here we can throw away the ladder and do it right.

But perhaps we should keep the ladder around. The challenge of reaching a basically functional social order has not been achieved everywhere. And, further, it appears that just taking solutions that work atop the ladder – such as progressive income taxes – and trying to use them in so-called developing countries has not been successful. In developing economies, incremental, bespoke reforms, likely not entirely consistent with the benefit principle or ability-to principle or any other principle, are now seen as the way to proceed.

And so the issue of financing framework goods is not so abstract in some places, but this is not the kind of place that Dworkin was referring to. I will argue that, under certain conditions, developed countries can be seen as in a similar situation. Basic universal health care is, perhaps, not a framework good like, say, a minimum of physical security. Yet I would argue that, assuming certain other facts are true, that such a good is close enough such that not finding some way to finance it, even in a confused way as a matter of tax policy, is, indeed, a disgrace.

II. Framework Goods

The first step in the argument is to determine what kinds of goods we are considering as potentially so important that we ought to relax our ordinary thinking about the best way to raise revenue. I will sketch out what these goods might be through the public goods literature; though note, as I point out below, I am not committed to the framework goods being *goods* at all.

A. Some Public Goods are More Equal than Others

The literature on public goods is enormous, but there is broad consensus on what they are and why governments are justified in providing them.[6] Public goods are non-excludable and non-rivalrous. If clean air and physical security is provided for me, then it must also be provided for my neighbour whose enjoyment of the good

---

[5] L Wittgenstein, *Tractatus Logico-Philosophicus* [1921] (DF Pears and BF McGuinness, trans) (London, Routledge, 1961) Proposition 6.54.

[6] Though not necessarily directly. Coase showed that the government did not need to provide lighthouses itself, but it did need to enforce collection of lighthouse fees. See RH Coase, 'The Lighthouse in Economics' (1974) 17(2) *Journal of Law and Economics* 357.

104 *Darien Shanske*

does not diminish my enjoyment. The possibility of free-riding indicates that both my neighbour and I are likely to under-invest in such goods. But not all public goods are created equal. Fireworks are another example of a public good, but these are clearly not essential in the same way. Using vocabulary from David Miller we might say that there is a much weaker independent justice reason for fireworks versus, say, clean air.[7] With due regard to fireworks, this chapter is addressed to public goods on the clean air end of the spectrum.

Note that I am starting with public goods, the public provision of which is broadly supported to some extent on efficiency grounds, and then adding the justice criterion. This is not because I believe justice is secondary nor that a government need not provide what justice requires. Rather, going back to the beginning of this chapter, I recognise broad dissensus as to what justice requires – if anything. Rawls' Difference Principle and Dworkin's resource egalitarianism will lead to substantively different results if operationalised. I don't think either result would be disgraceful.

Back to public goods and distinctions between them. There are, in fact, relatively few 'pure' public goods, as most are subject to congestion and competition at some point. This is true of a classic example such as roads. Furthermore, many public goods also throw off some private benefits – excludable benefits – consider education or health care. Indeed, lots of the most important public goods have this characteristic, namely that they are so important that individuals would seek to acquire them even without the state. This fact is not generally taken to indicate that the government should not provide the most important goods, just that policy designers need to take due account of crowding out private efforts. As to this chapter, I am concerned with essential public goods, even if they are impure, though, of course, I am particularly interested in that component of them that would not be supplied without government help.

There is yet another common distinction made between public goods, again along a spectrum. There is, for example, a certain level of security needed to pursue any life plans in a reasonable way, and then there is attending to security beyond that. We might say that people need to feel safe going about their business during the day at a minimum and feel secure if they stay indoors at night. Being safe

---

[7] D Miller, 'Justice, Democracy, and Public Goods' in K Dowding, R Goodin, and C Pateman (eds), *Justice and Democracy: Essays for Brian Barry* (Cambridge, CUP, 2004) 136–37. As concerns Miller, I am further sub-dividing his 'category A goods' into those that are independently justified *and* framework goods versus those that are 'merely' independently justified. Patten follows Miller in distinguishing different categories of public goods, with some differences. Patten reasonably argues that some public goods have a lesser claim to be financed by compulsory taxes. A Patten, 'Public Good Fairness' in D Butt, S Fine and Z Stemplowska (eds), *Political Philosophy Here and Now: Essays in Honour of David Miller* (Oxford, OUP, 2018). Neither author addresses whether the rules of taxation itself should be different as to different types of public goods. I am arguing here that as public goods become more essential, then financing them optimally becomes less important. The converse is also true – the less essential a public good is, then the more important that we get the financing right lest the poor choice of financing tool nullify the whole exercise.

A Brief Theory of Taxation and Framework Public Goods   105

walking around *after* dark is clearly a public good to be pursued, but perhaps not as essential. I don't feel strongly about the example, but I think the basic distinction is sound – consider the difference between basic medical care and cutting edge medical interventions. The basic amount of the basic goods has a greater claim to be provided than a surfeit. First, this is because the minimum is even more morally significant as to enabling individuals to lead their lives. Second, without a minimum provision of these goods then subsequent decisions about distribution of goods etc cannot be reached.

These goods have another characteristic, which is that they are bundled in a manner that cannot be disentangled, at least to any great extent. How can one disentangle clean air, clean water, sufficient food etc?

And so we are talking about public goods with powerful independent justifications that are primary and bundled. For the sake of simplification, I will call these framework goods.

This is an apt time to observe that I am not committed to the framework goods being goods at all. Sen's point that a discussion of 'goods' is fetishistic and that we must instead focus on what people can do is well taken.[8] I think it is sensible to speak of framework capabilities; without a certain level of reasonable flourishing by enough people, further meaningful distribution in order to equalise capabilities is not possible. I will continue to speak of framework goods in order to anchor the discussion in the more familiar notion of public goods, but I don't mean by that to take a side on the goods/capabilities debate. Indeed, it is because I am quite sympathetic to the more expansive capabilities approach that I think it quite likely that even a developed country will not supply all of the framework goods/capabilities of high moral significance.

The final characteristic of framework goods is that financing them poses a riddle, as they are in part necessary preconditions to (all?) other considerations of justice or anything else. We can't decide if we are financing them fairly or efficiently unless property rights are secure enough to know where individuals stand. It is a hard question whether engaging in a cost benefit analysis as to the marginal benefit of a public good can be done meaningfully against a just background,[9] but it is not a hard question as to the framework goods. It simply cannot be done, and so even an optimist on our ability to calculate marginal costs and benefits in a world where the framework goods have been provided, like Wicksell or Kaplow,[10] just

---

[8] A Sen, 'Equality of What' in J Rawls and S McMurrin (eds), *Liberty, Equality and Law: Selected Turner Lectures on Moral Philosophy* (Salt Lake City, University of Utah Press, 1979).

[9] See A Raskolnikov, 'Accepting the Limits of Tax Law and Economics' (2012) 98 *Cornell Law Review* 523, 554.

[10] K Wicksell, 'A New Principle of Just Taxation' (J Buchanan trans) in R Musgrave and A Peacock (eds) *Classics in the Theory of Public Finance* (New York, St Martin's Press, 1958) 72, 78; Kaplow (n 4) 207: '[P]reexisting public goods and services can be taken as given for most purposes.' Murphy and Nagel also start their analysis against a background of a just distribution. L Murphy and T Nagel, *The Myth of Ownership: Taxes and Justice* (Oxford, OUP, 2002) 79–80.

106 *Darien Shanske*

abstract away from this prior question as not relevant because we have provided the framework goods. I don't think this question is so readily evaded.

B. Two Basic Approaches to Financing Framework Goods

As to financing these goods, I can imagine two theoretical approaches. On the one hand, we are currently living in a society that has enough of the framework goods such that we can have a sensible discussion about the best way to finance these goods and other goods, even non-public goods. We should therefore apply whatever normative framework we think is the right one generally. For example, if one assumes that the initial fiscal structure that provided the framework goods was not terribly progressive, then that is not a reason not to finance these goods and all others progressively – assuming one is convinced that a progressive tax system is appropriate. I will call this the kicking away the ladder approach; we made it here, and how we got here has no particular import.[11]

On the other hand, one might think there is some residual import of the framework goods as framework goods that changes the usual financing rules. Again, once the framework goods are provided, then progressivity is possible and so the issue here is not our ability to impose such taxes. Rather, we might argue that the usual argument for progressivity (or any other post-framework rule) is weaker as to the framework goods that make progressivity possible. These good are relevantly different from others because they are both primary and bundled. The primariness indicates their importance for any conception of a good life;[12] the bundledness indicates that a substantial number need to be provided at once. That is, there needs to be sufficiently clean air and clean water and security and property rights and ... Financing this bundle in the right way is less important than financing it at all. Usually we have to be careful that financing a new government service is not undermined by the costs imposed by financing the service, but in the case of these goods that is more unlikely because of their great value.

Similar reasoning presumably underlies Rawls' brief embrace of a proportionate expenditure tax to fund the payments required by the difference principle.[13] Rawls is aware that such a tax is not progressive, but that is alright with him because it is part of an overall system financing the core goods required by justice. Again, this is not to say that Rawls does not think progressive taxes are appropriate for other ends, for example, to protect fair equality of opportunity, just that the

---

[11] I am not sure it is fair to claim that anyone in particular has embraced this view because, as noted above, the main thinkers I know of abstract from the question and assume the framework goods. That said, because thinkers as diverse as Kaplow and Murphy and Nagel do not discuss the possibility of some other special rule for framework goods (as Rawls does), it is perhaps fair to characterise *all* these thinkers as embracing the idea that we should kick away the ladder.

[12] I am basically following Rawls on primary goods. Rawls (n 2), 62.

[13] ibid 278–79.

A Brief Theory of Taxation and Framework Public Goods   107

special ends to which these revenues will be put changes how one can justify *how* these taxes are collected.

C. Back and Forth

The 'kick the ladder away' approach could critique Rawls' approach on related theoretical and pragmatic grounds. First, as a matter of theory, if one knows the just way to distribute the tax burden, then what justifies a deviation? Second, and pragmatically, using a less just way to distribute the tax burden only complicates the spending analysis. Put simply, if we are raising too much from the poor, then we will simply need to give that amount back – and we will need to raise that further amount through taxes that themselves distort. Why not raise the money correctly to begin with?

Yet getting it right all the way down to framework goods is problematic for two related reasons. First, even if one is supremely confident that one has the right master theory, room has to be made for reasonable disagreement. Once that room is made, then it becomes important to permit suboptimal financing as a matter of practical politics. Second, even if there were consensus among policymakers about the best way to go, the world may resist. In the face of practical hurdles, abandoning theoretical purity will be necessary. Here are a few scenarios to consider.

i. Scenario 1: Developing Countries

The standard prescription for developing economies was once to adopt the right taxes according to a more general theory. If taxing income was compelling normatively for developed countries, then why should that be different in developing countries? This type of thinking led first to the prescription of progressive personal income taxes and then to value added taxes.[14]

The current consensus does not challenge the idea that broad ideas about the optimal tax system could be true in the abstract, but a system of taxation needs to take into account institutional capacity across various dimensions, and a progressive income tax, for example, puts a lot of pressure on institutions. Though the overlap between the institutions needed to levy an income tax and those need to provide the framework goods do not necessarily overlap perfectly, the overlap is considerable. Obviously, there needs to be the stability to create wealth, but also an educational/legal system capable of putting into place and enforcing an income tax.

Accordingly, tax policy in developing countries is best done as a bespoke and pragmatic enterprise.[15] The implication of this – abstracted and stylised – discussion

---

[14] R Bird, 'Taxation and Development: What Have We Learned from Fifty Years of Research?' ICTD Working Paper 1 (2012), 7–8.
[15] ibid 15.

of taxation in developing countries is an illustration of Rawls' insight that heterodox tax structures can be justified by their ends.

ii. Scenario 2: Developed Countries and Near-Framework Goods

However a developed country might be defined, it would seem definitional that the framework goods have been financed. If that is so, then in a developed country perhaps we need to compromise on the best theory of taxation because others do not agree on the best theory, but we certainly do not need to compromise because the facts on the ground resist, as was the case with the developing countries. Yet this is not necessarily the case.

The first step towards seeing how the question of financing framework goods remains relevant is to see that there is a broad category of *near*-framework goods. We know that such a category must exist – and might be substantial – based on our sketch of framework goods. For one thing, we understand that the framework goods are a matter of degree, with the lines necessarily arbitrary. If basic security requires a reasonable expectation of law and order until dusk, then it is likely that security until a bit after dusk can also yield outsized benefits, both economic and otherwise.

This arbitrariness might well also apply to portions of the population. The provision of the framework goods is, at least in many cases, not going to be sufficient for many individuals; the framework goods are enough to get the collective going but might leave many behind. Yet if the provision of basic security to 60 per cent of the population is enough as a matter of the framework, it is hard to see why providing basic security to the next increment of the population will not also be very compelling as a matter of justice and efficiency.

The framework goods also come as a bundle and so it might be that a developed country has a functional bundle that is deficient in some way – perhaps the country has a particularly strong legal regime, but bare bones provision for primary education.

So far we are discussing goods that maybe should be framework goods, but there are going to be goods that we might accept are not framework goods, such as medical care beyond basic preventive care, but are nearly so. Remember, a framework good has a strong independent justification to be provided because, among other possible reasons, of its centrality to a person leading a choiceworthy life.

iii. Scenario 2A: Tax Averse Developed Country

With the near-framework goods, we have the possibility that even a developed country might not be providing core goods such that it raises the question of whether or not we are in a situation where using suboptimal revenue instruments is justified. But how likely is that possibility to be realised? After all, at least in a democracy, one would expect public goods to be broadly defined and broadly

A Brief Theory of Taxation and Framework Public Goods 109

provided. And there is evidence that this has generally been the case as compared to other forms of social organisation.[16]

I will consider two not very hypothetical scenarios. First, there might be tax aversion of some kind, such that a democratic majority will not fund any goods beyond the minimum and in some cases maybe not even reaching that minimum. This aversion might itself result from any number of factors. There could be a problem in the political process such that voters do not vote for their 'true' interest.[17] Alternatively, voters might have an informal theory of moral desert, such that they believe they are strongly entitled to their pre-tax earnings, and it is a particular problem to transfer pre-tax earnings from taxpayers to others so that the others can receive mixed public/private goods, such as education or health care.[18] There could also be much more problematic reasons for the aversion, such as a particular aversion to providing aid to a particular set of people.[19]

If any of these reasons are operative, then a developed society might provide a limited, or lumpy, set of public goods, such that many near-framework, even framework, goods, are not provided. In such a situation, using suboptimal tools to provide such goods, as would have been necessary to provide sufficient framework goods to begin with, appears justified.[20]

iv. Scenario 2B: Developed Country with 'Broken' Federal System

A second, related, scenario in which a developed country might be failing to provide framework goods has to do with federalism. It is a traditional prescription of fiscal federalism that major redistribution should be done by the central

---

[16] D North, J Wallis and B Weingast, *Violence and Social Orders: A Conceptual Framework for Interpreting Recorded Human History* (Cambridge, CUP, 2009) 10–11, 116–25.

[17] L Bartels, 'Homer gets a tax cut: Inequality and public policy in the American mind' (2005) 3 *Perspectives on Politics* 15.

[18] For discussion of the desert theory see, for instance, S Sheffrin, *Tax Fairness and Folk Justice* (Cambridge, CUP, 2013) 58–64. Stark makes a related argument to the effect that there can be an expressive value to tax aversion. Put roughly, one might argue that one is averse to progressive income taxes because one is signalling the value that one assigns to work. KJ Stark, 'The Role of Expressive Versus Instrumental Preferences in U.S. Attitudes Toward Taxation and Redistribution' in HP Gaisbauer et al (eds), *Philosophical Explorations of Justice and Taxation* (Springer International, 2015).

[19] C Grogan and S Park, 'The Racial Divide in State Medicaid Expansions' (2017) 42(3) *Journal of Health Politics, Policy and Law* 539.

[20] I stand on the shoulders of giants in making this point, though the giants do not apply it to framework goods. Liscow takes Stark and Sheffrin's insight a step farther and argues that if there is taxpayer resistance to progressive taxation based on folk justice norms (or other reasons), then using administrative tools for redistribution is appropriate – even if suboptimal relative to a tax solution in the abstract. Z Liscow, 'Democratic Law and Economics', *Working Paper October 2019*, available at https://www.law.nyu.edu/sites/default/files/Democratic%20Law%20and%20Economics%20-%20 Liscow.pdf. Liscow's argument is a particularly stunning application of McAdams and Fennell's argument that the traditional prescriptions of law and economics need to take into account political frictions. LA Fennell and RH McAdams, 'The Distributive Deficit in Law and Economics' (2016) 100 *Minnesota Law Review* 1051.

government; this is because it is much easier for wealthier individuals to move out of smaller subnational units, thereby defeating progressive taxation at the subnational level. In the ideal scenario then, we should have the subnational units fund those goods, including framework goods (eg local roads), that admit of a benefit rationale, while the central government funds those goods, including framework goods (eg interstate highways) that cannot be financed using benefit levies.

And so now consider the following scenario: a developed country has a central government that refuses to finance key public goods, including framework, or near-framework, goods. Perhaps this is because of tax aversion or some other cultural/historical reason. In such a case a subnational government would have a compelling reason to finance framework goods. But the subnational government will have a much harder time using progressive financing tools to finance these framework goods. For technical reasons, a subnational government might also have considerable difficulty using other theoretically-superior taxes, progressive or not. For instance, it is probably not possible for the American states to implement a credit-invoice VAT without help from the federal government.

If a subnational government within such a federation finds itself in such a situation, then, again, cobbling together sub-optimal revenue tools appears well justified.

III. A Short Theory of Public Finance Disgrace

With this outline of a theory of framework goods and public finance in place, I am ready to flesh out a theory of public finance disgrace. First, *there must be a developed country that is not providing framework or near-framework goods*. As to health care in the contemporary United States, and even more when Dworkin was writing (ie before the advent of Obamacare), it looks clear that a near-framework good is not being provided.[21] A certain amount of health care, for example vaccinations, are clearly a public good. We don't need to parse whether annual check-ups or coverage for medical disasters also qualify as framework goods, as the moral (and economic) arguments are so strong that they are close enough. Even if merely near-framework goods, such goods should be provided – if possible.

And this brings us to the second presupposition: *a country must easily have the fiscal capacity to fund the good in question*.

As outlined above, one might quite reasonably believe that the contemporary United States has the two structural challenges sketched out above: it is not providing framework and near-framework goods when it has the capacity to do so. But this only gets us so far. Yes, on balance there is, to this point, an argument

---

[21] For some of the depressing data, see ED Kleinbard, *We Are Better than This* (Oxford, OUP, 2015) 191–98, 314–24.

that Americans should get over their tax aversion and provide additional revenues in order to finance near-framework goods. This is, essentially, a version of the famous argument made by Murphy and Nagel [MN]. In a nutshell, MN argue that our pre-tax earnings should not be used for assessing the justness of the distribution of goods in society. This is because pre-tax earnings are themselves a result of the social order created by those taxes, and thus saying that one has a right to the pre-tax earnings is to misunderstand that one's gross earnings represent an accounting convention.[22]

This part of their argument has been subject to significant criticism, however. For one thing, attributing all of our earnings to a mere social convention flies in the face of moral intuitions about work and desert; moral intuitions that also have strong psychological foundations.[23] Furthermore, just because our pre-tax earnings do represent, at least in part, a convention, it does not follow that there is not a pre-tax baseline with some moral significance.[24]

In short, the taxpayers have a point and, in any event, labelling acting according to a deeply held and roughly consistent moral psychology 'disgraceful' overstates the problem. Of course, on the other side it cannot be that attributing to (some, all?) taxpayers an amorphous moral desert theory somehow relieves them of straightforward moral obligations.

So where then is the disgrace? So far as I know, few seriously doubt the basic MN point that our *exact* pre-tax earnings are a matter of convention and that, therefore, whatever that amount might be is of limited moral significance. The various philosophical critiques canvased above, which I think have at least some bite, lose their strength in inverse proportion to the increase in the proposed tax. Suppose my pre-tax earnings are $100,000. MN have the better of the argument as to whether it is significant if my after-tax earnings are changed to $99,000. It is a different matter if we were to argue that my income should be shifted to $50,000.

A similar result follows from the objection from the actual psychology of taxpayers. Here the argument is *not* that small changes are ok because taxpayers will not notice. Rather, the argument is that taxpayer/voters ought not object to small increases because a small adjustment to taxable income does not trigger deep moral intuitions about desert. We might call this the MN neutral zone.

Note that the size of the neutral zone might depend on something other than the tax rate change. Consider the difference between imposing a new 5 per cent tax on income and moving from a 95 per cent tax rate on income to 100 per cent. As rough rule of thumb, it seems reasonable to assume increasing moral significance if one is adding a tax to a higher base, though nothing hangs on this intuition of mine being correct. What matters is that the concept of a neutral zone is a coherent one.

---

[22] Murphy and Nagel (n 10) 36–37.
[23] Sheffrin (n 18) 58–64.
[24] KA Kordana and DH Tabachnick, 'Tax and the Philosopher's Stone' (2003) 89 *Virginia Law Review* 647, 651.

112   *Darien Shanske*

This leads to an empirical question, namely whether a tax increase in the MN neutral zone is sufficient to raise the revenue for the near-framework goods. If it is, *then* we have a disgraceful situation. The zone of fiscal capacity that can create disgrace is broader than the neutral zone created by one tax, even if it is the theoretically preferred tax. We have already established that there is a good argument for a multitude of imperfect levies in order to raise funds for the framework goods. This argument should hold true for the near-framework goods in proportion to how near framework goods they are. As to each of these levies, there is a neutral zone, with the combined neutral zone potentially significantly greater than that for any one tax.

It is worth taking a moment to consider why different taxes might produce different neutral zones. The personal income tax runs most directly into intuitions about desert; I *worked* for this salary. The desert theory might object to the property tax, but the property tax also offends against a notion of place; I am just sitting here in a home I have owned for years: why does *that* trigger a tax, especially a tax that might be so high so as displace me from my home?

Note that this argument about multiple tax instruments and moral weight has an analogue in the world of traditional considerations of efficiency. I note this parallel as further illustration, but also in order to make sure the core point is not misunderstood. The idea is not that small changes are easier to 'hide', but rather that the small changes really represent less of the good that taxpayers are valuing.

The argument for multiple instruments on efficiency grounds has two steps.[25] First, a fundamental tenet of tax economics is that the amount of deadweight loss generated by a tax increases at the square of the tax rate. The jargon is convoluted, but the intuition is simple. Consider how much trouble you would go to avoid a 5 per cent tax. Now imagine how much more trouble you would go to avoid a 20 per cent tax. You might not do anything to avoid a 5 per cent tax, but you would do a lot to avoid the 20 per cent tax – hence the exponential growth in wasteful tax planning and lost government revenue.[26] This step is the analogue to there being a morality of tax neutral zone; small steps matter less.

The second step requires making the observation that different taxes can be evaded in different ways. I can avoid paying income tax by deferring the sale of appreciated assets, but this does not help me avoid paying sales tax on my new car. I used to be able to evade the sales tax by purchasing from a remote vendor online, but this never helped with the income tax. If the tax rate on income is sufficiently low, say 5 per cent, then I will not defer the sale of assets that I otherwise wish to sell, and if the sales tax rate is sufficiently low, say 5 per cent, then I will not search

---

[25] Argument drawn from: D Gamage, 'How Should Governments Promote Distributive Justice?: A Framework for Analyzing the Optimal Choice of Tax Instruments' (2014) 68 *Tax Law Review* 1, 56–63; D Gamage, 'The Case for Taxing (All of) Labor Income, Consumption, Capital Income, and Wealth' (2015) 68 *Tax Law Review* 355, 375–81.

[26] To be precise, when a tax is imposed, say on gasoline, both the producers and consumers lose out on otherwise efficient transactions in an amount greater than the revenue the government raises by imposing the tax. See J Gruber, *Public Finance and Public Policy* 4th edn (New York, Worth Publishers, 2012) 591.

for an internet seller who will not collect the tax. This will be true even though at a rate of 10 per cent I might engage in evasion of either tax. Similarly, I might consider a 10 per cent tax increase to pay for health care to the poor an unacceptable transfer, but be alright with a 5 per cent shift.

But wait. It is well understood that, assuming a taxpayer consumes all their income, that an income tax and consumption tax are the same. And so I have smuggled in a 10 per cent tax on income! This objection is partially just an artefact of the illustration. My intuition, for what it is worth, is that 5 per cent is probably at the upper limit of the neutral zone (abstracting from other questions, such as the baseline rate). Furthermore, I am not assuming that no one notices that the increase in the consumption tax also amounts, at least in part, to a tax on income. What I am claiming is that taxpayers may have reasonably different moral intuitions about the two taxes, even if economists do not. The consumption tax is predicated on a choice to consume and taxpayers may properly evaluate such a tax differently – at least enough to accord it its own neutral zone.

And so now, at long last, we can return to the fiscal presupposition of disgrace. There is disgrace if a developed country is not providing (near) framework goods when it can easily do so even through some combination of small revenue increases which are themselves of little moral import. It is an empirical question whether this is true in the United States, but there is compelling evidence that this is so. It would cost about $18bn to provide insurance coverage to 2 million more people.[27] This is real money, of course, but raising this amount, or even multiples of it, would seem to be within the MN neutral zone. The tax cuts of 2017, for example, were estimated to cost $1.5tn over 10 years.[28] Just increasing the top personal income tax bracket from 37 per cent back to 39.6 per cent would likely raise multiples of $18bn per year, and it is hard to see how that increment is morally weighty.

IV. Conclusion

Perhaps all of this is obvious.[29] Dworkin himself gestures to the basic argument of this chapter in his introduction:

> The prosperous democracies are very far from providing even a decent minimal life for everyone – though some come closer to that goal than others – and we might therefore

---

[27] J Liu and C Eibner, 'Expanding Enrollment Without the Individual Mandate: Options to Bring More People into the Individual Market', Commonwealth Fund (August 2018), available at https://www.commonwealthfund.org/publications/fund-reports/2018/aug/expanding-enrollment-without-individual-mandate.

[28] Joint Committee on Taxation, *Estimated Budget Effects of The Conference Agreement For H.R.1, The 'Tax Cuts And Jobs Act'* (18 December 2017).

[29] Kleinbard also makes a similar argument. Kleinbard has argued quite convincingly that we need to focus on the spending half of the public finance system; we need not worry too much about getting the revenue system just right so much as the overall system. Kleinbard (n 21) 355, 372–83. Kleinbard

114   *Darien Shanske*

think it wise to concentrate on urging that lesser requirement and ignore, at least for the foreseeable future, the more demanding one of full equality. But once it is established that the comfortable members of a community do not owe their uncomfortable citizens equality, but only some decent minimum standard of living, then too much is allowed to turn on the essentially subjective question of how minimum a standard is decent, and contemporary history suggests that the comfortable are unlikely to give a generous answer to that question.[30]

Quite reasonably, Dworkin does not want to rely on the subjective choices of the haves as to how much the have-nots should minimally have. Yet Dworkin did not unpack the significance of his parenthetical claim that 'some [prosperous democracies] come closer to the goal [of providing a decent minimum] than others'. I think he relied on a similar intuition when he labelled a certain non-provision of public goods a 'disgrace'. I have endeavoured to unpack the presuppositions of public finance system disgrace in this chapter, and I want to conclude by agreeing with Dworkin that just because a society provides the near-framework goods when it can readily do so does not release it from any further moral obligation. However, as I have argued here, making such provision *does* shield that society from being 'disgraceful'. No one and no society should be satisfied at simply being not disgraceful, but, for the United States in 2019 at least, I think not being disgraceful is actually quite an ambitious place to start.

---

grounds his account of what goods should be provided on a loosely Rawlsian approach as to what level of social insurance we would agree to in the original position. Ibid, 345–46. Kleinbard does not, however, address whether some further relaxing of our preferred approach to taxation should occur as to some core goods, which has been the project in this chapter.

[30] Dworkin (n 1), 3.

PART III

Citizenship

7

A Critical Analysis of How Formal and Informal Citizenships Influence Justice between Mobile Taxpayers

YVETTE LIND*

Ongoing globalisation and increased taxpayer mobility illustrate a complex and highly present problem, as globally mobile individuals such as those working in several states, guest workers, immigrants and asylum seekers often find themselves excluded from voting privileges in the source state due to the lack of formal citizenship. The aim of this chapter is to describe and analyse how both formal and informal citizenships impact mobile taxpayers' inclusion in communities other than the state in which they have formal citizenship. This is done through a study of three principal legal frameworks in Sweden: taxation; access to welfare benefits; and access to voting rights.[1] These legal frameworks are all applicable to globally mobile workers and as such are pivotal when discussing justice between taxpayers in a democratic setting.[2]

---

* This chapter is a part of my project *Political (Tax) Equity in a Global Context* which was initialised during my stay at the Max Planck Institute for Tax Law and Public Finance as a scholarship holder in 2019. I am as a result grateful to Wolfgang Schön for scholarship funding and fruitful discussions. Further, I am also grateful to the Nordic Tax Research Council as they financed my stay as a visiting scholar at Levin College, University of Florida in 2020. For feedback on earlier versions of this chapter, I thank Mats Tjernberg, Åsa Gunnarsson, Neil H Buchanan, Diane Ring and all the participants of the Cambridge Tax Policy Conference of 2019. I am also grateful to those attending and commenting at my brownbag lunch which was held at the Max Planck Institute for Tax Law and Public Finance in August 2019 in addition to all the participants of the 5th Max Planck European Postdoctoral Conference on Tax Law. Finally, thank you to Dominic de Cogan for his dedication and patience when editing my text. All errors are mine.

[1] The Swedish system alone is used as the example of this chapter as it is not possible to discuss citizenship in a broader context due to the limited format, yet the findings and discussions are still relevant to many other states as formal citizenship is required in most states in order to receive the right to vote in general elections.

[2] Naturally, one may acknowledge a wider range of aspects within international taxation which may have democratic implications, for instance multinational corporations linked to tax avoidance versus the financing of welfare states, yet issues such as these are beyond the scope of this chapter.

To discuss the allocation of voting rights is naturally a sensitive subject due to its highly political nature. The hope is that this chapter will be able, through the trailblazing example of international taxation in which states at present time have been able to start agreeing on the allocation of taxing rights on a global level through both the G20 BEPS project and the EU's new anti-tax avoidance package, to illustrate both the need for a reform on how voting rights are awarded and the possibility for such reform.

I. Background and Aim of Research

As of lately, ongoing globalisation and increased taxpayer mobility has shown us that these phenomena not only exacerbate pre-existing shortcomings when allocating taxing rights between states, but also challenge the way that states traditionally award formal citizenship and as a result allocate political rights and benefits (this chapter primarily considers voting rights). This is brought on by the fact that states have expanded their tool box of tax incentives, already containing a wide range of tax benefits, to include so-called golden visas and citizenships (facilitating easier access through, for instance, investment in the state) when attempting to attract high-income earners, high-skilled workers and high-net value individuals to their jurisdiction.[3] This practice challenges the traditional perception of formal citizenship, as one may argue that it contributes to an erosion of its value and meaning, in addition to highlighting the differentiation between individuals with reference to economic status, as states give preferential treatment to those who chose to move (high-income earners, high-skilled workers and high-net value individuals) compared to those who are forced to move (refugees). Such differentiation naturally evokes not only the issue of justice between states,[4] but also between state and individual, and between individuals.

Formal citizenship in itself comprises much more than merely political rights and benefits. This is of course acknowledged, and therefore it should be clarified that in this chapter citizenship is primarily discussed in the sense of being the carrier (proxy) for political rights and benefits, thus excluding other rights and obligations generally linked to it, such as holding public office, permanent residency, being able to own land or being eligible for certain employments. Formal citizenship as the proxy of certain rights and benefits is as a result placed in a broader context through the inclusion of informal citizenships. In this chapter, the phrase 'informal citizenship' is used to capture the idea that formal citizenship is

---

[3] A Christians, 'Buying in: Residence and Citizenship by Investment' (2017) 62(1) *St Louis University Law Journal* 51.

[4] Ongoing discussions on global justice and cosmopolitan justice deal with this relationship, see for instance P Hongler, *Justice in International Tax Law – A Normative Review of the International Tax Regime* (Amsterdam, IBFD, 2019) and T Dagan, 'International Tax and Global Justice' (2017) 18(1) *Theoretical Inquiries in Law* 1.

A Critical Analysis of Formal and Informal Citizenships   119

not the only way that inclusion and exclusion of individuals may be established. This is also achieved through the application of other legal rules; for example those who are eligible to receive (social) welfare benefits in accordance to the legislation are considered social citizens. Just as those who reside and participate in a society belong to a community through inclusion and joint goals, those who pay taxes, for instance, could as easily be claimed to be part of a specific community. The application of Swedish legal rules linked to the distribution of social insurances clearly establishes an informal citizenship (commonly referred to as 'social citizenship' within Nordic welfare research, specifically research with a gender perspective).[5] Ideal citizenships such as these become normative as they dictate the factual outcome regardless of formal neutrality and equality, not unlike how formal citizenship is normative for voting rights when determining political citizenship. These informal citizenships add another layer of complexity to citizenship.

Previous papers within the *Political (Tax) Equity in a Global Context* project initially focused on the extent of inclusion (social, fiscal and political) in a state other than that gained through formal citizenship, concluding that (through both tax technical and more theoretical studies) formal citizenship is rarely mandatory in order for an individual to gain access to (social) welfare systems, nor is it the basis for tax liability (with a few exemptions, where the United States would be the most obvious example).[6] Furthermore, additional papers explored to what extent individuals could influence their tax situation (tax legislation and public spending) other than through traditional voting, concluding that taxpayers could indirectly influence tax and spend through various tax benefits embedded in domestic tax codes and constitutional safeguards such as the principle of equality, judicial review and taxpayer standing in court.[7]

This chapter attempts to add additional findings to these studies when discussing formal and informal citizenships as greater or lesser kinds of memberships in community. Thus, attempting to illustrate that a mobile taxpayer may in some cases be a member of said community (through residence, payment of taxes, economic activity, access to welfare benefits as well as inclusion in social and political life) without necessarily having formal citizenship. This level of membership participation will differ between various taxpayer groups, just as it differs between citizens

---

[5] See, eg, Å Gunnarsson, 'Hur jämställt är vårt sociala medborgarskap?' in L Vahlne Westerhäll (ed), *Legitimitetsfrågor inom socialrätten* (Stockholm, Nordstedts Juridik, 2007).

[6] Y Lind, 'Political (tax) equity in a global context as a part of Social Sustainability – some advice for researchers who wish to explore democratic influencing of taxation and public spending' in C Brokelind (ed), *Tax Sustainability in an EU and International Context* (Amsterdam, IBFD, 2020); Y Lind, 'Voting rights compared to income taxation and welfare benefits through the Swedish lens' (2020) 23(2) *Florida Tax Review*; Y Lind, 'Political (tax) equity in a global context – Voting rights compared to income taxation and welfare benefits from the Swedish perspective' (2019) 9(5) *Max Planck Institute for Tax Law and Public Finance working paper series*.

[7] Initially see Y Lind, 'Political (tax) equity in a global context – Some initial reflections on how individuals may indirectly influence tax legislation and public spending in Sweden, Germany and the US' (2019) 1(8) *CBS Law Legal Studies Research Paper Series*; Y Lind, 'Initial findings on how individuals may indirectly influence tax and spend in Sweden, Germany and the United States' (2020) *Intertax* 48(5) 482.

120   *Yvette Lind*

(an expat compared to a citizen living in the residence state for instance). A large part of these additional findings will be discussions on justice between individuals when considering their level of participation in their source state, meaning the state they work and pay taxes in when cross-border working.

As a result, this chapter aims to supplement the already existing body of research which has explored the relationship between fiscal policy and citizenship rather than portraying taxation as merely a source of material resources.[8] This is achieved through the analysis of globally mobile taxpayer groups, as most existing work has focused on a purely domestic setting in which citizens and non-citizens are more or less fixed actors within a community rather than being mobile between various communities. Furthermore, this chapter also contributes through discussion and analysis of how informal citizenships are ranked between themselves and how this ranking could, and possibly should, influence the inclusion or exclusion of mobile taxpayer groups in a community in which they are not formal citizens.

Equity is used as a tool to capture to what extent differing groups of mobile taxpayers have an equal footing when considering inclusion in a community and by doing so analysing if, how, and to what extent, formal and informal citizenships influence justice between these taxpayers as regards to this access. Naturally, when discussing equity between taxpayers one will also need to consider the relationship between individual and state in order to understand why the state may have, intentionally or unintendedly, chosen to award taxpayers differing rights and benefits. Other papers within the project have used equity as a tool for such discussions and this chapter will follow suit.[9] A more comprehensive discussion on equity is therefore not done here, as this has been covered in previous papers.

Furthermore, this chapter applies a broader sense of justice than would traditionally have been found within the Nordic legal scholarship. Nordic scholars often separate between justice referable to taxation (tax justice) and justice referable to the welfare state dimension (social justice). This practice contributes to a tradition of having a more pragmatic approach to justice as a concept or theory compartmentalised to different areas of law, for instance tax law or social insurance law, rather than applying justice more coherently and across several areas of law.[10] For instance, tax scholars rarely include, or even consider for that matter, social transfers in their research, as these would be considered as part of social insurance law or simply of a more political nature. It is natural, and logical, to make such a distinction if one perceives the structures of income (revenue) and expenditures (social transfers) as two differing entities instead of being not only linked but also dependent on each other.[11] Consequently, the social dimension of

---

[8] This body of research includes work done not only by AK Mehrotra, RA Musgrave and R Bellamy but also by W Schön, A Christians and G Beretta.

[9] Lind (n 6) and (n 7).

[10] See for instance above n 5.

[11] Recent discussions on revenue law support this broader inclusion of taxes. See for instance J Snape and D de Cogan, *Landmark Cases in Revenue Law* (Oxford, Hart, 2019). Additionally, the linking between social policy objectives and tax expenditures has been discussed in R Mason, 'Tax Expenditures and Global Labor Mobility' (2009) 84(6) *NYU Tax Law Review* 1540.

taxation is an underdeveloped field of research as more emphasis has historically been placed on tax justice in the context of revenue collection rather than both revenues and expenditures.[12]

This chapter favours this broader inclusion, and justice is therefore not considered as exclusive to just one legal field, as it is instead applied more holistically when analysing justice across those legal regimes which are associated to taxation, access to welfare benefits and voting privileges when considering mobile taxpayers. Such an approach would be necessary for justice to form a normative coherence rather than fragmented perceptions of it.[13]

This chapter is structured as follows. Section II provides some initial statements on how increased taxpayer mobility may impact democracy, primarily through the influencing of tax and spend and challenges arising from increased global mobility. In Section III informal citizenship is introduced and described. Social, fiscal and political citizenships, and how these are created through the application of material law referable to social insurances, are discussed in Section IV. Section V discusses taxation and voting rights are introduced in Section VI. Section VII concludes with a more comprehensive analysis of how informal citizenships compare to formal citizenship as regards justice and equity between mobile taxpayers.

II. The Democratic Implications of Increased Taxpayer Mobility and the Significance of Formal Citizenship

Historically, states have awarded voting rights to those who either owned property and/or paid taxes.[14] Voting would be a way for the individual to *directly influence*

---

[12] Å Gunnarsson, 'The making of a critical tax policy framework' in R Banakar, K Dahlstrand and L Ryberg Welander (eds), *Festskrift till Håkan Hydén* (Lund, Juristförlaget i Lund, 2018).

[13] For support of such reasoning see for instance Snape and de Cogan (n 11) 3. Naturally, there is some (generally accepted) incoherence between these legal areas due to differing principles and parallel, but uncoordinated, development of material law. The area of tax law in itself provides proof of such incoherence as tax rules are under constant change due to its highly international context combined with the struggles of the legislator when keeping a balance between the upholding of general principles and coherence (within the tax system as well as adjacent areas of law such as accounting and civil law) while still enforcing detailed rules that ensure legal certainty that, ideally, also facilitates the collection of fiscal revenues (read: attempts to keep tax avoidance at bay). This chapter will naturally need to consider such incoherence between studied areas of law when (1) describing and analysing the relationship between them, and (2) critically analysing if, when, and how informal citizenships (created by the application of these material rules) can influence justice between taxpayers.

[14] See, eg, A Keyssar, *The right to vote: The contested history of democracy in the United States* (New York, Basic Books, 2009).

122   *Yvette Lind*

tax and spend in the state in which taxes have been paid.[15] At the present time, most states award voting rights in accordance to formal citizenship. Theoretically, this strengthens political equity between individuals, as there is no separation with reference to the economic status of individuals which strengthens political equity between individuals. However, formal citizenship will not automatically result in complete political equity, as there naturally will remain some mismatches as regards to the payment of taxes and formal citizenship.[16] As mentioned in Section I, ongoing globalisation and increased taxpayer mobility illustrate this complexity, as globally mobile individuals often find themselves excluded from voting privileges in the source state due to the lack of formal citizenship.

As a result, mobile taxpayers may contribute financially to state finances (in one or several states depending on the degree of mobility) simply on account of their residence in a state, yet without the possibility of influencing their tax situation or the taxes paid. Some efforts have been made in order to compensate this political inequity as states may allow individuals with territorial affiliation to vote. For instance, EU Member States allow EU citizens to vote in municipal elections on the same basis as citizens in said state on the basis of residing in the state as a result of EU law,[17] while at the same time applying other requirements (such as being registered in the municipality for a minimum of 3–5 years) on individuals originating from a state outside the EU. Safeguards such as these proves that states may overcome these obstacles both legally and politically, yet at the same time they may also enforce the unfair treatment of affluent taxpayers compared to those less privileged, as individuals are not treated equally due to a distinction based upon their territorial origin.

Additionally, in contrast, citizens without any territorial affiliation or tax liability, such as expatriates, are on the other hand generally given full access to voting privileges. This illustrates apparent mismatches between systems and states. These mismatches in practice separate taxpayers and invoke discussions regarding justice between taxpayers as citizenship holds a value that trumps the fulfilling of any social contract through tax payments and/or territorial affiliation. Consequently, some taxpayers, in particular those who are highly mobile and work in several states (guest workers, immigrants and asylum seekers), are often excluded from voting privileges in the source state due to the lack of formal citizenship. The lack of citizenship may exclude them from such political rights and benefits, yet it does not absolve them from their duties to the community in which they reside, for example to pay taxes and abide the law. This illustrates the fact that individuals may participate and contribute in a community as members, even though they

---

[15] The differentiation between direct and indirect influencing of tax and spend, in addition to the relationship between these and the theory of direct democracy was discussed more extensively in Lind (n 7).

[16] Lind (n 7).

[17] Council Directive 94/80/EC of 19 December 1994 laying down detailed arrangements for the exercise of the right to vote and to stand as a candidate in municipal elections by citizens of the Union residing in a Member State of which they are not nationals.

are not formal citizens. Which leads to the need to identify and analyse differing memberships in a community, other than that of formal citizenship. Or as Marshall stated early on: that modern citizenship rests on 'an image of an informal citizenship against which achievements can be measured and towards which aspirations can be directed'.[18] The fulfilment of obligations determined by material law therefore formalises an individual's obligations towards a community while at the same time determining who is to be considered a member of such a community. And in the process, such inclusion or exclusion define a variety of citizenships outside of the purely formal one.

III. The Significance of Informal Citizenships and their Identification Through the Swedish Example

Bellamy links to this thinking through his discussions on citizenship, of which the combination of three key components establishes a condition of civic equality: (1) *membership* of a democratic political community, (2) the collective *rights and benefits* associated with this membership, and (3) *participation* in the community's political, economic and social processes.[19] The first component deals with the question of who is to be considered a citizen. Internal exclusions to this membership have always existed in various forms. Historically, people of a certain gender have been excluded from the right to vote, as have those without property ownership or wealth. Presently, states still apply internal restrictions such as age requirements and the need for a fixed address. Most important for this chapter are not internal exclusions but rather external exclusions, such as those referable to refugees and immigrants, as increased global mobility presses the need for a reformation of the construction and meaning of citizenship at present day. The second component deals with rights and benefits and is often considered as the most crucial component of citizenship.[20] There is an extensive doctrine referable to the extent and definition of these rights and benefits, yet this discussion is left out of this chapter. Instead, it focuses specifically on rights and benefits referable to the three included legal regimes of taxation, social insurance law and voting. The third and final component encompasses participation and is used as a red thread when discussing the meaning and significance of informal citizenships in this chapter.

The meaning and significance of citizenship in general is inconsistent by nature. It is consistent in the sense that formal citizenship does not expressly separate individuals based upon gender, social class or religion (at present day at least). Neither is there (expressively by law) any establishment of first or second-class citizens

---

[18] TH Marshall, *Citizenship and Social Class* (Cambridge, CUP, 1950) 29.
[19] R Bellamy, *Citizenship – a very short introduction* (Oxford, OUP, 2008) 12.
[20] ibid 13.

124   *Yvette Lind*

within a state.[21] But, at the same time citizenship is inconsistent as there will be informal separations, both at international level (EU citizens receive preferential treatment compared to non-EU citizens as a result of the deep integration process between EU Member States) and at national level (the Indian caste system or the ongoing situation in Hong Kong would be two obvious examples). Looking at the Swedish situation, it is possible to identify a variety of groups residing on Swedish territory (temporarily or permanently) who experience citizenship (together with rights and obligations attached to it) differently compared to the norm ('the white Swedish man'), for instance Sami, Finnish-speaking nationals, Tornedalers, Roma, Jewish, voluntary immigrants, refugees (who, unlike the voluntary immigrants, never can return to their state of origin) and so forth.

These groups may not be separated expressively by law, but they will nonetheless experience a differentiation in treatment when subjected to various legal rules. For instance, both the Swedish legislator and the Swedish research community have acknowledged gender issues since the 1960s,[22] resulting in an ongoing aspiration to reform the legal system with the aim of making it gender neutral (similar to Nordic neighbours such as Denmark).[23] The Swedish system is, as a result, designed in a gender neutral fashion with no formally expressed favouring of one gender compared to the other. For instance, Sweden replaced widow's benefits (social security spousal death benefits targeting widows specifically) and replaced these with a provision for surviving dependants.[24] Further, the Danish legislator raised the retirement age of women from 62 to 67 in the 1970s in order to match the retirement age of men as a result of the implementation of the EU principle of equal treatment for men and women in social security matters.[25] However, when designing the legal system in such a fashion, the Swedish and Danish legislator assume (wrongly) that society in itself is gender neutral. This results in a discrimination of women compared to men as the factual situation of women is different compared to that of men, for example women work part-time to a greater extent, women take out parental leave and care for children to a greater extent, in addition to women living longer lives and often being younger than their partner in couple relationships. This results in the promotion of the male norm despite the system being formally gender neutral.

---

[21] For further discussions on this see LK Kerber, 'The Meaning of Citizenship' (1997) 84(3) *The Journal of American History* 833–54.

[22] See, eg, the extensive work done by Swedish legal scholars such as Anna Christensen, Yvonne Hirdman, Åsa Gunnarsson and Eva-Maria Svensson.

[23] EM Svensson, *Genus och Rätt - en problematisering av föreställningen om rätten* (Iustus Förlag, 1997).

[24] For a more detailed description of the historical development of this legal provision see R Mannelqvist, *Samband I socialförsäkringen - En rättsvetenskaplig studie av sambandet mellan förmåner och avgifter i socialförsäkringen* (Uppsala, Iustus, 2003) 47–48.

[25] The legislative change was a result of the implementation of Council Directive 79/7/EEC of 19 December 1978 on the progressive implementation of the principle of equal treatment for men and women in matters of social security [1978] OJ L 6/24. Also see K Ketscher, *Socialret Almindelige principper Retssikkerhed og administration* (Copenhagen, GadJura, 1998).

Principles linked to the distribution of welfare benefits, such as the principle of equality and economic efficiency, are therefore essential within Swedish social insurance law as they will determine the distribution of rights and obligations between the individual and the state.[26] There is of course the idea and political ambition that this will result in a gender-neutral outcome when applied, yet instead they result in a preferential treatment of men due to non-legal factors such as age differences in relationships, the tradition of the woman staying at home with younger children etc. As a result, these principles act as guidelines as they form a legal framework which in turn establishes a benchmark when determining the ideal social citizen and which individuals who should have complete access to the welfare system, and subsequently also determines which individuals that are to be excluded from the social dimension and subsequently social citizenship.

Such separation is apparent in the Swedish social insurance system as it is built upon the premise of individuals having full-time employment which factually favours men, as women often are unable to work full time due to having more responsibility in the home (taking care of the children in addition to doing most of the household work). Swedish social insurance law does not actively discriminate women through differing (legal) criteria based upon their gender as it is designed in a gender neutral fashion, yet this legal framework will nonetheless result in a hidden discrimination as men factually will have easier access to work-based welfare benefits (compared to women) as they work full-time to a greater extent. This establishes a social community in which men will become social citizens more easily than women.

Besides social citizenship we can also identify other informal citizenships established by the application of material law. Those who interact with the tax system through tax payments and tax filing can be considered fiscal citizens, and those who are eligible to vote (non-citizens cannot vote in national elections but in some cases at local level) can be considered political citizens. This suggests that mobile taxpayers working and residing in Sweden may lack Swedish citizenship yet still be considered as social, fiscal and/or political citizens. The following sections of this chapter analyse these different informal citizenships as expressions of membership and inclusion in a community and discusses justice between different groups of mobile taxpayers (primarily those who choose to be mobile on one hand and those who are forced to be mobile on the other hand) when assessing the extent of access.

IV. Social Citizenship Through Access to (Social) Welfare Benefits

The Nordic states do not traditionally separate between citizens and non-citizens when distributing welfare benefits. Instead, access to these welfare systems is

---

[26] For an extensive insight into Swedish insurance law see Mannelqvist (n 24).

126   Yvette Lind

generally based upon either economic activity and/or territorial affiliation, resulting in benefits primarily being provided to working individuals. For instance, the basic assumption within Swedish social insurance law is that individuals ought to be financially independent of others. Subsequently, individuals are assumed to be able to support themselves through full-time work. If, and when, individuals are unable to perform such work, the state steps in and supports them, a situation much like insurance. The individuals will pay the premium (taxes) with the knowledge that they will receive assistance if in need rather than expecting benefits corresponding to the taxes paid.[27]

This means that the Nordic social security system is not based upon the benefit principle,[28] and instead of a direct link between payment (taxes or social security contributions) and benefit (public goods) there is an indirect link which does not actually require a traceable payment, or even a payment at all in some cases, in order for an individual to be eligible for the benefit.[29] The Swedish practice of payroll taxes of course reflects some sort of a link between payment and benefit but this link is arguably weak as these social security contributions are not earmarked and subsequently cannot be linked to the individual or the benefit.

Funding the social security system on the ability-to-pay principle rather than the benefit principle is considered to result in a fairer (more equitable) tax system as the individual's contribution to the community is not directly linked to the individual's need for public goods but instead enforces the idea of a civic identity underpinned by egalitarian principles.[30] In short, affluent taxpayers are obliged to give back to the community in which they are a member, as the ability-to-pay principle underlines the importance of ethical duties and social solidarity.[31] Such reasoning will be discussed further in Section V, as it argues that an individual proves his or her entitlement to fiscal citizenship through the payment of taxes as he or she contributes a fair share to the public treasury. Or as Zelenak puts it: the taxpayer is 'doing one's part' in order to support the community of which the taxpayer is a member.[32]

---

[27] Social security in general may be financed through either income taxation or social security contributions (payroll taxes paid by the employer); alternatively through a combination of both. Sweden finances its system mainly through payroll taxes, which in practice means that the employer pays these taxes and not the individual.

[28] For further elaboration of the benefit principle and its function within taxation see RA Musgrave and P Musgrave, *Public Finance in Theory and Practise* (New York, McGraw-Hill, 1989).

[29] The discussion on direct and indirect linking between taxes and public goods can be found in D Williams, 'Social Security Taxation' in V Thuronyi (ed), *Tax Law Design and Drafting vol 2* (Washington DC, International Monetary Fund, 1998).

[30] For support of such reasoning see, eg, J Adams, *Democracy and Social Ethics* (London, Macmillan, 1902).

[31] AK Mehrotra, 'Fiscal Forearms: Taxation as the Lifeblood of the Modern Liberal State' in K Morgans and A Orloff (eds), *The Many Hands of the State: Theorizing the Complexities of Political Authority and Social Contract* (New York, CUP, 2017).

[32] L Zelenak, *Learning to Love Form 1040: Two Cheers for the Return-Based Mass Income Tax* (Chicago, University of Chicago Press, 2013) 17.

A Critical Analysis of Formal and Informal Citizenships   127

The Swedish system does not only grant access to welfare benefits through the payment of taxes (work-based benefits) but also through territorial affiliation (residence-based benefits). The Social Insurance Code (SIC)[33] applies two criteria when granting access to welfare benefits:[34] (1) the payment of fees[35] and/or income taxes which can be accounted for (work-based benefits which are of a more general and discretionary nature),[36] and (2) Swedish domicile (residence-based benefits which are of a social nature).[37] The first criterion (work-based benefits) grants access to benefits such as sickness allowance, income-based pension and occupational injury compensation, to those who have a Swedish full-time employment.[38] The application of this criterion establishes an informal social citizenship which (generally) includes men and excludes women due to the existence of inherent gender inequalities in society, resulting in social injustice between men and women. This shortcoming has been acknowledged by the legislator who has subsequently implemented the second criterion (residence-based benefits) as a safeguard primarily targeting women. These residence-based benefits are arguably family friendly by nature as they provide benefits such as parental allowance, child benefits and a guaranteed pension (ensuring that women will have a pension even if they have not been able to work full-time or have not worked at all) and are awarded in accordance to territorial affiliation rather than economic activity. This further emphasises the weak (or in this case, non-existent) link between payment and benefit.

In conclusion, social citizenship in Sweden is based upon territorial affiliation and economic activity (work and payment of taxes) and not on formal citizenship. Legal frameworks associated to the distribution of (social) welfare benefits will not only determine an inclusion or exclusion of the individual in the social dimension, but also will determine the idea of social justice in the context of social insurance law. Social needs that fall outside of the scope of material law forming social citizenship will not be acknowledged, legally or legitimately, as an obligation for the state to provide.[39] For instance, women may find themselves excluded from work-based benefits as they may work part-time, or not at all, in order to take greater responsibility for the household. The informal social citizenship in the Swedish welfare state is therefore arguably an expression of classical social contract theory as it presumes that an individual works full-time in order to contribute

---

[33] SFS 2010:110 Socialförsäkringsbalken.

[34] Additionally, some welfare benefits require the individual to pay a fee, yet these are not dealt with in this study.

[35] The differentiation between fees and taxes has been widely discussed within Swedish legal doctrine. Theoretically there is a clear line between the two, ie a fee is, unlike a tax, earmarked for a certain purpose. However, the line between the two is in reality rarely clear. It is generally accepted, since the introduction of the 1991 tax reform in Sweden, that social fees are to be considered as partially taxes, partially fees.

[36] 'Socialförsäkringsbalken' (n 33) ch 6.

[37] ibid ch 5.

[38] ibid ch 6.

[39] For support see Gunnarsson (n 5).

128   *Yvette Lind*

to the community through taxes. Those who are outside of social citizenship are actively excluded from the social dimension and basic welfare benefits such as sickness allowance and income-based pension.

Residence-based benefits act as a remedy to this exclusion as they provide an additional safety net (primarily benefiting families). The legislator may initially have designed this safeguard with the intention to support Swedish women, yet they are currently also acting as a safeguard for refugees and immigrants. Safeguards such as these are of great importance as they reinforce the notion of social justice by including otherwise excluded individuals. However, these safeguards should perhaps also be scrutinised as they were implemented in times with less global mobility. Individuals who have been registered in a Swedish municipality for a minimum of one year may at present time access the Swedish welfare system regardless of their economic activity.[40] This is a practice which has recently sparked intense political debate as refugees and immigrants in Sweden will, due to the gender-neutral design of the Swedish legal system which opens up for territorial affiliation, gain access to part of the welfare system without any payment through economic activity.

V. Fiscal Citizenship Through Economic Activity and the Payment of Taxes

Taxation is commonly considered to characterise one of the most widely and persistently experienced relationships between an individual and the state and not only institutionalises the notion of a social contract but also formalises the obligations a member has towards other members of the same community.[41] The process of paying taxes may therefore be considered to establish civic identity and as such the notion of a fiscal citizenship as the act validates the financial responsibilities an individual has towards the community of which the individual is part. This is rather straightforward thinking when considering a purely domestic context, ie a worker who is a formal citizen of the state and contributes through taxes on his or her employment.

However, this will be less obvious if one considers the international context and the wide group of mobile workers who may contribute financially to a state through taxation while being formal citizens in another state. For instance, a mobile worker may reside in the residence state in which he or she has citizenship while paying taxes to the source state on a temporary basis, due to temporary work or other income. The worker will only interact with the community in the source state through limited taxation and possibly a short period of work. Compare a

---

[40] 'Socialförsäkringsbalken' (n 33) §38.
[41] For support see Mehrotra (n 31) and RA Musgrave, 'Clarifying Tax Reform' (1996) 70 *Tax Notes* 731–36.

mobile worker who has taken up a more permanent residence in the source state and who is a more active member of the community through not only taxation but also social interaction. I would therefore argue that the extent of fiscal citizenship will vary with reference to the extent of the individual's liability to taxation in the community.

Therefore, some elaboration needs to be done with reference to the extent of the taxpayer's tax liability and how this may impact the extent of fiscal citizenship. If a non-resident taxpayer is considered liable for full taxation, he or she will be subject to progressive taxation on his or her global income with the possibility for double-taxation relief offered by an applicable tax treaty. On the other hand, if the taxpayer is subject to limited taxation, a state will only tax income stemming from its territory (source taxation) and potential double taxation is once again relieved through the application of the relevant tax treaty. In the latter case, a taxpayer with income stemming from a Swedish source is subject to a lower, non-progressive tax rate of 25 per cent on the source income,[42] instead of full progressive taxation with a marginal tax rate of 60 per cent on the global income.[43] Similar to practices in many other states, the Swedish legislator justifies this lower taxation on the grounds that an individual who is only residing in the source state for a short time period (less than six months in this case, otherwise the taxpayer would be liable for unlimited taxation) does not need to financially contribute as much to society as a citizen since this individual will (presumably) take less advantage of public services and social welfare.[44]

The separation between limited and unlimited taxation is of importance in this context as taxpayers who are subject to limited taxation could arguably be excluded from fiscal citizenship as they do not contribute through progressive taxation and therefore their financial solidarity to the community is lacking. Furthermore, one may argue that these taxpayers will identify themselves more strongly as members in the community of their residence state in which they are subject to unlimited taxation rather than that of the source state in which they are subject to limited taxation. To conclude, mobile workers who are subject to limited taxation may not fulfil requirements on fiscal citizenship, while mobile workers who are subject to unlimited taxation in addition to having a limited/non-existent taxing liability in the state or origin would be considered to be fiscal citizens.

Interestingly enough, one could extend fiscal citizenship and include aspects than other than full liability to taxation and factual payment of taxes. Zelenak makes a distinction between filing and paying taxes, arguing that low-income earners who ultimately do not pay taxes could still constitute engaged citizens due to their interaction with the tax system and public sector in their

---

[42] Inkomstskattelag (1999:1229) ch 3, §17.

[43] F Carlgren, *Marginalskatt I Sverige och internationellt*, available at https://www.ekonomifakta.se/fakta/skatter/skatt-pa-arbete/marginalskatt/ (accessed 31 July 2019).

[44] Which would be in line with the benefit theory, ie those who benefit more from government expenditure should pay more taxes to support expenditure.

filing activities.[45] Such reasoning broadens the perception of fiscal citizenship as it includes individuals who not directly pay taxes, yet potentially could have done so. Zelenak supports this reasoning on the basis that the payment of taxes through tax filing propels taxpayers to be more politically engaged as the action in itself constitutes a concrete externalisation of the social contract between individual and state.

In conclusion, the act of paying (or filing) taxes represents a ceremony of fiscal citizenship. In the main, states impose tax liability with reference to territorial affiliation (the individual resides in the territory of the state; alternately, the income of the individual stems from a source within the territory) rather than citizenships (with a few exceptions such as the US and Eritrea).[46] The extent of the individual's tax liability may have an impact when determining the level of inclusion in a fiscal community, depending on how conservatively one determines fiscal citizenship.

VI. Political Citizenship Through the Ability to Vote

In order to understand how taxpayers may exercise influence on their taxing situation (tax legislation and public spending) through voting it is necessary to review the power to tax and to vote. In Sweden, the mandate to legislate on taxes is reserved to the national level because the Swedish constitution prohibits municipalities from enacting their own taxes through the principle of legality;[47] however, Swedish municipalities still have a strong position as they are free to set their own municipal tax rates in order to finance themselves. These rates are proportional and normally somewhere between 29–35 per cent,[48] depending on the fiscal needs of the respective municipality. Individuals who are registered in a Swedish municipality may vote in municipal elections and subsequently influence public spending. Those who hold Swedish citizenship are automatically qualified to vote in the municipality in which they are registered.[49]

Non-citizens in Sweden may be allowed to vote in municipal elections if they fulfil a territoriality requirement (ie having been registered in the municipality for a minimum number of years). EU citizens only need to have been registered

---

[45] Zelenak (n 32).

[46] For a more extensive studies on this see G Beretta, 'Citizenship and Tax' (2019) 11(2) *World Tax Journal* 227–60; A Christians, 'A Global Perspective on Citizenship Taxation' (2017) 38(2) *Michigan Journal of International Law* 193–43; A Christians, 'Cross-Border Mobility of Individuals and the Lack of Fiscal Policy Coordination Among Jurisdictions (Even) After the BEPS Project' (2019) 47(1) *Intertax* 91–112.

[47] Swedish Instrument of Government (Regeringsformen) ch 1, 4§.

[48] Statistics, Local tax rates 2020, by municipality, available at https://www.scb.se/en/finding-statistics/statistics-by-subject-area/public-finances/local-government-finances/local-taxes/pong/tables-and-graphs/local-tax-rates-changes-by-municipality/ (accessed 24 January 2020).

[49] Kommunallag (2017:725) ch 1, 7§.

in a Swedish municipality for a minimum of one year,[50] whereas non-EU citizens must have been registered for a minimum of three years.[51] Finally, as in most other states, citizenship is a mandatory requirement for individuals to participate in Swedish general elections in order to influence tax and spend on a national level.[52] Expatriates who have permanently moved from Sweden, but have kept their citizenship, are allowed to vote in general elections, but not in municipal elections as they are not physically present.

In conclusion, paying taxes (or interacting with the tax system) represents a ceremony of fiscal citizenship, while voting represents a ceremony of political citizenship. Non-citizens in Sweden can only gain access to voting at local level while citizens without territorial affiliation or economic activity (such as expatriates) can gain access to voting a state level. Additionally, an apparently preferential treatment is given to EU citizens as they can access voting on local level on the same conditions as Swedish citizens. Formal citizenship can therefore be considered to decrease political equity between globally mobile taxpayers, as those who are actively engaging in the Swedish community through taxation and/or inclusion in the welfare system (in addition to the community in general) are excluded from political rights and benefits if they do not hold formal citizenship in Sweden or another EU Member State.

VII. Concluding Commentary

Initially, this chapter has, through description and analysis of relevant Swedish law, concluded that there are indeed informal citizenships which may be extracted from social, fiscal and political dimensions. *Social citizenship* is determined in accordance to the individual's work capacity and ability to pay taxes, while *fiscal citizenship* is determined by an individual's ability to pay taxes, or possibly (if following the reasoning of Zelenak) an individual's interaction with the tax system through, for instance, tax filing. *Political citizenship* is based upon either territorial affiliation combined with a time-based threshold (for participation in municipal elections) or formal citizenship (for participation in general elections alternatively EU citizenship in order to gain instant access to local elections).

It becomes apparent that there are different levels of inclusion in a community depending on what group of citizenship one belongs to. One could, rather harshly, claim that those individuals who are both residing and participating in a community (through either social or fiscal citizenship) are still at best mere guests, or at worst mere subjects, compared to citizens of the state as long as they are excluded from the right to democratically influence (through political citizenship) their

---

[50] EU Directive on voting rights for EU citizens at local level (n 17).
[51] Kommunallag (n 49).
[52] Swedish Instrument of Government (Regeringsformen) ch 3, 4§.

own situation and the community in which they participate in and contribute to. In contrast, those non-citizens who are accepted as political citizens due to either their EU citizenship or the fulfilment of territorial affiliation (combined with the fulfilment of the time-based threshold) will be placed in a more equal situation compared to citizens of the state.

This results in a hierarchy where political citizens are placed on the top and political citizenship takes precedence over both social and fiscal citizenship. This is mainly because it is voting rights within a state that influences the terms of which all the residents in said state can pursue their lives.[53] Interestingly enough, the findings of this chapter illustrate that political membership in a state is a highly exclusive club in which citizens (not only formal citizens but also EU citizens) are given preferential treatment compared to those who originate from outside of state, or the EU, regardless of whether these individuals reside in its territory and/or contribute financially through taxation (resulting in both social and fiscal citizenship). Participation in a community through social or fiscal inclusion alone does therefore not matter when put to the test. It is therefore possible to conclude that there is an apparent need for a reformation at state level and/or international level when allocating political rights and benefits in order for there to be political equity between globally mobile taxpayers. Or as Bellamy expressed it:

> So membership, rights and participation go together. It is through being a member of a political community and participating on equal terms in the framing of its collective life that we enjoy rights to pursue our individual lives on fair terms with others.[54]

[53] Bellamy (n 19) 15.
[54] ibid 16.

8

Immigration, Emigration, Fungible Labour and the Retreat from Progressive Taxation

HENRY ORDOWER

With emphasis on the US, this chapter explores the role that taxation plays in the movement of people and capital. The chapter addresses the relationship between taxes and retention of capital, including tax incentives for capital investment, shifting tax burdens from capital to labour as progressive taxation wanes, and rules preventing the escape of capital from its current taxing jurisdiction. Next, the discussion moves on to consider how taxes supplement immigration policy to attract capital currently outside the jurisdiction. The chapter then queries whether taxes play any significant role in attracting or retaining skilled labour before identifying how tax trends disadvantage 'less desirable', fungible, frequently immigrant labour in response to anti-immigration and anti-immigrant public sentiment. The chapter concludes by observing a relationship between taxation and the unwillingness of societies to help those who culturally, ethnically, racially or religiously differ from the bulk of the membership in the society as that society may change from time to time.

I. Introduction

Family unity has driven US immigration policy for legal, permanent immigration.[1] Admission categories other than family immigration are 'merit-based' even within the special category for diversity immigration.[2] Merit criteria assign priority to exceptional individuals with critical skills and education. Unskilled, fungible[3] workers are often admitted seasonally but permanent status is elusive[4] – even

---

[1] 8 USC §1151 et seq.
[2] ibid.
[3] See discussion of fungible workers in text attached to n 121.
[4] ibid.

134 Henry Ordower

those holding work permits under temporary asylum status may face removal from the US.[5]

Despite the apparent national origin-based immigration policy advanced early in President Trump's administration,[6] recent immigration policy emphasises economic rather than cultural or religious distinctions.[7] Consistent with merit- and economic contribution-based immigration, the President has instructed federal agencies to enforce a longstanding, but historically unenforced, require- ment that sponsors of immigrants reimburse governmental expenditures on behalf of sponsored immigrants, including healthcare and welfare payments.[8] A new regulation[9] denies 'green cards'[10] to lawful immigrants on the basis that they are 'public charges'[11] when they claim public benefits.

Economic immigration restrictions also underlie an interim final rule[12] precluding asylum seekers from applying for US asylum if they pass through a third country without applying for and being denied asylum in that country.[13] The rule is comparable to the EU priority for asylum application in the first country of entry.[14] A grant of admission and asylum permits the asylum seeker to move freely throughout the EU. Most US asylum seekers come from Central American coun- tries, are economically stressed, and travel over land through Mexico. If granted asylum in Mexico, they have no right of admission to the US.

---

[5] ND Schwartz, 'Washington Wants to Deport Washington's Builders', *New York Times* (15 September 2019) Business 1 (Salvadorans' proposed removal).

[6] Bans on immigration from predominantly Muslim countries. US Department of Homeland Security (DHS), 'Executive Orders on Protecting the Homeland', available at https://www.dhs.gov/executive-orders-protecting-homeland (accessed 3 December 2018).

[7] MD Shear, 'Trump Immigration Plan Emphasizes Immigrants' Skills Over Family Ties', *The New York Times* (15 May 2019), available at https://www.nytimes.com/2019/05/15/us/politics/trump-immigration-kushner.html (accessed 17 May 2019).

[8] M Talev and Justin Sink, 'Trump Looks to Threat of Welfare Bills to Curb Immigration', *Bloomberg* (23 May 2019), available at https://www.bloomberg.com/news/articles/2019-05-23/trump-orders-government-to-collect-bills-for-immigrant-welfare (accessed 24 May 2019).

[9] US Citizenship and Immigration Service (USCIS), DHS, *Inadmissibility on Public Charge Grounds*, 84 FR 41292 (August 14, 2019) (effective 15 October 2019).

[10] 'Green card' is the identification card that the USCIS issues to immigrants qualified to reside and work permanently in the US. USCIS, DHS, 'Green Card', available at https://www.uscis.gov/greencard (accessed 12 September 2019).

[11] 8 USC §1201(a)(4) (individuals who are likely to become public charges are ineligible to immigrate to or remain in the US).

[12] USCIS, DHS and Executive Office for Immigration Review, *Temporary Final Rule, Asylum Eligibility and Procedural Modifications*, 84 FR 33829 (July 16, 2019).

[13] A Ahmed and P Villegas, '"This Takes Away All Hope": Rule Bars Most Applicants for Asylum in US', *New York Times* (12 September 2019), available at https://www.nytimes.com/2019/09/12/world/americas/asylum-seekers.html (discussing the Supreme Court decision to remove the lower court injunction barring enforcement of the rule).

[14] Regulation (EU) No 604/2013 of the European Parliament and of the Council of 26 June 2013 establishing the criteria and mechanisms for determining the Member State responsible for examin- ing an application for international protection lodged in one of the Member States by a third-country national or a stateless person (29 June 2013), available at https://eur-lex.europa.eu/legal-content/EN/TXT/?uri=CELEX:32013R0604 (accessed 7 September 2019).

Immigration, Emigration, Fungible Labour and Progressive Taxation   135

The Social Security Administration sends 'no match letters' to employers of low wage immigrants in industries that may employ unauthorised workers notifying them that some employees' names do not match their social security numbers.[15] The notices do not require employers to take action but exert implicit pressure to screen for unauthorised workers. Employers may dismiss workers rather than investing the time and expense to correct possible errors.

Historically, immigration was a key source of much-needed labour in growing economies. The US was built by immigrants and guest workers, who sometimes were denied permanent residence and whose contributions were not always acknowledged.[16] European countries relied heavily on guest workers from the mid-twentieth century to the earlier twenty-first century, often without granting the workers the right to reside permanently or to become citizens.

In the twenty-first century, conflict zones and weak economies drive immigration from those areas to wealthier and more stable areas, while high taxes and regulation fuel emigration from wealthy stable economies to lower tax, less regulated jurisdictions. Labour flight to lower tax jurisdictions historically has not been prevalent because rendition of services was location dependent. The rapid growth of technology, however, has made many industries independent of the location of their service providers.[17] Cross-border competition for some labour has grown.

While top scientists and medical professionals have been in demand since the early years of the twentieth century, demand for technology expertise has accompanied growing international reliance on technology. The emergence of English as the international technical language has removed linguistic barriers to commerce. Individuals with technical expertise are able to work remotely or relocate. Competition in many realms has become international. Developing countries which devoted their limited resources to training their citizens to develop technical skills are concerned those educated individuals may move to countries offering higher salaries and better living circumstances.[18]

---

[15] Miriam Jordan, 'Letters From Washington: Your Employees Could Be Undocumented' *New York Times* (16 May 2019), available at https://www.nytimes.com/2019/05/16/us/immigrants-undocumented-no-match.html (accessed 17 May 2019). The policy of sending 'no match letters' was suspended from 2012 to 2019.

[16] Chinese labourers' contribution to building the transcontinental railroad in the US was not celebrated until the 150th anniversary in 2019. J Katz, 'The Transcontinental Railroad Wouldn't Have Been Built Without the Hard Work of Chinese Laborers' (2010) *Smithsonian Magazine*, available at https://www.smithsonianmag.com/smithsonian-institution/transcontinental-railroad-chinese-labourers-180971919/#d40bEvGCK1RTcGYh.99 (accessed 25 May 2019); GH Chang, *Ghosts of Gold Mountain The Epic Story of the Chinese Who Built the Transcontinental Railway* (Boston MA, Houghton Mifflin Harcourt, 2019).

[17] Call centres for product support or marketing are examples, while technological services lend themselves to remote contact between clients and providers.

[18] Y Brauner, 'Brain Drain Taxation as Development Policy' (2010) 55 *Saint Louis University Law Journal* 221; M Lister, 'A Tax-Credit Approach to Addressing Brain Drain' (2017) 62 *Saint Louis University Law Journal* 63.

136   Henry Ordower

Whatever the reasons one chooses to emigrate, the immigrant expects equal and fair treatment by the receiving country. Tax burden distribution in the US discriminates somewhat against people of colour[19] and low wage immigrants.[20] Yet immigration has been largely absent from tax policy debate.[21] With emphasis on the US, this chapter inquires whether the taxation system provides fair treatment to all immigrant taxpayers or favours some immigrants over others.

This chapter first reviews the question of tax fairness in the distribution of tax burdens and whether tax structure discriminates against or favours taxpayers with differing characteristics. The chapter then addresses the relationship between taxes and retention of capital, including tax incentives for capital investment, shifting tax burdens from capital to labour, and rules preventing the escape of capital from its current taxing jurisdiction. The section following considers how taxes supplement immigration policy to attract capital currently outside the jurisdiction. Next, the discussion contemplates whether taxes play any significant role in attracting[22] or retaining skilled labour.[23] The final portion looks at taxes and tax trends and identifies how they disadvantage or benefit fungible labourers who often are immigrants and then concludes.

II. Tax Fairness: From Progressivity to Regressivity

One fundamental principle of tax fairness – 'horizontal equity' – requires the tax law to treat like taxpayers alike. US tax law is racially neutral on its face. While no discriminatory intent manifests itself in tax legislative history and strong public policy principles preclude enactment of expressly racist legislation, critical tax scholars have identified provisions of the US tax law that discriminate racially[24] or sexually.[25] Advantageous treatment of investment income favours higher income taxpayers.[26] Wealthy and high income taxpayers capture most charitable

---

[19] DA Brown, 'Teaching Civil Rights through the Basic Tax Course' (2010) 54 *Saint Louis University Law Journal* 809, 813–15 (blacks receive fewer tax benefits from home ownership because they tend to be renters).

[20] See nn 121–143 and accompanying text.

[21] Cf H Ordower, 'Taxing Others in the Age of Trump: Foreigners (and the Politically Weak) as Tax Subjects' (2017) 62 *Saint Louis University Law Journal* 157 (discussing tax elements disadvantaging lower income immigrants).

[22] PR Dukmedjian and N Girleanu, 'Luxembourg Offers Tax Incentives to Attract Highly Skilled Employees', *Tax Notes* (6 December 2018), available at https://www.taxnotes.com/worldwide-tax-daily/employment-taxes/luxembourg-offers-tax-incentives-attract-highly-skilled-employees/2018/12/06/28l6b (accessed 1 October 2019).

[23] See n 18 for literature examples.

[24] Brown (n 19).

[25] NC Staudt, 'Taxing Housework' (1995–1996) 84 *Georgetown Law Journal* 1571.

[26] H Ordower, 'Schedularity in US Income Taxation and its Effect on Tax Distribution' (2014) 108 *Northwestern University Law Review* 905.

Immigration, Emigration, Fungible Labour and Progressive Taxation   137

contribution tax benefits.[27] Among higher income taxpayers who enjoy tax expenditures, racial minorities are underrepresented.[28]

During the middle part of the twentieth century, a progressive income tax became a principal revenue source in advanced democracies.[29] Progressivity in taxation became the second fundamental principle of tax fairness: 'vertical equity'. The principle assumes that as an individual's income or wealth increases, the individual's ability and responsibility to pay tax increases disproportionally. In their seminal article on progressive taxation,[30] professors Blum and Kalven catalogued arguments for progressivity observing that regressive taxation is anathema to fair distribution of the tax burden and lacks support: '[i]t is so clear no one today favors any tax because it is regressive that the term itself has become colored'.[31] They concluded that smoothing economic inequality through redistribution of wealth is the strongest justification for progressive taxation,[32] understanding that 'the drawbacks of progression in terms of productivity must be weighed against its possible merits in allocating the tax burden fairly'.[33]

Despite its foundation in horizontal and vertical equity principles, basic tax structure tilted toward proportional and regressive taxes during the latter half of the twentieth century under the pressures of political influence of wealth and growing governmental revenue needs. A progressive income tax was difficult to collect efficiently and its high marginal rates imposed on mostly middle-income individuals from whom the state had to collect the bulk of its revenue were unpopular.[34] Legislatures sought other sources of revenue, especially in the welfare states of Northern Europe where less progressive and even regressive taxes emerged to carry the welfare state burden. Chief among those regressive taxes was value added tax (VAT).

VAT is somewhat hidden because the tax is built into the cost of goods and services. Taxpayer liquidity concerns of income taxes are absent because its inclusion in the price leaves the consumer a choice to pay the tax or not buy the item.

---

[27] H Ordower, 'Charitable Contributions of Services: Charitable Gift Planning for Non-Itemizers' (2014) 67 *Tax Lawyer* 517. Cf JJ Thorndike, 'Tax History: Charity Deductions Are for the Rich – and That Was Always the Plan' (2019) 164 *Tax Notes* 1856.

[28] US Dept of Commerce, Census Bureau, *2012 Statistical Abstract*, Section 13. Income, Expenditures, Poverty, and Wealth, Table 697. 'Money Income of Households – Percent Distribution by Income Level, Race, and Hispanic Origin, in Constant (2009) Dollars', available at https://www2.census.gov/library/publications/2011/compendia/statab/131ed/tables/12s0697.pdf?# (accessed 4 May 2020).

[29] The top marginal rate of tax in the US was 92% in 1952. Tax Foundation, 'US Federal Individual Income Tax Rates History, 1862–2013 (Nominal and Inflation-Adjusted Brackets)' [31], available at https://taxfoundation.org/us-federal-individual-income-tax-rates-history-1913-2013-nominal-and-inflation-adjusted-brackets/ (accessed 15 September 2019). Similarly, high marginal rates were prevalent or soon to be so in most European countries not in the Soviet sphere of influence.

[30] WJ Blum and H Kalven Jr, 'The Uneasy Case for Progressive Taxation' (1952) 19 *University of Chicago Law Review* 417.

[31] ibid 419.

[32] ibid 520.

[33] ibid 444.

[34] SO Lodin, 'Swedish Tax Reforms 1971–77 – Why So Many?' (1977) 56 *Acta Universitatis Stockholmiensis Studia Juridica Stockholmiensia* 181.

VAT has been so popular that the EU harmonised VAT taxation at a minimum rate of 15 per cent.[35]

For many moderate- and middle-income taxpayers, income from wages is their significant source of income. Since those taxpayers consume most of their wages for living expenses subject to VAT, VAT is effectively a tax on labour. VATs tend to be regressive because the lower the individual's income and wealth, the more the individual must dedicate their limited resources to basic living expenses subject to VAT. By contrast wealthier taxpayers devote significant amounts of income and wealth to investment rather than consumer purchases. Since purchases of intangible investment property such as corporate shares and bonds are not subject to VAT, income devoted to such investments remains free from VAT.

VAT rates have increased and income tax rates have declined over the last half century. Taxes on income from investment have declined disproportionally to taxes on income from personal services while supplemental wage taxes have grown. Frequently the wage taxes are indirect taxes that are imposed upon the employer but probably borne by employees in the form of lower wages than they otherwise might receive if there were no tax.[36]

Retreat from progressive taxation is an international trend that coincides with changing immigration patterns and increasing need to accept diverse refugee populations. Some immigrants will find work and invest capital and begin to pay income taxes quickly; others may not. Rules governing admission of immigrants to stable, developed countries try to anticipate income productivity.[37] Even if they differ ethnically, racially and religiously from the majority populace, wealthy and highly educated immigrants receive favourable admission decisions from immigration authorities more frequently than do conflict and economic refugees.[38]

Progressive taxation of the mid-twentieth century yielded to proportional and even regressive taxation in the twenty-first century as the burden of taxation shifted from capital to labour. While capital mobility can account for the shift from taxing capital to taxing labour, immigration also may have contributed to that shift.

III. Retaining Rich People and their Capital

Professor Winters argues that civil oligarchs use their wealth to influence tax system changes that reduce progressive taxes and substitute regressive ones. He sees the

---

[35] Council Directive 2006/112/EC of 28 November 2006 on the common system of value added tax, available at http://eur-lex.europa.eu/LexUriServ/LexUriServ.do?uri=OJ:L:2006:347:0001:0118:en:PDF (accessed 15 September 2019). Exemptions and reduced rates are not uniform throughout the EU.

[36] M Friedman, 'Transfer Payments and the Social Security System' (1965) 11 *The Conference Board Record* 7.

[37] Compare the US shift to merit based immigration: see text at n 7 above.

[38] L Adim, 'Between Benefit and Abuse: Immigrant Investment Programs' (2017) 62 *Saint Louis University Law Journal* 121; A Christians, 'Buying In: Residence and Citizenship by Investment' (2017) 62 *Saint Louis University Law Journal* 51 (both articles discussing 'golden visas' for investors).

Immigration, Emigration, Fungible Labour and Progressive Taxation   139

reduction of the maximum marginal income tax rate to be a result of oligarchical activity in order to gain anti-progressive taxation allies by including increased numbers of the wealthy but not obscenely wealthy as allies against progressive taxes by pushing them into the highest marginal brackets.[39] Alternative or additional forces driving a retreat from progressive taxation may have been growing tax avoidance and the international focus on retaining wealthy taxpayers in the face of international competition for their capital[40] and their skills.

High marginal income tax rates arguably encourage taxpayers to engage in aggressive tax planning. The tax sheltering industry in the US developed during the years of high marginal rates of income tax.[41] Yet, taxpayers often try to avoid even low rate taxes too.[42] Experience shows that even as income tax rates declined, taxpayers continued to seek aggressively structured planning opportunities to avoid or decrease the tax. So-called 'son of boss' structures in the US avoided the federal income tax largely on low rate long term capital gain then capped at 15 or 20 per cent.[43] Similarly, the S corporation payroll tax shelter avoided at most a 2.9 per cent combined employer-employee payroll tax.[44]

Expatriation to avoid very high taxes long has been a matter of concern in high marginal rate jurisdictions having territorial income tax systems.[45] Some

---

[39] JA Winters, 'Civil Oligarchies' in JA Winters, *Oligarchy* (Cambridge, CUP, 2011) ch 5 (distinguishing oligarchs from the merely wealthy and demonstrating that the extremely wealthy oligarchs bear an ever decreasing share of the tax burden in the US).

[40] A Alstadsæter, N Johannesen and G Zucman, 'Tax Evasion and Inequality' (2019) 109 *American Economic Review* 2073 (using leaked data showing that offshore tax evasion is highly concentrated among the rich in Scandinavia and highlighting the importance of factoring in tax evasion to properly measure inequality).

[41] H Ordower, 'The Culture of Tax Avoidance' (2010) 55 *Saint Louis ULJ* 47.

[42] Ordower (n 41); Alstadsæter, Johannesen and Zucman (n 40) (current lower than historical rates under Scandinavian income taxes do not stop offshore tax avoidance or evasion by wealthy taxpayers).

[43] 26 USC §1(h) (imposing a reduced rate of tax to net capital gain relative to the rate imposed on income of other types). Unlike the federal income tax that applies a reduced income tax rate to net capital gain, state income taxes generally apply an identical rate to net capital gain as they apply to income of all other types. State income taxes vary considerably from state to state and add an additional tax of as much as 3% in Indiana or 13% in California, for example, using 2019 rates. K Loughead and E Wei, 'State Individual Income Tax Rates and Brackets for 2019' (*Tax Foundation Fiscal Fact No. 643*, 2019), available at https://files.taxfoundation.org/20190515164552/State-Individual-Income-Tax-Rates-and-Brackets-for-2019-FF-643.pdf (accessed 29 May 2019). 26 USC is the Internal Revenue Code of 1986, as amended (the 'Code'). In the following, sections of the Code will be referred to as 'IRC §' followed by a number.

[44] Citizens for Tax Justice, 'Payroll Tax Loophole Used by John Edwards and Newt Gingrich Remains Unaddressed by Congress' (6 September 2013), available at https://www.ctj.org/payroll-tax-loophole-used-by-john-edwards-and-newt-gingrich-remains-unaddressed-by-congress/ (accessed 17 September 2019).

[45] Consider the Beatles and their tax moves described in N Irwin, 'The Beatles were the Mitt Romney of the 1960s, and other policy lessons from the Fab Four', *The Washington Post Blog*, 10 January 2014, available at http://www.washingtonpost.com/blogs/wonkblog/wp/2014/01/10/the-beatles-were-the-mitt-romney-of-the-1960s-and-other-policy-lessons-from-the-fab-four/. Under a territorial system, taxpayers who are not resident in the taxing jurisdiction are subject to tax only on their incomes from sources in the taxing jurisdiction and not on their income from performance of services outside the taxing jurisdiction. The US taxes its citizens and permanent residents on their worldwide income so US taxpayers must relinquish their citizenship or green cards to free themselves from the US income tax. 26 CFR §1.1-1.

140   *Henry Ordower*

countries address part of the impact of expatriation with continuation taxes,[46] but those anti-avoidance limitations on expatriation to avoid tax are an imperfect solution. Decreasing marginal rates of income tax and repeal or reduction in taxes at death has not staunched the flow of capital to low tax jurisdictions[47] or expatriations from the US and other countries.[48] Improved communication technology and stable, safe residential environments in many low-tax or no-tax island jurisdictions enable US and European nationals to emigrate without losing contract or control over businesses operating in their home countries.

Nevertheless, as global competition for capital increased in the latter decades of the twentieth century, the steeply progressive income taxes with high maximum rates of tax characteristic of developed countries during the middle years of the twentieth century yielded to systems with moderate or flat progression and moderate maximum rates of tax.[49] Schedularity under income tax systems has increased with its nearly discrete tax bases to which differing tax rate schedules apply.[50] Under schedularity, taxes have tended to increase on less mobile income from labour and to decrease on more mobile income from property.[51] As VAT rates and wage taxes on labour increased, taxes on capital gain stabilised or became preferential;[52] taxes on income from capital, as opposed to gain on the appreciation in the value of capital, also enjoyed a preference in some instances;[53] and rates of tax on corporations declined and continue to decline.[54] Recently the US enacted a preferential schedule for income from the conduct of businesses, other than the business of an employee, through a 20 per cent deduction of the amount of income from the business.[55] The new deduction favours capital intensive businesses and would seem to violate the horizontal equity principle. Periodic wealth taxes and gift and estate taxes on the transmission of wealth similarly have declined or

---

[46] Sweden, for example: 3. Kap. 3 § 3., 7 § Inkomstskattelag (1999:1229) (Income Tax Law Sweden), available at https://lagen.nu/1999:1229 (accessed 3 October 2019) (taxing expatriates on their income from all sources (obegränsad skattskyldighet) for five years following expatriation if they continue to have substantial connection with Sweden).

[47] Alstadsæter, Johannesen and Zucman (n 40).

[48] Department of the Treasury, Internal Revenue Service, 'Quarterly Publication of Individuals, Who Have Chosen To Expatriate, as Required by Section 6039G' (1st quarter, 2019), 84 FR 20954 (13 May 2019) (showing 1019 individuals).

[49] OECD Tax Database, available at http://www.oecd.org/tax/tax-policy/tax-database.htm#pit (accessed 3 October 2019).

[50] Ordower (n 26).

[51] OECD Tax Database (n 49).

[52] IRC §1(h) (net capital gain taxed at a maximum 20% marginal rate). As late as 1989, Sweden's maximum marginal rate of income tax was approximately 80%. Sweden now imposes a flat rate of 30% on income from capital but a maximum rate on income from labour of approximately 55% – with some variation a function of the local income tax. Sven-Olof Lodin et al, *Inkomstskatt – en läro- och handbok i skatterätt* (Lund, Studentlitteratur, 2011).

[53] IRC §1(h)(10) (qualified dividend preference in the US); dual income tax with a 30% rate on income from capital in Sweden.

[54] In 2018, the corporate income tax rate declined from a maximum of 35 to a flat 21% rate. IRC §11.

[55] Effective in 2018, qualified business income yields a 20% deduction so only 80% of qualified business income is taxable. IRC §199A.

Immigration, Emigration, Fungible Labour and Progressive Taxation   141

disappeared.[56] Such changes in rates and schedular tax structures may discourage wealthy individuals from emigrating and settling in lower taxed countries or transferring their income producing personal property to low tax jurisdictions but the success of such tax reductions is not at all certain.[57]

Decline in maximum rates of tax and occasionally complete disappearance of taxes on transmission of wealth have limited impact on funding of governmental services and public benefits. While steeply progressive taxes are associated historically with public benefits and welfare states, even confiscatory taxes on the wealthiest residents are unlikely to yield sufficient revenue to maintain extensive governmental functions and services. Moderate income taxpayers must provide the revenue to fund the demands of modern governments.[58] The policy supporting steeply progressive and high income tax rates and taxes on transmission of wealth at death served primarily to level disparities between wealthier and poorer residents and limit the growth and maintenance of a privileged and dominant class in the society.[59] Perceptions of worthiness of tax objects changed during the last decades of the twentieth century. Increasing capital mobility challenged the commonly held view that income from labour should not be disfavoured in taxation relative to income from capital.[60] Arguments prevailed that capital is more productive than labour so should be taxed at a lower rate than labour is taxed.

If decreased rates of tax and preferential tax treatment of capital gain and other income from capital do not constrain taxpayers from removing their capital from their home countries, exit taxes or continuation taxes following exit have become popular for the home country to capture otherwise lost future tax revenue. The US has used both a continuation tax[61] and an exit tax.[62] A continuation tax imposes an obligation on the taxpayer to pay tax on some or all the taxpayer's income following change of residence or citizenship.[63] Most continuation taxes have limits on

---

[56] In 1976 estates in excess of $600,000 were subject to estate tax in the US, but in 2019 estates become taxable only in excess of $11.4 million. IRC §2010 (exemption from tax). The maximum estate tax rate in the US declined from 77% of taxable estates in excess of $10 million in 1976 to 40% of taxable estates in excess of $11 million. IRC §2001. Sweden repealed its inheritance tax in early 2005, retroactively to 17 December 2004, and its wealth tax in December 2007, retroactively to 1 January 2007. Sweden and Austria are unusual among OECD members in not having an inheritance or estate tax.

[57] See text at nn 40–45, above.

[58] Lodin (n 34).

[59] Blum and Kalven (n 30) 487.

[60] AW Mellon, *Taxation: The People's Business* (London, Macmillan, 1924) 56–58.

[61] IRC §877.

[62] IRC §877A.

[63] H Ordower, 'The Expatriation Tax, Deferrals, Mark to Market, the *Macomber* Conundrum and Doubtful Constitutionality' (2017) 15 *Pittsburgh Tax Review* 1, 7. Sweden's continuation tax(n 46), in addition to taxing income from all sources for 5 years (obegränsat skattskyldighet), also imposes limited tax liability of some expatriates on income from capital (begränsat skattskyldighet) for 10 years following change of residence. 3 ch. 19 § Inkomstskattelag (Svensk författningssamling [SFS] 1999:1229) (Swed.) (taxing Swedish citizens and permanent residents who leave Sweden on income from capital). Similarly, Germany has a 10-year continuation tax based on tax avoidance intent as described in D Gutmann, 'La lutte contre "l'exil fiscal": du droit comparé à la politique fiscale', *Le Cercle des fiscalistes* (24 May 2012), available at http://www.lecercledesfiscalistes.com/publication/la-lutte-contre-lexil-fiscal-du-droit-compare-a-la-politique-fiscale/234 (accessed 6 June 2019).

142 *Henry Ordower*

duration, commonly five or 10 years. The US tax had a 10-year durational limit.[64] An exit tax imposes a single incident of taxation on the taxpayer's deferred income and unrealised gain at the moment of expatriation.[65] In the US payment of all or part of the tax may be deferred if the taxpayer assures payment of the tax through a bond or through withholding by the third party payer of the income to the taxpayer.[66]

Historically, US persons have valued their status as citizens and permanent residents of the US. Stable governments and developed banking and communication systems in low tax jurisdictions now make US citizenship or the right to reside permanently less compelling than they once were. Expatriation for wealthy individuals has become an alternative to continued citizenship or residence when it diminishes the individual's tax burden substantially.[67] High net worth individuals' sources of income have globalised. US source income remains taxable in the US even after expatriation but foreign source income ceases to be so. Some income follows the residence of its owner and becomes foreign source following expatriation. For example, unrealised gain on corporate stock, bonds, collectibles, gemstones, artwork and other personal property would have been US source if realised and recognised before a US person's expatriation. If recognition is deferred until after expatriation, its source shifts to the new residence of the owner[68] and it becomes free from US tax. The expatriation tax is designed to capture the unrealised appreciation as taxable gain to the date of expatriation.[69]

The US makes it more difficult to shift the incidence of taxation to low tax jurisdictions than other countries with territorial systems do, because the US taxes its citizens, residents, and domestic corporations[70] on their income from all sources worldwide.[71] Despite worldwide taxation, the US generally cedes primary taxing jurisdiction for income produced outside the US to the country where the income is produced by crediting foreign taxes paid by the US person.[72] If the foreign taxes

---

[64] IRC §877(d)(2).

[65] AG Abreu, 'Taxing Exits' (1996) 29 *UC Davis Law Review* 1087 (analysing various proposals to counteract the tax loss from expatriation with the income tax and the transfer tax systems).

[66] IRC §877A (expatriation tax). The French expatriation tax Code général des impôts (Tax Code) art. 167a (Fr.) (as in effect in 1999) was determined to violate the EU treaty when applied to a French national moving within the EU. Case C-9/02 *Hughes de Lasteyrie du Saillant v Ministère de l'Économie, des Finances et de l'Industrie* [2004] ECR I-2452 (European Court of Justice). The French expatriation tax was permissible, however, when a French national relocated to Switzerland. Case C-355/16 *Christian Picart v Ministre des Finances et des Comptes publics* (15 March 2018) in which the ECJ determined that the 1999 EU-Switzerland agreement on free movement of persons does not preclude France from imposing an exit tax on the unrealised gains of a taxpayer who moved to Switzerland but was not engaged in a trade or business there.

[67] Ordower (n 63) 6.

[68] IRC §865 (personal property sourced at residence).

[69] IRC §877A.

[70] Corporate residence for US tax purposes follows place of incorporation rather than seat of management. IRC §7701(a)(4).

[71] IRC §61 (defining gross income as all income from whatever source derived). Treasury reg §1.1-1 (worldwide taxation).

[72] IRC §901 (foreign tax credit).

are less than the US tax on the income, the US captures a tax amount equal to the difference between the higher US tax and the foreign tax credited.[73] If the foreign taxes are greater than the US tax, the credit may not exceed the amount of the US tax.[74]

To avoid US tax, US investors have two choices – one lawful, one not. There are also opportunities to defer US tax on the increase in the value of the taxpayer's investments. The lawful choice is to relinquish US citizenship or, for non-citizen residents, the right to reside in the US. That expatriation subjects the former US citizens and permanent residents to the expatriation tax.[75] Tax administration also has the power to certify seriously tax delinquent individuals to the Department of State for revocation or denial of issuance of the individual's passport.[76] Tax clearances are a requirement for non-residents exiting the US.[77]

The unlawful choice has been to secrete investments in foreign jurisdictions with strong bank secrecy laws so income and wealth remains hidden outside the US taxing jurisdiction, free from US tax.[78] The option of concealing income and income producing assets in a low tax, bank secrecy jurisdiction came under intense attack with the enactment of the Foreign Accounts Tax Compliance Act (FATCA) in 2010.[79] That legislation imposed substantial penalties on US taxpayers who failed to disclose their foreign accounts and pay tax on their income from those accounts. The Act also sanctioned foreign financial institutions accepting accounts from US taxpayers, which were not reported to US taxing authorities, by preventing them from participating in US programs, including reduced withholding on investments in the US – a feature important to the institution's underlying non-US investors.

Deferring US tax on increase in value is straightforward. Investors may operate businesses through or invest in domestic or foreign corporations and defer individual tax on the income until the individual shareholder receives distributions or sells the corporate shares. A peculiarity of the US tax system permanently eliminates the individual tax on gains but not dividends if the shareholder dies before selling the corporate shares as the decedent's property receives a new, fair market value tax basis at the owner's death.[80] A foreign corporation also permits the deferral of the US corporate-level income tax. Even if its shareholders are US persons, a foreign corporation is not subject to US taxing jurisdiction except on that portion of its income from US sources or effectively connected with its

---

[73] IRC §904 (limitation to US tax on the income).

[74] ibid.

[75] IRC §877A (see text to nn 65–66).

[76] IRC §7345 (certification under section 32101 of the FAST Act, Pub L 114-94 (2015) enacted as a revenue offset).

[77] IRC §6851(d); IRS, 'Departing Alien Clearance (Sailing Permit)', available at https://www.irs.gov/individuals/international-taxpayers/departing-alien-clearance-sailing-permit (accessed 3 October 2019).

[78] Compare for Scandinavia, Alstadsæter, Johannesen and Zucman (n 40).

[79] 124 Stat 71, Pub L 97-117 (2010).

[80] IRC §1014.

144   *Henry Ordower*

conduct of a US trade or business.[81] Most distributions of foreign source earnings of the foreign corporation to its non-corporate US owners become taxable in the US.[82] Since 2018, distributions of foreign source earnings to corporate shareholders that own at least 10 per cent of the voting rights in or the value of shares in the foreign corporation, that is, corporate US shareholders,[83] are free from US income tax on distributions from a foreign corporation under the 100 per cent dividends received deduction.[84]

The US has deployed an array of complex anti-avoidance or anti-deferral rules to prevent taxpayers from exploiting corporate limitations on US taxation of foreign source income. Some income of CFCs is taxable to the corporation's US shareholders if the placement of foreign source income serves no non-tax business purpose.[85] Passive investment income as well as sales and service income unrelated to the CFC's country of incorporation[86] trigger the inclusion to the shareholders as if the CFC were a tax transparent entity similar to a partnership.[87] US persons who invest in foreign investment companies may defer inclusion of the foreign investment company's income but when they sell their interests in the foreign company or receive distributions, the gain does not enjoy preferential rates on capital gains, and the gains and dividends become subject to an interest charge.[88] A decedent's estate does not get a new basis in foreign investment company shares so the estate's beneficiaries remain subject to the interest charge on the increase in value of the investment in the foreign investment company.[89] US corporations converting to foreign corporations to avoid US taxation on their foreign source income are caught by the anti-inversion provisions[90] subjecting them to continuing taxation of their foreign source income in the US.

---

[81] IRC §881 (fixed and determinable periodic income); IRC §882 (effectively connected income).

[82] IRC §316 (defining dividend as a distribution from any corporation's earnings and profits); IRC §301 (including dividends in the shareholder's income).

[83] Under IRC §951(b) (defining United States (US) shareholder except under IRC §245A the distributing corporation need not be a controlled foreign corporation ('CFC'). A CFC defined in IRC §957 (e) is a corporation in which US shareholders own more than half the voting power and share value.

[84] IRC §245A (anti-avoidance rules limit the value of the exclusion). IRC §951A taxes returns in excess of 10% of a CFC's tangible assets as subpart F income under the CFC provisions as global intangible income. IRC §59A imposes an additional base erosion alternative tax on related party transactions.

[85] IRC §951.

[86] Foreign base company income is subpart F income under IRC §952 included to the shareholders under IRC §951(a). IRC §954(a) (foreign base company income).

[87] IRC §951(a). Inclusion of CFC income is not fully transparent. Subpart F income that would have been capital gain to the corporation does not retain its character as capital gain to the US shareholders.

[88] IRC §1291 (income from a passive foreign investment company defined in IRC §1297). A taxpayer may avoid the unfavourable effect of these rules by electing to include the income of the foreign company in US income annually. IRC §1295 (qualified electing fund); IRC §1293 (inclusion of pro rata share of qualified electing fund income).

[89] IRC §1291(e).

[90] IRC §7874 (taxing all or part of a foreign entity's income in the US either as if it were a US entity or under a continuation tax following expatriation of the entity).

IV. Investors and Investor Immigrants (Commodifying Immigration)

As the US and other countries seek to limit expatriation of revenue, capital and people to protect the domestic tax base, there is active competition among jurisdictions, including the US, to attract cross-border capital and people. The global competition for capital is powerful and possibly destructive when it becomes a 'race to the bottom' of income inclusion and tax rates.

The US taxes the US-source investment income of non-resident alien individuals[91] and foreign corporations on its gross amount by requiring the person making any payment of US source income to a non-resident alien or foreign corporation to withhold[92] 30 per cent of the gross payment.[93] The US competes for the foreign investment capital with double tax treaties that reduce that rate of tax on interest, dividends, royalties and other investment income[94] and with exemptions from the withholding tax for the interest paid on deposits in financial institutions[95] and on portfolio indebtedness.[96]

State and local governmental units offer a variety of direct and tax subsidies to induce the enterprises planning to operate in the US to choose a specific locale. The practice of tax subsidy competition has generated a robust bidding process among states and localities in the US with questionable returns to the locality in exchange for considerable loss of tax revenue. The subsidies often do not require a permanent commitment from the enterprise and occasionally leave the locality with an ongoing facilities' burden after the enterprise ceases its operations there.[97]

Some low tax jurisdictions have competed actively for investor capital by offering bank secrecy and low or no income tax on the earnings of non-residents. The OECD targeted these jurisdictions as engaging in harmful tax practices in a 1998 initiative[98] leading to increased transparency and information sharing by

---

[91] IRC §7701(b)(1)(B) (defining nonresident alien as an individual neither a citizen nor resident of the US).

[92] IRC §1441 (withholding requirement).

[93] IRC §871 (tax on fixed, determinable, annual or periodic income of nonresident aliens); IRC §881 (similarly, foreign corporations).

[94] For example, Art. X of the United States – Canada Income Tax Convention, available at https://www.irs.gov/pub/irs-trty/canada.pdf (accessed 8 June 2019) reduces the withholding rate of dividends to 10% for certain corporate recipients and 15% for others.

[95] IRC §871(i).

[96] IRC §§ 871(h), 881(c). Portfolio interest is non-contingent interest paid pursuant to a registered debt instrument.

[97] H Ordower, 'Les Impôts Relatifs aux Investissements Étrangers aux États-Unis d'Amérique (observations générales)' (1996) 1996-2 *Revue Internationale de Droit Economique* 185.

[98] G Makhlouf, 'Current Status of OECD's Harmful Tax Practices Initiative A statement by the Chairman of the OECD's Committee on Fiscal Affairs' (2002), available at http://www.oecd.org/general/searchresults/?q=unfair%20tax%20competition&cx=01243260174851139151 8:xzeadub0b0a &cof=FORID:11&ie=UTF-8 (accessed 8 June 2019).

the targeted jurisdictions.[99] A second initiative on base erosion and profit shifting (BEPS) has continued the effort to achieve greater transparency with uniformity in tax rules to prevent arbitrage especially through use of hybrid structures.[100]

Such international efforts to limit tax competition may have motivated investors to become immigrants seeking the most favourable living and investment bases rather than simply moving capital. An emerging international competition issue has focused on 'golden' visas, including money laundering and similar concerns surrounding their issuance.[101] Rather than offering tax or direct subsidies for investment, countries with golden visa regimes expedite the immigration process for investors who bring substantial investment capital to the receiving country.

Under golden visa programmes, investor immigrants invest designated minimal amounts in the receiving country in exchange for the privilege to enter and reside there.[102] Some Caribbean island states exchange immediate citizenship for a fee rather than an investment commitment.[103] The amounts and industries in which the investments must be made are not uniform among countries. Economically developed countries like the US require a larger investment commitment than do countries looking to capture international capital to assist the country's lagging economic development.[104] Several countries also provide investor immigrants with temporarily favoured tax treatment.[105] Others are low tax jurisdictions that welcome investors from high tax jurisdictions who may wish to avoid or evade taxes in their home countries by changing their residence or citizenship.[106] Investor immigrants are desired and desirable as they add capital to the receiving country's economy.

Investor immigrants to the US are subject to general US taxing jurisdiction under the US worldwide taxation system when they become US residents. Their foreign source income draws a credit for taxes paid to foreign jurisdictions. Immigration for tax reasons is practical only for investors subject to taxes equal to or higher than US taxes in the country from which they are emigrating.

---

[99] OECD, *Harmful Tax Practices – 2018 Progress Report on Preferential Regimes; Inclusive Framework on BEPS: Action 5*, available at https://www.oecd.org/tax/beps/harmful-tax-practices-2018-progress-report-on-preferential-regimes-9789264311480-en.htm (accessed 9 June 2019).

[100] OECD, 'Base Erosion and Profit Shifting', available at http://www.oecd.org/tax/beps/ (accessed 3 October 2019).

[101] C Yeginsu, 'What Are Britain's "Golden Visas," and Why Are They Being Suspended?' *New York Times* (6 December 2018), available at https://www.nytimes.com/2018/12/06/world/europe/uk-golden-visa-suspended.html (accessed 4 October 2019) (expressing concern about Russian oligarchs' use of the British programme for money laundering).

[102] Adim (n 38); Christians (n 38).

[103] Adim (n 38) 122.

[104] Christians (n 38) 57.

[105] Ibid, 51 (discussing Italy's new programme, and comparison with Portugal, Malta, Ireland); RA Papotti and L Ferro, 'Italy's Attractive New Tax Regime for Wealthy Pensioners' *Tax Notes International* (29 April 2019) 343.

[106] FATCA legislation in the US (n 79); harmful tax competition and BEPS initiatives of the OECD (nn 98 and 100).

Immigration, Emigration, Fungible Labour and Progressive Taxation 147

Where their emigration jurisdiction has lower taxes than the US, investor visas are desirable only from non-tax perspectives – opportunities, lifestyle, safety, etc. As investors they enjoy the tax advantages currently favouring capital over labour in the US,[107] including the absence of any social security tax on income from capital,[108] preferential rates for net capital gain and dividends,[109] deferral of inclusion in income of appreciation in the value of their property,[110] rapid tax recovery of many capital expenditures,[111] and a deduction of 20 per cent of the income from the conduct of a trade or business in the US.[112]

V. Educated and Skilled Labour

A. Skilled Immigrants

Countries also tend to welcome immigrants or temporary workers with specific skills in a variety of fields. The US has many immigration priority programs for educated and skilled workers.[113] Jobs for individuals with skills or training often pay better than jobs in the immigrant's country of origin. Like investor immigrants, skilled immigrants are subject to the general taxing jurisdiction of the US on their worldwide income. Unlike investor immigrants, skilled immigrants receive payment for services and do not enjoy the advantages of the current US preferences for income from capital. Since their visa status is employment dependent, they may not conduct an independent trade or business yielding the qualified business income deduction.[114] They must pay social security taxes but those with high demand skills may draw wages exceeding the social security earnings cap so only part of their wages are subject to the social security tax.[115] Some skilled employee visas permit conversion to permanent residence[116] and access to social security benefits at retirement age unavailable to other temporary workers who may not work in the US sufficiently long to qualify for benefits.[117] Employers also

---

[107] Generally n 39 (text accompanying and following).

[108] IRC §3101 (6.2% tax on wages); IRC §1401 (tax on self-employment income).

[109] IRC §1(h) (maximum rate on net capital gains and dividends).

[110] IRC §1001 (gain from sale or other disposition of property).

[111] IRC §168(k) (bonus depreciation).

[112] IRC §199A (n 55 and accompanying text).

[113] For example, USCIS, 'H-1B Specialty Occupations', available at https://www.uscis.gov/working-united-states/temporary-workers/h-1b-specialty-occupations-dod-cooperative-research-and-development-project-workers-and-fashion-models (accessed 4 October 2019).

[114] IRC §199A (n 55 and accompanying text) (qualified business income).

[115] IRC §3101. In 2019, wages in excess of $132,900 are free from the social security tax. 'Social Security Fact Sheet 2019 Social Security Changes', available at https://www.ssa.gov/news/press/factsheets/cola-facts2019.pdf (accessed 9 June 2019). Those who never become permanent residents are unlikely to draw any benefits under the social security system.

[116] H1-B visas are dual purpose and permit application for green cards while other temporary work visas do not (text to n 113, above).

[117] nn 125–126, below, and accompanying text.

148   *Henry Ordower*

may offer various deferred compensation arrangements and, for some occupations, provide non-taxable benefits including housing and meals.[118] High wages may give the workers the opportunity to accumulate disposable income for investment to capture capital taxation benefits as investor immigrants do.

B. Skilled Emigrants

Economically developing countries educate promising young citizens at government expense to develop an indigenous pool of skilled and educated workers. Those individuals are among the most desired candidates for immigration to economically developed countries where their skills also are needed. Salaries higher than those possible in their home country and better opportunities for family members are seductive, despite any privileges their education might afford them at home. Emigration thwarts the home country's plans for those individuals to fulfil important societal roles and advance the country's development. Prohibiting emigration provides a solution but raises human rights concerns. These privileged individuals consumed considerable amounts from limited national wealth to become who they are. Repayment in some manner may be appropriate.[119] Other countries impose a special fee or tax requiring an emigrant to repay all or part of the cost or value of the education or training as an exit tax or a continuation tax following emigration.[120]

VI. Fungible Labour: Authorised and Unauthorised Immigrants

Many jobs require limited skills and training. The workers doing the jobs are substantially fungible. While unskilled jobs require some training – even specialised training in many instances – the necessary skills are relatively easy to learn and the shift from one unskilled job to another carries a moderate or low retraining cost. Unlike skilled and educated workers,[121] fungible workers receive limited amounts of nontaxable fringe benefits. Most fungible workers are subject to wage taxes on all their income because they do not earn more than the social security

---

[118] IRC §119 (exclusion from gross income of meals and lodging provided for the convenience of the employer).

[119] US Army, 'Earn Your Degree Through ROTC', available at https://www.goarmy.com/benefits/education-benefits/earn-your-degree-through-rotc.html (accessed 18 September 2019) (example of US service commitment military education programmes).

[120] T Boeri, H Brucker, F Doquier and H Rapoport (eds), *Brain Drain and Brain Gain The Global Competition to Attract High-Skilled Migrants* (Oxford, OUP, 2012); G Block and M Blake, *Debating Brain Drain: May Governments Restrict Emigration?* (Oxford, OUP, 2015); and literature cited at n 18, above.

[121] nn 113–120 above, and accompanying text.

Immigration, Emigration, Fungible Labour and Progressive Taxation 149

tax ceiling. They spend the bulk of their income on necessaries, leaving them little opportunity to accumulate wealth. In countries with VAT, substantially all of a fungible worker's income is subject to VAT as well as wage taxes. Fungible workers constitute much of the taxpaying public, bear a considerable portion of the burden of paying for government,[122] and are affected most profoundly as tax burdens shift from capital to labour.

Included in the pool of fungible labour are many immigrants who are low wage workers invited – sometimes temporarily as guest workers, sometimes as immigrants – to fill labour shortages. They are the Chinese labourers who built the US transcontinental railway;[123] the Mexicans, Central Americans and Filipinos who harvest crops; the Ukrainians, Lithuanians, Latvians, Caribbean islanders and Central Americans who provide cleaning services and home care for children, the elderly and individuals with disabilities. Some immigrate with the receiving government's authorisation and permission to work temporarily[124] or permanently, but many others enter without authorisation or with authorisation that does not permit them to work.

Once immigrants, whether temporary or permanent, reside in the US, their incomes become subject to the income tax and their wages to social security and Medicare taxes, although many will not reside in the US for the 10 years necessary to become eligible for retirement benefits under social security.[125] Many temporary workers and some immigrants who later reside outside the US lose benefits after six months outside the US.[126] Anyone buying items in the US pays state and local sales and use taxes even if the items are necessities for living. States vary with respect to items they may exempt from the state sales tax.[127]

In the US low wage earners qualify for a negative income tax[128] on their labour income.[129] The credit is substantial[130] but as the taxpayer's income increases, the credit rapidly phases out.[131] The credit does not help unemployed individuals and the phase out effectively imposes an additional 21 per cent tax on increases in wages in the phase-out range. Taxpayers lose the credit if they have income

---

[122] n 34 above, and accompanying text.

[123] n 16, above, and accompanying text.

[124] USCIS, 'H-2A, B temporary workers', available at https://www.uscis.gov/working-united-states/temporary-nonimmigrant-workers (accessed 18 September 2019).

[125] Social Security Administration, 'Retirement Benefits', available at https://www.ssa.gov/pubs/EN-05-10035.pdf (accessed 10 June 2019).

[126] 20 CFR § 404.460 (nonpayment of monthly benefits to aliens outside the United States).

[127] For example, New York State Department of Taxation and Finance, 'Lists of Exempt and Taxable Clothing, Footwear, and Items Used to Make or Repair Exempt Clothing', *Tax Bulletin ST-530 (TB-ST-530)* (10 March 2014), available at https://www.tax.ny.gov/pubs_and_bulls/tg_bulletins/st/clothing_chart.htm (accessed 10 June 2019).

[128] IRC §32 (inflation adjusted, refundable credit designed originally to balance the social security tax).

[129] IRC §32(c)(2) (wages plus self-employment income).

[130] IRC §32(b) (as much as 45% of the taxpayer's earned income not exceeding $14,570 in 2019 if the taxpayer has three or more qualifying children).

[131] ibid. The phase-out is 21.06% of each dollar over $24,820 for married taxpayers filing jointly: Rev Proc 2018-57, 2018-49 IRB 19 (phase-out tables).

150   Henry Ordower

from capital exceeding a low threshold, thus discouraging any accumulation of wealth by low income individuals.[132] Fear of examination by the taxing authority may discourage taxpayers from claiming the credit since taxpayers claiming the credit are examined more frequently than taxpayers with much greater incomes.[133] Taxpayers who do not have social security numbers are ineligible for the credit even if they have alternate taxpayer identification[134] and meet the other qualifications for the credit. Unauthorised workers may pay social security and income taxes but may not claim the earned income credit.[135]

Unauthorised immigrants are subject to deportation and have little hope of gaining authorised status. Unless they secure false papers or alternative taxpayer identification,[136] unauthorised immigrants may not accept work in the formal economy of the country. They participate primarily in the informal economy in which they receive payment for their services or the goods they sell in cash or in barter goods and services. Generally they accept payments for their services at rates substantially below the formal economy market rate.[137] Such service value discounts are necessary to entice service recipients to use unauthorised workers' services rather than those offered in the formal market. Unauthorised workers frequently find employment in occupations in which supplies of authorised workers are inadequate or that authorised workers do not want. Many unauthorised workers are in household occupations where their employer is in need of the services but is unwilling or unable to pay formal market rates. The payments generally would yield no tax deduction for the employer so payments in cash outside the formal economy are not of any consequence to the employers.[138] Even when they might provide a tax benefit to the employer,[139] the wages may be sufficiently low that the tax benefit would not match the wage differential for authorised workers.

Many unauthorised workers without tax identification do not report their income for income tax purposes. Failure to report income poses risks of both civil and criminal penalties since their obligation to report and pay taxes is

---

[132] IRC §32(i)(2); Rev Proc 2018-57 (n 131) (threshold amount in 2019 is $3,600).

[133] P Kiel, J Eisinger, and Propublica, 'The Golden Age of Rich People Not Paying Their Taxes', The Atlantic (11 December 2018), available at https://www.theatlantic.com/politics/archive/2018/12/rich-people-are-getting-away-not-paying-their-taxes/577798/ (accessed 4 October 2019).

[134] The US issues individual taxpayer identification numbers (ITIN) on request to individuals not authorised to work in the US but who have income to report in the US. IRS, 'Instructions for Form W-7', available at https://www.irs.gov/pub/irs-pdf/iw7.pdf (accessed 4 October 2019).

[135] In some cases they may claim the child tax credit under IRC §24 because the child is a citizen of the US by birth in the US and has a social security number.

[136] US taxpayer identification, for example (see n 134).

[137] The informal (or underground economy) operates primarily in cash outside the banking system and government regulation. Workers are paid at below market rates and have no little or no job protection. International Labour Organization, 'More than 60 per cent of the world's employed population are in the informal economy' (8 April 2018), available at https://www.ilo.org/global/about-the-ilo/newsroom/news/WCMS_627189/lang--en/index.htm (accessed 4 October 2019).

[138] Homecare workers for children, infirm and aged individuals, for example, generally nondeductible in any event as a personal expense under IRC §262 or the low wages in the informal economy being more valuable than a tax credit in those instances in which a credit is available. IRC §21.

[139] IRC §21 (dependent care expense credit, for example).

Immigration, Emigration, Fungible Labour and Progressive Taxation   151

independent of immigration status. If they were authorised workers, the incomes of many would lie below the threshold at which an income tax otherwise might be payable[140] but, in most instances, a wage-based social security tax would be payable. In the US such low income workers if authorised to work in the US might qualify for the earned income credit.[141] Thus, they are disadvantaged relative to authorised workers both in wage levels and access to a low wage tax benefit. While many unauthorised immigrants may not pay an income tax, they do pay consumption taxes[142] and excise taxes as they consume and indirectly pay property taxes in their housing rent.[143]

VII. Conclusion

Taxation plays a role in immigration and emigration and seems to drive some decisions to migrate from high to low tax jurisdictions. Capital mobility and labour immobility argue in favour of decreasing taxes on capital to prevent capital flight even if the decrease means shifting tax burdens to labour. Decreased taxes on capital, however, do not guarantee that capital will not flee. Another jurisdiction may offer still lower taxes and generate conditions for tax decrease competition, depriving the taxing jurisdiction of needed revenue. A race to the bottom on capital taxes enhances disparities between wealthy and poor residents and is unlikely to benefit developed economies. Growth of a privileged class undercuts longstanding commitments in advanced democracies to equality and equal opportunity.

Uncertainty for fungible, immigrant workers, both authorised and unauthorised, as to whether they will be permitted to remain in the country to which they have migrated often leaves them targets for exploitation. The immigrants accept low wages with few opportunities to organise to demand fairer wage treatment. Withholding to pay income and social security taxes from which they are unlikely to benefit further reduces already low wage income. Anti-immigrant government policies amplify uncertainty for fungible, immigrant workers and further exert downward pressure on wages assisting American business in keeping wages low and enhancing profitability.

Ability to pay – vertical equity – as a fundamental principle of taxation and resulting redistribution of wealth through strong welfare systems that provide for

---

[140] The income tax system of each developed economy does not tax incomes that fall below a minimum amount. That amount differs from country to country. In the US, the standard deduction under IRC §63 currently is $12,000 so that incomes less than that amount are not taxable. In Germany, a subsistence minimum must remain free from the income tax under the Constitutional Court's decision BVerfGE 82, 60, 85 (29 Mai 1990, 1st Senat).

[141] IRC §32 (n 128 above, and accompanying text).

[142] The US has no national consumption tax but most of the states of the US have retail sales taxes.

[143] A Stevenson (A Jurow Kleiman), 'Improving the US Guest Worker System through Tax and Social Welfare Reform' (2014) 17 *Harvard Latino Law Review* 147 (providing an excellent discussion of these issues).

the needs of all remain as compelling today as they were when many economically developed countries chose to impose steeply progressive taxes. Yet the focus on competing for capital resources seems to have supplanted principles of fairness and ability to pay and resulted in increasingly flat or regressive taxation. Tax rate competition for capital seems a doubtful strategy heading toward a zero tax on capital income and raises the question of whether something else – immigrant exploitation, wealth-based power disparities – motivates countries to shift tax burdens from capital to labour.

PART IV

International

9

What May We Expect of a Theory of International Tax Justice?

DIRK BROEKHUIJSEN AND HENK VORDING

In this chapter, we discuss what may be expected of a theory of international tax justice. After looking at the most important distributive as well as procedural theories of tax justice, we conclude that none of the existing theories can provide a standard of international tax justice that is satisfactory on all accounts. We therefore propose an alternative, more pragmatic approach. When making recommendations about social improvements, knowledge of perfect justice in international taxation is not necessarily required, just as one does not need to know the height of Mount Everest to find out that the Mount Blanc is higher than the Matterhorn.

I. Introduction

Before entering into questions of justice in international taxation, we will start by defining the problem. Within Western countries, we have become familiar with raising 'justice' arguments with respect to modest, sometimes trivial, questions of tax legislation. When we look at justice on a worldwide scale, the issues are not at all trivial. They have to do with access to a decent life either in one's country of birth or in some other place, with exploitation of natural resources, with corruption and failing states, with the incidence of climate change, etc. Taxation is just one part of the problems facing the worldwide community, and not the most vital part. Nevertheless, the problem of international taxation exists, institutions tackling the problem have stepped up their efforts in recent years, and the question whether progress is being made in terms of justice is very relevant. We will argue that the answer is simplification of the international tax system.

The tax problem, we assume (rather than demonstrate) consists of two parts with one cause. One part is that developing countries tend to be engaged in forms of tax competition that should be considered harmful to their interests. The other part is large-scale tax planning by multinational enterprises, at the detriment of developing countries. The single underlying cause is that the 'rules of the game' of international taxation are not particularly fit to protect the taxing rights of developing countries.[1] Effective international protection of source state taxation requires reasonably effective taxation worldwide, and acceptance of substantial withholding tax rates in particular. Both have been lacking, though very recent developments suggest some change.

More fundamentally, protection of developing countries' taxing rights may require a much less knowledge-intensive method of international taxation. Wealthy countries can afford to have thousands of academically trained people work in the field of international tax. Developing countries should be allowed to put their more limited human capital (in terms of educational level attained) to better use.[2] Recent (OECD) efforts to strengthen the international tax system have, however, tended to provide further refinement of already highly technical rules and norms; stepped-up 'technical assistance' to developing countries may increase rather than soften that tendency.

We first argue that tax justice, if understood to refer to tax burden distribution, has become a dead end. We then move to a Rawlsian idea of procedural justice, which may shed light on the OECD 'Inclusive Framework'. And we end with Sen's pragmatism, applying it to the OECD proposal of a global anti-BEPS set of rules which would, we suggest, effectively support the taxing rights of developing countries.

II. Distributive Justice in Taxation

A. Justice in Tax Burden Distribution: The National Level

Our thinking about taxation is imbued with notions of distributive justice. Countries' tax policies are usually inspired by some notion of fair distribution of the tax burden over their citizens.[3] The tradition of normative thought on just taxation is strong, and it has tended to focus on tax burden distribution within a single jurisdiction. And when considering questions of international tax justice, we tend to take that tradition with us. Nevertheless, even if the normative tradition

---

[1] T Dagan, 'The Tax Treaties Myth' (1999) 32 *New York University Journal of International Law* 939.

[2] It is interesting to see how many (not all) of the contributions in T Pogge and K Mehta (eds), *Global Tax Fairness* (Oxford, OUP, 2016) still focus on knowledge-intensive instruments like country-by-country reporting, improvement of the arm's length standard, financial transparency and exchange of information.

[3] See: T Plümper, VE Troeger and H Winner, 'Why is There no Race to the Bottom in Capital Taxation?' (2009) 53 *International Studies Quarterly* 761; SJ Basinger and M Hallberg, 'Remodelling the Competition for Capital: How Domestic Politics Erases the Race to the Bottom' (2004) 98 *American Political Science Review* 261. As Plümper, Troeger and Winner note, 'voters reduce political support when governments run large deficits, cut spending on relevant issues, and implement policies which voters perceive as unfair'. Concerns – however vague – about equitable tax burden distribution hence play a role: governments may engage in tax competition, but this comes at a political cost.

What May We Expect of a Theory of International Tax Justice? 157

was unproblematic (which it is not), it would not translate easily into a norm for 'fair shares' of countries in taxing cross-border activities, let alone in worldwide tax revenues. And a quick discussion of the traditional problems may well be sufficient to see why such a translation would stand little chance of success.

Any ideal of distributive tax justice runs into a number of problems. The first problem to be faced is that tax justice cannot be more than a partial ideal.[4] The judgment of a tax burden distribution (eg John pays 10, Mary pays 50) cannot be separated from the distribution of government benefits (eg whether all tax revenue is spent on John's behalf, or on Mary's behalf, or whether they each get some share of it). It is the overall distribution of government action that is the proper basis of assessment for any theory of distributive justice.[5] It could only be different – as a historical explanation for the strong tradition of normative thinking on tax burden distribution – in a past age when governments were small in size and their expenditures concerned pure public goods.

Even if we confined the issue to tax burden distribution for any given and morally irrelevant distribution of government benefits, new problems would turn up. The first is that the traditional thinking on tax burden distribution relies heavily on the libertarian benchmark of competitive market outcomes. That is, differences in people's starting positions are taken to be irrelevant, as is the distribution of good and bad luck over people's life courses.[6] To put it more precisely: a tax system based on the benefit or the ability-to-pay principle might well result in John paying less tax than Mary because he is worse-off, but it could never compensate him for the reasons why he is worse-off in the first place.[7] Nor would such a system be able to discriminate between John, who has little tax base because he had a poor starting position plus all the bad luck that one can have in later life, and Fred, who has little tax base because he declines to work.

The second and additional problem is that alternative (non-libertarian) approaches to tax burden distribution do not fare much better. The maximin rule of John Rawls[8] looks quite powerful, but it cannot have much application to taxation without taking into account government spending. It has been argued that almost any tax burden distribution could satisfy the maximin criterion, provided the tax revenue is spent on improving the position of the worst-off.[9] That result

---

[4] T Nagel and L Murphy, *The Myth of Ownership: Taxes and Justice* (Oxford, OUP, 2002).

[5] As Murphy and Nagel argue, this total benefit could be the difference between an individual's actual position in the world and her position in the Hobbesian world that lacks social institutions.

[6] This explains the attractiveness of endowment as a measure of ability-to-pay, though both Rawls and Dworkin rejected the idea. H Vording, 'Talents, Types and Tags: What Is the Relevance of the Endowment Tax Debate?' in Monica Bhandari (ed), *Philosophical Foundations of Tax Law* (Oxford, OUP, 2017) 233.

[7] This is Murphy and Nagel's 'baseline problem'.

[8] J Rawls, *A Theory of Justice* (Cambridge MA, Harvard University Press, revised ed. 1999).

[9] L Sugin, 'Theories of distributive justice and limitations on taxation: what Rawls demands from tax systems' (2003) 72 *Fordham Law Review* 1991.

158 *Dirk Broekhuijsen and Henk Vording*

relies on a weak interpretation of the maximin rule[10] – but the strong version of the rule would still provide few answers to the question of how the tax burden should be distributed over citizens.[11]

An alternative to Rawls is utilitarianism. Utilitarianism is relevant to tax burden distribution, but it is not a theory of distribution. As utilitarianism aims at maximizing total utility, the only reason to care about tax burden distribution is its impact on total utility. That recalls Rawls' objection to utilitarianism: it ignores individuals (except for their quality of generating utility). However, utilitarianism has had two clear results for the design of tax systems. First, it offers a basis for progressive taxation, under the assumption of declining utility of money (or, in the optimal taxation version, under the assumption of a benevolent planner who maximizes some social welfare function). Second, it offers support for neutrality of taxation as a guideline for maximising utility, and hence, for export and import neutrality as guidelines of international taxation.

Summing up, there is a lack of theoretical underpinning for our intuition that tax burden distribution should somehow be 'just'. The explanation for this intuition may be historical. The idea that tax burden distribution is a policy goal (and not a contingent result of taxes as they exist) has its roots in the eighteenth century. It developed into a battle cry of 'just taxation' throughout the nineteenth century, in a context of arbitrary taxes as described by, *inter alia*, Adam Smith. At that time, government activity was still limited to services of a 'public good' nature. As a consequence, taxation was the main if not the only policy instrument that mattered to distribution. The twentieth century development of state activities made taxation one of many government instruments and, hence, implied that tax burden distribution had lost its particular relevance to the positions of individual citizens. Government activity in fields like education, housing and health care has done much to reduce inequalities within states. At least in Western countries, remaining inequalities among citizens are evidently smaller than in, say, 1850 or 1900. Whenever we think of justice in taxation in terms of distribution of burdens, we are returning to ideals that mattered to the nineteenth century.

B. Justice in Tax Revenue Allocation: The International Level

As the tax burden debate has traditionally been limited to the scale of the national state, it cannot simply be transferred to a world level. The issue is not, we believe,

---

[10] Ie the maximin criterion is satisfied whenever a (tax) policy change brings benefit to the worst-off. The strong version holds that no additional change should be possible that would further increase the benefits to the worst-off.

[11] Assume that the government is able to maximise the position of the worst-off through its expenditure side. Ie neither an in/decrease of spending, nor another pattern of spending could possibly be better for the worst-off. In that case, the only task of tax policy is to raise the required revenue in a way that harms the position of the worst-off as little as possible (given the fact that taxation, when viewed in isolation, imposes a deadweight loss on society). It is a matter of economic expediency to find the tax

What May We Expect of a Theory of International Tax Justice? 159

that states are the representatives of national interests and (therefore) cannot carry responsibility for redistributive schemes aimed at other states' citizens. Such a pure 'statism' has been losing relevance due to increasing spill-overs between countries (be it pollution, migration or FDI flows).

Nevertheless, the statist view of sovereign states balancing their taxing rights through agreements has shaped the international tax regime as it stands today.[12] And as a consequence, the relevant issue is the share of nation states in the 'international' tax base, that is, the tax base that is not tied to a single jurisdiction but can be claimed by several jurisdictions.

Traditional tax principles have of course been used to allocate this 'international' tax base to national states. The benefit principle can justify taxation of non-residents over their tax base in a source country just like the ability-to-pay principle can justify taxation of residents over their worldwide tax base. Moreover, these principles generate utilitarian outcomes. Exclusive source-state taxation supports the limited goal of national maximalisation of utility (ie a level playing field for resident and non-resident investors) while residence taxation (with full foreign tax credit) achieves the wider goal of worldwide maximalisation (ie investors base their location decisions on before-tax returns as their home state determines their tax burden). These insights brought Richard and Peggy Musgrave to postulate a norm of 'international tax equity'[13] that effectively takes the taxing rights of the state of residence as self-evident, and the taxing rights of the source state as something that needs justification. To them, the purpose of a concept of international tax justice is to offer that source state justification. This justification, they argue, may be stronger in bilateral relations marked by differences in economic welfare. Hence, rich countries could allow more taxing rights to poor countries (tax treaty partners) than they would do to other rich countries.

This approach to 'international tax equity' poses several problems. The first one is that, like the distributional norms discussed in the previous section, it relies on a benchmark of competitive market outcomes. Whenever these outcomes are unjust, for example because countries face very different levels of human capital

---

bases and tax rates that produce this outcome. In principle, there should be a single optimal solution; in practice, the connection to actual questions of tax policy is remote. In addition, Rawls puts restrictions on optimisation by giving precedence to the requirement of liberty. This, in his opinion, rules out an endowment tax (a differentiated head tax) which might well be optimal.

[12] We discussed the distributional nature of international taxation in D Broekhuijsen and H Vording, 'The Multilateral Tax Instrument: How to Avoid a Stalemate on Distributional Issues?' [2016] *British Tax Review* 39.

[13] RA Musgrave and PB Musgrave, 'Inter-nation Equity' in RM Bird and JG Head (eds), *Modern Fiscal Issues: Essays in Honor of Carl S. Shoup* (Toronto, University of Toronto Press, 1972) 63. Their reasoning takes its starting point in 'national neutrality': the notion that foreign taxation should not reduce the return to foreign investment below the domestic before-tax return to investment. See the appreciative discussion in K Brooks, 'Inter-nation Equity: The Development of an Important but Underappreciated International Tax Policy Objective' in JG Head and R Krever (eds), *Tax Reform in the 21st Century: A Volume in Memory of Richard Musgrave* (Alphen aan den Rijn, Kluwer Law International, 2009) 471. See also N Kaufman, 'Fairness and the taxation of international income' (1997) 29 *Law and Policy in International Business* 145.

and natural resources, the benchmark is unreliable. The poorest countries are hardly helped by allowing them more taxing rights over international investors, as these investors are simply not there. Second, the account given for taxation of non-residents is not satisfactory on a normative level. It may be true that non-residents will avoid a country if they consider its tax claim uncompetitively high. In that sense, a country cannot tax a non-resident at effective rates that exceed the non-resident's perceived benefit of opting for this country instead of some neighbouring alternative. But such a (presumed) factual finding is not a norm for 'just' taxation. Of course, it can be replaced by a political judgment: the legislator of (wealthy) country 1 concludes a tax treaty with (developing) country 2 that allows the latter to tax country 1 investors at a high effective rate. But that is indeed a political judgment – and even if that judgment relies on some theory of distributive justice, it must be a general theory, not just about tax. And this brings us to a third and decisive objection. That objection is not necessarily that current tax treaty practice would not be able to accommodate an agreement between country 1 and country 2 on, for example, mutual corporate income tax rates cuts and increases. The content of tax treaties has evolved over time and will continue to evolve as new interests must be taken into account. The objection is that two countries cannot agree on increased (developing) source country entitlement (eg more generous crediting) to tax without taking into account third parties. The current practice of international tax planning simply does not allow bilateral agreements of that nature to be effective. A multilateral agreement may be used, but considering the type of 'game' played in international tax law, it is unlikely to be helpful to change source country entitlement, as we have shown elsewhere.[14]

Nevertheless, the attractiveness of some international tax equity norm that would support the taxing rights of (developing) source countries is evident. The Musgraves' proposal to found an 'inter-nation tax equity' norm was not taken up quickly, perhaps because it did not address a problem felt to be urgent at the time. That only changed over the last two decades, and NGOs like Oxfam and Tax Justice deserve credit for it. Cases of international tax planning at the expense of developing countries, as published by NGOs over recent years,[15] convey a feeling of indignation even if that feeling cannot be supported by a solid normative theory. In that sense, justice in taxation has the same battle cry meaning that it had on the national level, back in the nineteenth century.

The academic literature responded by developing alternative foundations for a duty of wealthy countries to strengthen developing countries' taxing rights.

---

[14] Broekhuijsen and Vording (n 12); D Broekhuijsen, *A Multilateral Tax Treaty: Designing an Instrument to Modernise International Tax Law* (Alphen aan den Rijn, Kluwer Law International, 2018).

[15] Eg J Henry, 'The price of offshore revisited' (Tax Justice Network, 2012); UNCTAD, *World investment report 2015: Reforming international investment governance* (UN, 2015), available at https://unctad.org/en/PublicationsLibrary/wir2015_en.pdf.

What May We Expect of a Theory of International Tax Justice? 161

Christians' contribution[16] considers why and how states could be under obligations not just to respect but to actively support other states' taxing rights. She argues (well ahead of the BEPS project) that the OECD is working towards a notion of 'sovereign duty' – a duty not to create tax policy spillovers that damage other states' tax sovereignty. As to the further question whether states are under a positive duty to support other states, especially developing countries, in effectively taxing non-resident investors, she is more cautious. Such a duty should rest on an obligation to provide every citizen of the world with access to basic goods. In an attempt to avoid outright cosmopolitanism, Benshalom[17] argues that wealthy countries do have a duty to support developing countries' taxing rights; this duty is however 'relational', based on the intensity of economic ties between two countries.

On a more technical level, Musgrave's 'international tax equity' norm has been taken up in several directions. Rosenzweig advocates that the residence state has a claim to some minimum return, to be calculated at arm's length; any MNE profits in excess of this normal return should be divided among all states involved, using formulary apportionment.[18] This reflects an idea that the rents of cross-border investment cannot simply be allocated to one jurisdiction or another. A more fundamental approach is offered by Infanti, in a proposal to make tax treaties a normal instrument of foreign policy.[19] When we want to help developing countries to combat inequality, discrimination and poverty, there is no reason why we would try to do that with, for example, trade and investment treaties, direct money transfers etc, but not with tax treaties. These treaties could offer developing countries the protection needed to effectively tax non-resident investors – and more so as these developing countries perform better on some index of social progress. While Infanti's proposal is highly impracticable in a world with tax planning opportunities, it does raise an interesting question – how is any obligation to assist and support developing countries affected by the socio-economic and/or political performance of those countries? To put it more bluntly: what if a country's tax revenues are funnelled to the offshore bank accounts of the ruling class?

The ongoing debate how base allocation of taxing rights to states depends on some notion of justice opens interesting viewpoints. The relevant literature is usually well-received in classrooms. It does, however, face the considerable challenge of founding a norm that has independent meaning towards the actual process of international policy-making. The tendency is to generate variants of

---

[16] A Christians, 'Sovereignty, taxation and social contract' (2009) 18 *Minnesota Journal of International Law* 99.

[17] I Benshalom, 'The New Poor at Our Gates: Global Justice Implications for International Trade and Tax Law' (2010) 85 *New York University Law Review* 1.

[18] A Rosenzweig, 'Defining a Country's Fair Share of Taxes' (2014) 42 *Florida State University Law Review* 373. Remarkably, Rosenzweig does not mention the Musgraves' work.

[19] A Infanti, 'Internation Equity and Human Development' in Y Brauner and M Stewart (eds), *Tax, Law and Development* (Cheltenham, Edward Elgar Publishing, 2013) 209.

162   *Dirk Broekhuijsen and Henk Vording*

neutrality norms, or to end up with proposals that would need a highly cooperative international tax environment.

III. Procedural Justice in Taxation

The alternative approach to justice in taxation is procedural, or as Rawls called
it: 'justice as fairness'. The basic idea is that a social institution (be it a norm, an
agreement, a set of rules) is just when all participants accept it as just. Such an
institution has been called a 'social contract', beginning with Hobbes and Locke,
and was developed into a widely accepted analytical tool by Rawls. Its acceptance
may be due to its plausible foundation in individual self-interest: I agree with obligations when I see the point for doing so. As a theory of social obligations, or as a
foundation of state power, it is evidently a-historical. That is not Rawls's concern.
He wants to show how individual self-interest can support not just cooperation
(an insight shared by libertarians) but obligation. The vital condition is that all
participants in contract-making are prepared to put their immediate concerns and
interests aside, realising that their current position in life may radically deteriorate
by plain bad luck. This 'veil of ignorance' (dubbed 'veil of uncertainty' by others[20])
is symbol to enlightened self-interest.

Rawls himself denied the possibility of a worldwide social contract; he considered the nation state the natural ambit for mutual acceptance of obligations. He
was strongly criticised for that by others, as 'being born in a rich country' is as
contingent as 'being born in a rich family'.[21] Both conditions should therefore be
hidden behind the veil of ignorance, and people from all nationalities should be
accepted at the negotiation table for a worldwide social contract. And, indeed, his
arguments against redistribution among states (in his *Law of Peoples*[22]) seem quite
akin to the libertarians' criticism of the maximin rule (as proposed in his *Theory
of Justice*). Wealthy states (or peoples, in Rawls's wording) have a limited obligation to help developing states on the path towards a well-ordered society; if these
states remain poor, that is not a reason for further help. And if states attain different levels of prosperity from comparable starting positions, that is no reason for
redistribution either.[23]

There is an analogy between Rawls's objection to endowment taxation (in his
Theory of Justice) and his claim that differences in prosperity among nations do
not create structural obligations to redistribute. Rawls objected to endowment
taxation primarily because such a tax would make some people (the talented)
instrumental to others (the worst-off). Those with high earning power would not

---

[20] G Brennan and JM Buchanan, *The Reason of Rules: Constitutional Political Economy* (Indianapolis,
Liberty Fund, 1999).

[21] T Dagan, 'International Tax and Global Justice' (2017) 18 *Theoretical Inquiries In Law* 1.

[22] J Rawls, *The Law of Peoples* (Cambridge MA, Harvard University Press, 2001).

[23] ibid, 114–17.

What May We Expect of a Theory of International Tax Justice?   163

be able to choose a leisurely life, but would be expected to work for the benefit of the poor. His argument against redistribution among states rests on his 'statist' foundation of international law. The rules that he derives in the *Law of Peoples* are created behind a veil of ignorance. The representatives of the states involved in creating the rules have no knowledge about the size and prosperity of the people they represent. What they do know is that it is their job to defend the interests of their own people. And that (statist) assumption rules out any agreement on helping poorer states, let alone on worldwide redistribution schemes. Again, one group of people should not be made instrumental to the needs of others.

We will not dig into this debate further (it has been done by many others).[24] Instead, we take the social contract as an analytical tool to help us define what participants in international decision-making may expect if that decision-making is to generate 'justice as fairness'.[25] The key to fair decision-making is what Rawls calls 'reflective equilibrium'. It requires that participants do not just advocate their interests and voice their concerns, but are prepared to accept criticism and inquire into the premises of their arguments. This process continues until all arguments have been exchanged, tested, and rejected as ill-founded or accepted as valid. And vitally, the process assumes that all participants have an equal say – an equal opportunity to participate and be heard.

This procedural approach has been pursued by Dagan. She starts at the domestic level to argue that 'the state's ability to ensure justice is critically diminished if the stronger segments of society are able to opt out of its tax system' through tax planning schemes that may not even require them to actually move. The pursuit of domestic distributive justice may therefore require international tax coordination. But critically, Dagan argues 'that mere cooperation among nations is not enough to ensure justice. A multilateral regime established through cooperation is just, I contend, if and only if it improves (or at least does not worsen) the welfare of the least well-off constituents in all the cooperating states.' The reason is that multilateral cooperation, while required to allow states to implement their own ideas on justice, is not itself an institution supported by citizens. The justification of multilateral cooperation must be that for any participating state, justice (as measured by the position of the worst-off) is indeed improved or at least, not deteriorated. And while states may not care about each other's ideas of distributive justice, nor about each other's worst-off citizens, they are still under a duty not to engage in multilateral cooperation that reduces the ability of other states to pursue their own ideas of justice. In the end, it is 'unjust for a state to promote domestic justice at the expense of justice in other states'.

In effect, Dagan is relaxing the limits of liberal non-interference as advocated in Rawls's *Law of Peoples*. She offers a specification of the 'sovereign duty' proposed by

---

[24] For an overview of the reception of Rawls, with application to international taxation, see P Hongler, *Justice in International Tax Law* (Amsterdam, IBFD, 2019).

[25] For an early application to issues of tax design: CR O'Kelly Jr, 'Rawls, Justice, and the Income Tax' (1981) 16 *Georgia Law Review* 1.

164   *Dirk Broekhuijsen and Henk Vording*

Christians: states should not contribute to unjustness in other states. We believe that her argument shows how unfruitful the statist distinction between states and citizens is. States are acting like black boxes; citizens are passive or at least invisible for our understanding of international relations. Dagan offers a way out by effectively deepening states' duties. But, probably, she allows for more cosmopolitanism than many states would be prepared to accept. For example, her approach seems to rely on an assumption that all states share a comparable standard of justice, or a comparable notion of which of their citizens are the 'worst-off'. Just as we saw with notions of tax revenue allocation, it seems hard to underpin a plausible intuition with sound reasoning. The way out, we believe, has already been shown by Benshalom. His solution was to mix up citizens' relational duties with states' redistributive obligations: relational duties can only be effected through state action. This reflects a world in which NGO's are actively engaged in reform of international taxation.

Leaving Rawls's statist position aside, his method of searching for reflective equilibrium focuses on deliberation. As a general approach towards justice, the quest for (some level of) reflective equilibrium may be as demanding as any theory of distributive justice. Developed states are reluctant to give up powerful political positions, as, for example, was shown by the failure of the 2015 Addis Ababa initiative for an equal voice of developing countries in setting international tax policy.[26] A truly open debate about climate change, mass migration, and indeed, taxation might come closer to full-fledged cosmopolitanism than any wealthy country would agree with. Nevertheless, the merit of a theory of justice is its providing guidance even if the prospect of realisation is remote. The idea of justice as fairness can be used to evaluate the 'inclusiveness' aimed at by the OECD.

A. Inclusive Framework

The G20/OECD Inclusive Framework on BEPS is an intergovernmental network open to all states (or so it seems), with the purpose of implementing the BEPS proposals. The OECD invites countries and jurisdictions to join the framework as associates, to participate on equal footing and commit to implement the BEPS Package.[27] The question is, however, whether the Inclusive Framework is as inclusive as it says, ie whether it truly allows developing countries to operate on an equal footing within its law-making processes and, most importantly, to allow them to influence setting the agenda. As Pendergast notes, the agenda 'is one of the most important structural aspects of any negotiation as well as a significant determinant

---

[26] UN General Assembly, *Resolution adopted by the General Assembly on 27 July 2015: Addis Ababa Action Agenda of the Third International Conference on Financing for Development* (2015) UN A/RES/69/313.

[27] OECD, *About the Inclusive Framework on BEPS*, available at https://www.oecd.org/tax/beps/beps-about.htm.

of negotiating power and influence'.[28] Yet, as Christians and Van Apeldoorn argue in their study on the OECD Inclusive Framework, the OECD's opaque institutional hierarchy makes it difficult (if not impossible) to assess how non-OECD members participate and with what consequences.

> The Inclusive Framework continues the OECD's expansion of tax cooperation beyond its member states, but it unfortunately also continues an OECD tradition of institutional and procedural opacity. As such its emphasis on inclusivity is intuitively appealing but elusive. The question for non [OECD] member states is whether, in the long term, the Inclusive Framework can adequately define and then deliver on the promise of equality on an equal footing.[29]

Yet, as the agenda determines the purview of rules created and implemented, it is the most significant element of the cooperation and negotiation process for developing countries. Developing countries participating in the inclusive framework are expected to implement rules; once these are formulated and agreed upon by the international community, there is no way back to the drawing table. This poses a problem, as a preliminary survey of BEPS implementation outcomes shows. In that study, Sadiq, Sawyer and McCredie suggest that the level of engagement in implementing the BEPS agenda is dependent on a country's level of development, with underdeveloped countries performing low. Of the 16 countries studied, countries with the lowest levels of engagement are the Philippines, Thailand, Vietnam and Malaysia.[30] And in introducing her similar study on the implementation of the BEPS Project in 12 countries in Africa, Asia, Europe, and North and Latin America, Mosquera Valderrama notes that developing countries facing the inclusive framework's implementation deadlines are concerned about the technical expertise required, suggesting that meeting these deadlines may come at the cost of paying attention to (more important) domestic matters of tax collection and tackling evasion.[31]

The OECD aims to provide, together with the G20 Development Working Group, 'toolkits and guidance' as well as 'the opportunity to receive coordinated and targeted capacity building support' to participants of the Inclusive Framework for them to implement BEPS outcomes.[32] But if it is indeed true that the level

---

[28] WR Pendergast, 'Managing the Negotiation Agenda' (1990) 6 *Negotiation Journal* 135.

[29] A Christians and L van Apeldoorn, 'The OECD Inclusive Framework' (2018) 72 *Bulletin for International Taxation* 226.

[30] K Sadiq, A Sawyer and B McCredie, *Tax Design and Administration in a Post-BEPS Era: A Study of Key Reform Measures in 16 Countries*, ir.canterbury.ac.nz/handle/10092/16099.

[31] I Mosquera Valderrama, 'Output Legitimacy Deficits and the Inclusive Framework of the OECD/G20 Base Erosion and Profit Shifting Initiative' (2018) 72 *Bulletin for International Taxation* 160.

[32] OECD, 'About the Inclusive Framework on BEPS', available at www.oecd.org/tax/beps/beps-about.htm. Also note the activity of the Platform for Collaboration on Tax, founded by the IMF, the OECD, the UN and the World Bank. The 'major aim of the Platform is to better frame technical advice to developing countries as they seek both more capacity support and greater influence in designing international rules'. The focus seems to be on technical support and advice on domestic reforms, not on simplification of international tax rules: see further World Bank, 'Platform for Collaboration on Tax', available at www.worldbank.org/en/programs/platform-for-tax-collaboration.

of resources demanded by the (implementation of) BEPS outcomes is excessively high for underdeveloped countries, the OECD cannot limit itself to providing developing countries with a basic phrasebook and a tour guide to navigate new additions to the complexities of international tax law. As a matter of reflective equilibrium, international tax law should provide an environment that is as hospitable to all those concerned, even if this means throwing overboard some of the existing paradigms of international tax law.

Procedural justice, we argue, requires a more open agenda for reform of the international tax system. It does, however, leave important questions unanswered, especially about the scope of inclusiveness. Recall the distinctions that Rawls made in his *Law of Peoples* between liberal states, decent hierarchical states and rogue states. Intuitively, one feels that any duty to support developing countries cannot simply ignore differences in political regimes, attitudes towards cooperation, etc. Indeed, states' internal conditions restrict the extent to which procedural tax justice can be achieved at the international level. Anarchy and corruption may lead to unfair outcomes of international tax rules reached in an otherwise fair way. Problems arise when leaders or institutions have no legitimacy. This may be the case when the moral justification to rule is absent, for instance because a state does not represent and cannot held accountable by its people.[33]

IV. Is Pragmatism the Remaining Option?

Amartya Sen famously argued against the *Theory of Justice* that it worded a transcendent ('other-worldly') concept of justice that says nothing about how justice is actually advanced.[34] Instead, to provide the footing for his 'capabilities' approach, Sen made use of Adam Smith's 'impartial spectator' to provide a comparative approach to justice that may be used to practically guide the reasoned choice of policies, institutions, etc. The perspective of the imagined 'impartial spectator' is an approach to justice that deemphasizes personal interests and priorities. Instead, the impartial spectator may identify social improvements as a disinterested observer who is not himself party to the social decisions to be taken.[35] This allows comparative assessments of justice, where, in identifying social improvements, knowledge of perfect justice is not required, just like one does not need to know the height of Mount Everest to find out that the Mount Blanc is higher than the Matterhorn. This pragmatist approach, when applied to international tax justice, may help us to accept our intuitions even when we find it hard to offer full justifications.

---

[33] See A Buchanan and R Keohane, 'The Legitimacy of Global Governance Institutions' in LH Meyer (ed), *Legitimacy, Justice and Public International Law* (Cambridge, CUP, 2009); A Buchanan, 'The Legitimacy of International Law' in S Besson and J Tasioulas (eds), *The Philosophy of International Law* (Oxford, OUP, 2010).

[34] A Sen, *The Idea of Justice* (London, Allen Lane, 2009). For transcendentalism, one can think of Plato's parable of the cave: our actual experiences are imperfect shadows of the world of Ideas.

[35] A Sen, 'What Do We Want from a Theory of Justice' (2006) 103 *Journal of Philosophy* 215.

In February 2019, the OECD published a consultation document on the tax challenges of the digitalisation of the economy.[36] Formally, it is a next step in a process that started with BEPS Action 1 and goes back to discussions in the late 1990s on 'digital presence' of non-resident businesses. As such, it is very much a debate between the US (the home state of the internet industry) and the EU (where about half of the users of that industry live). That part of the consultation document may have little relevance to most developing countries (nor to China, which has effectively closed its markets to Google, Facebook etc). The second part of the document takes a much broader perspective and may prove highly relevant to the tax position of developing countries. In October 2019, the document was followed up by an OECD secretariat paper further outlining the proposal.[37]

The 'Global anti-base erosion proposal' seems to offer what it promises: a form of worldwide minimum tax on intracompany income flows. The idea is, of course, not new. But it was always received with scepticism, due to evident problems of policy coordination. The OECD proposal is, however, very timely for two reasons. One is that the US, as an element of its 2018 tax reform, has returned to effective worldwide taxation of its corporate residents, at least partially. This allows the rest of the world to impose taxes on US investors to the extent that these are creditable against US tax. The second recent development is the emergence of conditional withholding taxes.[38] These taxes, at least conceptually, avoid the traditional residence versus source entitlement debate, and are just aimed at taxing an income flow when nobody else does. The incentive effect of each of these rules is to invite states to raise their effective tax rates on outbound corporate income flows.

Both the US tax reform 2018 and the idea of conditional withholding taxation may largely be a response to the GAFA (Google, Amazon, Facebook, Apple) problem that the fastest-growing industries largely escape taxation. Both are also broader in scope, and as a by-product, they may positively affect the tax position of the non-OECD world. Developing countries will find it easier to effectively apply withholding taxes on outbound income flows.

V. Summing Up

It seems completely plausible that the rules of international taxation, especially where developing countries are involved, should be evaluated against a standard of 'justice'. In fact, it is hard to find such a standard. Traditional thought on tax

---

[36] OECD/G20 Base Erosion and Profit Shifting Project, *Addressing the Tax Challenges of the Digitalisation of the Economy*, Public Consultation Document, 13 February 2019.

[37] OECD, Public Consultation Document, 'Global Anti-Base Erosion ("GloBE") Proposal – Pillar Two: Tax Challenges Arising From the Digitalisation of the Economy, 8 November – 2 December 2019', available at http://www.oecd.org/tax/beps/public-consultation-document-global-anti-base-erosion-proposal-pillar-two.pdf.

[38] J Vleggeert and H Vording, 'Conditional Withholding Tax: a Tax on Tax Planning' (2017) 71(8) *Bulletin for International Taxation* 452.

burden distribution is not helpful, both because it is in disarray and because (even if it was not) it cannot easily be translated to a world scale without requiring strong cosmopolitan premises. Notions of substantive 'international tax equity' tend to be either neutrality norms or expressions of some political preference. Turning to a procedural notion of justice, signs are more promising. The most practical conclusion is that developing countries should have a stronger role in agenda-setting. It might well be in developing countries' interest to get simpler international tax rules rather than more technical advice. We end with a positive note by relying on Sen's pragmatism. Even if we do not have a fully coherent account of justice in international taxation, we can still identify improvements. And such improvements, we suggest, can even happen to be the result of OECD countries pursuing their own interests.

10

Re-Imagining Tax Justice in a Globalised World

TSILLY DAGAN

In this chapter I explain why designing a country's tax policy with the elasticity of taxpayers' choices of residency in mind, although a rational welfare-maximising move by the state as a whole, and possibly even for its immobile as well as mobile constituents, is a policy that may not be justified under a liberal-egalitarian social contract.

I discuss two polar views of the social contract. One endorses the state with the coercive power to promote the joint interests of its constituents. The other views the coercive power of the state as a way to fulfil the collective will of its constituents as a society of equals, in order to promote who they are as people. If states' coercive power is based on equal respect and concern, a policy that undercuts such equality might not be justified. The state thus faces a dilemma: taking into account the increased electivity of taxation (by some) could undermine the normative foundations of the power of the state to tax. Ignoring such increased electivity, on the other hand, may limit the potential of *some* individuals and the state as a whole to flourish.

I. Introduction

Income taxation is considered a key tool (the *optimal* tool, some even argue) for promoting justice. Under canonical thinking, the monopolistic coercive power of the state could and should be used in order to promote justice. This belief in the power of tax to promote justice is based, however, on the assumption of a closed economy, where sovereign power reigns and the state has both the will and the power to impose and enforce its taxation.

This assumption of a closed economy, in turn, is challenged under globalisation. Globalisation is transforming the state-citizen relationship by increasingly turning states into market actors who compete for residents (individuals as well as businesses), for factors of production, and for tax revenues. Instead of powerful

170   *Tsilly Dagan*

sovereigns with the capacity to make and enforce mandatory rules, impose taxes and set redistribution, states are increasingly becoming actors in a competitive global market, where their ability to govern is affected by supply and demand. With the rise of mobility among residents and factors of production, the state increasingly functions as a regime that is to a large extent elective (at least for some), where certain individuals and businesses have the ability to choose from a broad range of legal jurisdictions. This electivity applies only to a limited set of the countries' constituents and resources, thus creating a new rift within the state: between the mobile (important among them are the rich and talented) and the immobile.

This new competitive market reality dramatically weakens states' ability to promote their goals through taxation, and presents them with fundamental dilemmas. Competition among states pushes them to lower the 'prices' (ie taxes) they charge, and, moreover, to 'price discriminate' among taxpayers, allowing them to collect lower taxes from the mobile segments of society, in order to stay competitive and maximise welfare. Thus, the question arises: are there domestic limitations on states, as competitive actors, in terms of justice? Should domestic taxation be based solely on the ability of states to collect whatever taxes they can, from whoever cannot avoid them, much like firms in a competitive market? Or should there be any limitations on income taxation even in a competitive world? This question is especially acute in a world where taxes become elective only *for some*,[1] while for others – those with limited mobility and limited ability to pick and choose among jurisdictions – taxation is still a coercive measure. Should taxation – in order to be defensible, let alone to be fair – comply with some basic requirements of justice and, if so, what are such requirements?

In this chapter I present the dilemma faced by sovereign states' taxation systems in a competitive world: between maximising the combined welfare of their constituents through market-inspired mechanisms on the one hand and maintaining a society of equals on the other hand. Each of these (extreme) options not only entails different consequences for states, their constituents, and the relationships among them, but is also based on a very different rationale for the state.

On the one hand, where states embrace market measures and choose to tax some of their constituents more leniently based on their elasticity (ie to grant mobile taxpayers with reduced tax liability in order to encourage them to stay), they might face serious consequences in terms of the stability and fairness of their social contract. This may be justified under a utilitarian perception of the state – one that sees the interaction between the state and its constituents, and among the constituents themselves, as strictly based on maximising their combined self-interests. This marketised version of the state – which is based on the supply and demand for states' services, and on the attractiveness of potential taxpayers

---

[1] The ability to move one's activities, or parts thereof, is not equally distributed among taxpayers. Taxpayers with international activities (eg foreign consumers), opportunities to operate overseas or more modular components within their operations will be better able to opt out of the system if they so wish.

– highlights citizens' independence, stresses their ability to exit and forms a thin conception of citizenship.

On the other hand, where states embrace equality – pursuing equal concern and respect – they must, as I explain below, look beyond maximising material resources, and should not let demand considerations take over. While under this rationale the state respects equality, it may entail considerable costs in terms of welfare, and – if not properly designed – undermine the autonomy of mobile residents.

The practical dilemma, too, is considerable. In the extreme case, sovereign states would present mobile taxpayers with a dichotomous choice: join us (and subject yourselves to our tax regime in its entirety) or exit (and we will be happy to host your business on a non-membership basis). Or, alternatively, they can choose to commodify their membership and subject it to the rules of the market, thus undermining their state-citizen relationship.

This chapter will continue as follows: Section II will discuss the shift in income taxation from benefit taxation to viewing taxation as part of one's civic identity, delinked from the value of the goods and services one receives from the state, and describe the different rationales for each. Section III wonders whether globalisation and tax competition – by highlighting mobility and fragmentation – brought with it a hybrid idea of taxation 'benefits taxes *for some*'. Finally, Section IV presents the sovereign state's dilemma – juxtaposing the two ideal types of state-taxpayers' relationships: a market-inspired version of the state (an 'exit based state') and a community of equals (a 'loyalty based state') and asking whether a choice between the two is inevitable (or even desirable).

II. Income Taxation: From Benefit Taxation to Ability to Pay

Taxation is anchored in the sovereign power of the state. It facilitates social cooperation within the state – by collecting the resources necessary for its operation,[2] and, at the same time, it operates thanks to the states' coercive power. Coercion is essential as – at least within a sizeable population – we cannot trust only the goodwill of individuals to pursue (even) their mutual interest.

> The only way to provide that assurance is through some form of law, with centralized authority to determine the rules and a centralized monopoly of the power of enforcement. This is needed even in a community most of whose members are attached to a common ideal of justice, both in order to provide terms of coordination and **because it doesn't take many defectors to make such a system unravel**.[3]

---

[2] D de Cogan, *Tax Law, State-Building and the Constitution* (Oxford, Hart Publishing, 2020) 7 (describing the prominence of tax in constructing states and social relations within them).

[3] T Nagel, 'The problem of global justice' in *Secular Philosophy and the Religious Temperament: Essays 2002-2008* (Oxford, OUP, 2010) 64 (emphasis added).

172   *Tsilly Dagan*

This raises a delicate question, which is at the core of our discussion as to 'the appropriate relation of the individual to the collectivity, through the institutions of the state.'[4] As Murphy and Nagel explain:

> A state has a near monopoly of force within its territory, and it has the authority 'to coerce individuals to comply with decisions arrived at by some non-unanimous collective choice procedure. What are the legitimate aims for which such power may be used, **and what, if anything, limits the way it may legitimately be exercised over individuals?** These are questions about what we may be said to owe to our fellow citizens, and what kind of sovereignty we should retain over ourselves, free from the authority of the state, even when we are members of it and subject to its control in certain respects. Those questions define the issue of political legitimacy.[5]

There are two very distinct ways to think about the coercive power of the state. One could think of it as a way for individuals to promote their joint interests. Under this view external coercive power is necessary where individuals cannot achieve this goal due to collective action problems. Alternatively, we could think of the coercive power of the state as a way to fulfil the collective will of its constituents as a society of equals in order to promote who they are as people.

Each justification for the state's coercive power dictates a different set of goals for income taxation. If coercion is only a way to more effectively promote the collective self-interest of states' constituents, tax policy should focus on the instruments that would maximise the collective welfare pie. If, on the other hand, coercion is necessary in order to promote the collective will of states' constituents, it demands a richer account not only of distributive justice, but also of horizontal equity; not only of maximising welfare but also on equal concern and respect – as will be explored below.

The evolution of income taxation seems to reflect a shift in the perception of the state. In the past, taxation was implicitly perceived to be a cost that a person paid for the public goods he consumed, and the rationale of benefit taxation was widely supported.[6] Under the benefit principle the tax relationship between the state and its constituents was limited to a deal, a quid-pro-quo, a 'cash nexus' as Ajay Mehrorta describes it in the American context of the nineteenth century.[7]

> Citizenship itself was reduced to a commodity. The benefits principle seemed to subordinate the social aspects of the social contract. For a subsequent group of theorists and political activists, such an impoverished vision of taxes and community would be unacceptable. But during the last decades of the nineteenth century few doubted this logic and characterization of taxes.[8]

---

[4] L Murphy and T Nagel, *The Myth of Ownership: Taxes and Justice* (Oxford, OUP, 2002) 41.

[5] ibid (emphasis added).

[6] Hobbes famously supported paying taxes in proportion to what people consume in society: 'But when the impositions are laid upon those things which men consume, every man payeth equally for what he useth.' T Hobbes, *Leviathan: Book II* (revised edition, Broadview Press Canada, 2010) 295. See AK Mehrotra, *Making the Modern American Fiscal State: Law, Politics, and the Rise of Progressive Taxation 1877–1929* (Cambridge, CUP, 2013) 64.

[7] See ibid.

[8] ibid.

Payment according to the benefits one receives from the state can make a lot of sense. It aligns the costs of government with the preferences of its constituents (assuming these could be accurately measured), it prevents the government from spending money on goals that are of no interest for its constituents and it provides a simple (some would say simplistic) utility-maximising version of the social contract. Especially for those who perceive of their own resources as 'naturally' belonging to them, benefit taxation provides an intuitive and easy to support rationale for taxation. When providing quid-pro-quo in public services, the government does not deprive constituents of their resources but rather serves their interests in solving their collective action problems in promoting such interests.

The justification for taxation in political theory evolved, however, from this initial (Hobbesian) justification of taxes as a payment for the public goods that taxpayers consume (ie benefit taxation) into a concept of state-imposed allocation of the fiscal costs of the budget, irrespective of such benefits.[9] In modern times, it is commonly assumed that tax should be de-linked from the benefits that a person receives from the state.

Under this version of the social contract, states' constituents subject themselves to the coercive powers of their states (only) in order to be able to effectively pursue their collective will. This creates a unique political interdependency where individuals are simultaneously 'subjects in law's empire and citizens in law's republic'.[10] This unique combination of coercive power and co-authorship, of relinquishing one's power in order to pursue the collective will of himself along with others, brings with it unique duties, as states' coercive powers must '... be justified to their co-authors'.[11] In Nagel's words:

> adherence to ... [political institutions] is not voluntary: Emigration aside, one is not permitted to declare oneself not a member of one's society and hence not subject to its rules, and other members may coerce one's compliance if one tries to refuse. An institution that one has no choice about joining must offer terms of membership that meet a higher standard.[12]

'The state', claims Nagel, 'makes unique demands on the will of its members ... and those exceptional demands bring with them exceptional obligations, the positive obligations of justice'.[13] Importantly, according to Cohen and Sable, 'not just any justification will do ... the justification must treat each person ... in whose name the coercion is exercised – as an equal'.[14] The reason for this is that 'states not only foster cooperation by coercively enforcing rules but implicate the will of those subject to their coercive authority by making, in the name of all, regulations

---

[9] K Vogel, 'The Justification for Taxation: A Forgotten Question' (1988) 33 *American Journal of Jurisprudence* 19, 24–33.

[10] J Cohen and C Sabel, 'Extram Republicam Nulla Justitia?' (2006) 34 *Philosophy and Public Affairs* 147, 148.

[11] ibid 160.

[12] T Nagel, 'The Problem of Global Justice' (2005) 33 *Philosophy and Public Affairs* 113, 133.

[13] ibid 130.

[14] Cohen and Sable (n 10) 160.

174   Tsilly Dagan

that apply to them all'.[15] Will-implication is significant since 'it is impermissible to speak in someone's name ... unless that person ... is ... given equal consideration in making the regulations'.[16] Regulations made by the state must therefore be justified to their co-authors.[17]

Or, as Ronald Dworkin, expresses it:

> A political community that exercises dominion over its own citizens, and demands from them allegiance and obedience to its laws, must take up an impartial, objective attitude toward them all, and each of its citizens must vote, and its officials must enact laws and form governmental policies, with that responsibility in mind. Equal concern ... is the special and indispensable virtue of sovereigns.[18]

Under this conception of the social contract, equal respect and concern is thus an inherent part of the power of the state to tax. Hence, taxes should be allocated among taxpayers as equal members in a political community. Underlying this approach is the idea that the state has grown so distinct and meaningful that it is no longer feasible (since it is extremely hard to measure how much one benefits from the state) and, more importantly, it is no longer appropriate, to base people's tax obligation on the benefits they receive from the state, as they are not merely consumers of public goods, but rather equal members in a political community. The duty to pay taxes cannot thus be based on the benefits one gets from the state but rather on a sense of membership and a civic obligation.[19] Though the exact level of this obligation is debatable, a widespread belief seems to have been entrenched that taxpayers should pay their fair share (Mill's 'equal sacrifice'[20]) in financing the public fisc based on their being equal members of the political community.[21]

Under a closed economy, tax law seemed like an optimal domain for implementing the social contract between states and their constituents and, in particular, a locus for states to apply their norms of justice. Globalisation and the tax competition it entailed seem to have changed this reality, and challenge the common

---

[15] ibid.

[16] ibid.

[17] ibid.

[18] R Dworkin, *Sovereign Virtue: The Theory and Practice of Equality* (Harvard, Harvard University Press, 2000) 6.

[19] See Murphy and Nagel (n 4) 16 and 19, who note that '[m]any have thought that fairness in taxation requires that taxpayers contribute in proportion to the benefit they derive from government' and criticise the benefit principle as being 'inconsistent with every significant theory of social and economic justice'.

[20] The idea of equal sacrifice is attributed to JS Mill, *The Principles of Political Economy with Some of Their Applications to Social Philosophy* (Boston, CC Little & J Brown 1848) 354 ('all are thought to have done their part fairly when each has contributed according to his means, that is has made an equal sacrifice for the common object'). But see Murphy and Nagel (n 4) 20–25, opposing equal sacrifice, indeed vertical equity, on the basis that justice of tax burdens cannot be separated from the justice of the pattern of government expenditure.

[21] Discussion of what are the exact attributes subject to such equality in tax law, especially under mobility and fragmentation, is the subject of Section IV of this chapter.

beliefs underlying our tax system. The next section will explain how the decentralised structure of international taxation affects the interaction between sovereign states and their constituents. Specifically, it will argue that competition brings with it a unique hybrid that distinguishes between parts of the constituents who pay taxes according to their ability and others who pay according to their benefit. In other words, the current international tax regime brings back benefit taxes, but only *for some*.

III. States under Competition: Benefit Taxation *For Some*

Under globalisation, taxpayers are increasingly mobile. This enables them to choose from among alternative jurisdictions to relocate their places of residence, investments and business activities. States often encourage such mobility by offering certain privileges and incentives to desirable potential residents and investors. Residents-in-demand relocate to more appealing jurisdictions, as states lure away investors, as well as sought-after residents. With this intensified mobility, sovereign states have found themselves in a new position: once defined by their coercive powers and control over their citizenry and territory, they now often need to lure residents and investments away from competing sovereigns, as they fight to keep their own desirable taxpayers.

By providing taxpayers with a viable alternative, tax (and often other regulatory) competition between states has effectively changed the role of the state. The state can no longer necessarily be perceived as making compulsory taxation demands on its subjects in order to promote the collective goals of a given group of constituents but, rather, it increasingly solicits investments in order to facilitate increased economic activity and bids for prospective residents in an attempt to build the best possible team. Tax rates and rules as well as other legal rules have become part of the considerations for the globally mobile when weighing their residency and investment options. Hence, they have become, to a large extent, the currency of state competition.

Under competition, tax has increasingly become a price taxpayers are willing to pay for residing, investing and conducting their business in an attractive state as opposed to a civic obligation they should fulfil as members in a political community. Moreover, under competition, tax rates and public policies have become subject, to a considerable extent, to the rules of supply and demand of the market among states. In its extreme version, tax competition changes taxation from a mandatory regime to a regime that is basically elective or, to be more precise, elective *for some* – ie those that can and will move elsewhere for more favourable tax and public services. Thus, in conditions of tax competition, if and when they obey the rules of the competitive market of tax competition, states increasingly resemble

176   Tsilly Dagan

business actors that offer goods and services that will appeal to (and keep) investors and residents, including attractive taxing and spending deals.[22]

Under the rules of this market, policymakers target the most valuable taxpayers and those most likely to move for tax reasons. They pursue taxpayers that will bring with them the most benefits to the state, such as spillover of technological and managerial skills, investments and simply talent. In terms of tax policies, this means offering the public goods and services that are most attractive to such constituents and lowering taxes for the most mobile.

In short, competitive sovereignty focuses on assembling the most attractive 'team' of constituents by offering the most attractive public services deals at an attractive price. This is very different from sovereignty that seeks to provide the best possible public services to a set group of constituents who share common goals and projects, and that wields the power and legitimacy to accomplish this using coercive measures so as to prevent collective action problems and to promote its collective will.

A. Unbundled Sovereignty

Mobility of residents and their resources – and the accompanying marketisation of the government-constituent relationships it entails – are only the tip of the iceberg. No less significant and too often overlooked is the ability of (certain) individuals and businesses to unbundle and then reassemble packages of sovereign goods tailored to their specific needs. In the current market of states, individuals and businesses are able not only to shop for their jurisdiction of choice but also to buy 'a-la-carte' fractions of regimes of different state sovereignties. This fragmentation of sovereignty occurs in many areas of state regulation, but tax – formerly the quintessential tight, all-encompassing coercive legal regime – seems particularly vulnerable to such tailoring by skilled tax planners.

The conditions that can trigger the application (or non-application) of tax laws in different jurisdictions vary widely, which has produced a fragmented international tax landscape with a diversity of mix-and-match components: differing residency rules; a wide assortment of source rules; conflicting rules for allowing deductions; differing tax and withholding rates; and a vast number of tax treaties between different jurisdictions. Even under the increasingly tightening international tax regime, sophisticated and well-advised taxpayers can and do still assemble these diverse components into a tax regime that is favourable to them and does not necessarily overlap with any of the regimes governing their other affairs.

Tax planners employ a host of techniques to de facto opt-out of a tax jurisdiction, without actually moving their human clients' residency or, in extreme cases, even their activities. Tax planners often incorporate subsidiaries or trusts

---

[22] For the classic theory for such regulatory competition in local government, see C M Tiebout, 'A Pure Theory of Local Expenditures' (1956) 64 *The Journal of Political Economy* 416.

in tax havens to reduce the taxation of their income or defer it to when the profits are repatriated, if at all. They siphon off income through beneficial tax treaties to and from low-tax jurisdictions, thereby avoiding taxation at source, as well as a host of other techniques to reduce the total tax liability of individuals and their businesses.[23] As a result, tax-planning taxpayers can often simultaneously reside in one jurisdiction (and consume its publicly provided goods and services); incorporate in another (and thus enjoy its corporate governance); do business in a third (and use the local court and banking systems), invest in an industrial plant in a fourth (and reap the benefits of publicly provided services such as an educated workforce and a developed transportation system); register its IP (and/or move its R&D activity over there) in a fifth; and be subject to the tax rates, if any, of a sixth jurisdiction.

The reason such arrangements are possible is that different factors trigger the application of different duties and rights, including tax obligations. Some rights and duties apply to residents (and the factors that make one a resident also vary across jurisdictions), while others apply to property owners, consumers, investors, or citizens of certain states. Many of these rights and duties are related to a person's permanent place of residence, place of abode or key place of business. Others are tied to citizenship, to the location of one's property, to one's (even temporary) presence or to specific actions within the state's jurisdiction.[24]

In contrast to the classic mobility story, which tends to be constructed around a market of states offering take-it-or-leave-it package deals of legal rules, public services and taxes, the fragmentation perspective highlights the electivity and flexibility of these packages. Instead of looking at individuals' and businesses' ability to shift their choice of jurisdiction en bloc by moving their residency to a new jurisdiction, fragmentation stresses the leeway to mix-and-match legal jurisdictions. The fragmentation of the state-citizen relationship and the fact that individuals and businesses are not exclusively connected to a single state but, rather, interact simultaneously with many states on various planes, mean that this relationship cannot, and does not, necessarily bundle together all of the dimensions of the potential interaction between taxpayers and states. This reality impacts the strategies used by taxpayers as well as states, and for better or worse, alters the meanings of such interactions. Whereas absent this jurisdictional fragmentation, the optional strategies for residents are essentially either voice (using their political power to shape state policy) or exit (relocating to a jurisdiction that offers a more favourable regulatory package), they now have an option that will maximise their benefits: to *diversify* their state-related interactions. Thus, in this market for public goods, *some* people can choose not only between jurisdictions in their entirety but also among different combinations of fractions of these jurisdictions. This feature of fragmentation has a liberating effect *for some* constituents – who can now better

---

[23] For some more detail, see T Dagan, *International Tax Policy: Between Competition and Cooperation* (Cambridge, CUP, 2018) ch 2 and references there.

[24] T Dagan, 'The Global Market for Tax and Legal Rules' (2017) 148 *Florida Tax Review* 168–170.

178   Tsilly Dagan

tailor their interaction with the state to match their needs and preferences. But, at the same time, if successful, it could have a rather dramatic impact on what membership in a state means for taxpayers who have the opportunity to unbundle states' sovereignty as well as what such membership means for those with limited such capacity.

States face hard choices in this reality of electivity under fragmentation. Fragmented competition occurs in multiple markets simultaneously. Hence, trade-offs between various aspects of their public services are much harder to pull off. In other words, a state's advantageous geographical location, excellent school system, or strong legal tradition will not necessarily compensate for a high corporate tax rate or strict deduction rules, as residents and businesses can often simply choose to opt out of the less desirable restrictions. Sadly, fragmentation, and the creative tax planning it facilitates, also allows taxpayers to free ride some of the public goods which states offer. While states can vow to collect taxes and make significant efforts in this direction, enforcement is a challenge. Where a state cannot collect the taxes from individuals and businesses that find ways to avoid them by tax planning, the fact of the matter is that states cannot ensure the participation of all taxpayers in the financing of public goods and services.

To be sure, states have come up with a variety of mechanisms in order to apply and enforce their rules on 'their' residents: a worldwide tax base; CFC rules for the corporations owned by their residents; and restrictive regimes for overseas trusts. States vigorously try to fight (and increasingly succeed in fighting) tax evasion and tax planning, by using GAAR rules, or by cooperating with other states.[25] But it seems as if we are still quite far from a state where rich and mobile taxpayers actually pay taxes at rates that are similar to those with less opportunity to opt out of the system.

B. Benefit Taxes *for Some*

Because of competitive pressure and the considerable difficulty for states to enforce their rules on mobile taxpayers, they are pressured to offer mobile constituents – or those with better planning opportunities – with either significant tax benefits or increased leeway in planning their world-wide tax operations. The rational choice for a state in a competitive market is a regime that is a hybrid between ability to pay and benefit taxation. *For some* taxpayers – the ones with lower ability or a smaller inclination to move – coercive world-wide taxation of their income would

---

[25] See eg European Commission, 'Council Directive 2011/16/EU on Administrative Cooperation in the Field of Taxation and Repealing Directive 77/799/EEC', 9; OECD, *Action Plan on Base Erosion and Profit Shifting* (Paris, OECD Publishing, 2013) 15, available at https://doi.org/10.1787/9789264202719-en (accessed 7 January 2020); OECD, *CRS by jurisdiction*, available at https://www.oecd.org/tax/automatic-exchange/crs-implementation-and-assistance/crs-by-jurisdiction/ (accessed 7 January 2020); for a description of some of the recent cooperative accords see also Dagan, *International Tax Policy* (n 23) ch 5.

make sense. Yet for others – those with available alternatives – a regime which is more lenient, at times even elective, is the more beneficial option in terms of tax revenues.[26] In other words, tax competition brings back benefits taxes in a unique version: benefit taxes *for some*.[27]

In more detail: by adjusting their policies to match them with the varying degrees of elasticity among their constituents, states could increase the tax revenues they collect. Assuming the marginal cost of providing much of the public services to such mobile taxpayers is zero, or close to zero, elasticity-based taxation could result in net gain for the state. Any taxes thus collected would be used to serve the entire population– not only the mobile residents who will pay lower taxes would benefit, but also immobile constituents (as whatever taxes collected will increase the collective revenues). Where, on the other hand, elasticity is low – as in the case of immobile taxpayers – there is no reason for the state not to collect higher taxes, as long as the incentive of taxpayers to work is intact. The bottom line is that in order to maximise the welfare pie, tax should be imposed in inverse relation to how elastic taxpayers are.[28] This means that the most inelastic (ie immobile taxpayers and the ones unable to opt out) should pay the highest (coercive) taxes, while the ones with the greatest elasticity should get a more lenient treatment.

When viewed from a strictly utilitarian perspective the choice of a flexible regime – adjusting rates and rules to the elasticity of taxpayers' choices in order to attract as much revenues and benefits as possible – may seem like an almost inevitable move by states. But is it? Is the state free to choose among these strategies? Or are there any limitations on the state when considering these options? The rest of this chapter will focus on justice and ask whether providing elastic taxpayers with tax benefits is justified.

IV. Benefit Taxes *For Some*: Between Two Ideals of the State

Under taxpayers' electivity (or lack thereof) among jurisdictions, the question arises whether catering to their electivity, granting them privileges in order to

---

[26] Some taxpayers are sometimes lured into countries which offer them residency combined with attractive tax deals. Interestingly, though, taxpayers may not have to actually relocate in order to attain better tax treatment. Some of them get preferable treatment by tax planning, eg by operating via offshore corporations and trusts.

[27] While tax benefits to certain groups of residents are available at the domestic level as well, global competition among states adds a considerable dimension to the preferable treatment of some taxpayers – stressing mobility and cross-border planning ability.

[28] True, if the mobile are also the rich (which is often the case) inequality between mobile and immobile constituents would likely increase. However, if – faced with increased taxation – the mobile leave, the result will be levelling down both the gaps between remaining (less mobile) constituents, along with a reduction in the national welfare pie.

180   *Tsilly Dagan*

attract (or keep) them, is justified under the social contract. The answer to this question depends on the rationale for the social contract in each state.[29] Does the social contract follow a utilitarian ideal of maximising our collective interests (the market-inspired ideal)? Or is it about creating a community of equals (the membership ideal)?

In a different world this choice might have been one of domestic political processes within states – free to shape their unique contracts, allowing constituents that prefer alternative arrangements to opt for them in a different jurisdiction. Under competition, however – and especially the imperfect competition among jurisdictions we currently observe – we are presented with a significant dilemma. Under current competition only *some* residents have a real choice of opting for a different jurisdiction. Others have no real alternative as (foreign) states are under no obligation to welcome newcomers and, thus, social contracts in their countries of origin are non-negotiable for them. In other words, under competition, only certain people have a choice: those who are both willing to exit and who are most attractive in the eyes of other states.

When choice is limited *for some* taxpayers, both the utilitarian ideal and the membership ideal raise considerable challenges. The utilitarian ideal caters to the needs of the mobile segments of society, supports their independence and maximises the national welfare pie. Such a model, however, may undermine equal respect and concern for the immobile factors of society, that is, the people that have no or lesser choice among jurisdictions. The membership-based ideal, on the other hand, supports equal respect and concern for immobile taxpayers, but at a cost to collective welfare, *and* it forces mobile taxpayers to make a binary choice between staying and leaving – thus undermining their self-determination and disrespecting their choice of a life plan that is not necessarily tied to a single jurisdiction.

A. Utilitarian Ideal of the State

If our social contract is about the joint promotion of the combined self-interests of all of the state's constituents, and assuming we focus on material resources, the fact that *some* taxpayers (the mobile and fragmented, in our case) pay less taxes, should not bother us, as long as the state's welfare pie grows, and the slice each of us gets is no smaller than under the alternative (ie if we tried to impose higher taxes on the mobile). Surely, it would not have been in our best interest to attempt to tax the mobile if the result would have been their opting out of the state's system which would result in a net loss.

---

[29] Whether or not there are justice considerations that (should) limit the ability of the state to choose between a 'thin' social contract, under which the state merely promotes the collective interests of its constituents, or a 'thick' social contract, which focuses on equal respect and concern, depends on the alternatives available for the constituents. Assuming that there is a variety of other states of all shapes and kinds and that people are, in practice, free to choose among them, I believe states should be free to choose among such alternatives.

As explained above, under the utilitarian ideal, states under competition must offer attractive 'deals' for mobile taxpayers. Just like firms on the market, the 'price' they charge for their public goods and services must be competitive and thus subject to the elasticities of the supply and demand curves of the market. Mobile taxpayers, and taxpayers that prefer to diversify their membership and split their lives between a number of jurisdictions may benefit from such policies, as such policies enable them to live their lives without fully committing to (and paying the taxes of) a single jurisdiction. If, on the other hand, their country of residence demands that they pay full taxes (and assuming such a demand is enforceable), they would be forced to either obey or exit. This welfare-maximising policy (ie calibrating taxes to such elasticities), while supporting the independence of taxpayers in high demand, undermines equality. Not only does it limit the ability of the state to redistribute income (and perhaps even increase economic gaps),[30] it also – as explained below – undermines equal respect and concern.

B. An Equality-based Ideal of the State

If the basis for our entrusting the state with our collective power is not only the need to coerce us to cooperate in the promotion of our own self-interests, but also to implicate our will as co-authors, then the limitation it (should) impose on our tax system is more stringent. In speaking on our behalf, the state has a duty not only to serve our material interests but also to treat us all with equal respect and concern. The tax system has an important role in shaping our political communities. Under this ideal of the state it has a role in supporting a community of equals. Under global competition, in particular, it also has a role in determining who belongs to us and what rights and duties such inclusion may involve.

C. The Market-based Ideal Undermines Equality

The global demand for certain people is a result of their willingness to exit (or their ability to fragment their interaction with the state) and their use value in the eyes of competing jurisdictions (ie how attractive they are for other jurisdictions). These features are often based on taxpayers' age, their talents, their family status and fortune, even their language and vocational skills. It is thus often attributes that are beyond individuals' control (or choices that are a crucial part of their identity) that make them more or less attractive for other jurisdictions – and thus enable them (and not others who lack such options) to choose among alternative jurisdictions.

Should these features be the basis for favouring them (or discriminating against others) if we are to equally respect all constituents for tax purposes? Favouring the

---

[30] If the rich are also the ones most mobile. See Dagan, *International Tax Policy* (n 23) 36–37.

182 Tsilly Dagan

ones that can opt out, I believe, treats the others unequally. If the state is to build a political community of equals, a person's option value – her 'net worth' elsewhere – cannot be a reason for her paying lower rates of taxation. If taxes are part of our civic duties, if they are – like voting – a sign of our membership in an egalitarian community of equals, we can certainly decide to exit, but we should not be allowed to base our share of contributing to the country's fisc on how credible our threat of exit is.

Both constituents' readiness to opt out and their use value are criteria, the consideration of which in the tax context challenge justice (in the sense of equal respect and concern). Favouring the mobile – like favouring the tall, or the handsome or the smart – undermines equality based on attributes that the immobile are simply unlucky to have. The fact that one is luckier than others to have options to move elsewhere, or to shift their income to another jurisdiction, should not be taken into account if we were to treat all of our constituents with equal respect and concern for who they are.[31] If mobility provides its holders with privileges that others do not enjoy it becomes the new status. The consideration of attributes that subject some of us to heavier duties than others based on attributes that are beyond their control undermines, I believe, our social contract understood as equal respect and concern.

Finally, operating under the threat of exit – keeping our relationships with our co-citizens on a tentative basis – allows mobile taxpayers to argue or even imply that they will stay if the price were right but threaten to leave if it were not, and even more so – allows them to contribute less to the public fisc *because* they have other options available elsewhere (which other taxpayers don't necessary enjoy). This, I believe, does not treat immobile constituents with equal concern and respect. Instead, it presents them with an ultimatum: a take-it-or-leave-it deal. Such an ultimatum and equal respect and concern are contradictory in terms. As Elizabeth Anderson, in her famous critique of the nature of equality argues '[democratic] equality … regards two people as equal when each accepts the obligation to justify their actions by principles acceptable to the other, and in which they take mutual consultation, reciprocation, and recognition for granted'.[32] Ultimatums inherently disrespect this ideal.

When equality is undermined, the justification of the state in imposing its coercive power declines with it. Under the social contract we agree to endorse the state with our collective power only because we trust it to treat us equally. Treating some of us better than others, simply because of attributes they were lucky enough to have – their threat power, in particular – is simply not under the mandate of

---

[31] See eg K Lippert-Rasmussen, 'Justice and Bad Luck' in *The Stanford Encyclopedia of Philosophy*, Summer 2018 Edition, available at https://plato.stanford.edu/archives/sum2018/entries/justice-bad-luck/ (accessed 7 January 2020).

[32] E Anderson, 'What Is the Point of Equality?' (1999) 109(2) *Ethics* 297, 303.

Re-Imagining Tax Justice in a Globalised World 183

the state. And using market power as a criterion for our civic duties challenges the social contract on which state coercion (at least today) is based.[33]

D. Why Ignoring Elasticity Also Undermines Equality

On the other hand, as explained above, mobility and fragmentation are not only a result of how attractive one is in other jurisdictions, it is also a result of one's personal desires, dreams, unique features and life plans. Think, for example, of a renowned scientist or a famed athlete who seeks an opportunity to pursue her professional career under the auspices of the world's leading research institute or finest league. Subjecting them to the full scope of taxation at their country of origin pushes them to choose between their old allegiances and new ones. Despite the fact that subjecting mobile taxpayers to residence-based taxation might disrespect their choices to be citizens of the world, and their desire not to commit to a single jurisdiction, it does not undermine state power in ways similar to the alternative (of taxing in inverse relation to one's elasticities). The reason is that with elasticity comes the (real) choice of exit. Exit, although different than voice, still allows mobile individuals to effectively resist the coercive power of the state by emigrating. This, I believe is a lesser infringement on their autonomy and hence on the legitimacy of the coercive power of the state.

And yet, the question remains whether exit is good enough an answer in order to maintain equal concern and respect. After all, shouldn't mobile residents too have a claim to stay part of their country of residence *and* be able to live a cosmopolitan-style life? Hence, shouldn't they be able to argue that they would like to stay *and* have the state respect their wish to split their allegiances among different jurisdictions, instead of pushing them to leave (or stay)? I believe the answer to this claim by mobile taxpayers is both yes and no. Taxpayers' split allegiance should be respected in order to allow them to run their lives as they wish, without pressuring them to leave. But such taxpayers should *not* be allowed to pay only for the public services that they actually consume. Hence, ability to pay residence-based taxation should be sustained, in order to protect an equality-based social contract. At the same time, such taxpayers should be allowed to credit any foreign taxes they pay (so as not to impose double taxation on those wishing to split their lives between jurisdictions). This logic, alleviating some of the excess burden imposed on mobile taxpayers without allowing them to pay only for the public services they actually consume, may also demand a more nuanced understanding of residency

---

[33] If we were to think of a different structure of the international order – if, for example, we could set states under a classic Tiebout model, with unlimited mobility, and opportunities for individuals to join and establish political communities freely and without limitations – we could, theoretically think of alternative communities of equals who decide, for example, to limit public goods and services (and the need for coercive power) to a bare minimum. This, obviously, is currently utopian (due to limited mobility of some) if at all desirable.

184   *Tsilly Dagan*

where individuals are entitled to split their taxes between various jurisdictions. This could be achieved, perhaps, by adopting a 'number of days' or other split of residency among various jurisdictions,[34] or by allowing taxpayers to split their entire world-wide income tax base between different states according to their level of allegiance.[35]

But even if policies for the prevention of double taxation succeed in ameliorating the equality concern of the mobile, without undermining the equality of the immobile, they still don't eliminate tax competition and with it the incentive which high overall taxes provide for mobile residents to exit.

E. The Sovereign's Tax Dilemma

This is the crux of the sovereign's dilemma: states under competition must decide whether to consider their taxpayers' mobility in determining their tax liability. If they choose to ignore the varying elasticities of their constituents (ie subject all of their constituents to similar rules and rates of taxation, irrespective of how elastic their choices of residence are), they may lose the ones that are most mobile and wealthy. If, on the other hand, they choose to give weight to taxpayers' varying elasticities – they risk undermining equal respect and concern for the immobile ones. Moreover, not only considering mobility, but also allowing fragmentation may undermine equal respect and concern for the immobile. Ignoring mobility and curtailing fragmentation may provide the immobile with equal respect and concern, but disrespect the mobile. Credits for foreign taxes may resolve some of the issues, and yet, residence-based taxation with or without a credit comes at a cost to the collective welfare pie, by pushing taxpayers subject to increased taxes to leave.

The significance of this choice for state governance in tax matters cannot be overstated: it juxtaposes two very different ideal types of state-taxpayers' relationships: a market-inspired version of the state ('exit-based state') and a community

---

[34] Thus, a resident splitting her life between country A (10% tax, where she spends 100 days each year) and country B (40% tax, where she spends the rest of the year) and producing income in country C (15% tax), should pay taxes on her entire ability to countries A and B (at a 100:265 ratio) and get a credit for the 15% country C taxes.

[35] This scheme echoes Seligman's famous contribution in the 1923 league of nations report. Seligman was part of a panel of four tax experts that were nominated to study the issue of double taxation. The experts weighed the relative strengths of the various allegiances – political ties, temporary residency, permanent residency, location of wealth – and concluded what has become widely accepted ever since: that a state is justified in taxing income where the taxpayer owes it a certain degree of economic allegiance. Similarly to the case described in this chapter, the approach expressed in the experts' report recognised the possibility that taxpayers may have multiple allegiances. Hence, the report's recommendations are premised on the assumption that allegiances can be shared among states as well as ranked or proportioned. For a review of the report's conclusion and a critical analysis, see Dagan, *International Tax Policy* (n 23) 44–45.

of equals ('loyalty-based state'). Under the first, states surrender to the rules of the market, and operate more like a profit maximising organisation, which optimises the tax revenues (and other benefits) they can collect from current and potential residents. To do that they must give considerable weight to the elasticities of taxpayers' choice of jurisdiction. The result is that exit power prevails over voice and loyalty. Under the second, the state ignores such elasticities in the name of equal respect and concern and reinforces a loyalty-based taxation where one's belongingness to the state dominates her taxation, pushing her to make binary choices between staying of leaving.

In between these two extremes – strict exit and strict loyalty – lies the third component in Albert Hirschman's prescription formulation: Voice.[36] Allowing *all* constituents to have a say in the political negotiations of a tax system that provides them with a welfare system that avoids leaving *some* people behind and allows them freedom to pursue their life plans within the state and beyond it. This, of course, is the great challenge for states under the current international tax regime: how to preserve the benefits of globalisation and avoid its harms without incurring the faults and injustices of the market on the one hand and the constraints of restrictive loyalty on the other. Whether this justice-based taxation can be achieved is left unanswered.

V. Conclusion

Competition has dramatically undermined the state's centralised monopolisation of the power of taxation and thus altered the relationships of states with their constituents. Mobility, the relocation options it opened up, and the opportunities for fragmentation of one's attributes and activities have allowed *some* taxpayers to opt for lower taxes. This has put states in a serious dilemma: how should states deal with these options? The answer, I have argued, involves meaningful choices: between playing by the rules of the market for states – focusing on maximising collective welfare on the one hand *and* practicing equal concern and respect by subjecting mobile and immobile taxpayers alike to tax rules that ignore elasticities. Both options have their costs. The first undermines equality. The second undermines collective welfare, and (potentially) the autonomy of *some* taxpayers to choose to split their lives among various jurisdictions. Whether a system that achieves a reasonable compromise of both can be achieved is left unanswered.

---

[36] AO Hirschman, *Exit, Voice, and Loyalty: Responses to Decline in Firms, Organizations, and States* (Harvard, Harvard University Press, 1970).

11

Between Legitimacy and Justice in International Tax Policy

IVAN OZAI

This chapter compares and contrasts two accounts of normative evaluation of the present international tax regime. One builds on the tradition of international political legitimacy and points to the lack of inclusivity of less powerful countries in the international tax policy decision-making process. The other builds on the tradition of international distributive justice and points to the imbalance of taxing rights impacting less affluent countries. This chapter suggests that these two normative dimensions are frequently confounded in discussions of international tax policy, leading to what can be called the Legitimacy-Justice Fallacy.

I. Introduction

The international tax regime has been increasingly criticised over the years from varied perspectives, from its complexity and susceptibility to exploitation by multinationals' tax avoidance schemes, to its inability to tackle the increasingly digitised economy.

This chapter suggests that many of the common criticisms over the international tax regime can be grouped into two distinct narratives that reflect a division in how justice is perceived and discussed in the political philosophy literature. One set of concerns centres around distributive justice, which generally relates to how burdens and benefits should be distributed throughout society. The other normative dimension focuses primarily on democratic legitimacy and asks the conditions for the legitimate exercise of political power.

This chapter investigates how matters of legitimacy and distributive justice relate to one another. Both issues are somewhat connected since political legitimacy should comprise to some extent the set of conditions for a political institution to effect a just distribution of burdens and benefits.[1] However, each of

---

[1] K Dowding, 'Are Democratic and Just Institutions the Same?' in K Dowding, RE Goodin and C Pateman (eds), *Justice and Democracy: Essays for Brian Barry* (Cambridge, CUP, 2004) 25.

188   *Ivan Ozai*

these dimensions builds on distinct normative foundations and entails different requirements. Modest attention has so far been given to the relationship between these two normative realms in the political philosophy literature,[2] and a similar gap exists in the international tax scholarship.[3]

This chapter argues that the failure to understand the different aspects of these two dimensions of justice has allowed for what can be called the Legitimacy-Justice Fallacy, that is, seeking to either solve legitimacy problems by addressing distributive justice concerns or solve distributive problems by addressing legitimacy concerns. International institutions such as the Organisation for Economic Co-operation and Development (OECD) and the European Union (EU) seem to have historically relied on this fallacy either to impose allegedly just standards on non-member countries without legitimate decision-making procedures or, as seen more recently, to eschew distributive justice concerns by suggesting that an inclusive procedure should suffice in delivering just outcomes, as if legitimacy and justice were interchangeable from a normative standpoint.

II. Legitimacy Problems in the International Tax Regime

The international tax regime poses some significant legitimacy problems, particularly to developing countries. First, international tax policy today is primarily driven by the OECD, and the policy-making process significantly excludes the participation of non-OECD countries. Although the OECD has sought to include non-member countries in some of the tax policy discussions,[4] the reasons

---

[2] See S Thompson, 'On the Circularity of Democratic Justice' (2009) 35(9) *Philosophy and Social Criticism* 1079, 1080.

[3] The distinction addressed in this chapter between *justice* and *legitimacy* is not to be confounded with the distinction between *input* (process) and *output* (outcome) legitimacy. Similar to an assessment based on justice, output legitimacy is concerned about outcomes of institutional processes. However, output legitimacy is still about legitimacy in the sense that it requires outcomes of institutional processes to be aligned with stakeholders' interests. It is still a democratic question of how well institutions connect with interests. In other words, conditions for legitimacy focus either on including individuals' inputs in the process (input legitimacy) or achieving results that realise those same interests (output legitimacy). On the other hand, distributive justice follows a different philosophical tradition and, despite also focusing on outcomes, speaks to how benefits and burdens can be fairly distributed throughout society. Whereas outcome legitimacy builds on the democratic tradition and speaks to the accountability of a given institution to stakeholders, distributive justice consists of a moral evaluation of a given distribution rather than on whether such a distribution aligns with stakeholders' interests. For a more comprehensive discussion on the legitimacy-justice distinction, see Dowding, Goodin and Pateman (eds) (n 1).

[4] OECD, *OECD/G20 Inclusive Framework on BEPS: Progress Report July 2017-June 2018* (Paris, OECD, 2018) 6. Along with the group of 46 countries (OECD and G20 members), 83 jurisdictions have joined the Inclusive Framework, amounting to a total of 129 participating jurisdictions. See OECD, *Members of the Inclusive Framework on BEPS*, available at www.oecd.org/ctp/beps/inclusive-framework-on-beps-composition.pdf (accessed 5 April 2019).

seem to have less to do with increasing their actual participation in setting the rules than with securing their engagement and fostering a public perception of inclusiveness.[5] Participation of developing countries in international tax policy is mostly circumscribed to the endorsement stage, with virtually no participation in idea conception and negotiation phases.[6]

A second legitimacy problem arises from path dependence.[7] Even if formal equality were achieved at some point through greater participation, many rules and concepts have already been established in favour of developed countries and some entrenched rules may be difficult to change. Throughout decades of tax policy-making process, stakeholders who have become involved at an early stage tend to enjoy greater influence over international tax policy due to the lock-in effect and the costs associated with changing the existing standards and the ongoing process. This suggests the existing agenda, concepts and standards of the international tax regime not only tend to favour more powerful countries but are also less likely to change to a more balanced division with less powerful countries even if participation over tax policymaking were equalised.[8] Having entered the discussion as latecomers, developing countries also have reduced experience and resources to keep pace with developed countries.[9]

III. Justice Problems in the International Tax Regime

From a distributive perspective, a significant problem facing developing countries is that the present allocation of taxing rights among countries significantly favours richer nations. The international tax regime consists of a network of bilateral tax treaties – most to some extent based on the OECD Model Tax Convention – that determine how taxing rights are divided between home (residence) and host

---

[5] See M Lennard, 'Base Erosion and Profit Shifting and Developing Country Tax Administrations' (2016) 44(10) *Intertax* 740, 745; IJM Valderrama, 'The EU Standard of Good Governance in Tax Matters for Third (Non-EU) Countries' (2019) 47(5) *Intertax* 454, 461.

[6] See IJM Valderrama, 'Legitimacy and the Making of International Tax Law: The Challenges of Multilateralism' (2015) 7(3) *World Tax Journal* 343; A Christians, 'Taxation in a Time of Crisis: Policy Leadership from the OECD to the G20' (2010) 5(1) *Northwestern Journal of Law and Social Policy* 19.

[7] Path dependence refers to the causal relevance of preceding stages in a temporal chain of events. It suggests that once institutions have started down a track, the costs of reversal become significantly high due to the entrenchments of certain institutional arrangements. See P Pierson, 'Increasing Returns, Path Dependence, and the Study of Politics' (2000) 94(2) *The American Political Science Review* 251, 252.

[8] See T Dagan, *International Tax Policy: Between Competition and Cooperation* (Cambridge, CUP, 2018) 173–74: 'In other words, in designing the treaty mechanism to favor countries of residence in the allocation of tax revenues, the network initiators were able to extract monopolistic rents at the expense of late-coming developing (host) countries.' See also R Lall, 'Timing as a Source of Regulatory Influence: A Technical Elite Network Analysis of Global Finance' (2015) 9 *Regulation and Governance* 125 (pointing out the importance of first-mover position in setting the agenda in global rulemaking, especially in influencing distributional outcomes by ensuring that proposals made by first movers are increasingly difficult to change at later stages of rulemaking).

[9] I Burgers and I Mosquera, 'Corporate Taxation and BEPS: A Fair Slice for Developing Countries?' (2017) 1 *Erasmus Law Review* 29, 38.

190   *Ivan Ozai*

(source) countries in cross-border transactions. Some argue that they actually reallocate taxing rights from source (developing) to residence (developed) countries, since in the absence of such treaties, source countries would first enjoy taxing rights over income, leaving the residence country to double tax or provide relief for the source country tax.[10]

The OECD tax treaty model came to dominate the international tax arena, and the costs of not being part of the network gradually increased for late-coming developing countries. The result is that the tax treaty regime has allowed developed countries to benefit from a model so widespread that it is unlikely to change.[11] Although a competing network may provide a fairer distribution of tax revenues to developing countries, many countries might be unwilling to join for fears of decrease in cross-border investment due to the path dependence phenomenon.[12]

More fundamentally, the tax treaty network provides the legal infrastructure for the principles and concepts that shape the international tax regime today, so that the overall structure of international tax law is based on standards, principles and methods that lead to an inequitable distribution of taxing rights between developing and developed countries.

It is not the purpose of this chapter to engage in the global justice debate.[13] However, by taking a practice-dependent approach rather than adopting a cosmopolitan conception of global justice,[14] it embraces an intermediary position on global justice which suggests that international cooperation requires minimal mutual respect between political communities, which might not imply full global distributive justice but demands the absence of grave injustices.[15] The minimum base for international cooperation involves respect for human rights worldwide, prevention of international exploitation of weaker political communities, and opportunities for political self-determination.[16] Cooperation thus requires that institutions do not worsen the situation of the least advantaged, and the strength of the duty to reduce poverty and inequality is positively related to the capabilities of the different countries.[17]

---

[10] K Brooks and R Krever, 'The Troubling Role of Tax Treaties' in GMM Michielse and V Thuronyi, *Tax Design Issues Worldwide* (Kluwer Law International, Alphen aan den Rijn, 2015) 159, 166.

[11] See Dagan (n 8).

[12] See Pierson (n 7).

[13] For a brief summary, see S Scheffler, 'The Idea of Global Justice: A Progress Report' (2014) 20 *The Harvard Review of Philosophy* 17. For a more comprehensive account, see G Brock (ed), *Cosmopolitanism versus Non-Cosmopolitanism: Critiques, Defenses, Reconceptualizations* (Oxford, OUP, 2013).

[14] For the distinction between the cosmopolitan perspective and institutional theory, see M Blake, 'Global Distributive Justice: Why Political Philosophy Needs Political Science' (2012) 15 *Annual Review of Political Science* 121, 128–29 (pointing out that cosmopolitanism argues that a concern with relative distributive justice is always important no matter what institutions exist, whereas an institutional approach suggests that a concern with relative distributive justice matters for particular and contingent reasons).

[15] D Miller, 'Against Global Egalitarianism' (2005) 9 *The Journal of Ethics* 55, 77–78.

[16] ibid 78.

[17] See J Mandle, *Global Justice* (Cambridge, UK, Polity Press, 2006) 102 (arguing that this duty of justice is stronger among wealthy states and those that played a historical role in making the social order unjust such as through colonialism).

IV. Does Justice Dismiss Legitimacy Claims?

Discussions on global distributive justice frequently leave aside any consideration of the institutions required to deliver the form of justice they support.[18] Yet, most would arguably agree that democratic values are an important requirement of justice and would hardly favour autocracy even if it may lead to a better outcome on the long run.[19] One could ask whether a normative evaluation of the international tax regime can preclude matters of legitimacy when it has passed the test for distributive justice. More concretely, suppose we determine that some normative standards in international tax policy are just, can we apply them to all stakeholders even if they are not derived from democratic institutions and through democratic procedures? Can distributive justice replace democratic legitimacy as a measure for normative evaluation?

Substantive discussions on distributive justice are effective when determining general principles of justice, but they can be problematic when translating these principles into concrete solutions for real-world problems. The problem with a substantive approach that overlooks normative conditions for legitimacy is that it is insensitive to context and fails to appreciate that institutional implementation requires political judgment.[20] Even if we are able to determine guiding principles for international taxation based on specific conceptions of justice, we still need to discuss how they should apply and be implemented. And given the considerable disagreements on what justice entails, participation in the decision-making process of those affected by policy decisions is necessary to avoid arbitrariness and favouritism. There are several potential solutions for international tax problems which can be justified by a standard of justice. Determining which of these justifiable solutions should be adopted requires a broader discussion through democratic procedures.[21]

One example of what this could lead to is unilateral sanctions imposed on countries that do not follow standards based on unilateral understandings of what international tax justice entails. A recent case is the EU list of non-cooperative tax

---

[18] K Dowding, RE Goodin and C Pateman, 'Between Justice and Democracy' in Dowding, Goodin and Pateman (eds) (n 1) 1, 5.

[19] For a different position, see RJ Arneson, 'Democracy Is Not Intrinsically Just' in Dowding, Goodin and Pateman (eds) (n 1) 40 (arguing that the value of democracy is dependent on its ability to produce justice according to an independent standard of assessment and that the choice between autocracy and democracy should be determined based on which delivers morally superior results).

[20] As Nancy Fraser points out, adopting a 'mindset of latter-day philosopher kings' implies ignoring the political aspect of justice and the plurality of reasonable perspectives on how best to interpret the requirements of justice. See N Fraser, 'Social Justice in the Age of Identity Politics: Redistribution, Recognition, and Participation' in N Fraser and A Honneth, *Redistribution or Recognition?: A Political-Philosophical Exchange* (London, Verso, 2003) 7, 71. For a similar position in international tax policy, see TD Magalhães, 'What Is Really Wrong with Global Tax Governance and How to Properly Fix It' (2018) 10(4) *World Tax Journal* 499.

[21] See A Buchanan and RO Keohane, 'The Legitimacy of Global Governance Institutions' (2006) 20(4) *Ethics and International Affairs* 405, n 10 (arguing that legitimacy provides a 'focal point' that helps stakeholders select one equilibrium solution among others).

jurisdictions,[22] which aims to address tax competition and includes countries that do not follow specific standards relating to tax competition.[23] The list is not limited to a 'naming and shaming' approach but is expected to result in the application of defensive measures if the listed jurisdiction does not make the changes requested by the EU.[24] The EU's initiative was based on an idea of 'fair taxation'[25] and the criteria for determining the standards for the list did not include the participation of non-EU member countries. Based on a unilateral conception of distributive justice, the initiative raises problems relating to normative legitimacy.[26]

V. Does Legitimacy Dismiss Justice Claims?

From the opposite perspective, one may ask whether we need to discuss distributive justice principles at all, or whether we should leave justice to be determined by the outcomes of democratic procedures. Some philosophers focusing on conditions for fair decision-making procedures forswear detailed accounts of justice and assume that stakeholders should themselves decide what justice is.[27] They argue that since any conception of justice can be disputed and politicised, concerns about global justice should give rise to a quest to democratise systems of global governance.[28]

This section will challenge that assumption in the context of international tax policy and argue that legitimacy and justice are not interchangeable as normative requirements. It is true that principles of justice cannot be imposed without proper democratically legitimate procedures. That said, democratic institutions do not always lead to just outcomes, and an in-depth discussion on distributive justice is also necessary to ensure fairness in international tax policy.

---

[22] The original list and subsequent adjustments are available at: ec.europa.eu/taxation_customs/tax-common-eu-list_en (accessed 8 January 2020).

[23] EC, *Council Conclusions on the criteria for and process leading to the establishment of the EU list of non-cooperative jurisdictions for tax purposes* [2016] OJ C 461/02.

[24] ibid.

[25] EC, *Council Conclusions on the EU list of non-cooperative jurisdictions for tax purposes* [2017] OJ C 438/04.

[26] The list has sparked criticism for lack of both transparency and objective criteria as it omits EU Member States as well as some countries that are commonly viewed as tax havens. See eg D Boffey, 'EU Blacklist Names 17 Tax Havens and Puts Caymans and Jersey on Notice', *The Guardian* (5 December 2017), available at www.theguardian.com (accessed 8 January 2020); Francesco Guarascio, 'EU Adopts Tax Haven Blacklist, British Territories Spared', *Reuters* (5 December 2017), available at www.reuters.com (accessed 8 January 2020). See also A Christians, 'Sovereignty, Taxation and Social Contract' (2009) 18(1) *Minnesota Journal of International Law* 99, 101 (observing that the naming and shaming in harmful tax competition is problematic and represents the decision of taxing rights of sovereign nations by a relatively small and elite group of individuals). For general criticism of the practice of blacklisting, particularly by supranational institutions, see LL Carvalho, 'The Ills of Blacklisting for International Taxation' (20 September 2018), available at kluwertaxblog.com/2018/09/20/ills-blacklisting-international-taxation (accessed 8 January 2020).

[27] Thompson (n 2).

[28] See eg H Patomäki, 'Global Justice: A Democratic Perspective' (2006) 3(2) *Globalizations* 99. A similar argument is advanced in the international tax literature in Magalhães (n 20), fn 32: 'Philosophers,

A. The Gap between Political Equality and Substantive Equity

As noted earlier, the OECD introduced in 2016 the BEPS Inclusive Framework to address legitimacy concerns.[29] The framework aims to allow non-OECD jurisdictions to participate on an 'equal footing' in developing standards, review, and monitor the implementation of the Base Erosion and Profit Shifting (BEPS) project, which is a comprehensive action plan put forward by the OECD to address tax avoidance and tax competition through a coordinated and collaboratively approach.[30]

The Inclusive Framework has been criticised because it limits participation of non-OECD and non-G20 jurisdictions to reviewing and monitoring the implementation of standards that were in great part already determined through the development of the BEPS project.[31]

However, the main problem with improving participation of developing countries in those terms is determining what 'equal footing' means. The BEPS Inclusive Framework seems to build on what is called a pure proceduralist conception of democratic legitimacy. The pure proceduralist account takes political equality as the paramount egalitarian value and confines democracy to the idea of equality in the decision-making process, dismissing any consideration of its outcomes,[32] as opposed to instrumentalist defences of democracy which suggest that democratic legitimacy requires that decision-making procedures lead to just outcomes or to the morally best among the alternative policies.[33]

The main problem with the pure proceduralist view of democracy is that it neglects that giving all stakeholders an equal opportunity to express their preferences does not always lead to a fair aggregation of these preferences, as the problem of entrenched minorities often reveals.[34] In that respect, the instrumentalist view does not reject the importance of democratic procedures but submits that the consequences of its implementation should also determine its justifiability.[35]

One may suggest that developing countries constitute the great majority of the global community, and therefore giving them an equal say in the decision-making

---

like the ones discussed below ... behave as experts when they put disagreement and political deliberation aside and perform the monological role of enlightened philosopher kings, offering her (or, more usually, his) own view of what justice consists in, what rights we have, what fair terms of social co-operation would be, and what all of this is based on.'

[29] OECD, *BEPS Progress Report* (n 4) 6.

[30] See OECD, *Addressing Base Erosion and Profit Shifting* (Paris, OECD, 2013).

[31] See, e.g., IJM Valderrama (n 6) 350.

[32] For a firm defence of the proceduralist account of normative legitimacy, see F Peter, 'Democratic Legitimacy and Proceduralist Social Epistemology' (2007) 6(3) *Politics, Philosophy and Economics* 329.

[33] See eg RJ Arneson, 'Defending the Purely Instrumental Account of Democratic Legitimacy' (2003) 11(1) *Journal of Political Philosophy* 122; Steven Wall, 'Democracy and Equality' (2007) 57(228) *The Philosophical Quarterly* 416.

[34] Wall (n 33) 437.

[35] Arneson (n 33) 124. Arneson does point out that the instrumentalist approach takes various forms and argues for a specific version which holds that a political decision is legitimate only if over the long haul it produces morally superior results to ones that would result from any feasible alternative.

194 *Ivan Ozai*

process would likely result in a regime leaned toward favouring poorer over richer economies. However, developing countries face increasing competition for access to foreign investment and markets and are divided by significant levels of political, social, and economic heterogeneity which prevents them from acting collectively. As commentators note, strong economic or political stakeholders, such as powerful states or wealthy investors, frequently take advantage of these divergences to practice 'divide and rule' strategies and erode the capacity of weak countries for collective actions by confining them to 'different "cells" in a maze of prisoners' dilemmas'.[36]

Merely ensuring that countries have an equal say in the decision-making process might not suffice to produce a fair result or to include the interests of the less powerful stakeholders, primarily because of background inequalities in resources, technical knowledge, and general bargaining position.[37] This is illustrated in the ongoing BEPS project, in which the OECD has managed to monopolise the reform process through a top-down approach with agenda-setting on a higher level.[38] Even within the Inclusive Framework, the project is still under the command of the OECD, and since its secretariat is bound to defend the interests of the OECD, it should not depart much from its institutional aims, which includes 'achiev[ing] the highest sustainable economic growth and employment and a rising standard of living in Member countries, while maintaining financial stability, and thus to contribute to the development of the world economy'.[39] Moreover, political decisions are generally based on the technical work put forward by technical bodies primarily composed by nationals from OECD member countries[40] who are expected to hold at least informal commitments to represent the institution's interests.

An additional problem is the role of path dependence and first-mover advantage in policy decision-making. Initial institutional arrangements commonly produce significant advantage in setting agendas and standards. Once institutions have started down a track, the costs of reversal become significantly high due to the entrenchments of certain institutional arrangements. Even if an alternative

---

[36] E Benvenisti, *The Law of Global Governance* (The Hague, The Hague Academy of International Law, 2014) 208–09 (also noting that the term 'global governance' in itself indicates that global regulators do not simply implement consensual commitments but rather 'govern' through the exercise of discretion).

[37] Participation in international governance itself is questioned as genuinely voluntary, considering the costs weaker states would suffer by not participating. See Buchanan and Keohane (n 21) 414: 'Of course, there may be reasonable disagreements over what counts as substantial voluntariness, but the vulnerability of individual weak states is serious enough to undercut the view that the consent of democratic states is by itself sufficient for legitimacy'.

[38] T Büttner and M Thiemann, 'Breaking Regime Stability? The Politicization of Expertise in the OECD/G20 Process on BEPS and the Potential Transformation of International Taxation' (2017) 7(1) *Accounting, Economics, and Law: A Convivium* 757.

[39] *Convention on the Organisation for Economic Co-operation and Development* [1960].

[40] See *OECD Frequently Asked Questions – Jobs*, available at www.oecd.org/general/frequently askedquestionsfaq.htm (accessed 8 January 2020).

policy could be considered fairer and more efficient from an ideal perspective, the existing institutional arrangements might make it an infeasible alternative. In this respect, commentators frequently note how the OECD has advanced a rhetorical strategy in the BEPS project based on the notions of economic substance and value creation not only to strengthen its epistemic and governance authority but primarily to evade committing a more substantial overhaul of the current system.[41]

In short, political equality does not ensure substantive equity. Improving participation of countries on an equal footing with no consideration to background inequalities and differences in bargaining position might not lead to a fair allocation of taxing rights, particularly to the least developed countries. Unless there is a more serious discussion on distributive justice and substantive equity in how taxing rights are allocated, poorer countries will be left with only a formal right to participate in the policy-making process.

B. Normative Framework for Equal-Standing Negotiation

Most international tax reform proposals discussed today, aimed at addressing the allocation of taxing rights, have an underlying concern with economic substance. They hold an implicit assumption that states are entitled to benefit from (and thus to tax) resources they control and the wealth created in their territory.[42] However, what frequently goes unnoticed is that the commitment to economic substance is ultimately based on a fundamental notion of international justice, that is, on a specific moral standard for determining how the rights to tax should be allocated among countries. Such standard is so entrenched in the literature and the policy-making debates that commentators rarely acknowledge it as a contentious matter of distributive justice.[43]

Policy negotiations involving technical concepts and significant distributional outcomes often result in stakeholders supporting technical arguments which will maximise their share of benefits.[44] The lack of a normative framework that challenges the dominant theoretical model impairs the ability of less powerful stakeholders to discuss and negotiate policy on an equal standing. Reviewing

---

[41] See eg Büttner and Thiemann (n 38).

[42] For a discussion on this assumption and a critique from a philosophical standpoint, see L Apeldoorn, 'Exploitation, International Taxation, and Global Justice' (2019) 77 (2) *Review of Social Economy* 163.

[43] For a critical assessment, see A Christians, 'Taxing According to Value Creation' (2018) 90 *Tax Notes International* 1379 (portraying economic substance and value creation as well-worn tax mantras and noting it camouflages the distributive nature of the international tax system as neutral and apolitical).

[44] From the perspective of political legitimacy, the lack of distance between 'author' and 'subject' of international law is sometimes seen as problematic and resulting in states proceeding in a self-interested manner when crafting legal obligations for themselves. See J Ellis, 'Stateless Law: From Legitimacy to Validity' in H Dedek and SV Praagh (eds), *Stateless Law: Evolving Boundaries of a Discipline* (Ashgate, 2015) 133.

196   *Ivan Ozai*

the normative foundations for allocating taxing rights among countries fairly is necessary for improving distributive justice, but it is also vital to allow developing countries to counter a rhetoric based on entrenched principles with significantly weak normative support.

Even for an equal-standing negotiation, there is a need for expanding the discussion on the normative criteria to determine the allocation of taxing rights. Limiting discussions to legitimacy concerns might not suffice in view of the lack of proper theoretical framework and language that help developing countries make a case for improving their taxing rights. A serious discussion on distributive justice is an important way to provide a counter-hegemonic framework to shift the balance toward a more equitable division of rights.

C. The Reciprocally Supportive Roles of Consent and Content Stakeholders' Protection

Another reason why legitimacy discussions should not replace the need for distributive justice concerns is that a scenario where normative conditions for the legitimacy of global governance institutions are fully met seems far. First, a pervasive problem in international governance institutions is the long chain of delegation from the individual citizen to the international policy decision-making, where the impact of popular will on the decision-making process becomes merely nominal at the international level.[45] Second, there is no political structure today that could ensure democratic control over global governance institutions.[46] Third, an attempt to create such a structure in the form of a global democratic federation would have to rely on existing states as federal units, but since many states themselves lack conditions for state legitimacy, they could not confer legitimacy to a global governance institution.[47]

The prospects for legitimacy in international tax policymaking are poor. The OECD's BEPS Inclusive Framework, an attempt to increase inclusiveness, has been harshly criticised for limiting participation of non-OECD and non-G20 members to the implementation phase. Similarly, calls for a global tax body under the United Nations (UN) are systematically rejected and undercut by the world's most influential countries, and the UN itself is decried for lack of democratic procedures.[48]

---

[45] Buchanan and Keohane (n 21) 414–15. See also Ellis (n 44) (arguing that access to the structures and processes of international law by civil society remains limited and concentrates on organisations rather than on individuals and informal groups).

[46] Buchanan and Keohane (n 21) 416.

[47] ibid.

[48] See S Fung, 'The Questionable Legitimacy of the OECD/G20 BEPS Project' (2017) 10(2) *Erasmus Law Review* 76, 81 (pointing out that proposals to hand the BEPS Project over to the UN do not solve all the democratic deficits of international law-making and is most likely utopian); Magalhães (n 20) 533 (noting the UN has repeatedly failed to act on behalf of poor countries); RO Keohane, 'Global Governance and Legitimacy' (2011) 18(1) *Review of International Political Economy* 99 (pointing to

Regional arrangements are another possible solution for improving legitimacy, but it is unclear whether they will gain enough influence at a global level and how they will connect to each other in a way that leads to global cooperation.

Given this scenario, even if we were to concede that legitimate institutions should necessarily lead to fair outcomes, forgoing discussions on distributive justice in international tax policy in favour of a democracy-oriented solution implies waiting for legitimate structures to take place when it is not clear if they ever will. The bleak prospects for global democracy have led some to suggest that a standard for normative legitimacy of global governance institutions should not rely on conventional requirements for democracy but should rather build on minimum moral reasons which can be agreed upon despite the persistence of significant moral disagreement.[49] Likewise, in domestic tax systems, stakeholders have historically relied on fixing substantive principles of tax justice (content) whenever participation in tax policy decision-making (consent) was limited.[50] Taking consent and content as mutual complementary ways of protecting weaker stakeholders, protection by content acquires an even more important role where protection by consent is limited.[51]

VI. The Legitimacy-Justice Fallacy and its Role in International Tax Policy

Although the distributive justice issues in the international tax regime have long been identified and acknowledged in the relevant literature,[52] a broad and in-depth discussion on the normative implications of global justice for addressing these tax

---

the lack of transparency and accountability of the UN). See also R Domingo, *The New Global Law* (Cambridge, CUP, 2010) 59 (arguing that the UN hand over the governance of the world to an exclusive club of sovereign powers and excludes an entire group of global actors who are dismissed as simple consultants).

[49] ibid 435.

[50] See W Schön, 'Taxation and Democracy' (forthcoming) 72 *Tax Law Review*, available at https://ssrn.com/abstract=3267279 (accessed 8 January 2020) (noting that while decision-making in tax matters is hardly constrained by any material constitutional limitations in the UK and the US, European and Latin American countries have largely resorted to hard-wired constitutional constraints on tax legislation to ensure a high degree of judicial review by constitutional courts).

[51] ibid (arguing that a content-oriented principle of tax equity should take charge of those who are not entitled to make tax policy dependent on their consent).

[52] See eg V Thuronyi, 'Tax Treaties and Developing Countries' in Michael Lang et al (eds), *Tax Treaties: Building Bridges Between Law and Economics* (Amsterdam, IBFD, 2010) 441; Dagan (n 8); M Hearson, 'When Do Developing Countries Negotiate Away Their Corporate Tax Base?' (2018) 30(2) *Journal of International Development* 23. For general tax policy challenges and constraints on developing countries, see eg A Christians, 'Global Trends and Constraints on Tax Policy in the Least Developed Countries' (2010) 42(2) *University of British Columbia Law Review* 239; M Carnahan, 'Taxation Challenges in Developing Countries' (2015) 2(1) *Asia and the Pacific Policy Studies* 169, 179; R Collier and N Riedel, 'The OECD/G20 Base Erosion and Profit Shifting Initiative and Developing Countries' (2018) 72(12) *Bulletin of International Taxation* 704.

198   *Ivan Ozai*

policy problems is still lacking.[53] One important reason for this scholarly gap is that the literature tends to conflate legitimacy with distributive justice problems.[54] Proposals to address the latter (that is, reducing the existing inequities of the international tax regime) frequently focus on improving the former (that is, securing greater participation of developing countries in tax policy decision-making). Whereas improving legitimacy in the international tax regime by strengthening participation of developing countries in the decision-making process is expected to result in distributive improvements, this is not a necessary result, and addressing legitimacy deficits may not suffice to meet the requirements of global justice.[55]

There is a logical causal gap between the moral requirements for distributive justice and the solutions for addressing legitimacy. Democratic legitimacy largely focuses on procedural requirements to formally capture interests of stakeholders and translate them into outcomes and has only tangential connections to just outcomes.[56] Conditions for legitimacy and justice are grounded in related but different moral values and justifications, and imply distinct normative requirements. Improving legitimacy is likely to help advancing distributive justice due to the mutually supportive roles of consent and content mentioned above,[57] but attempting to address one problem (distributive justice) with the solution for another (legitimacy) neglects that these constitute two separate issues.

Conflating these two normative realms produces what can be called the Legitimacy-Justice Fallacy. While distributive justice focuses on how burdens and benefits should be distributed, political justice (or legitimacy) considers who should exercise power and how they should do so.[58] Collapsing the notion of legitimacy into one of distributive justice undermines the social function of legitimacy assessments.[59] On the other hand, the problem with an exclusive concern with

---

[53] Two notable exceptions are P Dietsch, *Catching Capital: The Ethics of Tax Competition* (New York, OUP, 2015); Dagan (n 8).

[54] The tax literature rarely discusses separate solutions for these two issues, and calls for improving legitimacy in the international tax regime frequently eclipses an in-depth discussion on solutions focused on distributive justice. See eg RM Bird, 'Reforming International Taxation: Is the Process the Real Product?', *International Center for Public Policy Working Paper* 15–03 (2015); Burgers and Mosquera (n 9); RS Avi-Yonah and H Xu, 'Evaluating BEPS' (2017) 10(1) *Erasmus Law Review* 3; Collier and Riedel (n 52). From a different perspective, Tarcísio Magalhães makes an explicit distinction between discussions on legitimacy and justice but argues that given the conditions of multiplicity of interests and values, philosophers and tax scholars should not attempt to build rational principles of international tax justice but rather work toward improving democratisation of global tax governance. See Magalhães (n 20).

[55] See Dowding, Goodin and Pateman, 'Between Justice and Democracy' (n 18) 5 (noting that there is nothing inherent in democracy that necessarily makes it just).

[56] ibid 5–6.

[57] Thompson (n 2) (arguing that justice and legitimacy stand in a circular relationship, where democratic political arrangements constitute a requirement of justice, but democratic deliberations should meet the standards of justice).

[58] S Caney, 'Justice and the Basic Right to Justification' in Rainer Forst (ed), *Justice, Democracy and the Right to Justification: Rainer Forst in Dialogue* (London, Bloomsbury Academic, 2014) 147, 152–56.

[59] See Buchanan and Keohane (n 21) 412 (arguing that there are two reasons not to mistake legitimacy for justice, the first being that there is sufficient disagreement on what justice entails so that

democratic legitimacy is that it does not seem able to legitimate every result it generates, and it neglects that outcomes that are undeniably democratic can be palpably unjust.[60]

The OECD seems to particularly rely on this fallacy in promoting its goals and standards for international tax policy. In an earlier attempt to tackle tax competition, it built on a unilateral conception of justice to impose specific standards for 'acceptable' tax competition and called for defensive measures and economic sanctions against countries that would not comply with its standards.[61] Although such standards were unilaterally established by the OECD, they applied indifferently to both OECD and non-OECD members. The lack of legitimacy in the decision-making process was seemingly taken by the OECD as justified based on its own understanding of 'fairness' and 'neutrality'.[62]

More recently, the focus shifted toward legitimacy. The OECD seems to rely on the Legitimacy-Justice Fallacy to circumvent discussions on distributive issues, when it suggests that its BEPS Inclusive Framework, aimed at addressing the Legitimacy Problem, might resolve the Distributive Justice Problem. Although not making the argument that the framework aims to produce a fair allocation of taxing rights among jurisdictions, it implicitly suggests that it eventually will.[63] Similarly, when describing its Inclusive Framework, the OECD largely takes for granted that it 'ensures [developing countries] can influence norms and standards in their favour'.[64]

Generally, the exclusive focus on creating an inclusive framework when discussing fairness to developing countries seemingly indicates an attempt to sidestep a more serious discussion on a fair allocation of taxing rights for developing countries. In a recent public consultation document, the OECD discussed different proposals to reconsider the current allocation of taxing rights by revising profit allocation and nexus rules.[65] Although acknowledging that the proposals 'chiefly relate to the question of how taxing rights ... should be allocated among

---

a standard for legitimacy requires a different concept for securing coordinated support for valuable institutions, and the second that withholding support from institutions because they fail to meet the demands of justice would mean ignoring that progress toward justice requires effective institutions).

[60] See eg RE Goodin, 'Democracy, Justice and Impartiality' in Dowding, Goodin and Pateman (eds) (n 1) 97, 98; LH Meyer and P Sanklecha, 'Legitimacy, Justice and Public International Law: Three Perspectives on the Debate' in LH Meyer (ed), *Legitimacy, Justice, and Public International Law* (Cambridge, CUP, 2009) 1, 12.

[61] See OECD, *Harmful Tax Competition: An Emerging Global Issue* (Paris, OECD Publications, 1998). For a comprehensive and critical analysis of the OECD's harmful tax practices initiative, see Christians, 'Sovereignty' (n 26).

[62] See OECD, *Harmful Tax Competition* (n 61).

[63] OECD, *BEPS Progress Report* (n 4) 14 (pointing out that although 'BEPS measures do not necessarily resolve the question of how rights to tax are shared between jurisdictions ... the OECD/G20 Inclusive Framework will continue working towards a consensus-based long-term solution').

[64] ibid 28.

[65] OECD, *Addressing the Tax Challenges of the Digitalisation of the Economy*, Public Consultation Document (February 13, 2019).

countries',[66] the document provided no discussion on how to make the allocation fairer to poorer countries or how the proposed changes would affect their existing rights. Nonetheless, the Inclusive Framework was mentioned 20 times throughout the 29-page document, apparently as a way to emphasise that the fairness of the discussion is implicit in its purported inclusiveness and to eschew distributive justice concerns by framing the process as normatively legitimate.[67]

A normative evaluation of the international tax regime requires that both the legitimacy and the distributive justice dimensions be considered and that specific solutions be discussed for each of them. Given the considerable disagreements on what justice entails, participation in the decision-making process of those affected by policy decisions is necessary to avoid arbitrariness and favouritism. On the other hand, political equality does not ensure substantive equity, and an inclusive decision-making process might still lead to an unfair allocation of taxing rights due to existing inequalities and differences in bargaining position among countries. Moreover, an equal-footing negotiation requires a counter-hegemonic framework based on distributive justice grounds to shift the balance toward a more equitable division of rights. And given the bleak prospects for democratic legitimacy in the existing international governance institutions, forgoing discussions on distributive justice in favour of a democracy-oriented solution implies waiting for institutional changes that might never take place.

---

[66] ibid 5.

[67] Similarly, a more recent document released by the OECD in May 2019 acknowledges that the international tax reform proposals currently discussed 'will have an impact on revenues and the overall balance of taxing rights' and mentions the Inclusive Framework 43 times throughout its 40 pages. See OECD, *Programme of Work to Develop a Consensus Solution to the Tax Challenges Arising from the Digitalisation of the Economy* (Paris, OECD, 2019). However, the report gives no consideration to whether or how reform could address the existing inequities in the current allocation of taxing rights between developed and developing countries.

PART V

Justice and Procedures

12

Tax Justice in the Post-BEPS Era: Enhanced Cooperation Among Tax Authorities and the Protection of Taxpayer Rights in the EU

CHRISTIANA HJI PANAYI AND KATERINA PERROU

Justice, let alone tax justice, is a highly contested concept, subject to a plurality of interpretations.[1] Lately, the concept of tax justice seems to have been used prominently by groups that promote rules against tax avoidance or aggressive tax planning of multinationals – ie rules that enhance the powers of the state and its authorities to tax, whether by closing loopholes or by extending cross-border administrative cooperation. This is evident also by the agendas of most European Parliament groups, many of which seem to use the terms tax justice and tax fairness interchangeably.[2] Therefore, one could say that tax justice is at the top of the EU's agenda. This chapter reviews another aspect of tax justice, which has been eclipsed by the international developments of the post-BEPS era: tax justice as protection of taxpayer rights.

I. Tax Justice and the OECD BEPS Action Plan

The notion that profits should be taxed where economic activities generating the profits are performed and where value is created lies at the core of international tax justice.

---

[1] See S Douglas-Scott, 'Human rights as a basis for justice in the European Union' 8(1) *Transnational Legal Theory* 59, available at DOI: 10.1080/20414005.2017.1321907 (accessed 8 January 2020).

[2] See eg the agenda of the Confederal Group of the European United Left – Nordic Green Left, available at http://guengl-panamapapers.eu/ (accessed 8 January 2020); the Green Party's 10 point plan for tax justice, available at https://www.greens-efa.eu/en/priority/group/tax-justice/ (accessed 8 January 2020); and the European People's Party' mandate on fairness in taxation, available at https://www. eppgroup.eu/how-we-make-it-happen/working-groups/wg-economy-and-environment/financial-crimes-tax-evasion-and-tax-avoidance (accessed 8 January 2020).

204 *Christiana HJI Panayi and Katerina Perrou*

The aim of the OECD Action Plan on Base Erosion and Profit Shifting (BEPS) was to target specific tax-planning strategies that exploited gaps and mismatches in tax rules in order to allow enterprises to artificially shift profits to low- or no-tax jurisdictions where there was little or no economic activity. It was thought that this mismatch between the place where value was created and the place where such value was taxed, undermined the fairness and integrity of tax systems not only among countries, but also among businesses. It appeared that businesses that could operate across borders were able to use BEPS schemes to gain a competitive advantage over enterprises that operated only at a domestic level. As a result, both developing and developed countries lost tax revenues to the benefit of interme-diary countries.[3] Through specific recommendations,[4] the OECD BEPS Action Plan targeted schemes that used intermediary countries to artificially divert profits in order to avoid taxation in the jurisdictions where those profits were actually created. It is beyond the purview of this chapter to discuss the technical recommendations.

Another way to attempt to counter this situation – and in addition to the technical recommendations – was to demand greater transparency both from taxpayers and states.

Transparency formed one of the three pillars of the BEPS Action Plan (the other two being coherence and substance). Three out of the 15 BEPS Actions were related to transparency and created a net of intertwined obligations for the taxpayers: Action 12, which contained recommendations regarding the design of mandatory disclosure rules for aggressive tax planning schemes; Action 13, which contained guidance on transfer pricing documentation, including the template for country-by-country reporting, to enhance transparency; and Action 14, which developed solutions to address obstacles that prevent countries from solving treaty-related disputes under the mutual agreement procedure, via a minimum standard as well as a number of best practices.

At the same time instruments providing for the exchange of information between tax authorities (automatic, spontaneous and upon request exchanges) had

---

[3] See eg Dagan who points out that competition undermines the ability of states (rich and poor) to maintain the domestic background conditions that are necessary to sustain their legitimacy; T Dagan, 'International Tax and Global Justice' (2017) 18 *Theoretical Inquiries in Law* 1, 4. The 2013 OECD BEPS report refers to data that show that in 2010 Barbados, Bermuda and the British Virgin Islands received more FDIs (combined 5.11% of global FDIs) than Germany (4.77%) or Japan (3.76%). During the same year, these three jurisdictions made more investments into the world (combined 4.54%) than Germany (4.28%). On a country-by-country position, in 2010 the British Virgin Islands were the second largest investor into China (14%) after Hong Kong (45%) and before the United States (4%). For the same year, Bermuda appears as the third largest investor in Chile (10%). Similar data exists in relation to other countries, for example Mauritius is the top investor country into India (24%), while Cyprus (28%), the British Virgin Islands (12%), Bermuda (7%) and the Bahamas (6%) are among the top five investors into Russia; see OECD, Addressing Base Erosion and Profit Shifting (Paris: OECD) para 36; available at https://dx.doi.org/10.1787/9789264192744-en (accessed 8 January 2020).

[4] For example, Actions 5, 6, 7 and to an extent, also Actions 2 and 4.

increased exponentially.[5] The EU, following these developments, established its own measures to tackle tax abuse and ensure fairer taxation in the EU.[6]

One characteristic of the post-BEPS era is that the whole BEPS project provides only for enhanced powers for the tax administrations and in no way deals with the position of the taxpayer in the new international tax environment. However, tax justice can only be served, and perceived by the taxpayers as being served, when the rules applied contain not only (often burdensome) obligations for the taxpayers, but when they contain legitimate and proportionate limitations on the powers of the tax authorities.

Arguably, the lacuna concerning the protection of taxpayer rights that is observed in the BEPS project's results can be explained by the fact that it is not really a matter of international tax law to provide guarantees for the protection of the taxpayer. This is a matter for the domestic law of each state. However, two questions arise: is the existing model for the protection of the taxpayer adequate to address the challenges of the post-BEPS era and the combined power of the tax administrations, which work in many cases as one super-tax authority? Also, given this new global tax environment, can it still be convincingly supported that taxpayer protection should be left uncoordinated at a global level?

Indeed, the existing human rights system, which is based on the Universal Declaration of Human Rights and elaborated in the various regional human rights conventions,[7] provides for worldwide coverage. In reality, the level of protection in each country may vary significantly, especially across continents. The case of the European Union represents a highly integrated area, with legal systems based

---

[5] For a historical overview of the development of the bilateral and multilateral rules on exchange of information, see analysis in V Wöhrer, *Data Protection and Taxpayers' Rights: Challenges Created by Automatic Exchange of Information*, online book (IBFD, 2018) ch 3. Instruments developed in order to facilitate exchange of information between tax authorities include the OECD Common Reporting Standard Multilateral Competent Authority Agreement, the OECD Model Agreement on Exchange of Information on Tax Matters (Model TIEA); the Convention between the Member States of the Council of Europe and the Member Countries of the OECD on Mutual Administrative Assistance in Tax Matters (25 January 1988) (as amended through 2010); the US Foreign Account Tax Compliance Act (FATCA); and EU Council Directive 2011/16/EU of 15 February 2011 on administrative cooperation in the field of taxation and repealing Directive 77/799/EEC (DAC) (as amended through 2018).

[6] For a detailed overview, see C HJI Panayi, *Advanced Issues in International and European Tax Law* (Oxford, Hart Publishing, 2015) ch 5 and C HJI Panayi, 'The Europeanisation of Good Tax Governance' (2018) 36(1) *Yearbook of European Law* 442.

[7] Following the adoption of the Universal Declaration on Human Rights (adopted on 10 December 1948, available at http://www.un.org/en/documents/udhr (accessed 8 January 2020); see also the Official UN Universal Declaration of Human Rights home page, www.ohchr.org (accessed 8 January 2020) and of the International Covenant on Civil and Political Rights (ICPPR) (adopted on 16 December 1966 and in force since 23 March 1976), three major regional human rights systems were developed: the European system in the 1950s (the European Convention for the Protection of Human Rights and Fundamental Freedoms (ECHR), in force since 1953, text available at http://conventions.coe.int (accessed 8 January 2020)); the Inter-American system in the 1970s (see the American Convention on Human Rights 'Pact of San Jose, Costa Rica' that was adopted in 1969 and entered into force in 1978); and the African system in the 1980s (see M Evans and R Murray, *The African Charter on Human and People's Rights, The System in Practice, 1986–2006*, 2nd edn (Cambridge, CUP, 2008).

on the rule of law, where the level of protection of taxpayer rights is rather high and, to a great extent, uniform. Still, concerns are raised, as a number of issues are emerging from the case law of the European courts (the European Court of Human Rights (ECtHR) and the Court of Justice of the EU (CJEU)) that have created uncertainty and confusion even for the courts that are called to decide upon them. Although the scope of this chapter is to discuss such concerns from an EU point of view, these concerns are not only EU-specific; on the contrary, these are global issues.

Our chapter seeks to identify the risks of potentially arbitrary tax authority intervention to the taxpayer's private business that the new tax environment has created as a result of the expansive use of exchange of information. In addition, it assesses the level of protection of the guarantees that are provided under existing rules to limit such arbitrary intervention. Our chapter concludes that the introduction, by means of soft law, of a universally accepted charter of taxpayer rights is urgently needed, as a complement to BEPS, in order to limit the risk of arbitrariness by the tax authorities.

II. Exchange of Information and Protection of Taxpayer Rights in the EU

It is undisputable that tax authorities must have timely access to accurate information in order to be able to effectively implement tax legislation.[8] In the last few years, the world has witnessed an enormous increase in the volume and detail of tax information that is collected and subsequently shared among tax authorities on a global level. At the same time, concerns of taxpayers about the use of their tax information have also increased and a number of challenges have arisen regarding various aspects of the access to and use of tax information by the tax authorities.[9]

At EU level, multiple levels of protection of taxpayer rights exist. Firstly, at domestic law level, taxpayers enjoy the protection granted by the Constitutions of the Member States. Second, at the EU level, after the entry into force of the EU Charter of Fundamental Rights ('the EU Charter')[10] on 1 December 2009, taxpayers enjoy the protection of the rights and guarantees provided in the Charter. At the same time, the European Convention for the Protection of Human Rights and Fundamental Freedoms (ECHR) is also applicable in the EU, as all Member States are signatories and subject to the jurisdiction of the ECtHR. Even though the

---

[8] See eg S Hemels, 'Administrative Cooperation in the Assessment and Recovery of Direct Tax Claims' in P Wattel, O Marres and H Vermeulen, *European Tax Law*, 7th ed, Vol 1 (Netherlands, Kluwer Law International, 2018) 541; see also M Stewart, 'Transnational Tax Information Exchange Network: Steps towards a Globalized, Legitimate Tax Administration' (2012) 4 *World Tax Journal* (June) 152, 154.

[9] See eg P Baker, 'Privacy Rights in an Age of Transparency: A European Perspective' (2016) 82 *Tax Notes International* 6, 584.

[10] OJ C 326/391.

scope of application of the two instruments is not the same as regards the rights and guarantees included therein, their territorial scope covers the whole of the EU and, therefore, subject to the conditions provided in each instrument, they are also available to taxpayers in the EU.

Taxpayers have relied on the ECHR to challenge the compatibility of various domestic tax measures.[11] Both substantive and procedural aspects of taxation have been the subject of interesting case law by the ECtHR. The rules concerning the access to, the use of and the exchange of information are usually part of the procedural law of a state. As such, in this context, procedural rights and guarantees provided for in the ECHR are more relevant. Such procedural rights and guarantees, in relation to issues concerning tax information, are mainly protected under Article 6 ECHR, which provides for the right to a fair trial, and under Article 8 ECHR, which provides for the right to respect for private and family life, home and correspondence. The corresponding provisions of the EU Charter are also increasingly invoked in cases before the CJEU.[12]

In the following sections the specific guarantees that are applicable in relation to the disclosure of information by taxpayers and the use and exchange of information by the tax authorities will be examined in light of the case law of the two European courts.

A. Use of Information Obtained by the Taxpayer Himself: The Right to Remain Silent (No Self-Incrimination; *Nemo Tenetur*)

The right to remain silent is protected under Article 6 ECHR; it is one of the elements of the fairness of the proceedings covered by Article 6, including tax proceedings. Indeed, although it is not specifically mentioned in Article 6, the right not to incriminate oneself lies at the heart of the notion of a fair procedure, since, by providing the taxpayer with protection against improper compulsion by the authorities, the aims of Article 6 are secured.

In an early case, dating back to 2001, *JB v Switzerland*, the ECtHR heard a case that involved the right to remain silent in the context of a tax case.[13] The taxpayer was assessed with income taxes in arrears for unreported interest income that was

---

[11] See eg the factsheet published by the European Court of Human Rights on 'Taxation and the European Convention on Human Rights', April 2019, available at https://www.echr.coe.int/Documents/FS_Taxation_ENG.pdf (accessed 8 January 2020).

[12] See P Pistone, 'The EU Charter of Fundamental Rights, General Principles of EU Law and Taxation' in Wattel, Marres and Vermeulen (n 8) 153.

[13] *JB v Switzerland* (Application no 31827/96), ECHR 2001-III. See also analysis of ECtHR case law in R Luja, 'Accounting Disclosure of Tax Liabilities, Fair Trial and Self-incrimination: Should the European Commission endorse IFRS in the light of the European Human Rights' in G Kofler, MP Maduro and P Pistone (eds), *Human Rights and Taxation in Europe and the World*, online (Amsterdam, IBFD, 2011) 263.

208   *Christiana HJI Panayi and Katerina Perrou*

linked to an investment he had made through companies in which he participated. The taxpayer was assessed with the income tax evaded and tax surcharges. He was also charged with tax evasion by the tax authorities.

The tax authorities, after having assessed the taxpayer with income tax for the returns of an investment he had made at some point in the past, sent him a request asking him to explain the source of the invested income, which had given rise to the interest income he had been assessed for. Within four years (between 1987 and 1990) the authorities found it necessary to request the applicant on eight separate occasions to submit the information concerned and, when he refused to do so, they successively imposed altogether four disciplinary fines on him.

The taxpayer complained against the imposition of multiple penalties, arguing that, under Article 6 ECHR, he had the status of an 'accused person' and he should not be obliged to incriminate himself.[14] The case was brought before the ECtHR, which affirmed the application of the criminal limb of Article 6 in the case,[15] and went on to examine the compliance of the domestic legislation with the rights and guarantees under Article 6 and especially with the privilege of no self-incrimination.

The ECtHR emphasised that the right not to incriminate oneself in particular presupposes that the authorities seek to prove their case without resorting to evidence obtained through methods of coercion or oppression in defiance of the will of the 'person charged'.[16] As such, there had been a violation of the right under Article 6(1) ECHR.[17]

This case, however, cannot be considered as a norm concerning normal tax proceedings. Although it is not made clear in the judgment, it appears that the determining factor for the ECtHR's decision was the inability of the Swiss tax authorities to separate the normal tax proceedings from the (criminal) tax evasion proceedings that applied simultaneously in the case. As a result, any additional findings regarding evaded income tax were liable to result not only in additional taxes being assessed but also in an additional penalty for tax evasion.

This is confirmed by the subsequent case law of the ECtHR.

The case *van Weerelt v the Netherlands*[18] concerned requests for information addressed to the taxpayer made by the Dutch tax authorities, as a result of information that these tax authorities had received through the German tax authorities, which showed that the taxpayer had a financial interest in a Liechtenstein foundation. Although the case was declared as manifestly ill-founded and was rejected, it still merits discussion, as very useful conclusions on the privilege of no self-incrimination that taxpayers enjoy in relation to tax authorities can be derived.

Although the ECtHR declared the case as inadmissible, it noted that the right to remain silent does not act as a prohibition on the use of compulsory powers to

---

[14] *J.B v Switzerland*, ibid para 22.
[15] ibid paras 44–51.
[16] ibid para 64.
[17] ibid para 71.
[18] *van Weerelt v the Netherlands* (dec.) (Application no 784/14), 16 June 2015.

require taxpayers to provide information about their financial affairs, as the obligation to make disclosure of income and capital for the purposes of the calculation and assessment of tax is a common feature of tax systems, and necessary for their effective functioning.[19] Furthermore, the ECtHR found that the Dutch Supreme Court acted pre-emptively to prevent the misuse of the information for the purposes of determining a 'criminal charge' against the taxpayer.[20] Notwithstanding the lacuna in the Dutch legislation, it was found that the Supreme Court followed the principles established by the ECtHR[21] and provided with its judgment the necessary guarantees against self-incrimination.[22]

The privilege of no self-incrimination that taxpayers may invoke against tax authorities, is, therefore, rather clearly delineated and may be summarised as follows:[23]

– Tax authorities can ask the taxpayer to disclose information which is relevant and crucial for the assessment of taxes, and the taxpayer has the obligation to provide such information.

– A distinction must be made between information that can be obtained only from the taxpayer (will-dependent information) and information that exists independently of the taxpayer's will (will-independent information).

– Will-dependent information can form the basis for tax assessments, but it cannot form the basis for the imposition of sanctions (penalties) and the initiation of criminal proceedings against the taxpayer for the tax obligations resulting from them.

However easy as this may appear in theory, it can be very difficult to apply in practice, as drawing the line between will-dependent and will-independent information may be very tricky. If the tax authority has the information required to assess the taxes due, then the disclosure by the taxpayer is not crucial, rendering the relevant requests irrelevant and even redundant: adding compliance costs without any visible benefit for either the taxpayer or the tax authority. If, on the other hand, the tax authority does not have the necessary information, and the taxpayer does not comply by voluntarily disclosing his tax affairs, the tax authority is in the dark. In such a case, the tax assessment may result either in no tax being assessed, when there is no information, or in the tax being assessed on a purely fictitious base; both results are bad. The tax-evading taxpayer is in a better

---

[19] ibid para 56.

[20] ibid para 62.

[21] The reasoning and conclusions of the Dutch Supreme Court were based on *JB v Switzerland*, to which the domestic court made express reference; see ibid para 60. Similar issues were raised in the communicated case of *de Legé v the Netherlands* (Application no 58342/15). It was questioned whether there was a breach of Art 6 ECHR where the taxpayer was coerced into producing incriminating evidence which had an existence independent of his will.

[22] ibid para 66.

[23] For additional issues that arise, such as timing issues and the existence of a 'charge', see analyses in Luja (n 13), and N Čičin-Šain, 'New Mandatory Disclosure Rules for Tax Intermediaries and Taxpayers in the European Union – Another "Bite" into the Rights of the Taxpayer?' (2019) 11 *World Tax Journal* 77.

position, in any case: first, because the tax authority is not able to establish any tax liability and, second, because the tax assessment may not stand in court, if the tax authority, having the burden of proof, does not fulfil its burden, based on will-independent information.

These considerations are especially relevant for the assessment of the mandatory disclosure rules provided for in BEPS Action 12 and, correspondingly, as far as the EU is concerned, in DAC 6.[24] Indeed, since in some cases the obligation to disclose is passed on from the intermediary to the taxpayer himself who is using the tax scheme,[25] the overlap (or conflict) between the right to no self-incrimination and these rules must be explored.

Interestingly, the final report on BEPS Action 12 (henceforth, 'the Final Report') contained a discussion on the relationship between the rules proposed under Action 12 and the right of protection against self-incrimination.[26] It was argued that the proposed rules should not create a problem with the right of no self-incrimination, because the information requested under the mandatory disclosure rules is, in general, no different from the information normally requested in the context of a tax audit. As such, no particular problems with the application of the principle of no self-incrimination were expected to arise. In addition, the Final Report claimed that for many countries the types of transactions targeted for disclosure under Action 12 were not generally the types of transactions that would give rise to criminal liabilities. A third argument was based on the timing of the request of information: the issues with the no self-incrimination principle were expected to arise only when criminal proceedings had already been initiated, and not in cases where the information was obtained early. In a case where a scheme was reported that had not yet been implemented, it appeared that no issue would ever arise.

In any case, the Final Report acknowledged that mandatory disclosure should not, in general, infringe upon the privilege against self-incrimination. To this end, two drafting suggestions were made to countries. First, it was suggested that countries may choose to simply exclude those transactions from the scope of the disclosure regime without substantially curtailing the scope of the regime. Second, it was suggested that countries could also specify that the privilege against self-incrimination was a reasonable excuse for not reporting a disclosable transaction and exclude taxpayers from the obligation to disclose such schemes.

The discussion in the Final Report does not seem to address all the potential issues that may arise. Indeed, when the disclosure takes place by third parties

---

[24] See Council Directive (EU) 2018/822 of 25 May 2018 amending Directive 2011/16/EU as regards mandatory automatic exchange of information in the field of taxation in relation to reportable cross-border arrangements (commonly referred to as DAC 6, as it is the sixth amendment of Directive 2011/16/EU).

[25] See Art 8ab, point 6 of the Directive.

[26] See, in particular, 'Annex B – Compatibility between self-incrimination and mandatory disclosure' in OECD, 'Mandatory Disclosure Rules, Action 12 – 2015 Final Report' 85, available at https://doi.org/10.1787/23132612 (accessed 8 January 2020).

(the intermediaries), the right of no self-incrimination *cannot* be invoked by the taxpayer but possibly only by the intermediary and to the extent that this concerns the intermediary's own liability, since the intermediary may also face similar sanctions and criminal prosecution. Furthermore, even when the disclosure is made by the taxpayer but the scheme has not yet been implemented, there is no place for the imposition of sanctions or the initiation of criminal proceedings. As a corollary, there is no conflict with the principle against self-incrimination either.

However, these cases are only marginal cases that do not represent the whole spectrum of issues that may arise under the mandatory disclosure rules.[27] In addition, the proposed solution for cases that may indeed give rise to conflicts with the principle of no self-incrimination is the surrender of the mandatory obligation rules in favour of the protection of the taxpayer's rights. This is the correct approach; however, it diminishes dramatically the desired effect of the mandatory disclosure rules.[28] Indeed, under the proposed treatment, the tax-evading taxpayer seems to be in a better position than the non-tax evading taxpayer: they both have an obligation to disclose reportable cross-border transactions, but a taxpayer who considers that such disclosure may result in criminal prosecution is released from that burden, whereas another taxpayer who does not reach the same conclusion is still under that obligation. It is unclear how the rules will be enforced and applied in those situations.

Interestingly, according to the recitals of the Directive 2018/822 (DAC 6), the fundamental rights are respected and the principles recognised in particular by the EU Charter are observed.[29] However, Article 16(1) of Directive 2011/16 provides that the information exchanged may be used in connection with judicial and administrative proceedings that may involve penalties, initiated as a result of infringements of tax law, without prejudice to the general rules and provisions governing the rights of defendants and witnesses in such proceedings. This provision already creates confusion regarding the potential use of the information disclosed by the taxpayer and subsequently exchanged among EU tax authorities, since it does not preclude the possibility of this information being used against the taxpayer in proceedings involving the imposition of administrative sanctions as well as the initiation of criminal proceedings. In this context, this latest amendment to the Directive, DAC 6, has indeed raised significant concerns regarding its compatibility with the no self-incrimination privilege that taxpayers enjoy.

In our view, the uncertainties surrounding the scope of application of the mandatory disclosure rules contained in DAC 6 as well as their compatibility with the no self-incrimination principle create doubts over the suitability of these rules to effectively serve the aim of restoring tax justice. It is rather unfortunate that the

---

[27] See also the analysis in Čičin-Šain (n 23) 98–99 and 101.

[28] See also ibid, 107, arguing that the 'solutions' proposed in the OECD Final Report would strip these rules of their intended efficiency.

[29] See recital 18 of the Directive.

212   *Christiana HJI Panayi and Katerina Perrou*

Commission's drive for tax fairness seems to be mainly channelled into initiatives that enhance the (tax collecting) powers of tax authorities and largely ignores the rights of taxpayers.

B. The Use and Exchange of Illegally Obtained Information: Fruits of a Poisonous Tree?

In principle, all information that a tax authority possesses may be exchanged with other tax authorities on the basis of specific international agreements.[30] There are, however, concerns regarding the use of such information by the recipient tax authority, if it can be proved that the information exchanged was obtained by the responding tax authority under questionable circumstances. It is important to examine whether there is scope to apply the doctrine of 'the fruit of a poisonous tree' in such cases. If so, this could render the information thus obtained useless (or inadmissible).

In the *WebMindLicences* case,[31] the CJEU had the chance to deal with the question of whether information that may have been illegally obtained could be taken into account for the assessment of additional VAT. The case concerned the use of evidence obtained without the taxable person's knowledge in the context of a parallel criminal procedure that had not yet been concluded; namely, through the interception of telecommunications and seizure of emails.

The CJEU pointed out that obtaining evidence in the context of a criminal procedure must be assessed in light of Article 7 of the EU Charter, dealing with the right to respect for private and family life. Since the latter contains rights which correspond to those guaranteed by Article 8(1) of the ECHR, Article 7 of the Charter (in accordance with Article 52(3) of the Charter) is to be given the same meaning and the same scope as Article 8(1) of the ECHR, as interpreted by the case law of the ECtHR.[32]

Accordingly, the CJEU held that the national court which reviews the legality of the decision founded on such evidence has the duty to verify, first, whether the interception of telecommunications and seizure of emails were means of investigation provided for by law and were necessary in the context of the criminal procedure and, second, whether the use by the tax authorities of the evidence obtained by those means was also authorised by law and necessary.

The CJEU went on to hold that if the national court finds that that evidence was obtained in the context of the criminal procedure, or used in the context of the

---

[30] The OECD Global Forum Working Group on Effective Exchange of Information has developed a Model Agreement on the Exchange of Information in Tax Matters (Model TIEA), available at https://www.oecd.org/ctp/exchange-of-tax-information/taxinformationexchangeagreementstieas.htm (accessed 8 January 2020).

[31] Case C-419/14 *WebMindLicences* EU:C:2015:832.

[32] ibid para 70. For an analysis of the data protection guarantees under Art 8 ECHR and Art 8 of the EU Charter, see Wöhrer (n 5), sections 6.2 and 6.4, respectively.

administrative procedure, contrary to Article 7 of the Charter, it must disregard that evidence and annul that decision. Such evidence must also be disregarded if the national court cannot verify that the evidence was obtained in the context of the criminal procedure in accordance with EU law or cannot at least satisfy itself, on the basis of a review already carried out by a criminal court in an *inter partes* procedure, that it was obtained in accordance with EU law.

Arguably, the standard adopted by the CJEU is quite high. It appears that, irrespective of what the national law stipulates on the use of illegally obtained evidence, the CJEU demands that a separate and autonomous assessment should be made, based on the guarantees protected by the EU Charter. However, this is not yet settled.

Indeed, in a judgment published in 2016, in *KS and MS v Germany*,[33] the ECtHR was called to examine the compatibility of a tax assessment in Germany, which had taken place as a result of a search warrant that had been issued due to evidence that had been obtained in breach of international and domestic law. The ECtHR's conclusion here differed from the one reached by the CJEU.

The ECtHR acknowledged that a search in someone's private house constitutes an infringement of the right of respect of a person's home. Since the rights of Article 8 ECHR are not absolute but can legitimately be limited, the ECtHR went on to examine whether such an interference was justified. The ECtHR observed that the safeguards provided by German legislation and jurisprudence against abuse in the sphere of searches in general could be considered adequate and effective; as such, they were compliant with Article 8.[34] The ECtHR observed that the search was ordered in order to find further evidence in order to establish whether the taxpayers were in fact liable for tax evasion. The Liechtenstein data, which were the only evidence available at the relevant time, suggested that the applicants might have evaded paying tax but this was not sufficient proof.[35] Lastly, the ECtHR pointed out that under the well-established case law of the German Federal Constitutional Court there is no absolute rule that evidence which has been acquired in violation of the procedural rules cannot be used in criminal proceedings.[36]

In light of the above considerations, the ECtHR held that the interference with the taxpayers' rights as protected under Article 8 was justified.

This judgment was delivered at a time when few, if any, relevant data sets other than the one at issue had been purchased by German authorities. Furthermore, only a few sets of criminal proceedings relying on unlawfully obtained tax data as an evidential basis had been instigated. The ECtHR attached particular weight to this fact.[37] One could argue that the ECtHR accepted the justification of the

---

[33] See the judgment in the ECHR case, *KS and MS v Germany* (Application no 33696/11), 6 October 2016.

[34] ibid para 47.

[35] ibid para 49.

[36] ibid paras 28 and 51.

[37] ibid para 51.

interference with the rights protected under Article 8 after having established that this was an exceptional case and not a widespread practice of the tax authorities.[38]

These considerations may provide a useful guidance towards the future use of information obtained illegally. Indeed, the widespread exchange of information between tax authorities cannot mean that the guarantees against the use of illegally obtained information have been forfeited in favour of the tax authorities. On the contrary, this should be conceived as an exception which can only be interpreted (and applied) narrowly.

The legal issue in both cases was the same: the scope of application of the guarantees for the protection of the private home and the impact of these guarantees on the potential use of illegally obtained evidence. The fact that these guarantees as set out in the EU Charter seem to correspond to the guarantees provided for in the ECHR, create confusion as to the scope of application of the judgment in the *WebMindLicences* case. Although the CJEU is not limited by the judgments of the ECtHR and can provide for a higher level of protection,[39] the fact that the ECtHR used a lower level of protection regarding the use of illegally obtained evidence, in a case decided after the judgment of the CJEU in the *WebMindLicences* case, creates an overall uncertainty on the standard that is applicable within the EU.

C. Exchanging Information without the Knowledge of the Taxpayer Whose Information is Being Exchanged

In a number of instances, the taxpayers have challenged exchanges of information that took place without their knowledge.[40] Both the CJEU and the ECtHR have rendered decisions on the validity of the exchange of information rules and their compatibility with the right to a fair trial and the right to respect the taxpayers' private life.

In *Sabou*,[41] the CJEU was called to examine whether EU law, as derived in particular from Directive 77/799 (the predecessor to Directive 2011/16) and the fundamental right to be heard, conferred on a taxpayer from a Member State the

---

[38] See also ibid para 52, where the ECtHR also refers to the fact that no evidence was produced before it, indicating that the German authorities, at the relevant time, deliberately and systematically breached domestic and international law in order to obtain information relevant to the prosecution of tax crimes.

[39] This is explicitly provided in Art 52(3) of the EU Charter.

[40] In relation to the right to be informed, see CE Weffe, 'The Right to Be Informed: The Parallel between Criminal Law and Tax Law, with Special Emphasis on Cross-Border Situations' (2017) 9 *World Tax Journal* 431.

[41] Case C-276/12 *Jiří Sabou v Finanční ředitelství pro hlavní město Prahu* (Grand Chamber) EU:C:2013:678; see also the comments in CFE ECJ Task Force, 'Opinion Statement ECJ-TF 2/2014 of the CFE on the Decision of the European Court of Justice in *Sabou* (Case C-276/12), Concerning Taxpayer Rights in Respect of Exchange of Information upon Request' (2014) 54 *European Taxation* 318; F Chaouche and W Haslehner, 'Cross-Border Exchange of Tax Information and Fundamental Rights' in W Haslehner, G Kofler and A Rust, *EU Tax Law and Policy in the 21st Century* (Netherlands, Kluwer Law International, 2017) 179.

right to be informed of a request for assistance from that Member State addressed to another Member State; the right to take part in formulating the request addressed to the requested Member State; and the right to take part in an examination of witnesses organised by the requested Member State.[42] The CJEU found that there was no such right in the Directive itself and it was up to domestic legislation to protect the taxpayer's right to a fair trial.

The ECtHR followed this line of reasoning in the *Othymia* case,[43] where it found that the information exchanged was not in breach of Article 8 ECHR and the right to respect of private life. In particular, the ECtHR found that the exchange of information had taken place in accordance with the law (especially Directive 77/799/EEC). It pursued a legitimate aim, which was the payment of taxes and it was necessary in a democratic society, as, according to the judgment of the CJEU in the *Sabou* case, there was no obligation to inform the taxpayer who was the subject of the exchange of information. The ECtHR also held that in taxation, as in other areas, investigative methods may have to be used covertly. Accordingly, it cannot be a requirement of Article 8 ECHR that prior notice of lawful tax investigations or exchanges of tax-related information be given to all persons potentially implicated.[44]

In another case that was also brought before the ECtHR and was decided in 2015, the case of *GSB v Switzerland*,[45] the ECtHR dealt with an information exchange that had taken place between the Swiss tax authorities and the IRS and was based on a special agreement between the USA and Switzerland. The taxpayer complained that the transmission and subsequent disclosure of his bank details to the IRS amounted to a violation of his right to respect for his private life. The ECtHR held that the transmission of information that was made pursuant to the international agreement between the Swiss Confederation and the USA was provided in law, pursued a legitimate aim and was necessary in a democratic society. It was noted that the taxpayer had effective procedural safeguards at his disposal to challenge the surrender of his bank details, thereby protecting him against arbitrary implementation of the agreements between Switzerland and the USA.[46] In any case the data disclosed was of a non-personal nature. The ECtHR held that it was not unreasonable for Switzerland to prioritise the general interest of an effective and satisfactory settlement with the USA over the private interest of the taxpayer. As such, Switzerland did not overstep its margin of appreciation and no breach of Article 8 ECHR could be established.[47]

---

[42] Case C-276/12 *Sabou*, ibid para 30.
[43] See *Othymia Investments BV v the Netherlands* (dec) (Application no 75292/10), 16 June 2015.
[44] ibid para 44.
[45] See *GSB v Switzerland* (Application no 28601/11), 22 December 2015.
[46] ibid para 96.
[47] ibid para 97.

216   *Christiana HJI Panayi and Katerina Perrou*

This was the case law of the European courts until 2017. However, the *Berlioz* case,[48] decided in 2017, marked a shift towards greater protection of taxpayers' rights in relation to information exchanges.

In this case,[49] the CJEU found that the protection against arbitrary or disproportionate intervention by public authorities in the sphere of the private activities of any natural or legal person constituted a general principle of EU law.[50] Therefore, for the protection of that right, Article 47 of the EU Charter applied and a person from whom information was requested had the right to be informed in a way that allowed that person to challenge the validity of the request, without at the same time having the right to have full access to the request of information.

Although it might appear that the decision in the *Berlioz* case goes against the CJEU's previous judgment in *Sabou*, this, in fact, is not the case. Indeed, the two cases are different in many aspects and that could justify the different result. In the *Sabou* case, the exchange of information concerned the taxpayer himself, whereas the *Berlioz* case concerned the rights of a relevant person (a third person, other than the taxpayer) from whom information was requested based on the Directive on Administrative Cooperation. Therefore, the position of the taxpayer who is under investigation and who cannot be made aware of the proceedings during the collection of information from the tax authorities without this knowledge jeopardising the progress of the tax audit is not the same as the position of a person, other than the taxpayer, from whom information is requested pursuant to the provisions of the same Directive and who has a right to verify that the procedure complies with the provisions of the Directive, as he faces consequences in case of no compliance.[51]

In both cases the CJEU by accepting legitimate limitations to fundamental rights, seeks to safeguard the effectiveness of information exchange under the Directive on Administrative Cooperation 2011/16. In *Sabou*, the limitation was of a temporal nature: the taxpayer could not rely on fundamental rights during the early stages of the collection of information to challenge the lawfulness of the procedure; yet he must be able to do so in full at a later stage. In *Berlioz*, the limitation was of a quantitative nature: the relevant person could not have access to the full text of the request of information; yet he must have access to the minimum information referred to in Article 20(2) of Directive 2011/16.[52]

---

[48] Case C-682/15 *Berlioz Investment Fund SA v Directeur de l'administration des Contributions directes* (Grand Chamber) EU:C:2017:373.

[49] For comments see, indicatively, K Pantazatou, 'Luxembourg: Fundamental rights in the era of information exchange – The Berlioz case (C-682/15)' in M Lang, P Pistone, A Rust et al (eds), *CJEU – Recent Developments in Direct Taxation 2017* (Linde Verlag, 2018) 127; CFE ECJ Task Force, 'Opinion Statement ECJ-TF 3/2017 on the Decision of the Court of Justice of the European Union of 16 May 2017 in Berlioz Investment Fund SA (Case C-682/15), Concerning the Right to Judicial Review under Article 47 of the EU Charter of Fundamental Rights in Cases of Cross-Border Mutual Assistance in Tax Matters' (2018) 58 *European Taxation* 93; B Michel, 'Exchange of Information on Request: Whenever, Wherever? Shakira's (and Berlioz's) Right to Judicial Review of the Foreseeable Relevance Standard' (2019) 73 *Bulletin for International Taxation* 90.

[50] *Berlioz* (n 48) para 51, with further references to CJEU case law.

[51] See also ibid para 58 where the CJEU compares the two cases.

[52] ibid, para 100.

The impact of the *Berlioz* case is significant. First, it showed that tax transparency is not absolute and that fundamental rights such as the right to an effective remedy can limit its application. Second, after *Berlioz* it is very difficult for the tax authorities to rely on fishing expeditions, as the information holder may effectively challenge the validity of an information order, at least in cases of obvious lack of foreseeable relevance of the request. Last but not least, it must be pointed out that even in cases of doubt, a national court that has full access to the request of information, may always intervene, following a petition by the taxpayer, to ensure the validity of the request according to the standards of the Directive.

Again, with its latest decision on the matter, the CJEU seems to adopt a rather high standard of protection.

D. Inter-continental Exchange of Information: Which Standard of Protection?

Tax authorities have a duty to protect the information collected in the course of exercising their duties. The same duty applies for the information received by a tax authority in the context of exchange of information. Thus, for example, under Article 26(2) of the OECD Model Tax Convention, the recipient state is obliged to treat any information it receives in the same manner as it treats information obtained under its own domestic laws. However, this guarantee, which essentially reflects the principle of national treatment, may not always be the most suitable way to provide adequate guarantees of tax confidentiality. From the perspective of the taxpayer, this is certainly not the same.

A taxpayer disclosing information to the tax administration of their state of residence is covered by legislation protecting such information in that state. Furthermore, the taxpayer has the (judicial) means to enforce such protection at the level guaranteed by domestic legislation. Once the information is exchanged, however, this information is protected in the other state according to the level of protection that applies in that recipient state. Within the EU this may not be such a major problem, as the level of protection guaranteed in all Member States may be considered comparable. This is particularly so for individuals, who enjoy the protection of the General Data Protection Regulation.[53] However, for exchanges between EU and third countries, taxpayers cannot simply rely on an assumption that the level of protection in the recipient country will not be lower than the one accorded in the requested EU Member State.

---

[53] Regulation (EU) 2016/679 of the European Parliament and of the Council of 27 April 2016 on the protection of natural persons with regard to the processing of personal data and on the free movement of such data, and repealing Directive 95/46/EC, (2016) OJ L 119/1. See, however, Art 25 of Directive 2011/16, concerning data protection, where it is provided that the rights to data protection are superseded by the need for the effective functioning of the exchange of information mechanisms.

218 *Christiana HJI Panayi and Katerina Perrou*

This discrepancy and the concerns that it creates may be illustrated by the CJEU judgment in the *Schrems* case.[54] In this case Mr Schrems challenged the level of protection of his personal data, that he, as a Facebook user, gave to Facebook Ireland, and which was subsequently transferred from the European Union to the US, to servers of Facebook Inc. Although this was not a tax case, it offers useful insights on how the protection of tax information at the level of the recipient state should be treated. In its judgment of 6 October 2015, the CJEU held that Commission Decision 2000/520[55] did not contain any finding regarding the existence of US rules providing for the protection of persons whose data were transferred from the EU to the US. The CJEU pointed out that there was no evidence that measures were adopted by the US intended to limit any interference with the fundamental rights of those persons. Such measures were required even for cases in which the interference of the State entities of that country would be justified by the need to pursue legitimate objectives, such as national security. The examination of the adequacy of the protection afforded in the recipient country, as dictated by the CJEU, should not be merely formalistic. Rather, there must be a substantial assessment of whether effective legal protection against interference of that kind was indeed available in the recipient country.

The standard of protection within the EU, as confirmed by the CJEU, was the standard set by Article 47 of the EU Charter, which provided for the fundamental right of effective judicial protection against any kind of arbitrary interference by the State. Indeed, the very existence of effective judicial review designed to ensure compliance with provisions of EU law was inherent in the existence of the rule of law.

The CJEU conducted an examination of the remedies available in the USA in this respect and concluded[56] that legislation not providing for any possibility for an individual to pursue legal remedies in order to have access to personal data relating to him, or to obtain the rectification or erasure of such data, did not respect the essence of the fundamental right to effective judicial protection, as enshrined in Article 47 of the EU Charter. The CJEU pointed out that the Commission did not state in Decision 2000/520 that the USA in fact 'ensures' an adequate level of protection by reason of its domestic law or its international commitments.[57] As a consequence, the CJEU declared Decision 2000/520 that contained the safe harbour rules invalid.

---

[54] Case C-362/14 *Schrems v Data Protection Commission* (Grand Chamber), EU:C:2015:650. Stateside data protection is still under scrutiny: see AG's Opinion in Case C-311/18 *Facebook Ireland and Schrems v Data Protection Commission* EU:C:2019:1145.

[55] Commission Decision 2000/520/EC of 26 July 2000 pursuant to Directive 95/46/EC of the European Parliament and of the Council on the adequacy of the protection provided by the safe harbour privacy principles and related frequently asked questions issued by the US Department of Commerce (notified under document number C(2000) 2441), (2000) OJ L 215/7.

[56] Case C-362/14 *Schrems* (n 54) para 95.

[57] ibid para 97.

Arguably, the judgment in *Schrems* points to the path that EU Member States should follow regarding exchange of tax information with third countries. In *Schrems*, the CJEU emphasised that it was the duty of national data protection authorities to keep data transfers to third states under review, in order to ensure that EU persons will enjoy at the recipient country the same guarantees that they enjoy in the EU. Arguably, the same reasoning should apply to tax information, which is already protected under the General Data Protection Regulation. There is no reason why, on this point, individual taxpayers and corporate taxpayers should be treated differently. We are of the opinion that the same treatment should be extended to information concerning corporate taxpayers.

Tax authorities should not ignore the fact that they are dealing with the taxpayer's information and therefore do not have carte blanche regarding its treatment; on the contrary, tax authorities may be restricted in sharing this information with jurisdictions that do not provide the same level of protection.

III. The Way Forward: Remedying the Uncertainty

The international tax regime has undergone dramatic changes in the last few years. After it was observed that the porous borders (especially within the EU) and the digitalisation of the economy offered more complex opportunities for tax evasion, tax authorities responded by agreeing to instruments facilitating greater cooperation on a global level. Transparency has been a key element of the transformation of the international tax regime. However, greater transparency regarding the affairs of taxpayers, demands greater responsibility from the tax authorities regarding their handling of tax information they have access to and their powers to exchange or transmit such information to other tax authorities.

In this chapter, a number of problematic issues were identified and the responses that have been formed at EU level were presented. It was shown that the situation is far from ideal. In fact, there are serious concerns regarding the effectiveness of the protection of taxpayers' rights in this context. Up to now, such concerns have served as the basis for challenging various aspects of the handling of tax information by the tax authorities before the courts. Still, the fragmentation of the rules on the protection of taxpayers' rights and the overall uncoordinated response to some of the problems identified illustrate the limitations of the legal process – and to an extent of the international tax community – in this area. What is needed is the creation of an antidote.

The necessity to adopt a universal taxpayer bill of rights or minimum standards of protection is not something new.[58] In the past, some soft law proposals have

---

[58] See RG Anton, 'The Fragmentation of Taxpayers' Rights in International Dispute Resolution Settings; Healing Anxieties through Judicial Dialogue' (2018) 10 *World Tax Journal* 131, 133 with further references to the literature.

220 Christiana HJI Panayi and Katerina Perrou

been put forward,[59] for example, the European Commission's European Taxpayers' Code,[60] without much success. In our view, the time is ripe to revisit these initiatives, even though to some the protection of the tax base from BEPS practices and the protection of taxpayers' rights might seem counterintuitive. Ideally, the same soft law tools that were used for the development of the BEPS Actions and the minimum standards should now be used to develop a framework for the protection of taxpayers' rights, in which a Universal Taxpayer Bill of Rights would be prevalent.

Thanks to the Inclusive Framework, which has managed to bring together the vast majority of jurisdictions, a high level of consensus has been achieved in some areas covered by the BEPS project. Dialogue between tax authorities appears to continue in other areas. Drafting and agreeing on a catalogue of minimum standards and best practices, such as the one drafted by Baker and Pistone in their 2015 IFA General Report,[61] could be the starting point for creating a much needed *de minimis* level of protection of taxpayers' rights. Arguably, the effectiveness of the BEPS recommendations can only be enhanced by complementing them with basic minimum standards to protect the rights of taxpayers. This will go some way in showing that tax justice is not just a slogan for the increase of the powers of tax authorities.

---

[59] Anton, ibid, 134, argues that in the current post-BEPS era, setting up a new institutional system for the protection of taxpayers' rights, such as the one adopted by the ECtHR, will not likely prosper. Similarly, the introduction of a hard law taxpayer's code at the EU level by means of a directive would likely fail in meeting the subsidiarity and proportionality tests. In the field of human rights, states are traditionally quite reluctant to accept mandatory and binding jurisdiction of an international court entitled to monitor human rights in their national jurisdictions. Therefore, the current efforts are focused on instruments of soft law that encompass a catalogue of best practices and common standards of taxpayers' rights to be implemented by states. These legal instruments advocate for a major involvement of taxpayers in all administrative tax procedures, including tax assessment, tax audits, mutual assistance, cross-border dispute resolutions, etc.

[60] See European Commission, *Guidelines for a Model for A European Taxpayer's Code, TAXUD* (2016) 6598744 (EC 2016), available at https://ec.europa.eu/taxation_customs/sites/taxation/files/guidelines_for_a_model_for_a_european_taxpayers_code_en.pdf (accessed on 8 January 2020). On the possible introduction of a EU taxpayer's code see L Cerioni, 'The Possible Introduction of a European Taxpayer Code: Objective and Potential Alternatives' (2014) 54 *European Taxation* 392, who observes that although it is not legally binding, EU Member States should implement these rules into their national laws, if such rules do not already exist. See also B Peeters, 'Towards a More Coordinated Approach of the Relation Between the Taxpayer and Tax Administration: The European Taxpayers' Code' (2017) 26 *EC Tax Review* 178.

[61] P Baker and P Pistone, 'General Report' in *The Practical Protection of Taxpayers' Rights*, IFA, Cahiers de droit fiscal international, vol 100B (The Hague, Sdu Uitgevers, 2015).

13

Tax Justice and Older People: An Examination Through the Lens of Critical Tax Theory

JANE FRECKNALL-HUGHES, NASHID MONIR,
BARBARA SUMMERS AND SIMON JAMES*

'Tax justice' is a term commonly used in the context of ensuring that companies and individuals pay the 'right' amount of tax, although it is acknowledged that it also relates to promoting societal well-being through the use of the tax system, this last connotation linking to the wider, more general definition of (Western) justice as fairness in the way people are dealt with, doing what is morally right and giving everyone his/her due. In the latter sense, individuals and their tax affairs should always be dealt with equitably and without bias. However, the UK tax system contains inherent biases which impact adversely on older people, which are exacerbated by the advent of digitalisation, a key finding revealed by the study reported in this chapter.

The study was funded by the Chartered Institute of Taxation (CIOT), to examine the records of *Tax Help for Older People* (*Tax Help*), a charity which assists those (typically) aged over 55 with income of £20,000 or less who experience problems with taxation, chiefly income tax. It was an archive-based study which explored and analysed data in *Tax Help*'s case files to identify the types of problems that *Tax Help*'s clients experience and why such problems arise. The study followed up on an earlier scoping study into those same records, also funded by the CIOT. Details of 708 case files were recorded over a series of seven site visits during 2016–17, with the separate scoping study examining 169 cases. The data are viewed through the lens of critical tax theory, with the findings making a contribution to studies in this area, which have not hitherto examined the experiences of older people through this lens.

---

* The authors gratefully acknowledge funding from the CIOT, which enabled this research to be carried out, and the very generous assistance provided by the staff at *Tax Help*.

I. Introduction

Civil rights law considers as unlawful discrimination any unfair or unequal treatment of an individual, or group of individuals, based on certain characteristics, which are thus protected by law. The UK Equality Act 2010 lists nine protected characteristics, one of which is age. The others are: disability, gender reassignment, marriage or civil partnership (in employment only), pregnancy and maternity, race, religion or belief, sex and sexual orientation. Age differs from many other characteristics as it affects everyone, sooner or later (assuming they live long enough): it is not a condition into which anyone is born, or over which they have any choice. Individuals who may or may not share other protected characteristics will also be affected by age, which can bring with it yet other characteristics, for example disability, so older individuals may thus be affected by multiple layers of discrimination. This is further compounded in the context of a tax system, which older people find especially difficult to engage with for a number of reasons, such as being 'cast adrift' from Pay as You Earn (PAYE) systems previously implemented by their employer and not knowing whether they need to be in the self assessment regime. Added to this in recent years has been the further requirement to deal with these difficulties by digital means, which, we argue, superimposes another layer of discrimination. As we show in this chapter, older individuals, possibly already excluded from engaging with the tax system because of issues associated with old age, are then further excluded by the need to engage with a digitalised system. The UK tax system as it stands is designed for those of able body and mind, who are tax-educated/literate, and it inherently and increasingly discriminates against those who are not, or who cannot afford to pay for professional tax advice, all of which undermine the concept of 'tax justice'.

The past few years have seen a determined effort by HM Revenue & Customs (HMRC) in the UK to encourage individual taxpayers to engage with the tax system online, through either self assessment, or, more recently, the use of a Personal Tax Account (PTA). The reasons for this are in many ways understandable: we live in an age where use of computers and information technology is predominant, and these carry out routine work much more quickly, efficiently and cost-effectively. However, not everyone has a computer or access to one, or even knows how to use one. This is especially true for the older individuals who comprise a significant proportion of our society. Moreover, having to engage with the tax system online adds an additional layer of complexity to dealing with taxation, which many find difficult enough without this added complication. As the literature reviewed in Section II shows, older people's needs as regards digitalisation may be specific, owing to the particular vulnerabilities generated simply by being older.

The research objective of this chapter is to examine the experiences of older people in dealing with a digitalised tax system. Evidence is gathered from the records of the tax charity, *Tax Volunteers*, which runs *Tax Help for Older People* services (*Tax Help* hereafter). *Tax Help* was established in response to an initiative of the Low Incomes Tax Reform Group (LITRG), a committee of the Chartered Institute of Taxation (CIOT). In December 1998, LITRG published a report – *Older People on Low Incomes: The Case for a Friendlier Tax System*[1] – and in the absence of any real action on the part of HMRC to address the problems highlighted therein, LITRG initiated *Tax Help for Older People* in April 2001 as a one-year pilot project in Wolverhampton and in rural areas of the South West of England, chosen as representing very different areas but having in common a substantial population of older people on low incomes. The objective was to provide accessible tax help and advice for older, more vulnerable and unrepresented people on low or modest incomes. Funding for the pilot initially came from the CIOT and the Nuffield Foundation and it was established with the help of just a small number of volunteers. The success and take up of the service led to the eventual establishment of *Tax Volunteers* as a charity in 2004, specifically to run *Tax Help* services.[2] The charity is currently based at Salway Ash, near Bridport, in Dorset. To qualify for assistance, individuals will usually have income of less than £20,000 per annum and be aged over 55.

The evidence, viewed through the lens of critical tax theory (see later), finds a wide range of difficulties presented to older people by the digitalisation of the tax system. We might go so far as to suggest that, despite being a significant part of the UK population, they are overlooked and stigmatised, their needs are unaddressed, and they are left to fend for themselves at a time of life when they are increasingly vulnerable to a variety of other problems. This study makes a significant contribution to the literature on older people and computer/information technology use, as well as filling in a gap in the studies using critical tax theory, which have not specifically examined older people.

The chapter is structured as follows. Section II reviews previous literature on older people in terms of their tax problems, and of computers and information technology generally, then narrows the focus to the digitalisation of tax and digital exclusion. This is followed by a discussion of critical tax theory as the appropriate theoretical framework for this study in Section III, with Section IV then detailing the research methods adopted. The discussion of the findings follows in Section V, with Section VI offering our conclusions.

II. Review of Prior Literature

The UK today has a greater number of older people in its population than ever before. The increase has been steady over recent years. The population growth and demographic statistics provided by the Office of National Statistics (ONS) estimates the total UK population in mid-2017, for example, as being in excess of

---

[1] LITRG, *Older People on Low Incomes: The Case for a Friendlier Tax System* (London, Chartered Institute of Taxation, 1998).

[2] This information was taken from *Tax Help*'s website (www.taxvol.org.uk, accessed 23 April 2017). Tax Volunteers is an independent company limited by guarantee and is a registered charity in England and Wales (No 1102276) and in Scotland (No SC045819).

66 million, with 11.9 million (18.0%) being aged 65 or over and 1.6 million (2.4%) being 85 or over.[3] In mid-2015, the figures were 65.11 million, with 11.6 million (17.8%) being aged 65 or over and 1.5 million (2.3%) being 85 or over.[4] The ONS reported in its *National Life Tables, United Kingdom: 2012–14*[5] that this so-called 'Golden Cohort', born between 1926 and 1935, has 'experienced improvements in mortality throughout most of their lifetimes that no cohorts previously or since have experienced'. The *National Life Tables, United Kingdom: 2015–18* reveal that, although there have been slight decreases in recent years in life expectancy for women aged 65 (some two weeks), it remains unchanged for men, while the number of those aged 90 or over 'is still increasing due to previous improvements in mortality going back many decades'.[6]

It must also be borne in mind that the age range of those deemed 'older' is very wide – typically 55 and over. This is a non-homogeneous group, comprising the retired, the active and the inactive, and persons in both good and poor mental and physical health. Moreover, not all see themselves as 'old' or 'older'. Many people who receive pension income also actually still work to make ends meet, hence this older group is likely to have very limited financial resources. *The Telegraph*, for instance, reported in July 2016 that the 'number of pensioners with jobs has trebled since the 1980s and one in 10 of those over the age of 65 is now in work'.[7] Some of these individuals are members of this 'Golden Cohort', although many are younger. An Office of Tax Simplification (OTS) report on pensioners' taxation, published in 2014, opens with the remark that '[t]here is no such thing as a typical pensioner. They may be single or married; above or below sixty five; in work or taking their leisure; with or without a pension; with or without savings or investments'.[8]

The tax issues generally experienced by older individuals have been well documented by a series of reports by LITRG,[9] the National Audit Office (NAO)[10] and

---

[3] ONS, *Overview of the UK Population July 2017* (ONS, 2017), available at www.ons.gov.uk/releases/overviewoftheukpopulationjuly2017 (accessed 3 December 2018). This was the latest date for which figures were available at the time of writing.

[4] ONS, *Population Estimates for UK, England and Wales, Scotland and Northern Ireland: Mid-2015* (ONS, 2016), available at www.ons.gov.uk/peoplepopulationandcommunity/populationandmigration/populationestimates/bulletins/annualmidyearpopulationestimates/latest (accessed 24 April 2017).

[5] ONS, *National Life Tables, United Kingdom: 2012–14* (ONS, 2015) 8, available at www.ons.gov.uk/peoplepopulationandcommunity/birthsdeathsandmarriages/lifeexpectancies/bulletins/nationallifetablesunitedkingdom/2015-09-23 (accessed 24 April 2017).

[6] ONS, *National Life Tables, United Kingdom: 2015–18* (ONS, 2018) 7, available at www.ons.gov.uk/peoplepopulationandcommunity/birthsdeathsandmarriages/lifeexpectancies/bulletins/nationallifetablesunitedkingdom/2015to2017 (accessed 29 March 2019).

[7] *The Telegraph*, 'Number of Pensioners with Jobs Trebles Since 1980s, With 1 in 10 People Aged Over 65 in Work', available at www.telegraph.co.uk/news/2016/07/28/number-of-pensioners-with-jobs-trebles-since-1980s-with-1-in-10 (accessed 24 June 2017).

[8] OTS, *Review of Pensioners' Taxation: Final Report* (London, Office of Tax Simplification, 2013) 4.

[9] LITRG, *Tax Help For Older People (TOP) Pilot Projects in the South West And West Midlands, April 2001 to March 2002*, Final Report (London, Chartered Institute of Taxation, 2002).

[10] NAO, *Report by the Comptroller and Auditor General, HC 961 Session 2008–09, HM Revenue & Customs: Dealing with the Tax Obligations of Older People* (London, The Stationery Office, 2009).

the OTS.[11] An earlier LITRG report in 1998,[12] states that older people on low incomes: (i) have less access to support, such as a payroll department or a professional tax adviser; (ii) are more likely than younger people to suffer from physical disabilities, thus impeding their ability to deal with their tax affairs; (iii) often have to cope with tax issues, for the first time, following bereavement; (iv) face a tax system that is particularly complex for those aged 65 or over; and (v) must deal with PAYE and tax withholding systems which are not geared to their needs. The fact of digitalisation being superimposed compounds these existing issues. This, in a wider sense, encompasses within it the idea of 'tax literacy', not just in terms of coping with a tax system that is complex per se, but in using digital tools to deal with it. Research in this field, as a sub-set or dimension of financial literacy, is a recent development. Cvrlje suggests that 'discussions on tax literacy are not widespread and the concept is also not discussed widely nor is it generally defined or accepted',[13] although tax literacy generally is linked to 'tax complexities including tax revenues and tax compliance' and enables people to 'control their personal financial resources'.[14]

The ONS has also recently estimated that over 11 million adults in the UK lack basic digital skills, in that they cannot fill in online forms or find websites – and of this 11 million, 4.5 million have never used the internet. Of the 4.5 million, 2.6 million were older than 75.[15] The over-75s also comprise the group with the highest level of lapsed internet use, although internet use by those aged 65 and over has overall increased since 2011. Since the ONS began its survey in 2011, adults aged 75 years and over have consistently been the lowest users of the internet.[16]

While some older people will be very comfortable with computer and internet use, others may not. Younger people tend to grasp new ideas more quickly and thoroughly than older people, possibly because, for older people, new ideas involve 'unlearning' older, entrenched facts, which can be more difficult than learning something for the first time.[17] General levels of education are also relevant.[18]

---

[11] OTS, *Review of Pensioners' Taxation: Interim Report* (London, Office of Tax Simplification, 2012). For the 2013 Report, see n 8.

[12] See n 1 above.

[13] D Cvrlje, 'Tax Literacy as an Instrument of Combating and Overcoming Tax System Complexity, Low Tax Morale and Tax Non-Compliance' (2015) 4(3) *Macrotheme Review* 156, 158.

[14] ibid. See also T Chardon, B Freudenberg and M Brimble, 'Are Australians Under or Over Confident When it Comes to Tax Literacy, and Why Does it Matter?' (2016) 14(3) *eJournal of Tax Research* 650. The authors report on research carried out in Australia of 604 individuals (188 male, 416 female, including 65 people overall over 55 years in age), indicating that 19% of Australians had 'tax literacy scores classified as either "poor" or "low"'(at 652).

[15] ONS, *Internet Users in the UK: 2018* (ONS, 2018) 6, available at www.ons.gov.uk/businessindustry-andtrade/itandinternetindustry/bulletins/internetusers/2018 (accessed 29 March 2019).

[16] ibid.

[17] See HC Lehman, *Age and Achievement* (NJ, Princeton, 1953).

[18] See C Gagliardi, G Mazzarini, R Papa, C Giuli and F Marcellini, 'Designing a Learning Program to Link Old and Disabled People to Computers' (2007) 34(1) *Educational Gerontology* 15.

There are also other barriers/limitations to computer use for older people – financial reasons (cost of computers and internet access); complexity in locating information; navigation; using programmes; concerns about security and privacy; and lack of technical assistance.[19] Additional difficulties are caused by physical impairments like arthritis, visual impairments and ergonomic obstacles, such as small font size.[20] Individuals have also reported problems caused variously by lack of computer knowledge; having insufficient room in their living space; feeling too old to learn; lack of patience with the computers; a degree of laziness; lack of typing skills; no transportation to computer classes; fears about 'radiation'; and lack of interest[21] (some of which might apply to younger users as well). However, it must be remembered that, while some older people may have used computers in their working lives before retiring and gained the necessary basic skills to use them (eg typing), most people aged 65 or over will not have experienced them as part of everyday school or leisure activities in the same way as younger people currently do, so computer use may not be 'second nature'. This all needs to be considered in terms of the speed of technological change in recent years. For instance, the first smartphone went on sale fewer than 25 years ago, 'preceded only by a couple of years by the invention of the world wide web'.[22]

A considerable amount of academic research has been undertaken to date on older people's use of computers and information technology, with special reference to how older people respond, their attitudes and learning abilities.[23] The various studies often reveal conflicting results in their findings, although the same general themes emerge relating to whether older adults are technologically inadequate; whether they have difficulties in learning new technologies; whether they are more selective of the technology they use than younger people or have a more negative attitude towards it; and whether they are subject to the same or different influences as younger individuals. There are many 'common myths'[24] about older people in

---

[19] See BD Carpenter and S Buday, 'Computer Use Among Older Adults in a Naturally Occurring Retirement Community' (2007) 23(6) *Computers in Human Behaviour* 3012.

[20] See A Tatnall and J Lepa, 'The Internet, E-Commerce and Older People: An Actor Network Approach to Researching Reasons for Adoption and Use' (2003) 16(1) *Logistics Information Management* 56; and I Darroch, J Goodman, S Brewster and P Gray, 'The Effect of Age and Font Size on Reading Text on Handheld Computers' in MF Costabile and F Paternò (eds), *Human-Computer Interaction – INTERACT 2005, IFIP TCIB International Conference Proceedings*, Rome, Italy, September (Berlin, Springer, 2005).

[21] As noted by Carpenter and Buday (n 19).

[22] OTS, *Technology Review: A Vision for Simplicity* (OTS, 2019) 8, available at www.gov.uk/government/publications/will-tax-simplification-still-be-needed-as-technology-advances (accessed 9 February 2019).

[23] This body of work is summarised by T Broady, A Chan and P Caputi, 'Comparison of Older and Younger Adults' Attitudes Towards and Abilities with Computers: Implications for Training and Learning' (2010) 41(3) *British Journal of Educational Technology* 473.

[24] ibid 477.

relation to computers and technology: both young and old may be affected similarly. However, in reference to older people:

> [f]irst, consideration must be given to allow ample time for older people to master new skills. Second, care must be taken to treat any person learning to use technology in a positive manner that makes them feel like they are valued and that success is the expected outcome.[25]

Factors which assist older people in learning to use technology have been found to be, in order of importance: simple and clear written instructions; clarity of meaning of operating instructions; clarity of demonstrator; easy pace of demonstration; short sequence of instructions; one step operation; audio/visual prompts to indicate next steps; large print size of written instructions; colour coded instructions; and an accompanying sound, such as beeping.[26] However, it is a significant problem that older people's requirements 'are not often considered in the design of computer systems and software',[27] so it is not surprising to find them among the 'digitally excluded'.

'Digital exclusion' is defined in a report published in 2019 by the OTS as 'having no use of the internet – predominantly because of a lack of access at home (or in ... place of work for businesses), or for a small minority because of no use despite having access'.[28] The report acknowledges that certain elements in society are excluded from using digital technology. Research undertaken by HMRC in 2017 on the use of the Personal Tax Account (PTA) stated that 'around 10 to 15% of the overall HMRC customer population is digitally excluded'.[29] The 2019 OTS report summarises the reasons for digital exclusion as follows:

– *Lack of access.* There is limited or no broadband availability and/or the costs of hardware, software and internet access prohibit access.

– *Lack of skills.* Possible access exists to physical tools to enable internet connection, but there is a lack of knowledge or ability in using them.

– *Lack of motivation.* Individuals are not interested in bettering their digital skills and make no effort to improve them.[30]

---

[25] ibid.

[26] See C Irizarry and A Downing, 'Computers Enhancing the Lives of Older People' (1997) 16(4) *Australian Journal on Ageing* 161, 164.

[27] J Goodman, A Syme and R Eisma, 'Older Adults' Use of Computers: A Survey' (2003) in *Proceedings of BCS HCI 2003*, Bath, UK, 8–12 September, available at www.researchgate.net/profile/Audrey_Syme/publication/246993432_OLDER_ADULTS%27_USE_OF_COMPUTERS_A_SURVEY/links/0a85e533b24bfb50bb000000/OLDER-ADULTS-USE-OF-COMPUTERS-A-SURVEY.pdf (accessed 11 February 2019). This work, although available in pdf format, does not have page numbers. The quote is on the first page.

[28] OTS, *Technology Review* (n 22) 20.

[29] HMRC, *Personal Tax Account Research* (HMRC, 2017) 6, available at https://assets.publishing.service.gov.uk/government/uploads/system/uploads/attachment_data/file/726978/Personal_Tax_Account_Research.pdf (accessed 11 February 2019).

[30] OTS, *Technology Review* (n 22) 21.

The overall result may be a lack of confidence and increased dependency on assistance, for example individuals may need to borrow equipment and/or be helped to use it, often with someone sitting alongside to help complete online forms. This latter group HMRC recognises as 'Assisted Digital', finding that such individuals suffered from both reduced confidence and increased anxiety, because of the burden perceived as associated with digital issues, and 'a general lack of knowledge and experience of online interactions'.[31] This presents a barrier for this group of people in terms of HMRC's ambition to become one of the 'most digitally advanced tax administrations in the world', providing services that should be 'easy-to-use, convenient, and personalised for individuals, businesses and agents'; promoting 'digital take-up and voluntary compliance by designing for customer needs'; using 'data to help customers avoid errors through pre-population'; and providing 'assistance in using or accessing … services for those who need it'.[32] However, the OTS concludes that considerable work is needed before this vision can be achieved and comments that 'understanding the experience of the user, the taxpayer, is critical in identifying ways to simplify how people manage their tax affairs and improve understanding of their obligations on tax'.[33] The OTS has already reported earlier that more needed to be done to assist people technologically and to help them understand tax, potentially by developing the use of the PTA.[34]

A very important underlying aspect of all this is how well the digitalisation of tax progresses. In 2018, James and Sawyer, for instance, compared the New Zealand (NZ) and UK approaches and identified a number of risks, not least the low success rate of information technology (and related) projects, attributed mainly to poor project management.[35] In the present context, in both NZ and the UK, by the time the new systems are fully operational, the revenue authorities will have lost a substantial number of experienced staff, including those involved in face-to-face dealings with taxpayers. It may be that the consequences arising from a lack of personal engagement with taxpayers have been underestimated and that these fall relatively heavily on older taxpayers for the reasons mentioned above.

III. Theoretical Framework

The literature reviewed above is explicit that older people's needs are not addressed by the tax system, nor are their requirements 'often considered in the design of

---

[31] ibid.

[32] ibid 6.

[33] ibid 5.

[34] OTS, *Guidance for Taxpayers: A Vision for the Future.* (OTS, 2018) 16, available at https://assets. publishing.service.gov.uk/government/uploads/system/uploads/attachment_data/file/746076/OTS_ Guidance_for_taxpayers_041018.pdf (accessed 13 February 2019).

[35] S James and AJ Sawyer, 'Digitalization of Tax: Comparing New Zealand and United Kingdom Approaches' (2018), UNSW, Sydney, Australia, 13th International Tax Administration Conference, 5–6 April.

computer systems and software'.[36] This, together with the other problems identified that relate to their 'older' status, may mean that a significant proportion of the population is excluded from engaging with a tax system which, in theory, should have the capability to deal with all individuals' tax affairs, regardless of who they are or in whatever situation they find themselves – tax being 'the one area of law that affects everyone in our society'.[37] If individuals are prevented from engaging with the tax system, this indicates the presence of some form of bias or prejudice, which brings us into the area of critical tax theory as a lens through which to view the research reported in this chapter. One of the goals of critical tax theory is 'to uncover bias in the tax laws'.[38] In their edited work on *Critical Tax Theory: An Introduction*, Infanti and Crawford include chapters by various authors which address discrimination in the US tax system against race, ethnicity, socio-economic class, gender, sexual orientation, immigration and disability.[39] Old age differs in that it is not a characteristic that one is 'born into'. Many other aspects of the human condition identified by Infanti and Crawford are innate (even immigrant status may, perhaps controversially, transcend generations) and may be seen by an individual as core to their identity. Old age, however, affects everyone if they live long enough, so, on top of these other biases, individuals may find themselves subject to another form of discrimination as they grow older, and have to adapt to ageing and whatever accompanies it at a time when their resources are unlikely to improve. While older people may inherently be included in one or more of the groups identified by Infanti and Crawford, bias against them in the tax system is not addressed as a separate issue, hence this chapter makes a contribution to the body of work in the area of critical tax theory by examining this group. Infanti, in a later work, makes the point that US tax laws reflect the divisions in society, validating existing power and privilege, leading to an institutionalised exclusion of certain groups, saying that '[t]he truly "fundamental" tax questions concern not who gets which tax cut but how our system reflects on us as a society and what it says about how justly and fairly we treat each other'.[40] He goes on specify the differential impacts relating to race, gender, marriage, and the LGBT, immigrant and disabled communities of various aspects of the tax code. He follows up with case studies on the ideas implicit in critical tax theory that tax laws should both reflect and construct social meaning, and reinforces how they make certain individuals stigmatised. This is true also of the group considered in this chapter: older people.

---

[36] Goodman, Syme and Eisma (n 27).

[37] AC Infanti and BJ Crawford, 'Critical Tax Theory: An Introduction' (2009) 1, University of Pittsburgh Legal Studies Research Paper No 2009-04, available at https://ssrn.com/abstract=1333799 (accessed 7 September 2018).

[38] ibid 12.

[39] AC Infanti and BJ Crawford (eds), *Critical Tax Theory: An Introduction* (New York, CUP, 2009).

[40] AC Infanti, *Our Selfish Tax Laws: Towards Tax Reform that Mirrors Our Better Selves* (Cambridge, Mass, The MIT Press, 2018) 151.

IV. Research Methods

This was an inductive, archival study, which examined individual cases that *Tax Help* had dealt with. Over a series of seven site visits during 2016–17, 708 case details were recorded (351 men; 357 women; 35 persons in total being aged under 60). The details were extracted for each case selected on to an Excel spreadsheet for demographic-type details and on to a Word file for the narrative details of the issues involved. The 708 cases comprised in essence a convenience sample, aimed at being generally reflective of the issues which come to *Tax Help*. It would be difficult to obtain any other sort of sample in the context of individuals needing help.

Tax Help records all cases on its client database using a Client Advice Record (CAR), and every time anything is done for any client, an entry is made. Help is provided by a variety of means – post, phone, e-mail, 'surgeries' at venues close to clients' homes, and home visits – by the permanent staff at the charity and by a team of professionally qualified volunteers throughout the UK. The method of help depends on the nature of the problem identified.

The CAR is a key document, as it logs the name of any client, the address, telephone number and a variety of other personal information relevant for tax purposes, such as age, marital/partnership status, tax reference number, etc (though sometimes not all details are present). It usually records the source of the initial query to *Tax Help* (eg *Age UK, Citizens Advice*, previous client, etc), who dealt with it, and to whom, among the volunteer tax advisers, the case was referred, if this was necessary. If a volunteer tax adviser was involved, the CAR records the adviser's name, date, location for giving advice, and the amount of any tax payment/repayment due and whether the case was immediately resolved or required further input. All cases dealt with receive a unique reference number, which is the identifier used in this research, to ensure anonymity and confidentiality. Many individuals were 'returning' clients, and some had entries dating from the establishment of the electronic database in about 2008 (and before). Until a client record was accessed, it was not possible to tell whether a case was a single, anonymous phone call, dealt with almost at once, or whether it involved a returning client with multiple entries, going back many years. Some cases had 50 or so entries; a very long one might have 70; a short one might only have one entry. One-off (sometimes anonymous) queries by phone requiring no more than a few minutes' discussion/advice were not uncommon.

The CAR also logs the type of technical issue on which the client needed help, under broad categories, for example, self assessment, PAYE, advocacy, help with forms, general guidance and tax credits, etc, and listings of the kinds of problems arising are maintained. A basic analysis of the type of tax problems manifesting themselves was thus available a priori, but this did not indicate why such problems might have occurred, so a detailed thematic analysis of the recorded case details was carried out to determine reasons. Overwhelmingly, the issue of engaging with the tax system digitally emerged as a key reason for the problems experienced, as discussed in the next section.

V. Discussion of the Findings

It must be acknowledged first of all that a considerable amount of the work done by *Tax Help* is non-contentious in tax terms, for example the routine completion of tax returns, either by paper or online. Some older clients are very content to deal with their affairs online, but need help to do so, and just regard digitalisation as requiring a different way of doing things. Of the issues discussed below, many may equally apply to the population more widely, not just those over 55: we currently do not know.

A. Lack of Resources – Financial and Other

The effect of tax problems, especially digital ones, on this older group of people, is exemplified by the following case. A retired lady of 68, who had paid no tax since she retired at 60, contacted *Tax Help* when her pension provider deducted £67.40 in tax as a result of using incorrect codes supplied by HMRC. Her e-mail to *Tax Help* is worth quoting in full:

> I have written and telephoned the Tax Office and they agree there is no way I should be charged tax as my income is so small. However, they also say that they cannot issue a refund and I will have to wait till next September when the annual pension is paid for me to get that money back. They have supplied correct tax codes now to my pension provider and advised me to request that [the pension provider] just run me on the payroll again, using these codes and the refund would be automatic. [The pension provider] ha[s] refused to do this unless the Tax people write and ask them to do this. So far this has not happened.
>
> The amount may seem incredibly small to some people but I have to say that being nearly £70 short of the money I was expecting at that time of year was a problem for me. Also, I do not feel that as a 'small person' in society that I have been treated fairly by these organisations. I did nothing and yet have been penalised financially and now, with no sympathetic responses from either of these organisations feel hard done by and let down.
>
> Is there anything you can advise me to do which would not involve me in any further outlay. I have already made telephone calls and sent letters as I feel there is a principle to uphold here and do not see why unempowered people in our society should not be treated fairly, no matter how small the matter may seem to others.
>
> Thank you for offering this free service to pensioners, it is much appreciated. We are not all the 'rich pensioners' that our media would have us believe.

The above example is revealing in other ways, in that it shows how difficult it is to engage with the tax system, as there are so few mechanisms/resources whereby individuals can do so. This lady had at least obtained a response from HMRC: there are numerous instances of people not being able to do so, reporting being 'on hold' so long in trying to make contact by telephone that they abandoned the attempt. One lady reported that attempting to telephone from overseas proved not only impossible but prohibitively expensive, and as the above quote shows, the cost of telephone calls can still be a consideration in the UK (an issue frequently raised). Telephoning an HMRC help line or writing are the commonest ways to contact HMRC if there are problems (if one cannot afford professional advice), and if one does not have online access. While telephone response rates have improved since the problems widely reported on the introduction of a telephone helpline, the level of response still remains an issue – especially when, if there is a need to call back, after establishing contact, it is not possible to talk to the same person. Since HMRC closed its Enquiry Offices, individuals cannot go and talk to anyone face-to-face to try to deal with problems – problems that they cannot often articulate clearly. Digitalisation has removed interaction between human beings. The above example also shows that a relatively small sum of money can be critical to the financial well-being and security of individuals on very low incomes. This lady's income was well under £10,500 – and that is more than many *Tax Help* clients receive. It also shows how many of the problems people experience may be inter-related or overlap, which makes it difficult to classify problems definitively. We go on to report our findings, therefore, in broad general categories, some of which are inherent in the above quote.

B. 'Abandonment' and Tax Code Issues

It was very clear that individuals who had been formerly employed often felt 'cast adrift' from the PAYE system previously implemented by their employer, and might be unaware that they needed to be in the self assessment regime. Removed from the employer's PAYE system, they then had to engage directly with a digitalised tax system on their own, deprived of any support. There was great misunderstanding as to why tax was deducted from one source of income when it appeared to relate to different income, for example the state pension (which is not taxed at source). The issue of the correction of incorrect tax codes is a constant theme throughout the *Tax Help* records. Innumerable cases involved the incorrect calculation/application of 'K' codes by HMRC or a pension provider, often where individuals on retirement had small pensions from different sources.

A K code means that a person has income that is not taxed elsewhere (eg at source) and that is in excess of the tax-free allowance. An employer or pension provider will take the tax due on the untaxed income from wages or pension, even if a different organisation is the one paying the untaxed income. Employers and pension providers cannot take more than half of pre-tax wages or pension in tax when using a K tax code. However, problems can arise if a K code is not issued against the largest source of income. For example, if a K code is issued against the smallest source of income, rather than the largest, it will cause the tax due not to be collected. If this happens for several years, it may give rise to multiple years of under-payments, pushing individuals into self assessment and/or debt. Often uncollected debts will mean that the debt collection agency becomes involved, and things may rapidly spiral out of control, especially as individuals have a tendency to leave tax matters to 'take care of themselves' – a tendency possibly resulting from having an employer's PAYE department deal with tax at source on employment income, and/or because they do not understand the standardised, computer-generated documents they receive. Leaving tax matters to 'take care of themselves' can also result from illness or the forgetfulness associated with failing memory, and may follow years of non-problematic tax filing. This was a problem that had given rise to almost too many cases to count. Some individuals had also clearly tried to deal with their tax affairs online but had ended up in a terrible muddle (eg a wife including her income as that of her husband), covering several years of returns, which *Tax Help* have then sorted out. Others have made more successful attempts, and they have continued to file online on their own after *Tax Help* has shown them what to do, albeit with occasional requests for additional help for any items which fall outside their experience.

C. Access Issues and Errors

Issues regarding access to computers, and/or knowing how to use them, were major problems. Some individuals reported having to complete their self assessment returns via computers in public libraries, and thus not being able to print out their returns so they could retain a copy. Other clients without computer access commonly asked *Tax Help* if the charity could print out a form they needed so that they could complete it and post it to HMRC.

One lady needed a paper copy of her P60, the annual summary of gross pay and deductions provided by an employer. However, the employer only provided these online and as she did not have a computer, or access to one, it caused her considerable worry about how she might check that her income tax position was correct. It is not uncommon for employers/pension providers to apply a wrong code (see above). This might be caused, for example, by a delay in receiving information from HMRC, an error made by the employer/pension provider, or computer systems breaking down (including, in two reported cases, when HMRC experienced computer problems, one of which resulted in a duplicated request notifying an under-payment). The move to the Real Time Information (RTI) system had caused many difficulties and errors, often with individuals' records being duplicated. Some kinds of errors are difficult to explain. One lady received a letter from HMRC stating that she was the personal representative for a person recently deceased: she had never heard of the person in question. Another was very surprised to receive correspondence addressed to the personal representative of herself deceased, even though her National Insurance number was on the letter. Another elderly gentleman was extremely distressed to receive, inexplicably, a request for details of his wife's income, some 12 years after her death.

Access problems can be of several different kinds. There were several reports of *Tax Help* clients trying to deal with making disclosures under an HMRC 'Let

234 Jane Frecknall-Hughes, Nashid Monir, Barbara Summers and Simon James

Property Campaign', that needed an online form which clients could not access. The form could only be completed online: it could not be printed off and completed manually and then posted to HMRC. The case notes in one instance specifically refer to a particular client being 'digitally excluded', with the tax volunteer being prepared to 'go out of his way to help this client', who was aged 70, had no family support and suffered from depression.

Different kinds of access problems were commonly experienced by individuals in terms of filing an online return under self assessment, even where they had done so successfully on prior occasions, as there appeared to be problems over different access routes and problems with passwords not being recognised. Access via the 'Government Gateway' sometimes proved impossible, as did various verification procedures. Similarly, trying to access help through a telephone system using voice recognition proved impossible even for some people who were articulate and knew what they wanted, as well as for those who were confused by it.

Self assessment and whether individuals' tax should be dealt with via self assessment were on-going difficulties. One client, aged 90, was asked for the first time to file a self assessment return online, but the family member authorised to help her was unable to activate the authorisation code, despite a lengthy call with HMRC to take her through what needed to be done. The family member reported that the HMRC adviser 'told her that her computer was rubbish', so she hung up and asked *Tax Help* for assistance. It turned out that there was no reason for the client to be in self assessment, and as she also had not received the married couple's allowance to which she had been entitled, refunds of tax were actually due. (It was common to find that individuals had not claimed, or did not know about, the allowances to which they might be entitled – very commonly and incidentally discovered where individuals had contacted *Tax Help* for assistance on an unrelated matter.) In other cases, individuals had been removed from self assessment, when they should not have been, in numerous instances because a state pension exceeded the personal allowance. Notice to file online where an individual had not even filed a paper return before and did not have computer access could present problems which seemed insuperable at a personal level. Individuals who did not ignore the notices often struggled to find help – even though they wanted to be tax compliant.

D. Self Assessment: Paper Versus Online Filing

Individuals who normally receive paper returns expect that they will continue to file regularly using paper returns, but on a number of occasions HMRC issued 'notice to file' and did not send the paper return. Individuals who had become used to filing paper self assessment returns often found problems with the differences between the paper form and the online requirements. One lady had submitted paper returns for years without any difficulties, but found her attempt to file online for the first time was met by problems. She had always paid tax in previous years and was surprised that her online filing resulted in no tax being due. It turned out that she had a German state pension which was actually non-taxable, but which she had recorded as taxable income on the paper forms. She contacted *Tax Help* when HMRC advised her that this still needed to be recorded online as taxable when she queried no tax being due. She received a refund for four years of over-paid tax. Foreign income, especially pensions, often caused problems, requiring expert technical input from HMRC, as documents providing the necessary details might be in a language other than English. One client with a Danish pension had particular problems as his case had been dealt with by the Needs Enhanced Support (NES) unit of HMRC, which, after helping him file returns, refused to re-open his case in response to a query which was raised (via *Tax Help*) regarding their calculation showing tax was due: it was not. Another individual, who had regularly reported overseas income on the foreign income pages sent with his paper return, received that paper return without the foreign income pages being included. He could not download the necessary pages as he had no computer access.

E. Rectifying Online Problems

It is not always easy or possible to rectify simple errors made in online filing, and it gives rise to possibilities for errors that may not arise with paper returns. A client who received a late filing penalty immediately contacted HMRC, as he thought he had completed his self assessment online and had paid his tax liability on time. It was discovered that, although he had paid his liability, he had not fully submitted his return online (this was not uncommon), so he went back into his online record, submitted the return and appealed the fine. His appeal was refused, on the grounds that, although he had paid on time, he had filed online previously and so did not have a reasonable excuse for filing late. His appeal was then sent to [X city] where it was refused again, owing to the same reasons and outlining the deadlines for appealing to the Tribunal. He missed this deadline because he was away when the letter arrived advising the course of action he should then take. He had advised HMRC in an earlier phone call regarding his appeal that he would be away for two months and asked them to note this on his record and not to send a reply until his return. This was not done and he missed the chance to go to the Tribunal. The penalty here seems extremely harsh. The individual had never filed late before, was advancing in age – and when people use a system only once a year, it is easy to forget exactly all the procedures involved.

Failure to complete the online process is an easy error to make. One self employed person had previously used an accountant to file his self assessment return, but then decided to use online filing himself. In his first year of doing so, he reached the final calculation screen and thought that his filing was completed, not noticing the '95% complete' warning at the top of screen. This was the only indicator that filing was not formally completed. He then paid his bill (on time) and thought that everything had been completed satisfactorily. Late filing penalties followed, leading to the client protesting that he had actually filed and there must be some error at HMRC. Despite numerous contacts, HMRC were unable to explain adequately to the client that his filing was not fully complete, and daily penalties were then added. Eventually filing was completed at an Enquiry Centre, which was then still open for business (only after he had first visited a Centre shown on HMRC website which turned out to have closed), but penalties had reached £1,200 by that time. The client was unaware that his past protestations had been treated as penalty appeals (despite the self assessment return not being formally 'filed' at the time of some of those contacts). Having been told that he had exhausted his appeal chances and that a Tribunal appeal was now his only option, he approached *Tax Help*. After numerous unsuccessful approaches to HMRC by *Tax Help*, the case eventually reached a level of seniority within HMRC such that the penalties were cancelled, but not until the client had endured an extremely stressful 12-month period, caused by the difficulty of using HMRC's self assessment system and inappropriate management/consideration within the penalty appeal/complaint procedure. The case notes include a comment from the tax adviser: 'where else on the Internet can you reach the stage of "payment" without having completing [sic] all the required data input?'.

F. Forms

Individuals have frequently reported difficulties in trying to find the correct form they needed, even though they might know what they were looking for, such as the P53 form to reclaim tax deducted on taking a small pension lump sum, or the R40 form for reclaiming tax over-paid on savings income. The form to transfer the marriage allowance from one spouse to another has generated enormous difficulties, largely because in the first instance it simply was not available and ultimately could only be completed online. One client called HMRC to request marriage allowance transfer and, owing to the automated recorded message, decided to try to register online. However, he was unable to complete online so tried to call HMRC again and was put on hold for a long time; and when he spoke to an adviser, he was told by HMRC they were unable to action the transfer over the phone and he would have to register online. There was also much confusion between the marriage allowance and the married couple's allowance.

G. 'Scams'

Using computerised systems also gives rise to the opportunity for 'scams' in a way that paper returns do not. One *Tax Help* client moved house and consequently did not receive the normal paper return in time to complete and return it by post. In the following January the individual contacted the local *Citizens*

Advice office for assistance to complete the form online. Unfortunately, instead of accessing the HMRC website, the *Citizens Advice* adviser completed the tax return on a bogus site. Both the client and *Citizens Advice* were unaware of this error until the end of January. *Tax Help* assisted the client in contacting HMRC for agreement to file late.

In another case, a client had been coming to *Tax Help* for years for help with untaxed interest. *Tax Help* contacted the client to check the interest figures and to confirm that a refund was due. However, the client told them that her son had gone online to claim the refund – in her words 'my son has made a claim on his computer thing as you have to wait 45 days otherwise'. She had no idea how he did it and *Tax Help* could only assume that her son had opened a PTA for her. While in this case *Tax Help* felt sure that the son was acting in his mother's best interest, it does highlight the vulnerability of an elderly person. An unscrupulous son could easily have entered his own bank details to collect the refund or could have reported fictitious figures to create a larger refund. The refund in this case was wrong because HMRC held incorrect data on the interest the client received, but fortunately, she was owed more not less. However, her son could easily have claimed a refund that was not due.

Another case concerned a lady of 89, suffering from dementia, whose daughter was empowered to act on her behalf as she held power of attorney (POA). The daughter had recently cashed in two pensions for her mother under the trivial commutation rules, one in 2015–16 and one in 2016–17. As she believed that a refund might be due, the daughter contacted HMRC in December 2015, although she was at that time unable to talk to anyone because she had not yet registered the POA with HMRC. HMRC insisted on talking to the mother, who was extremely impolite that day. However, the outcome of the call was that the daughter was advised that the refund would be issued immediately. The second pension was commuted in July 2016. Since the daughter had not heard from HMRC regarding the 2016 commutation, she decided to search online and found 'claim a refund' on Gov.UK. She created a PTA for her mother and made a claim. She did not need to enter any income details, which seemed unusual, and shortly afterwards received an e-mail saying she was due a refund of £1,200. The e-mail gave reference numbers and advised her to visit HMRC to claim the refund, via a link embedded in the e-mail. She did not access the link but returned to her mother's PTA account. It would seem that she claimed again and this time was asked for bank details, which she entered but repeatedly received a message saying 'invalid details'. Finding this all very confusing, she called *Tax Help*, who advised her that this was suspicious and likely to be a scam. As it was difficult for her to explain what had happened, *Tax Help* spoke to HMRC on her behalf to ensure that the correct refunds for both years were issued. In the same week another family member (granddaughter) received an e-mail unexpectedly, advising she was due a refund. Unfortunately, she did access the link embedded into the e-mail and entered all her bank details. It seems that she had been caught by a scam and *Tax Help* advised her to contact her bank.

H. Double Discrimination

As mentioned earlier, and emergent from other findings discussed in this section, it is clear that many older people suffer from severe illnesses and disabilities (physical and mental) which often accompany old age. One of the 'scam' victims mentioned in the previous sub-section was a lady suffering from dementia. The *Tax Help* case records frequently note the effect of a severe physical or mental impairment on their clients, some of which themselves prevent engagement (eg the memory loss associated with dementia, or problems with movement). While younger individuals may also suffer disabilities, they appeared without doubt to be more common in older people, especially in those over 80, and had various impacts in terms of engaging with a digitalised system. A person with sight impairment (typically a problem affecting older people, but which can affect younger people too) might need screen-reading software to be able to complete a self assessment return or PTA online (if, indeed, screen-reading software could cope with such documents in the first instance). Moreover, even screen-reading software would not be able to locate particular forms if an individual needed to download them. Persons suffering from arthritis may not be able to type; and those with, say, Alzheimer's Disease, or being looked after in a care/nursing home, would not be able to engage at any level. Hence digitalisation adds an extra layer of difficulty – an impossibility in many cases – to engaging with a digitalised tax system. Similarly, it was clear that individuals whose first language was not English struggled not only with tax per se, but dealing with it online added an additional level of complexity, owing to more specialised language skills being needed.

VI. Conclusions

It is evident from our findings that many older people struggle in dealing with a digitalised tax system. Many do not have internet access and/or access to a computer, which is a problem added to the existing problems in dealing with tax in the first place. Difficulties are also compounded by the fact that older people may suffer the physical and mental impairments that often accompany the ageing process – and which may be superimposed on other barriers to engagement institutionalised into the system because of other biases against them, creating double discrimination. While some older people are willing to engage with a digitalised system, engaging with it successfully on their own or with only a little help, many need more assistance to do so (some become extremely muddled in trying to deal with their tax affairs online), and clearly fall into the category HMRC have deemed 'Assisted Digital'. They are often caused extreme distress by having to deal not only with 'the taxman', but with 'the taxman' online. Some case notes record individuals suffering severe depression in such circumstances. One client's *Tax Help* case notes carry a report of the client being told by HMRC, in relation to a demand for under-paid tax: 'if you pay it HMRC won't hound you anymore and we won't charge you interest'. She then paid the demand as she was too frightened not to do so. Further demands followed, but another individual at HMRC then referred her to *Tax Help*, who resolved the issue (at root, the problem was one of incorrect codes being issued).

As Infanti[41] has pointed out, the way the tax system is configured, in this context in relation to digitalisation, means that a significant proportion of the population is unfairly excluded from engaging with a tax system which should have the capability to deal with all individuals' tax affairs, given that tax is the one area of law which affects everyone. This is not a group of people who are trying to avoid or evade tax, but who will endeavour to meet their obligations if they know how to do so or can find out. They may, however, end up in a situation where they miss out on refunds or allowances due to lack of ability to engage. Those who do not have access to suitable computer equipment can be exposed to lack of privacy in their tax affairs, by having to use public computers, and this may cause concern to individuals (as well as meaning that they are unable to obtain paper records to take home). Given that many of these people are among the most vulnerable in society, this evidence supports the need for exclusion from the tax system to be addressed.

[41] ibid.

14

Tax Tribunals and Justice
for Litigants in Person

RICHARD THOMAS

On 1 April 2019 the Tax Chamber of the First-tier Tribunal (TC) celebrated (meta-phorically) its tenth anniversary. About seven weeks before that date I retired as a judge of the TC, having served nearly four years in that capacity, and before that, six years as a member, ie from the beginning. I also had extensive experience of appearing before a predecessor tribunal, the General Commissioners of Income Tax, and on occasion before another, the Special Commissioners.

With this background, this felt like an opportune time for me to reflect on my time with the TC and in the context of this volume to seek to examine the question not so much whether the TC provides justice to the parties appealing to it (I think it does in the vast majority of cases) but whether the performance of the TC over the last 10 years lives up to the expectations of those who established it and represents an improvement over previous arrangements.

I do this specifically by reference to the way in which the TC deals with litigants in person (LiPs). Unlike the position with the courts, the Upper Tribunal and some other Chambers of the First-tier Tribunal,[1] the majority of the appellants appealing to and appearing before the TC are LiPs.

I consider briefly what the system was like before the establishment of the TC in April 2009, and what benefits the First-tier Tribunal and the TC in particular were expected to bring.

I do this mainly by drawing on my own experience as well as certain contemporary documents. To judge properly and rigorously whether the TC has improved matters and enhanced the delivery of justice for LiPs would require a major research exercise. Instead, this is a much more subjective account, which also means that I have confined my consideration primarily to direct taxes.

---

[1] The other chamber dealing with large numbers of appellants, most of whom are not legally represented, is the Social Entitlement Chamber (SEC) which deals with benefits (including those administered, like tax credits, by Her Majesty's Revenue & Customs (HMRC)) and other similar matters such as Child Support.

242   *Richard Thomas*

I. Tax Dispute Resolution before 2009

Before the TC was set up, disputes between taxpayers and the income tax authorities which could not be resolved were adjudicated on by one of two bodies, the General Commissioners of Income Tax (GCs) and the Special Commissioners (SCs).

A. The General Commissioners

The GCs had a long history. They appear in Addington's Income Tax Act of 1803[2] as the Commissioners appointed to act 'in the Execution' of the Act, and to whom any person thinking 'himself, herself or themselves respectively overcharged'[3] could appeal. One can see similar types of arrangement in Pitt's 1799 Act and indeed in the Land Tax Acts. Until 1964 the GCs had a number of administrative functions to do with the making of returns and the assessing of income tax, but from then until their abolition their function was simply to decide tax disputes.[4]

The GCs were organised into divisions: there were hundreds of these, roughly corresponding to the hundreds (or rapes, lath(e)s and wapentakes) of the counties, at least in England and Wales. There was a very rough correlation between the area of a division of the GCs and the area of an office of HM Inspector of Taxes (HMIT) – but in cities one could find one body of GCs dealing with many districts (eg City of London) and in the country, one tax district dealing with many divisions. This arrangement was part of the major insistence on localism in tax affairs that allowed the income tax system to gain, if not public acclaim, a degree of support.

The GCs themselves were local worthies with, until 1964, a property qualification. Many were also magistrates.[5] Like magistrates they had a clerk who was usually a local solicitor[6] who gave the GCs legal advice and who was also responsible for the administration of the hearings, for example sending out the notices of appeal, and on the very few occasions when there was an onward appeal, preparing the stated case for the High Court.[7]

However, it was the Inspector of Taxes, an officer of the Board of Inland Revenue who did much of the donkey work, and was responsible for preparing the list of appeals to be heard. This to a great extent reflects the fact that until self assessment the 30-day time limit for making a return was never observed in practice and

---

[2] 43 Geo III (c 122).

[3] ibid s 57.

[4] Their assessing functions were abolished by the Income Tax Management Act 1964.

[5] Something which was readily apparent in the way some chairmen of GCs conducted proceedings and treated appellants.

[6] Occasionally the clerk was a retired Inspector of Taxes. This was notably the case in the City of London and in the Division of Becontree in East London (Becontree being a hundred of the county of Essex).

[7] In nearly all cases the GCs gave an oral decision. Only by seeking a stated case for transmission to the High Court (or Court of Session) could the reasons for the decision usually be discovered.

the procedure for seeking a penalty for this failure was excessively cumbersome. As a result, in the period from July to October each year the offices of HMIT were engaged in the exercise of making estimated Schedule D assessments[8] in round figures, usually a small amount larger than the returned profit of the previous year. These assessments were usually appealed against on the ground that they were estimated and not in accordance with the accounts and returns (which were not at that time in existence). Often little happened after the appeal unless the tax district listed the appeal for a hearing before the GCs. The GCs had the power to issue a notice (called a precept) for accounts or they could, usually after several adjournments, confirm the estimated assessments.[9]

This paper chase ended with the enactment of self assessment in the Finance Act 1994 and its practical introduction in 1996. As a result, the workload of the GCs dropped off significantly, replaced in part by appeals against penalties for the more stringent system for late returns.[10]

Except occasionally in what were known as 'contentious' cases, it was extremely rare for a taxpayer to be represented by a lawyer before the GCs. Many taxpayers were represented by an accountant, whose quality and usefulness varied.[11] But even the best accountants were often not familiar with the disciplines required in a GCs hearing, so their clients were in effect LiPs.

B. Special Commissioners

This body was established in 1842 by Robert Peel. Because of the intense localism of the GCs, some taxpayers who were not themselves Commissioners were understandably rather coy about disclosing their profits to their competitors sitting in judgment over them. The 1842 Act gave them the opportunity of having the appeal heard by a specialist central body, the Special Commissioners (SCs).

The SCs were almost always lawyers (often former Inland Revenue solicitors). Although their main diet was complex cases, whether technical or investigations, anyone could elect to have their case heard by the SCs – which some did as a way, they hoped, of delaying matters.

However, a much larger percentage of appellants before the SCs were legally represented.[12]

---

[8] Schedule D covered, importantly, profits from trades and professions, ie the self-employed.

[9] In theory the GCs could use their local knowledge to come to a figure. I have had only one experience of this, before the GCs for the Division of Southwark (in the County of Surrey, as the clerk was proud to call them). That division was apparently the smallest in the country in terms of the number of taxpayers apart from the GCs for each of the Inns of Court and the great universities (eg Cambridge, and no doubt if General Melchett from Blackadder IV is to be believed, Hull, but obviously not Oxford).

[10] There were many mergers of divisions of GCs after 1996 as a result.

[11] I was told on more than one occasion by a clerk to the GCs that accountants were always at a disadvantage with the GCs. Either the Commissioners did not know the accountant at all, unlike the local Inspector, or they 'knew them only too well'.

[12] This statement does not hold good for Northern Ireland where there were no GCs.

C. Matters Common to Both Bodies

Neither body was encumbered by any comprehensive procedural rules, save what appeared in the Tax Acts. These were in a small compass. The Taxes Management Act 1970 (TMA) as originally enacted had the following provisions which impinged on appellants, and LiPs in particular:

- If it was shown to the satisfaction of the Commissioners that 'owing to absence, sickness or other reasonable cause' a person had been prevented from attending, the Commissioners might postpone the hearing or admit the appeal to be made by any agent clerk or servant of his behalf (s 50(4)).
- The Commissioners had to permit any barrister or solicitor to appear before them on behalf of any party either orally or in writing and had to hear any accountant who is a member of an incorporated society (s 50(5)).
- A party to the appeal was entitled to adduce lawful evidence (s 52(1)).

The SCs did publish a leaflet to inform appellants what they were expected to do and what might happen at an appeal hearing. In 1994, however, Rules of Procedure were made for both bodies, being rather more complex for the SCs than the GCs. As a result of these rules coming into force s 50(4), (5) and s 52 TMA were repealed.

II. The Leggatt Report

In May 2000 the Government appointed Sir Andrew Leggatt, a retired Lord Justice of Appeal, assisted by Dame Valerie Strachan, retired Chairman of the Board of Customs & Excise, to review the delivery of justice through tribunals to ensure that, among many other things: 'There are adequate arrangements for improving people's knowledge and understanding of their rights and responsibilities in relation to such disputes, and that tribunals and other bodies function in a way which makes those rights and responsibilities a reality.'[13] This is the part of the terms of reference which had the most direct implications for LiPs.

The Review was published in March 2001. In its overview it said: 'this Review has as its four main objects: ... fourthly, to enable unrepresented users to participate effectively and without apprehension in tribunal proceedings.'[14] Further: 'All chairmen and members should be periodically assessed to ensure that they are applying the skills needed to assist unrepresented users without, however, favouring them.'[15]

---

[13] A Leggatt, *Tribunals for Users – One System, One Service: Report of the Review of Tribunals*, March 2001 (London, Department for Constitutional Affairs), Introduction, para 2.

[14] ibid, Overview, para 2.

[15] ibid, Overview, para 20.

It is notable that while in its discussion of individual tribunals the Report had much to say about the arrangements for dealing with unrepresented appellants (ie LiPs) in the Employment and Social Security Tribunals, it said next to nothing about the tax tribunals.

The Report made 361 proposals for change, but only para 356: 'Rules of procedure [of the tax tribunals] should be applied flexibly to recognise differences between the varied kinds of cases arising' seems to recognise that LiPs may form a substantial majority of appellants to the tax tribunals.

III. The Government's Response

The Government's response came in July 2004 in the form of a White Paper *Transforming Public Services: Complaints, Redress and Tribunals*.[16] It said that the Government accepted Sir Andrew Leggatt's key recommendation that tribunals provided by central government should be brought together into a unified system and that its mission should be to help to prevent and resolve disputes, using any appropriate method and working with its partners in and out of government, and to help to improve administrative justice and justice in the workplace, so that the need for disputes is reduced.

In an analysis of what the existing tribunals provided, the White Paper said (relevantly to LiPs):

> 5.1 This chapter analyses the effectiveness of the tribunal system today in providing redress. For these purposes we have worked on the assumption that potential users will want and are entitled to the following:
> – cases resolved without formal hearings if possible;
> – easily navigable, comprehensive and comprehensible information about the process;
> – hearings which are not daunting or legalistic ...

IV. The Creation of the Unified Tribunals: TCEA 2007

The next step towards creating a unified tribunals service and a single first instance tax tribunal was the enactment of the Tribunals, Courts and Enforcement Act 2007 (TCEA) and in particular Part 1. Chapter 2 of this part of the Act provided the structure of the unified tribunals system, in particular that there was to be a First-tier and an Upper Tribunal and that each of those tribunals was divided into 'chambers': a tax chamber was established for the First-tier Tribunal

---

[16] Cm 6243.

246   *Richard Thomas*

and a 'Tax and Chancery Chamber' for the Upper Tribunal. This Chapter of Part 1 of the Act also dealt with the review of decisions by both Tribunals and appeals to the Upper Tribunal and beyond and with the 'judicial review'[17] jurisdiction of the Upper Tribunal.

Section 22 and Schedule 5 provided power to make Tribunal Procedure Rules. For the TC, procedural rules were made in 2009. Rule 2 provides:

Overriding objective and parties' obligation to co-operate with the Tribunal

2(1) The overriding objective of these Rules is to enable the Tribunal to deal with cases fairly and justly.

(2) Dealing with a case fairly and justly includes—

(a)   dealing with the case in ways which are proportionate to the importance of the case, the complexity of the issues, the anticipated costs and the resources of the parties;
(b)   avoiding unnecessary formality and seeking flexibility in the proceedings;
(c)   ensuring, so far as practicable, that the parties are able to participate fully in the proceedings;
(d)   using any special expertise of the Tribunal effectively; and
(e)   avoiding delay, so far as compatible with proper consideration of the issues.

The overriding objectives set out in Rule 2 of the TC rules are not special to it. They appear in all the procedural rules for the chambers of the First-tier Tribunal and in the single set of procedural rules for the Upper Tribunal.

It is worth mentioning a few other of the procedural rules that are relevant to this chapter:

Representatives

11(1) A party may appoint a representative (whether a legal representative or not) to represent that party in the proceedings.

…

(5) At a hearing a party may be accompanied by another person who, with the permission of the Tribunal, may act as a representative or otherwise assist in presenting the party's case at the hearing.

Evidence and submissions

15(2) The Tribunal may—

(a)   admit evidence whether or not the evidence would be admissible in a civil trial in the United Kingdom; or
(b)   exclude evidence that would otherwise be admissible where—

    (i)   the evidence was not provided within the time allowed by a direction or a practice direction;
    (ii)   the evidence was otherwise provided in a manner that did not comply with a direction or a practice direction; or

---

[17] The quotation marks are the Act's.

(c)   it would otherwise be unfair to admit the evidence.

(3) The Tribunal may consent to a witness giving, or require any witness to give, evidence on oath, and may administer an oath for that purpose.

Determination with or without a hearing

29(1) Subject to rule 26(6) (determination of a Default Paper case without a hearing) and the following paragraphs in this rule, the Tribunal must hold a hearing before making a decision which disposes of proceedings, or a part of proceedings, unless—

(a)   each party has consented to the matter being decided without a hearing; and
(b)   the Tribunal considers that it is able to decide the matter without a hearing.

(2) This rule does not apply to decisions under Part 4 (correcting, setting aside, reviewing and appealing Tribunal decisions).

(3) The Tribunal may dispose of proceedings, or a part of proceedings, without a hearing under rule 8 (striking out a party's case).

Hearings in a party's absence

33. If a party fails to attend a hearing the Tribunal may proceed with the hearing if the Tribunal—

(a)   is satisfied that the party has been notified of the hearing or that reasonable steps have been taken to notify the party of the hearing; and
(b)   considers that it is in the interests of justice to proceed with the hearing.

The provisions of s 22(4)(b) and (d) TCEA and of Rules 2(2)(a)–(c), 11, 15(2)(a), 29(1) and 33 are, in my view, of particular relevance to LiPs appealing to the Tribunal.

V. Case Categorisation

For the first time the procedural rules of the TC recognised that different types of case required differences in case management and other procedures. The TC rules distinguish between Complex cases, Default Paper cases, Basic cases and Standard cases.

The categorisation of cases in the Tax Chamber, ie what types of case fall within each category, is governed by Rule 23 of the TC Rules (for Complex cases) and the Practice Statement 'Categorisation of Tax Cases in the Tax Chamber' made on 29 April 2013 by Judge Colin Bishopp, the then President.[18]

---

[18] Available at https://www.judiciary.uk/wp-content/uploads/2014/12/categorisation-of-case-in-the-tax-chamber.pdf (accessed 8 January 2020).

248 Richard Thomas

Complex cases are those which will require lengthy or complex evidence or a lengthy hearing, involve a complex or important principle or issue or involve a large financial sum.[19]

Default Paper cases are currently cases involving fixed penalties for late filing, late notice of liability or late payment not exceeding £2,000. In practice many cases in excess of that figure and some tax geared penalties are categorised as Default Paper.

Basic cases include appeals against penalties of all types, unless 'deliberate' action is involved or there is also a tax assessment under appeal; against information notices; and against PAYE codes. It also includes applications to make a late appeal; 'hardship' appeals; postponement of tax; and directions for closure of an enquiry.

Standard cases therefore are any others not falling into the other categories, most frequently appeals against tax assessments and other decisions by HMRC particularly in connection with VAT and other indirect duties. Standard cases are informally divided into 'high' and 'low' maintenance (ie case management) types: counsel or specialist tax advisers may well be engaged in the higher end of Standard cases.

VI. Litigants in Person

The vast majority of the TC's cases are not Complex cases and do not involve counsel or other legally qualified representatives. Hearings of Basic and most Standard cases usually therefore involve an LiP, and practically all Default Paper cases will involve LiPs.[20] This chapter includes in its classification of appellant as LiPs those (many) people who are represented by a person, usually an accountant who may be (but often is not) a member of a recognised accountancy body such as the Institute of Chartered Accountants in England and Wales or the Association of Chartered Certified Accountants.

In some cases an accountant or other adviser may have represented the LiP in their dealings with HMRC and with the Tribunal administration but does not appear at a hearing (often for reasons of cost). They may put in written submissions of behalf of the LiP, but again often do not as that would also add to the costs of the LiP. This is not surprising given that the appeal may be against penalties of £100 (or even less) and that the costs of representation may well exceed the amounts at stake, with no possibility of receiving an award of costs except in unusual situations.

This proliferation of LiPs in all Default Paper and most other cases puts a particular burden on the First-tier Tribunal, not only of course in the TC, and dealing with these cases in accordance with the overriding objective brings into prominence several of the paragraphs in Rule 2(2).

---

[19] Rule 23(4) and (5) of the TC Rules.
[20] I have dealt with hundreds of Default Paper cases and in none was a lawyer involved.

A. The General Commissioners and LiPs

Before considering how the TC has performed in its dealing with LiPs and whether its performance is an improvement on what went on before, it is worth noting how the GCs, who would have dealt with 99 per cent of LiPs in direct tax matters, were required to deal with their hearings from 1994 onwards. Rule 15 of the GC procedure rules[21] provided:

Procedure and evidence at hearing

15(1) At the beginning of the hearing of any proceedings the Tribunal shall, except where it considers it unnecessary to do so, explain the order of proceeding which it proposes to adopt.

(2) The Tribunal shall conduct the hearing in such manner as it considers most suitable to the clarification and determination of the issues before it and generally to the just handling of the proceedings and, so far as appears to it appropriate, shall seek to avoid formality in its procedure.

(3) The parties shall be heard in such order as the Tribunal shall determine and shall be entitled—

(a)   to give evidence,
(b)   to call witnesses,
(c)   to question any witnesses including other parties who give evidence, and
(d)   to address the Tribunal both on the evidence and generally on the subject matter of the proceedings.

(4) In assessing the truth and weight of any evidence, the Tribunal may take account of its nature and source, and the manner in which it is given …

(6) The Tribunal may receive evidence of any fact which appears to the Tribunal to be relevant to the subject matter of the proceedings notwithstanding that such evidence would be inadmissible in proceedings before a court of law in that part of the United Kingdom by reference to the law of which the proceedings before the Tribunal are to be determined …

It should be noted that LiPs before the GCs did not face an opponent who was legally qualified either. Cases before the GCs would be taken by the District Inspector or an assisting Inspector of Taxes who would have had some training in conducting appeals before the GCs, but whose expertise and qualifications were in tax.

What follows is the more subjective part of this paper. It is based on my own experience as a member (one who sat with over 30 judges) and then as a judge of TC and as one who, admittedly some time ago, appeared before many bodies of General Commissioners.

---

[21] The General Commissioners (Jurisdiction and Procedure) Regulations 1994 (SI 1994/1812).

B. The Tax Chamber and LiPs

i. Case Management

As far as concerns case management of proceedings involving LiPs, then whatever the tribunal does is an improvement, as there was no case management at all before the GCs. The parties would have been expected on the day of the hearing to provide whatever evidence by way of documentation each thought was relevant: whether there was any exchange of evidence or the production of a statement of case or skeleton arguments was left to the parties to agree. In the tribunal in Basic cases there is also little real case management,[22] but the Tribunal panel hearing the appeal will have been given the appellant's Notice of Appeal which will also include correspondence with HMRC including usually a review conclusion which will give the Tribunal a good idea of what the case is about and what the parties will be arguing. These Basic cases are characterised as 'turn up and talk', and LiPs are told to bring any documents they wish the Tribunal to see to the hearing.

In Standard cases there is active case management by the Tribunal.[23] First, as well as the Notice of Appeal HMRC is required to produce a statement of case.[24] Once that is received, standard form directions will be issued by the Registrar or one of the judges. These give various deadlines for things to be done and would be extremely familiar to any solicitor taking a case in the County Court for example, but could be a daunting document for a LiP to handle. In recognition of this (and in response to suggestions from judges) the Tribunal now issues a 'translation' of the directions into less formal English to help LiPs.

One matter that particularly seems to confound LiPs is the requirement in directions to list the documents they seek to rely on. In most Basic and the less complicated Standard cases, HMRC will provide a bundle which *should* include all the correspondence, notes of meetings and phone calls that have taken place and most LiPs assume that because of this they need do nothing. But HMRC are nothing like infallible in this area. Nor do most LiPs realise that when they are asked for details of their witnesses and possible witness statements that that technically includes any statement of the evidence that they themselves will (inevitably) be putting forward to explain why an assessment to tax or a penalty should not be imposed. All LiPs in my experience either say they have no witnesses or refer only to another person. They are also prone to bringing documents to the hearing and seeking to produce them but without having disclosed this to HMRC beforehand.

---

[22] Rule 23(2)(b) TC Rules defines them as 'cases ... which will usually be disposed of after a hearing, with minimal exchange of documents before the hearing'.

[23] As Rule 23(2)(c) TC Rules puts it, standard cases are 'subject to more detailed case management'.

[24] Rule 25(1)(b) TC Rules.

Tax Tribunals and Justice for Litigants in Person 251

This can cause problems although HMRC presenting officers usually raise no objections to such conduct.[25]

In Default Paper cases HMRC are also required to produce a statement of case, the vast majority of which include all the relevant papers, starting with the issue of assessments and the appeal to HMRC. Appellants in these cases are asked if they wish to respond to the statement of case and some do. This response takes the place of the appellant 'turning up and talking' in Basic cases.

A noticeable feature in recent years has been the readiness of some, but by no means all, HMRC appeal caseworkers and presenting officers to assist a LiP in the weeks before the hearing by explaining what is required for the hearing from them and what is not.

ii. The Hearing

As with preparation for the hearing, it is clear to me that in some cases the HMRC presenting officers will talk to the LiP before an oral hearing[26] of a Basic or Standard case to explain what is to happen, and in some cases to seek to agree a settlement of the case which can then be reported to the tribunal.

In hearings with LiPs it was my invariable practice to explain[27] that in a case where the appellant has the burden of proof, eg in an appeal against an amendment to a tax return, an assessment to VAT or a claim for relief (but not a penalty or fault based assessment), the usual practice is for the appellant to open and for HMRC to respond, but then continue that many LiPs unfamiliar with the procedure of the TC find it helpful if HMRC go first and explain the nature of the case and the reason for the hearing. LiPs mostly accept and HMRC are always content.

In Basic and most Standard[28] cases HMRC officers who are not themselves legally qualified present the case, although there are exceptions. In excise and import duty cases and those involving penalties under money laundering regulations HMRC is frequently represented by counsel in even the smallest cases. Such counsel often do more than HMRC officers to assist the appellant and help the appellant put forward points that might assist them but would not otherwise be raised.[29]

The usual problem with LiPs is that the grounds of appeal as set out in the notification to HMRC and to the Tribunal may be diffuse and contain a large number of separate strands. HMRC presenting officers seem more reluctant to adapt to the

---

[25] Sometimes in cases where had they objected, the Tribunal would have either regarded the evidence as inadmissible, or more likely given no weight to it.

[26] Parties are urged to attend half an hour before the time given for the hearing (usually 10 am or 2 pm).

[27] Consistently with Rule 15(1) of the GC Procedure Rules. I am aware that many other judges also do this because I sat with many of them during my years as a member of the Tribunal.

[28] Apart from some of the high maintenance cases.

[29] In a somewhat extreme example, I heard a case where counsel for HMRC even took on the cross-examination of his own, somewhat surprised, witness, a Border Force officer, on behalf of the appellant.

252   Richard Thomas

situation of LiPs. They are either reluctant to try to disentangle what is said by the LiP or say that because there is no clearly articulated ground of appeal, the appeal must fail.

This leaves the Tribunal in the position of having to decide how interventionist it should be in assisting appellants to put their case. This can involve simply asking questions of the appellant to clarify what the appellant is objecting to about what HMRC have done, but it may also involve raising an argument with HMRC that the appellant was ignorant of but which may be highly relevant to the appeal. Intervention by a Tribunal in the formulation of grounds of appeal is something of an inquisitorial approach to a dispute: suggesting a possible new ground of appeal definitely involves such an approach.[30]

Judges may sometimes feel it necessary to ask a LIP questions to clarify their evidence of fact and also involves adopting an inquisitorial approach. The issue of whether such an approach is permitted or necessary is an interesting one which affects other chambers of the First-tier Tribunal.

In the Social Entitlement Chamber (SEC) which deals with disputes about social security benefits and other matters such as child support there is the highest authority that an inquisitorial approach is not only permitted but that it should be employed.

In *Kerr v Department for Social Development (NI)*[31] Baroness Hale said:

> [61] Ever since the decision of the Divisional Court in *R v Medical Appeal Tribunal (North Midland Region), Ex p Hubble* [1958] 2 QB 228, it has been accepted that the process of benefits adjudication is inquisitorial rather than adversarial. Diplock J as he then was said this of an industrial injury benefit claim at p 240:
>
>> A claim by an insured person to benefit under the Act is not truly analogous to a lis inter partes. A claim to benefit is a claim to receive money out of the insurance funds ... Any such claim requires investigation to determine whether any, and if so, what amount of benefit is payable out of the fund. In such an investigation, the minister or the insurance officer is not a party adverse to the claimant. If analogy be sought in the other branches of the law, it is to be found in an inquest rather than in an action.
>
> [62] What emerges from all this is a co operative process of investigation in which both the claimant and the department play their part. The department is the one which knows what questions it needs to ask and what information it needs to have in order to determine whether the conditions of entitlement have been met. The claimant is the one who generally speaking can and must supply that information. But where the information is available to the department rather than the claimant, then the department must take the necessary steps to enable it to be traced.

If that sensible approach is taken, it will rarely be necessary to resort to concepts taken from adversarial litigation such as the burden of proof.

---

[30] Unless the new argument is a clear killer blow, HMRC will be asked in this situation if they want an adjournment to deal with the point, or more usually, directions to make written responses will be given.

[31] *Kerr v Department for Social Development (NI)* [2004] UKHL 23 (*Kerr*).

Lord Diplock's reference to an adjudication of benefits not being a *lis inter partes* is reflected in tax law. In *HMRC v Tower MCashback LLP1 & anor*[32] Moses LJ was addressing the question whether the jurisdiction of the GCs in an appeal had changed following the introduction of self-assessment. He said:

> [28] The retention of s.50 [TMA] in terms which closely follows that of its predecessor is a powerful indication that Parliament did not intend to change the jurisdiction of the Commissioners in as dramatic a fashion as the introduction of a system of self-assessment might have suggested. As Henderson J remarked, the public interest is that taxpayers pay a correct amount of tax (see [115]). In the exercise of their statutory functions the Commissioners are not deciding a case *inter partes*; they are determining the amount on which, in the interests of the public, the taxpayer ought to be taxed (see *R v Income Tax Commissioners ex-parte Elmhurst* [1936] 1 KB 487 at 493). That public interest has in no way been altered by the introduction of self-assessment.

In *Jamie Garland v HMRC*[33] the TC was considering an application by HMRC to strike out an appeal by a LiP on the basis that it had no reasonable grounds of success. Judge Christopher Staker said:

> [14] As regards HMRC's reliance on rule 8(3)(c), the Tribunal accepts that if the notice of appeal sets out no grounds of appeal with any reasonable prospect of succeeding, the Appellant risks a successful strike out application being made by HMRC. However, in cases involving unrepresented appellants, it can occur that the notice of appeal fails to disclose any arguable grounds of appeal, even though there is potential merit in the appeal.
>
> [15] In *Aleena Electronics Limited v Revenue and Customs* [2011] UKFTT 608 (TC), it was said at [60]:
>
>> It is the ethos of the Tribunal system and certainly that of the Tax Chamber of the First-tier Tribunal that a taxpayer can bring an appeal to a tax-expert Tribunal without the expense of instructing representatives. The Tribunal hearing a substantive appeal will be expert: it will know the law and will take the legal points at the hearing that an unrepresented appellant may not. Where the Appellant is unrepresented the Tribunal panel will take on a more inquisitorial role and will ask witnesses questions which an unrepresented Appellant may not think to ask.
>
> [16] Default paper cases and simple basic cases in particular may involve an unrepresented appellant who wishes to exercise the right of appeal to the Tribunal against a decision that the appellant considers to be harsh and unfair, even though the appellant has no knowledge of the law and is incapable of articulating a legally arguable ground of appeal. It is possible for the Tribunal in such a case to hear the appellant's account of the facts and to consider this together with all of the evidence presented by the parties, and for the Tribunal to satisfy itself as to the facts, and to determine for itself whether the HMRC decision is in accordance with the facts and the law. In such a case, even if it should turn out that the appeal was hopeless, the unrepresented appellant at least has the satisfaction of knowing that his or her case has been considered by an independent

---

[32] *HMRC v Tower MCashback LLP1 & anor* [2010] EWCA Civ 32 (*MCashback*).
[33] *Jamie Garland v HMRC* [2016] UKFTT 573 (TC) (*Garland*).

254   *Richard Thomas*

judicial body. Furthermore, the appeal may not turn out to be hopeless, and it may ultimately be allowed in whole or in part. In the case of an unrepresented appellant, failure of a notice of appeal to state an arguable ground of appeal should therefore not in every case necessarily lead automatically to a strike out application being granted.[34]

It can be seen that the comments about the Tribunal's role set out in the passages above do not perhaps go quite so far as Baroness Hale's dictum in *Kerr*. There is a distinction to be drawn between the cases considered by the SEC and those by the TC. All cases within the SEC's remits would be treated as Basic or low-end Standard cases in the TC: the SEC does not deal with Complex cases in which an adversarial approach is clearly the correct one. But there seems to be no reason why *Kerr* should not apply to many Standard cases as well as to Basic and Default Paper cases.

The Upper Tribunal (Administrative Appeals Chamber) which deals with appeals from the SEC regularly upbraids the SEC for not being inquisitorial. A recent example is in *DS v SSWP*[35] where Judge Poole said:

> [6] The system of social entitlement appeals has been set up to try to ensure affordable access to justice for vulnerable benefits claimants. The amount of money at stake in any particular case may be small in relation to some court actions, but it is recognised that cases may be very important to claimants, many involving subsistence. Provision is therefore made for appeals against decisions by the SSWP. So that appeals to the Social Entitlement Chamber of the First-tier Tribunal are accessible in practice, ordinarily there are no fees payable. Nor do claimants have to spend money on lawyers, because there is no requirement of legal representation, and the tribunal sits with a judge with legal expertise and has an inquisitorial function (*AP v SSWP* [2018] UKUT 307 and *AS v SSWP* [2018] UKUT 260).
>
> …
>
> To assist vulnerable claimants to cope with tribunal hearings, they are relatively informal, questioning tends to be led by the tribunal members rather than proceedings being adversarial, and hearings are not long.
>
> …
>
> The procedure before the tribunal is deliberately designed to be different from procedures in many courts; it is a simple and quick procedure, designed not to be over-complicated at all levels.

In my view what is said applies with equal force to LiPs in the TC.

As has been explained, this chapter is very substantially based on my experiences and practices. Talking to other judges and, in particular, members who themselves sit with many other judges apart from me gives me the strong impression that most, but not all, judges in the TC will follow the *Kerr* approach and be inquisitorial where it is relevant and will treat LiPs in a way which is consistent with the overriding objectives, as exemplified in *Jamie Garland*.

---

[34] This passage was approved by the Upper Tribunal in *HMRC v Liam Hill* [2018] UKUT 45 (TCC).
[35] *DS v SSWP* [2019] UKUT 347 (AAC).

C. The Equal Treatment Bench Book

That many TC judges do now follow the *Kerr* approach is, I think, substantially due to a publication aimed at all judges. For a few years now the courts and tribunals have been urged to follow the Equal Treatment Bench Book (ETBB) published by the Judicial College.[36] Chapter 1 of the ETBB is on LiPs, and at para 59 of that Chapter the ETBB says:

Difficulties at the hearing and how to help

59. The judge is a facilitator of justice and may need to assist the litigant in person in ways that would not be appropriate for a party who has employed skilled legal advisers and an experienced advocate. This may include:

- Attempting to elicit the extent of the LiPs understanding at the outset, and giving explanations in everyday plain language.
- Making clear the concept of a just trial on the evidence, ie that the case will be decided on the basis of the factual evidence presented and the truthfulness and accuracy of the witnesses called.
- Exercising considerable patience when LiPs demonstrate their scant knowledge of law and procedure.
- Not interrupting, engaging in dialogue, indicating a preliminary view or cutting short an argument in the same way that might be done with a qualified lawyer.

It also deals with introductory explanations by the judge, explaining the real issues in the case, and advocacy. The latter contains an important point at para 74, which the TC has had occasion to upbraid HMRC presenting officers and officers drawing up statements of case for Default Paper cases for failing to observe:

Opposition Counsel in a party-and-party case and the State's representative in tribunals where the State is the respondent, are expected to draw to the court/tribunal's attention a fair picture of the law and not omit cases which go against his or her side's interests. They should be reminded of this.

An example of HMRC officers ignoring the ETBB on this point was their approach to cases involving penalties on non-residents who were filing tax returns under self assessment but who did not report within 30 days, as they were required to do, the sale of a residential property in the UK, irrespective of whether any chargeable gain arose. A number of judges[37] had held that ignorance of this particular law, introduced without fanfare in 2015, could amount to a reasonable excuse for failing to file the return in time, while another (*Welland*) had held that it could not. HMRC always only referred in their statements of case to *Welland*.

---

[36] Judicial College, *Equal Treatment Bench Book*, February 2018 edition with September 2019 revision, available at https://www.judiciary.uk/wp-content/uploads/2018/02/ETBB-February-2018-edition-September-2019-revision.pdf (accessed 8 January 2020).

[37] Beginning in my decision in *McGreevy v HMRC* [2017] UKFTT 690 (TC).

The ETBB also deals comprehensively with certain categories of litigant, many of whom will be LiPs, including vulnerable persons, those for whom English is not their native language and people with disabilities. TC judges and members are frequently called upon to deal with cases of this sort.[38]

D. Is the Position Better Now Than before 2009?

Any views on this are again bound to be subjective and are not supported by any rigorous or academic research and my experience before the GCs was mostly before self-assessment. But my general feeling is that the TC is far better than most bodies of GCs when it comes to dealing with LiPs. I have no way of knowing whether it was the same before the SCs and the VAT Tribunal, but I suspect that there was not the same attention to informality and flexibility as there is in the TC and other Chambers.

I put this improvement down primarily to the consciousness, drilled into judges and members in training, particularly induction training, of the overriding objectives of the Tribunal and its Chambers and to the promulgation of the ETBB. Changes in the way the administrative staff of the TC handle LiPs and the attitude of some HMRC officers have also helped.

VII. Jurisdiction Issues and Litigants in Person

I referred above to the problems judges in appeals involving LiPs face in disentangling grounds of appeal and working out what are the issues the appellant wishes to air. It is commonplace in grounds of appeal put forward by LiPs to find that one, if not the only, ground relates to the perceived unfairness of the tax system and particularly penalties or of aspects of HMRC's conduct. Or there may simply be a ground that the TC cannot deal with because there is no right of appeal against it.

The TC is like any part of the Tribunals system a creature of statute, so that its jurisdiction must be found in statute and not in the common law. Rule 20 of the TC Rules relating to appeal proceedings says that they must be started by providing a notice of appeal to the Tribunal, but this may only be done where the appeal is 'under an enactment'.

Where an enactment does provide for an appeal, the available grounds are not usually circumscribed but the powers of the TC in deciding an appeal are. In the passage from *MCashback* quoted above, Moses LJ was referring to s 50 of the TMA

---

[38] HMRC, though, has some way to go in these kinds of cases. See eg *E v HMRC* [2017] UKFTT 348 (TC) and *Sandpiper Car Hire Ltd v HMRC* [2018] UKFTT 267 (TC).

which sets out the power of the TC in any appeal relating to income tax, capital gains tax and corporation tax. Its power is to find the correct amount of tax due by upholding quashing or varying the HMRC assessment or other decision. What it cannot do is to find for the appellant because of HMRC's conduct in an investigation or compliance check; because someone in similar circumstances has been let off or treated more leniently; because HMRC has not applied an extra-statutory concession; or because the appellant was led to believe that HMRC would not make the decision it had. The Court of Appeal and the Upper Tribunal have repeatedly said that the TC has no general power to consider public law matters in the abstract – in other words it has no general judicial review jurisdiction.[39] Attempts by judges of the TC to seek to find a way around this have been sternly rebuffed.

That is not to say that the TC does not in some limited circumstances consider public law matters: indeed in one area it can specifically intervene if it finds that a decision by HMRC, although not appealable, was flawed in the judicial review sense.[40] In other statutes, particularly those relating to indirect taxes, the TC has a supervisory jurisdiction, eg it has to decide whether the decision reached by HMRC is one which it could reasonably have come to.

Faced with the sort of grounds of appeal I have described, many judges of the TC will seek to advise LiPs what remedies may be open to them. These will include applications or appeal to other courts, such as the County Court in collection matters and the Administrative Court where an application for judicial review may be in point. It may well include information about remedies for maladministration and other improper conduct by HMRC, such as a complaint to the Revenue Adjudicator and the Parliamentary Ombudsman. On occasions HMRC presenting officers are willing to talk to appellants after the proceedings to advise them about possible remedies.

A. Seizures of Excise Goods: A Special Case?

An issue in one specific area involving the TC's powers which arises frequently before the tribunal and the problems it creates for LiPs have been the subject of much comment by TC judges many of whom are clearly uncomfortable with the result.

As most people know, within the EU the Treaty provisions on freedom of movement of people and goods prevent normal customs procedures and rules from applying. Most people also know that there is one tax – excise duty – where free movement is not unconstrained. While there are no specific limits on the amount of tobacco or alcohol that may be brought in from another part of the customs

---

[39] See eg *HMRC v Hok Ltd* [2012] UKUT 363 (TCC).
[40] This is where HMRC make a decision as to whether a penalty under certain provisions in FA 2007, 2008 and 2009 should (or much more usually should not) be reduced because of 'special circumstances'.

258 *Richard Thomas*

area of the EU, the Excise Duty Directive[41] allows officials to question passengers and that power may be exercised where the passenger had more than an indicative limit in their possession. The law is that a person may personally bring across the border as much as they like as long as it is for their own use or for gifts.

If a person is stopped and questioned by UK Border Force, the officer will seize the goods if they are not satisfied that they are for that person's private use.[42] Passengers who have their goods seized (which may include the car they are travelling in where they come by sea, road or rail) are given a notice of seizure which explains that they have 30 days to contest the seizure in the Magistrates' Court, a procedure they would start by asking Border Force to begin condemnation proceedings. They will also be told that if they do apply to the Magistrates' Court and lose, Border Force will seek costs, which are likely to amount to at least £2,000. Unsurprisingly most passengers do not contest seizure.

What is abundantly clear is that no passengers realise that probably up to a year later they will receive a letter from HMRC – not Border Force – telling them that they owe duty and will be subject to an assessment, and that they may be liable to a penalty for 'excise wrongdoing' of up to 70 per cent of the duty. Naturally, most people will appeal and will complain that they thought their trouble and expense was at an end when they abandoned their goods to Border Force. They will be told by HMRC (and the TC will be forcefully reminded by counsel for HMRC) that their failure to contest the seizure means that they cannot put to the TC any arguments that the goods were in fact for their private use. This is the outcome made clear authoritatively by the Court of Appeal in *HMRC v Jones & anor*[43] and specifically in relation to assessments to duty in *HMRC v Race*.[44] The basis for this ruling is either that the TC has no jurisdiction to entertain such an argument as the point has been conclusively determined by the deeming provisions in the Customs and Excise Management Act 1979 (CEMA), and so the TC must strike out the appeal[45] or the effect of the deeming provisions is that there is no reasonable prospect of the appeal succeeding, and so on an application by HMRC ought to be struck out.[46]

In these circumstances any success by such passengers will be very rare and will usually turn on technical points to do with the assessment and arguments about the level of penalty.

In my view, and those of other judges, this system is iniquitous. Passengers are faced with Hobson's choice: they must contest the seizure and win before the Magistrates Court to have any chance of defeating the duty and penalty assessments, but if they lose there they must pay costs in addition to losing the goods and paying the duty and penalty. The information given by Border Force to those

---

[41] Directive 2008/118/EC, Art 32.
[42] That includes cases where gifts are made to others.
[43] *HMRC v Jones & anor* [2011] EWCA Civ 824.
[44] *HMRC v Race* [2014] UKUT 331 (TCC).
[45] Rule 8(2)(a) of the TC Rules.
[46] Rule 8(3)(c) of the TC Rules.

whose goods are seized does not clearly spell out the possible assessment and penalty consequences of a failure to contest the seizure.

Jurisdiction, at least in relation to private persons importing goods, over the legality of the seizure should be transferred to the TC[47] and should be considered alongside any duty and penalty assessment, so that there is no risk of jurisdictional roulette of the type currently in operation. The Tribunal already deals with seizures indirectly as it has a supervisory jurisdiction over decisions by HMRC not to restore seized goods, including cars used to carry tobacco and alcohol.[48]

B. A Public Law Jurisdiction for the TC?

In relation to some of the other matters I have mentioned, where a LiP's remedy is limited to judicial review, I feel it is a much more finely balanced issue whether the TC should have a wider judicial review jurisdiction. I do not think that any such wider jurisdiction should be or could be confined to LiPs.

There is no doubt, as I have mentioned, that the TC does employ public law concepts in its supervisory jurisdictions – the name '*Wednesbury*' crops up often in reports of decided cases by the TC. It is therefore no argument to say that TC judges are not equipped to deal with public law matters.[49] They are also familiar with such matters as extra-statutory concessions and HMRC Guidance. TC judges will undoubtedly have much more familiarity with tax law and practice than most of the judges dealing with judicial review of HMRC decisions in the Administrative Court.[50]

In my opinion a very effective case for giving the TC a more general judicial review function has been put by Stephen Daly of King's College London.[51] It might be appropriate to introduce such a jurisdiction in stages to test the waters and in particular to cover those areas where the amounts at stake inevitably mean that the frustrated appellant would not go for judicial review because of the costs, not only of making the application but also the need to pay the costs of HMRC in the event of losing. It is also arguable that those complaints which fall within the jurisdiction of the Adjudicator should not be included, but there may be a case for some of them to be, and in any event an unsuccessful applicant to the Adjudicator might be allowed a right of appeal to the TC.

Reforms along these lines, and to the seizures jurisdiction, would allow LiPs to feel much happier with the system than they currently do.

---

[47] Some fairly simple amendments to Schedule 3 of CEMA are all that seems to be required.

[48] As with assessments, it is not open to the appellant to argue that the goods brought in in the car were for private use only, if the appellant did not contest the seizure in the Magistrates' Court.

[49] Many judges of the TC also sit in the Upper Tribunal where they do hear 'full blown' judicial review cases, and others handle public law issues in their practice as barristers or solicitors.

[50] An exception was Simler J (now LJ) who practised at the tax bar as well as the employment bar and who represented at three levels the respondent Inspector of Taxes in a complex case I handled in the Inland Revenue.

[51] S Daly, 'Public Law in the Tax Tribunals and the Case for Reform' [2018] *British Tax Review* 94.

15

New Wave Technologies and Tax Justice

BENJAMIN WALKER

This chapter analyses the impact of New Wave Technologies on tax justice. The fundamental question for this chapter is: Do New Wave Technologies promote or hinder tax justice? In order to answer this question the tool of administrative justice is adopted. Having laid the foundation, the chapter outlines how New Wave Technologies function. The primary focus is a discussion of the benefits and risks of New Wave Technologies. An analysis reveals several benefits that could promote tax justice; however, there are also potential risks that could hinder tax justice. The net result will ultimately depend upon the institutional framework. With that in mind, the chapter proposes a three-fold approach to promote tax justice.

I. Introduction

Tax administrations are responsible for collecting tax revenues that fund the provision of public services. They are constantly challenged by several issues that undermine their ability to collect tax revenues.[1] Information is the greatest ally that aids tax administrations. Tax administrations need to first collect information, then draw insights from it. The underlying technological infrastructure of any tax administration plays an important part in recording and storing information. The gradual shift from analog (paper) information to digital (computer) information has enabled better storage of information, and more of it. The emerging New Wave Technologies (NWTs), like all technology,[2] could unlock the exponential value of information by significantly expanding the insights derived from such data that could transform the nature of tax administrations.[3] NWTs consist of

---

[1] For example, under-reporting of income, over-reporting of deductions, tax evasion, tax fraud, etc.

[2] J Tomlinson, *Justice in the Digital State* (Bristol, Policy Press, 2019) 2: 'The essential promise of technology remains, as it always has done, of more and better for less effort'.

[3] For a useful discussion about the impact of technology on government, see M Bovens and S Zouridis, 'From Street-Level to System-Level Bureaucracies: How Information and Communication Technology Is Transforming Administrative Discretion and Constitutional Control' (2002) 62 *Public Administration Review* 174, 174–84.

262   Benjamin Walker

three components: data analytics, big data and computing power. The interaction between these three components of technology offers significant benefits to tax justice, but also several risks. A critical analysis of NWTs is timely as technologically advanced tax administrations are already adopting NWTs.

This chapter analyses the benefits and risks of NWTs. Given the breath of the topic, the chapter is not a comprehensive analysis of all relevant factors. What follows is a framework for thinking about NWTs, and their various impacts on tax justice. Further research questions will arise that will need answers.

Section II provides 'administrative justice' as a tool to analyse NWTs. Section III describes NWTs in greater detail, and outlines how some of these technologies have existed for decades. However, the doubling of computing power has created the emergence of big data that has fundamentally improved the value of data analytics. Section IV analyses the benefits and risks of NWTs and their impact on tax justice. It uncovers hope for tax justice: reduced tax compliance gap, increased legal certainty and greater efficiency. However, there are serious risks to tax justice, including over-reliance on machines, poor data, lack of transparency and little oversight. Section V offers a three-fold proposal to capture the benefits of NWTs and reduce the risks. Section VI concludes with closing remarks. The fundamental question for this chapter is: Does use of NWTs by tax administrations promote or hinder tax justice?

II. Tax Justice

The concept of 'justice' is a fundamental concern for every human. The concern for justice has been felt throughout human history. De Waal argues that equality is naturally imprinted onto our social DNA.[4] Homo sapiens have a natural inclination towards empathy and collective survival as social creatures. The development of this trait has allowed our species to dominate the planet.[5] Justice is today a pillar of modern society:

> Nothing is more fundamental to the character of a successful democracy than its citizens' trust in judicial and legislative processes that protect basic human rights and provide equal justice under the law.[6]

The demand for protection and equal treatment is so natural we often take it for granted,[7] especially in developed countries where citizens are spared the tragedies of life often encountered by citizens in developing countries. Some argue that

---

[4] F de Waal, *Our Inner Ape* (New York, Riverhead Books, 2005).
[5] This is contrary to Thomas Hobbe's popular claim that humanity is 'every man against every man'.
[6] E Steuerle, 'And Equal (Tax) Justice for All?' in J Thorndike and D Ventry (eds) *Tax Justice: The Ongoing Debate* (Washington, The Urban Institute Press, 2002) 252, 254.
[7] ibid 256: Justice is also a key purpose of regulatory systems. ibid 255: 'Regulatory processes are designed to allow anyone claiming unfair treatment access to an almost judicial consideration of their claim.'

justice is the chief purpose of the state.[8] The concern for justice often outweighs efficiency concerns: 'While constitutions and courts require "equal justice under the law", they do not require efficiency or simplicity'.[9]

The concept of 'justice' is notoriously difficult to define. It has developed into numerous sub-categories including 'social justice', 'distributive justice', 'legal justice', 'administrative justice', 'procedural justice' and 'commutative justice'.[10] Furthermore, these sub-categories often conflict with each other. Obtaining agreement on the meaning of 'tax justice' is no easy feat. There is scarce literature discussing tax justice,[11] hence this book is a timely contribution.

A. Administrative Justice as Tax Justice

The central problem of this chapter is the use of NWTs by tax administrations, and their impact on tax justice. Given that we are tackling a large state actor that makes countless decisions impacting taxpayers, the best tool to investigate the topic is 'administrative justice'.[12] Administrative justice, prominent in public and administrative law systems,[13] has no universally accepted definition; however, it is generally understood as 'processes through which the state makes decisions about people and the avenues by which they can challenge those decisions.'[14] The processes adopted by the tax administrations to make decisions has a huge impact on society. Administrative justice allows a more insightful understanding of the problem, and any potential solutions. Appropriate use of NWTs results in better implementation of law, fewer aggrieved taxpayers, enhanced taxpayer morale and lower operating costs.[15] Inappropriate use of NWTs could have the opposite effect.

There are two approaches to administrative justice: governmental approach and a legal approach. First, the governmental approach focuses on 'the entire volume of cases presented to government that then require decisions'.[16] The executive branch ideally makes decisions that are timely and proportionate with the

---

[8] T LeFevre, 'Justice in Taxation' (2016) 41(4) *Vermont Law Review* 763, 764.

[9] Steuerle (n 6) 257. For an alternative view, see FA Hayek, 'The Atavism of Social Justice: Social Justice, Socialism, and Democracy' (Centre for Independent Studies, 1979). Hayek argues that fixation on justice or equality has reinforced 'primitive' societies. Hayek points to technological discoveries made by scientists in the past 400 years as evidence of individualism triumphing. He argues that progress has occurred by individuals ignoring principles that 'held old groups together'.

[10] See D Daiches Raphael, *Concepts of Justice* (Oxford, Clarendon Press, 2001).

[11] A Jeorg, 'Tax Justice-Justice of Taxation (Ethics Discussion Paper III)' ('Tax Justice & Poverty' Research Project, 2018) 4.

[12] For the toolkit approach, see B Bogenschneider, 'A Philosophy Toolkit for Tax Lawyers' (2017) 50(3) *Akron Law Review* 451.

[13] Tomlinson (n 2) 1.

[14] ibid IX.

[15] A useful analysis of decision-making: R Thomas, 'Administrative Justice, Better Decisions, and Organisational Learning' (2015) *Public Law* 111.

[16] R Thomas and J Tomlinson, 'Mapping Current Issues in Administrative Justice: Austerity and the 'More Bureaucratic Rationality' Approach' (2017) 39(3) *Journal of Social Welfare and Family Law* 380, 380.

264 Benjamin Walker

available resources. Second, the legal approach focuses on redress through judicial review or statutory appeal for individual cases.[17] Both approaches are justified for this chapter as tax administrations are a key actor under both approaches, and they ultimately directly affect taxpayers.[18] A broad approach to administrative justice captures the full range of activities between state and taxpayers.[19] The values of administrative justice are a useful guide for testing NWTs: accuracy, fairness, cost-effectiveness and efficiency.[20] These values can act as yardsticks for assessing the impact of NWTs.

III. NWTs: The Basics

A. Introduction

The ability to concretely define and categorise technologies is a serious problem for the field of data science,[21] which creates problems understanding the various technologies. In this chapter the general term 'NWTs' is used to include three components:

(i) big data;
(ii) computer power; and
(iii) data analytics.

A clear understanding of each component is critical to understand their precise impact on tax justice.

There is no universal definition of big data, but it broadly 'refers to the gigantic amounts of digital data controlled by companies, authorities and other large organizations'.[22] For example, Facebook has more than two billion monthly active

---

[17] ibid.

[18] This position is supported by the United Kingdom Administrative Justice Institute. For discussion, see T Buck, R Kirkham and B Thompson, *The Ombudsman Enterprise and Administrative Justice* (London, Routledge, 2016) 57.

[19] More support for a wide definition: T Mullen and S O'Neill, *Administrative Justice in Scotland – the Way Forward: A Summary of the Final Report of the Administrative Justice Steering Group* (Scottish Consumer Council, 2009) 2.

[20] M Adler, *Administrative Justice in Context* (Oxford, Hart Publishing, 2010).

[21] C Gavaghan, A Knott, J Maclaurin, et al, 'Government Use of Artificial Intelligence in New Zealand: Final Report on Phase 1 of the New Zealand Law Foundation's Artificial Intelligence and Law in New Zealand Project' (The Law Foundation, 2019) 5.

[22] International Working Group on Data Protection in Telecommunications, 'Working Paper on Big Data and Privacy: Privacy principles under pressure in the age of Big Data analytics', Berlin Commissioner for Data Protection, available at https://www.edoeb.admin.ch/edoeb/en/home.html (accessed 21 January 2020). For a critical analysis of big data in taxation, see KA Houser and D Sanders, 'The Use of Big Data Analytics by the IRS: Efficient Solutions or the End of Privacy as We Know It?' (2017) 19 *Vanderbilt Journal of Entertainment & Technology Law* 4; F Başaran Yavaşlar and J Hey, *Tax Transparency* (Amsterdam, IBFD, 2019); M Hatfield, 'Taxation and Surveillance: An Agenda' (2015) 17 *Yale Journal of Law & Technology* 319; Mazzoni argues that a balance between taxpayer privacy and

New Wave Technologies and Tax Justice   265

users worldwide. Every day millions of comments are posted. Facebook can collect and store all the information from those two billion users. Before big data, this was unimaginable. There is currently a continuous 'dramatic reduction in the cost of acquiring and using information'[23] across society as technology advances. There are lower costs of producing information, which lowers the costs of individuals to understand their legal rights and obligations.[24] The cost of real time updating of specific information is also reducing.[25] Big data will only become bigger over time.

The second component, connected to big data, is computing power. Big data has been facilitated by the large improvement in computing power over the past 50 years that have drastically improved the performance of computers. Computer power is doubling every two years.[26] This allows tax administrations to collect more information.

More information is useless unless one can draw insights from the data. Data analytics is the third component that solves this problem. Data analytics refers to analysing data to make conclusions about that information. In its basic form, there are statistics that provide insights about data. 'Advanced analytics', a synonym for data analytics, is defined by the OECD as a 'set of statistical techniques and practices that can help distil insight and clarity from masses of information.[27] It can distil insight and clarity from the information that humans could never obtain due to our inherent processing capabilities. Data analytics includes various subcategories,[28] but the most relevant for tax administrations are:

(i) predictive analytics (statistical modelling and simulation); and
(ii) prescriptive analytics (Optimisation, heuristics and rules-based/expert systems).

Predictive analytics uses various techniques that analyse current data to make predictions about the future. Predictive models analyse the relationship between two variables in a data set and assess the likelihood that the future will exhibit the same relationship. For example, tax officials want to know where to target tax audits. A model may analyse the relationship between tax evasion and employment status, thereby offering a clue for investigations. Prescriptive analytics uses various techniques that provides options and their consequences. For example, a model may outline various options for tax officials (eg a combative approach or

---

public interest is required: G Mazzoni, '(Re)defining the Balance between Tax Transparency and Tax Privacy in Big Data Analytics' (2018) 72(11) *Bulletin for International Taxation* 656.

[23] AJ Casey and A Niblett, 'Self-Driving Laws', 5 June 2016, 3, available at https://papers.ssrn.com/abstract=2804674 (accessed 9 January 2020).

[24] See B Alarie, A Niblett and A Yoon, 'Using Machine Learning to Predict Outcomes in Tax Law', 15 December 2017, available at https://papers.ssrn.com/abstract=2855977 (accessed 9 January 2020).

[25] Casey and Niblett (n 23) 1.

[26] Alarie, Niblett and Yoon (n 24) 7.

[27] *Advanced Analytics for Better Tax Administration: Putting Data to Work* (Paris: OECD Publishing, 2016) 3.

[28] Other categories include diagnostic analytics and descriptive analytics.

266   *Benjamin Walker*

conciliatory approach) when assessing a possible case for audit. Depending on the question, both set of analytics can assist decision-making.

The use of statistical techniques dates back centuries. Johann Süssmilch developed a predictive model in the 1740s to predict marriage age and marriage rate.[29] A regression analysis, a statistical method that estimates the relationships between variables, is a helpful technique that is traced back to the early nineteenth century. The history of artificial intelligence (AI), a key tool in data analytics, attempts to replicate human cognitive dates back to the mid-twentieth century. The first use of AI and tax was seen in the 1970s. Thomas McCarty, the father of AI and law,[30] developed a machine tool for US corporate tax law aimed at company reorganisations called 'Taxman'.[31] Taxman could allegedly decide whether a company reorganisation in the USA was taxable or not. Tax is often viewed as a good fit for AI as it is highly technical and complex.

The long history of statistical techniques raises critical questions: If statistical techniques have existed for centuries, what is the relevance of NWTs? Is there anything inherently new or disruptive? I argue that the addition of big data and computing power has exponentially expanded the power of statistics. The value of statistical techniques is reliant on enough information to draw inferences. Statistical techniques were traditionally limited by the lack of data, and the limited ability of humans to make inferences from such data. The determination of causation based on a limited set of data was the highest goal within science. Recording, storing and using information was severely restricted to analog form before the widespread use of computers. Computers allowed humans to record and store information on a larger scale. The 'greater quantification of observable phenomena in the world',[32] ie big data, has dramatically increased the usefulness of statistical techniques as there is simply more information to analyse. The sample sizes have grown exponentially. Additionally, computing power has increased the automated use of information. Data analytics can now be automated allowing inferences from massive amounts of data within seconds.[33] These techniques or machines that learn (machine learning) outperform humans in certain domains including memory, objectivity and logic.[34] For example, research indicates that formal algorithms outperform human judgment using a clinical method in the vast number of cases.[35]

---

[29] S Kotz, 'Reflections on Early History of Official Statistics and a Modest Proposal for Global Coordination' (2005) 21(2) *Journal of Official Statistics* 139, 141.

[30] R Susskind, 'Pragmatism and Purism in Artificial Intelligence and Legal Reasoning' (1989) 3(1) *AI and Society* 28, 29.

[31] L Thorne McCarty, 'Reflections on "Taxman": An Experiment in Artificial Intelligence and Legal Reasoning' (1977) 90(5) *Harvard Law Review* 837.

[32] B Alarie, A Niblett and A Yoon, 'Law in the Future' (2016) 66(4) *University of Toronto Law Journal* 423, 425.

[33] Alarie, Niblett and Yoon (n 24) 5.

[34] ibid 7.

[35] See WM Grove and PE Meehl, 'Comparative Efficiency of Informal (Subjective, Impressionistic) and Formal (Mechanical, Algorithmic) Prediction Procedures: The Clinical-Statistical Controversy' (1996) 2(2) *Psychology, Public Policy, and Law* 293.

It is difficult to speculate about the future progress of NWTs, but the rate of current technological change is exponential.[36] Some predict that computers could have the capacity of a human brain in 20 years.[37] Grandiose predictions are seldom reliable, but even slow progress could deliver significant disruption.

B. Case Study: AI Interpretation of Law

AI is the cutting-edge component of data analytics that can be incorporated into various data analytical techniques. As previously mentioned, AI attempts to replicate human cognitive functions using sophisticated techniques. There are two categories of AI. First, Narrow Artificial Intelligence (NAI) is where a machine performs a narrow task defined by the programmers that optimises a certain goal using algorithms. For example, algorithms have been used in the United States to decide whether to grant bail or not.[38] Second, Artificial General intelligence (AGI) is where machines solve any general problem, rather than a specific problem. Problems are autonomously identified independently from human supervisors and solved. Machines have not reached this level yet. Some predict that machines will gain AGI by 2100.[39] Some predict a radical transformation of tax professional work beyond 2050, which will be shaped by technological developments, but not necessarily AGI.[40] For our present purposes, this chapter considers only NAI.

There exists today an AI tool that interprets law and provides probabilistic answers using application programming interface, which is a developing technology that uses 'machine learning to textually analyse all the relevant sources and provide a probabilistic answer to that question'.[41] Kuźniacki has developed an 'AI Tax Treaty Assistant' to interpret the principal purposes test recently introduced by the OECD.[42] He uses knowledge-based AI relying on supervised learning classifier system (question-answer) combined with semi-supervised pattern recognition (information retrieval by reading contracts between companies and

---

[36] G Moore, 'Moore's law' in DC Brock (ed), *Understanding Moore's Law: Four Decades of Innovation* (Philadelphia, Chemical Heritage Foundation, 2006) 67–84.

[37] R Kurzweil, *The Singularity is Near: When Humans Transcend Biology* (New York, Penguins, 2006) 167–81.

[38] Casey and Niblett (n 23) 5.

[39] See VC Mueller and N Bostrom, 'Future Progress in Artificial Intelligence: A Survey of Expert Opinion' in Mueller (ed), *Fundamental Progress in Artificial Intelligence* (Cham, Springer International Publishing, 2016) 553–71.

[40] B Alarie, 'The Path of the Law: Towards Legal Singularity' (2016) 66(4) *University of Toronto Law Journal* 443, 453.

[41] See AH Yoon, 'The Post-Modern Lawyer: Technology and the Democratization of Legal Representation' (2016) 66(4) *University of Toronto Law Journal* 467.

[42] See B Kuźniacki, 'The Artificial Intelligence Tax Treaty Assistant: Decoding the Principal Purpose Test' (2018) 72(9) *Bulletin for International Taxation* 524.

268   *Benjamin Walker*

descriptions of existing or planned tax schemes) to provide a prediction tool for stakeholders.[43]

Alarie, Niblett and Yoon, in conjunction with Thomson Reuters, have developed a similar tool called 'Blue J Legal' that can answer specific tax questions. Blue J Legal tags words (verbs, nouns, etc) from unstructured data to provide predictions.[44] For example, Blue J Legal can allegedly predict with 98 per cent confidence, based on 20 questions, whether a person is classified as an employee or independent contractor under Canadian Law.[45] The data set contains all relevant case law from the early 1990s until 2016.

Both AI tools use neural networks, which is an important feature of NWTs that could have significant impacts. A neural network is 'a collection of neuron-like unites that perform simple computations and can have different degrees of activation'.[46] Neural networks are inspired by brain computation. Each neuron is a processor that is connected by synapses. The network learns by modifying the strength of individual synapses. A typical network, a feedforward network, uses a set of input units that encode the input variables. The output units encode the outcome variables and the hidden units process the input variables to produce the output variables based on a function. The hidden units identify and organise the input variables independently of human control. They operate autonomously, and it is difficult for humans to understand exactly how the hidden units operate. The network can analyse variables and construct relationships among them, rather than a human constructing these relationships:

> Neural networks find hidden connections between the variables that we, as empirical modellers, do not specify and – probably – could not have identified even with unlimited time and resource using conventional approaches to legal research.[47]

Blue J Legal uses a neural network model to provide probabilistic answers. The case facts are the input units, based on a serious of questions answered by humans. The hidden units are constantly weighing relevant variables based on case law and the output units are the probabilities. The model arguably allows users to draw insights from case law that were not obtainable through purely human endeavours. It could save inexperienced stakeholders countless hours by drawing their attention to a probability and key cases.

---

[43] ibid 531–32. There are uses in other areas: ROSS Intelligence is used in bankruptcy law. Lex Machina uses prediction models for patent law. It aims to predict how likely it is that a judge will grant or deny a specific motion or how likely a judge is to find infringement of a patent, fair use of a trademark, etc: see Lex Machina, https://lexmachina.com/legal-analytics (accessed 9 January 2020).

[44] See Alarie, Niblett and Yoon (n 24).

[45] ibid 5.

[46] Gavaghan et al (n 21), 11.

[47] ibid 10.

IV. The Impact of NWTs on Tax Justice Benefits

A. Tax Compliance Gap

The tax compliance gap is a violation of tax justice.[48] The tax compliance gap is the difference between the total tax revenue that could be collected assuming 100 per cent compliance and the actual tax revenue collected.[49] Tax laws are notoriously complex requiring large amounts of information about taxpayers that are provided by taxpayers themselves or related parties (eg employers, banks, businesses, etc). Some of these requirements place a large burden on individuals to comply with tax laws. Where these compliance mechanisms fail, the tax administration does not have complete information to enforce the law, hence tax revenue is lost. This problem also violates the principle of enforceability, which holds that laws should be enforced fairly amongst citizens that protect basic human rights.[50] Honest taxpayers face a greater burden from tax administrations attempting to collect information, and dishonest taxpayers are able to fall through the cracks, and pay less tax.

Third party reporting of taxpayer information has gone some way to increasing compliance rates. But, tax revenues are still lost each year to non-filing, under-reporting of income, or over-reporting of deductions.[51] The estimates across the globe range from $190 billion to trillions.[52] As a result, there is less money available for public services, which disproportionately impact the least-advantaged in society. Furthermore, it violates tax equity as dishonest taxpayers face a lower taxer burden than honest taxpayers. Tax justice could be improved if tax administrations can increase the number of persons paying tax, and the correct amount. NWTs potentially offer tax administrations the ability to decrease the tax compliance gap through better enforcement.

NWTs could also decrease the tax compliance gap by improving decision-making. Information has only existed in analog (paper) form in significant

---

[48] Hatfield (n 22) 335.

[49] ibid 332.

[50] J Martikainen, 'Data Mining in Tax Administration- Using Analytics to Enhance Tax Compliance', Master's thesis, Aalto University, 42, available at https://aaltodoc.aalto.fi/handle/123456789/7398 (accessed 9 January 2020): 'As one of the main objectives of a tax administration is to ensure that right amounts of taxes are paid, the tax gap is a fundamental measure of the financial extent of tax risks. In 2007, the Swedish Tax Agency estimated that Sweden's annual tax gap would amount to approximately 133 billion Swedish crowns (equivalent to approximately 14 billion euro).'

[51] See P Janský, 'European Parliament, TAX3 Committee: Hearing on Evaluation of Tax Gap', 23 January 2019, available at http://www.europarl.europa.eu/cmsdata/161049/2019%2001%2024%20-%20Petr%20Jansky%20written%20questions%20-%20Ev_TAX%20GAP.pdf (accessed 9 January 2020).

[52] DM Kemme, B Parikh and T Steigner, 'Tax Havens, Tax Evasion and Tax Information Exchange Agreements in the OECD' (2017) 23(3) *European Financial Management* 519; A Cobham, 'Working Paper Number 129 Tax Evasion, Tax Avoidance and Development Finance' 20.

270 Benjamin Walker

quantities since the invention of the printing press. Tax administrations have traditionally centrally collected and held massive amounts of information. Near the end of the twentieth century, tax administrations started moving slowly towards digitalisation (information in digital form) and this process is still not over for some tax administrations. Taking digital information and allowing data analytics to analyse the data is another leap from digitalisation to datafication (digital information that is used for data analytics) that has the potential to dramatically improve decision-making.[53] Tax administrations could use the information to predict what is likely to take place (predictive analytics) and what to do about it (prescriptive analytics): 'Whether selecting cases for audit, determining the next steps for debt management, or in designing taxpayer communications, tax officials are constantly making predictions and drawing conclusions about the likely impact of their actions.'[54]

There are several countries already using NWTs to inform decision-making, thereby improving decision-making.[55] Australia, Singapore, Ireland, New Zealand, the United Kingdom and the United States are world leaders in the use of NWTs for numerous activities including audit case selection, filing and payment compliance, taxpayer service, debt management and policy.[56] Most countries use NWTs for at least one area of compliance. Neural networks are being deployed to identify false income-tax deductions (Australia) and under-reported income (Ireland).[57] These models could identify potential tax evasion that would otherwise go unnoticed.

NWTs are also proving helpful for policy decisions by forecasting the impact of policy decisions. China has used simulation modelling, which relies less on historical data but is based on economic theory, to build a Taxation Computable General Equilibrium (CGE) model.[58] The model can 'estimate the economic and social consequences of the VAT reform'.[59] Tax administrations are also using AI-based advanced analytics for the recovery of revenue and predictive communications with taxpayers.

The New Zealand tax administration, Inland Revenue (IR), one of the more technologically advanced tax administrations, is currently embracing NWTs to improve general compliance through its transformation program.[60] Brazil is at the forefront of AI technology: facial recognition technology is now commonplace for

---

[53] V Mayer-Schönberger and K Cukier, *Big Data* (Boston, First Mariner Books, 2013).
[54] *Advanced Analytics for Better Tax Administration: Putting Data to Work* (n 27) 11.
[55] 'D9 Members' include: Canada, Estonia, Israel, Mexico, New Zealand, Portugal, South Korea, United Kingdom & Uruguay, see https://www.digital.govt.nz/digital-government/international-partnerships/the-digital-9 (accessed 9 January 2020).
[56] *Advanced Analytics for Better Tax Administration: Putting Data to Work* (n 27) 20.
[57] ibid 23.
[58] ibid 29.
[59] Mayer-Schönberger and Cukier (n 53) 29.
[60] Inland Revenue, 'Transforming Inland Revenue', available at https://www.ird.govt.nz/transformation/transforming-ird.html (accessed 9 January 2020).

customs systems, connected to a tax database, that track individuals with luggage in Brazil, and systems are in place that track the importation of goods.[61] AI is also used in tax assessments[62] and the adjudication of cases relating to tax debts lower than approximately EUR 4,500. Furthermore, the Supreme Court of Justice (Supremo Tribunal Federal) actively uses AI, a machine called 'Victor', to actively select analogous cases to a factual scenario. Thus, AI is already being used to interpret and apply the law by a court. The use of AI is seen as an antidote to the slow wheel of justice in Brazil.[63]

Value added tax (VAT) fraud is a problem for tax administrations caused by highly sophisticated schemes devised by businesses that deprive the state of VAT revenue, thereby reducing the provision of public services. Previously, there was the limited use of data as humans could not ascertain useful knowledge from massive amounts of information. Based on the current wealth of data, prescriptive analytical tools could analyse the data to autonomously identify anomalies in datasets, predict future events and offer tax officials various options for certain aspects of VAT fraud and their respective implications. The identification of anomalies could greatly improve the knowledge of tax officials and their ability to respond to various problems. Another tool is social network analysis (SNA). SNA is the process of analysing social networks. SNA can identify links between risk groups that are not immediately obvious to a tax official.[64]

An empirical analysis of the impact of all these measures is difficult as tax administrations have a duty to protect their proprietary technology from misuse by taxpayers. For example, if taxpayers knew how tax audits were selected based on NWTs, they could possibly construct their affairs to fall outside of the audit selection. However, the limited evidence and the obvious utility of NWTs suggests that tax administrations are benefiting from their use. The ability of tax administrations to tackle non-compliance has likely improved, which is a positive step towards reducing the tax compliance gap.

B. Legal Certainty

Another potential benefit is increased legal certainty for all stakeholders. The cost of non-compliance with tax laws depends on the severity of the breach, but it can result in a prison sentence and large financial penalties in most jurisdictions.

---

[61] 'SISAM' – Sistema de seleção aduaneira por aprendizado de máquina (Custom selection system by machine learning) uses AI to analyse imports, available at https://www.jambeiro.com.br/jorgefilho (accessed 21 January 2020).

[62] 'SPED' – Sistema Público de Escrituração Digital (Public System of Digital Accounting), available at http://sped.rfb.gov.br (accessed 21 January 2020).

[63] M Margolis, 'Brazil's mercurial courts undermine growth and democracy', Bloomberg, 15 July 2018, available at https://www.bloomberg.com/opinion/articles/2018-07-15/brazil-s-mercurial-courts-undermine-growth-and-democracy (accessed 9 January 2020).

[64] *Advanced Analytics for Better Tax Administration: Putting Data to Work*, above n 27, 21.

272　*Benjamin Walker*

Furthermore, the tax liabilities can be detrimental to any business. Hence, legal certainty is critical. Laws are often drafted broadly to capture potential tax planning, and notoriously are so complex that only a limited number of professionals understand them. The use of AI to interpret and apply the law is attractive because of the increased legal certainty derived from a probabilistic answer. Many disputes between tax administrations and taxpayers debate what would happen in court with an adversarial nature. AI could create more objective predictions.[65] As noted earlier, Brazil is already experimenting with this AI tool. Looking to the future, there are even bolder predictions from scholars in this area. Casey and Niblett envisage a world of 'micro-directives' that use algorithms to automatically update laws.[66] Alarie predicts the achievement of 'legal singularity' that effectively eliminates legal uncertainty where the law is updated in real time, allowing a shift from fewer standards to more rules.[67] Ex-post decisions will reduce and ex-ante guidance to individuals will increase in capability. Alarie also argues that machine learning could achieve an 'efficient frontier' of public policy, extending beyond positive law.[68] This area of development is still in its early stages, but promising signs point to a world with more legal certainty. Improved legal certainty can facilitate a better relationship between taxpayers and tax administrations that could also potentially reduce the tax compliance gap.

C. Efficiency

NWTs offer potential improvements in operational efficiency for tax administrations. They can do more with less. Training a tax official is lengthy and costly. The tax profession suffers from the 'cost disease'.[69] The cost disease is where productivity of a particular employment is relatively constant; for example, it took musicians in 2019 the same amount of time to perform Puccini's *La Boheme* as in 1919.

Tax administrations are better placed to fight cost disease through technological development than a small organisation due to its large amounts of data and economies of scale. Instead of training tax officials and hiring numerous seasonal workers during tax-return season, NWTs can perform certain tasks better than humans. The New Zealand tax administration (IR) is currently in a process of reducing its staff numbers by nearly 35 per cent over a four-year period.[70] Their

---

[65] See D Katz, 'Quantitative Legal Prediction-or-How I Learned to Stop Worrying and Start Preparing for the Data-Driven Future of the Legal Services Industry' (2013) 62 *Emory Law Journal* 909, 936.

[66] Casey and Niblett (n 23) 2.

[67] Alarie (n 40) 445.

[68] ibid 453.

[69] W Baumol & W Bowen, 'On the Performing Arts: The Anatomy of Their Economic Problems' (1965) 55 *American Economics Review* 495.

[70] Inland Revenue, 'Budget 2017: Four-Year Plan: Covering Vote Revenue', November 2016, available at https://www.classic.ird.govt.nz/resources/d/7/d7d56768-e030-44bb-af63-cda63c06add0/budget-2017-four-year-plan.pdf (accessed 9 January 2020).

transformation project plans to incorporate more technology with fewer human inputs. In 2019, many taxpayers enjoyed their first automatic tax refunds. An algorithm calculates the taxpayer's position and issues a refund or notice of outstanding tax. Where the algorithm finds information missing, the taxpayer is asked for more information. Furthermore, an algorithm identified that many taxpayers were also paying the incorrect tax rate in New Zealand.[71] As NWTs play a greater role, greater efficiencies could reduce the long-term cost for taxpayers funding the tax administration.

D. Application of NWTs for Tax Administrations

It is difficult to predict the future use of such technology, but the current NWTs offer organisations the ability to unlock the value of their data. Companies such as Facebook and YouTube have become technology giants by unlocking the value of customer data for targeted advertising. NWTs have proven ideal for governments when attempting to improve the wellbeing of citizens in various facets of their life, most notably in public health where outbreaks of diseases can be more easily predicted. Tax administrations have massive amounts of data, hence the use of NWTs could have significant consequences for all members of society. There is a potential shift for tax administrations from questions such as: What are the problems? What happened? What action is needed? They could ask more insightful questions such as: Why is this happening? What if we try x? What will happen next? NWTs offers tax administrations the ability to draw better insights, which could allow them the ability to make better decisions.

E. Risks

i. Over-reliance on Machines

NWTs shift the role of the human from operator to supervisor, which creates new challenges for humans. The field of industrial psychology has demonstrated that this shift affects humans in several respects, and some of these are dangerous.[72] One major danger is the over-reliance on algorithms that results in errors being ignored or missed. This can lead to humans ignoring their own senses or their intuition.[73] For example, a neural network model identifies that a taxpayer could potentially be under-reporting income. The tax official's experience or intuition

---

[71] The Prescribed Investor Rate (PIR) is used to calculate the tax rate on Portfolio Investment Entity (PIE) taxable income.

[72] L Bainbridge, 'Ironies of Automation' (1983) 19(6) *Automatica* 775.

[73] K Pazouki, N Forbes, R Norman and M Woodward, 'Investigation on the Impact of Human-Automation Interaction in Maritime Operations' (2018) 153 *Ocean Engineering* 297, 299.

274 Benjamin Walker

suggests to her that there is an innocent explanation, but the tax official proceeds with a tax audit. This could be problematic to any tax official that has unique experience that cannot be replicated by NWTs. A common strategy against this problem is to only use NWTs where they are significantly better-than-humans.[74] A system can be further broken down into sub-categories of tasks where humans can complement algorithms.[75] For example, the final decision on whether a tax audit is carried out should be completed by a human unless NWTs demonstrate otherwise. Analysing the viability of NWTs is a lengthy process that should include repetitive trials before proceeding with implementation.

A related issue, predominantly with neural network models, is that the user does not understand how a model discovered an anomaly from massive amounts of data. It only knows that the model suggests potential under-reporting. The choice is either to proceed with further investigation or ignore the information. The process is unreviewable. Take a future case, if the investigation proceeds and a court process eventually occurs, how should the court treat the neural network when it cannot review it?

At one end of the spectrum, governments could prevent the use of neural networks. France has banned the use of data analytics relating to judges' rulings.[76] At the other end of the spectrum, governments could fully embrace NWTs by promoting their use in tax administrations and the adjudication of disputes (eg Brazil). In my view, this end of the spectrum appears more frightening. Open liberal democracies are based on the Montesquieu's separation of powers: legislative, executive and judicial. The judicial branch interprets and applies the law independently from the legislative and executive branches. It is a check on the power of the executive. If a sophisticated model using neural networks is adopted by the tax administration and this is unreviewable, the judiciary has a reduced role, and the tax administration could operate free from the law. Therefore, there is a potential risk associated with over-reliance on NWTs, and especially neural networks.

ii. Data

The most practical risk of NWTs is the problem of poor data being used that distort the output results, thereby undermining decisions. The usefulness of NWTs to infer clarity and insight is based on the quality of the underlying data. Data analytical tools require datasets to train their functions. The datasets cannot be automated. Human judgment is necessary for choosing which data is appropriate, ie they

---

[74] Gavaghan et al (n 21) 39.

[75] 'DCAF' approach (dynamic/complementary allocation of function).

[76] S Taylor, 'France Bans Data Analytics Related to Judges' Rulings', Legal Week, 4 June 2019, available at https://www.law.com/legal-week/2019/06/04/france-bans-data-analytics-related-to-judges-rulings (accessed 9 January 2020).

must make specific decisions and assumptions about the data.[77] The interaction effects between independent variables must be carefully considered. Furthermore, humans must oversee the training process. Humans must choose the appropriate variables for each case they attempt to deconstruct. Several errors in these processes can lead to bad output results. Anything less than a team of experienced professionals would lead to poor data that would distort the result.

More advanced models that use deep neural networks allegedly overcome most of these issues by autonomously constructing variables.[78] However, the problem of 'over-fitting', where an analysis corresponds too closely to a set of data that it fails to fit additional data, can still occur where too many independent variables are provided.[79] This occurs where the model is unable to detect the relevant variables in data that are 'finely tuned to the idiosyncrasies or biases in the training set such that they are not predictive of future, novel scenarios'.[80] This may be particularly relevant where tax officials are attempting to predict an outcome based heavily on data that may not be representative of future events. Where a future case involves new features, the data is less valuable in predicting the outcome.

The data science literature distinguishes between two types of biases: intrinsic and extrinsic bias. Intrinsic bias 'resides in a system by virtue of its design, structure and rules of operation, or as a consequence of inputs effecting a permanent change in these features'.[81] For example, limited access to tax services for certain people (Group A), due to the lack of economic resources, reduces their ability to effectively defend themselves in tax matters. Hence, the datasets used to train a neural network model will contain stronger correlations between successful prosecutions and Group A. Hence, the model is more likely to reinforce the prosecution of Group A in a self-fulfilling prophecy, and would reinforce underlying injustices within society. Research has suggested that the Inland Revenue Service's targeted practice of auditing lower and middle-class individuals in the United States has led to a regressive tax system in the United States.[82]

Extrinsic bias occurs where false inputs are used by a system. Extrinsic bias is the most prevalent problem for AI given the high dependence of data.[83] If the data collected is tainted, then the decisions reached will contain potential discriminative measures against certain groups. For example, if the dataset used to train a neural network model to detect under-reporting of income does not represent the diversity of the population (ie age groups, race, gender, sex, etc), it will entrench biases against groups over-represented in the dataset and favour

---

[77] Alarie, Niblett and Yoon (n 24) 6.

[78] ibid 7.

[79] ibid.

[80] H Surden, 'Machine Learning and Law' (2014) 89 *Washington Law Review* 29, 106.

[81] Gavaghan et al (n 21) 44.

[82] B Bogenschneider, 'Income Inequality and Regressive Taxation in the United States' (2015) 4(3) *Interdisciplinary Journal of Economics and Business Law*, 8.

[83] B Friedman and H Nissenbaum, 'Bias in Computer Systems' (1996) 14(3) *ACM Transactions on Information Systems* 330.

276 Benjamin Walker

groups under-represented in the dataset. For example, if the datasets are derived from London, the model will over-represent minorities in the United Kingdom due to the higher proportion of minorities living in London. This is discrimination against minorities and, thus, it violates tax justice. The neural network is far more difficult to control, and the potential damage caused is greater than could be caused by a human. A racist tax official would be relatively easy to identify if all that official's audits were directed at one group of people without a credible explanation. For example, you can see a rat crawling along your living room. A neural network is an army of rats working in the walls. The very faith in the rule of law is based on adjudication of the law, rather than non-law factors. The construction of hidden variables could entrench biases in the law against certain groups or individuals in society.[84]

Another important limitation is the lack of data. Some areas, such as VAT, may have enough data. However, other areas lack data. Substantive tax questions are often complex, and many areas lack enough sources of law to provide reliable predictions such as anti-avoidance rules.[85] Tax laws can operate in the grey areas, and legal certainty is often difficult to obtain especially in tax planning. Hence, NWTs should not be applied to every conceivable problem of tax administration. Distinguishing between applicable areas and non-applicable areas is critical to ensure net benefits.

iii. Transparency

Tax administrations are currently operating various tools that incorporate NWTs without any public explanations except for high-level descriptions about their use. Tax administrations admit using NWTs but will not explain how they use them in any detail. It is extremely difficult to analyse a tax administration's use of NWTs given that it has a duty to protect its proprietary technology from misuse by taxpayers.[86] One potential risk is that such a lack of transparency could lead to the tax administration making bad decisions that protect their interests, but negatively impact taxpayers. However, tax administrations have always operated with limited transparency even before NWTs. The question, therefore, arises: What do NWTs change?

One aspect of transparency is the ability to explain any given result.[87] Before NWTs, a decision by a tax official to launch an audit could theoretically be explained by an internal audit of the decision. The process is human. Neural networks are different: the internal processes operate independently of human

---

[84] Casey and Niblett (n 23); Surden (n 80) 106.

[85] ibid.

[86] Centre for Public Impact, 'Artificial Intelligence in Taxation: A Case Study on the Use of AI in Government', October 2018, available at https://resources.centreforpublicimpact.org/production/2019/01/CPI-AI-Case-Study-Taxation.pdf (accessed 9 January 2020).

[87] Gavaghan et al (n 21) 41.

control. Tax officials could be expected to explain their reasons for a tax audit; a neural network cannot. On the other hand, it is also impossible to audit the internal brain processes of decision-makers. Humans are often wrong about their real motivations and processing logic.[88] A tax officials may have no logical reason for auditing a taxpayer. Therefore, neural networks should not be held to a higher standard than human systems.[89] It is important to admit that human systems perform far below an optimal level.

The potential for wide-scale incorrect decisions is higher for NWTs. Previously, tax officials relying purely on limited information at hand without the assistance of NWTs would make a decision based on their knowledge and experience. They may make the wrong decision to audit, and this has a negative impact on tax justice. But, the potential risk of wide-scale incorrect decisions is limited by the overall knowledge, the experience of the tax officials and general human limitations. Furthermore, the internal processes of tax administrations generally reduce the probability of systematic errors. The potential wide-scale harm caused by a neural network is considerably larger due to the computational power of NWTs.

iv. Oversight

Another risk, linked to transparency, is the lack of oversight of the use of NWTs by tax administrations. There is usually a legal framework that governs how tax administrations collect information. In New Zealand, IR usually require information when it is deemed 'necessary or relevant'.[90] Tax administrations require information-gathering powers that can include collecting one-off taxpayer-specific and third-party information.[91] Ensuring clear rules that facilitate tax administrations access to datasets while maintaining taxpayer rights is essential. Tax administrations should be allowed to use information for other purposes, otherwise, the information has limited value. The United Kingdom expressly permits use of information for another function.[92] However, there appear to be few or no rules governing the use of NWTs. Tax administrations appear to have *carte blanche* when using NWTs. This is a serious concern given the power of NWTs.

---

[88] ibid 42.

[89] J Zerilli, A Knott, J Maclaurin and C Gavaghan, 'Transparency in Algorithmic and Human Decision-Making: Is There a Double Standard?' (2019) 32(4) *Philosophy and Technology* 661.

[90] New Zealand: Tax Administration Act s 17.

[91] New Zealand: *New Zealand Stock Exchange and National Bank of New Zealand v CIR* [1992] 13 NZTC 8, 147: 'The whole rationale of taxation would break down and the whole burden of taxation would fall only on diligent and honest taxpayers if the Commissioner had no power to obtain confidential information about taxpayers who may be negligent or dishonest.'

[92] United Kingdom: Commissioners of Revenue and Customs Act 2005 s 17: 'Information acquired by the Revenue and Customs in connection with a function may be used by them in connection with any other function.'

V. Proposal

As noted in section IV, the tax officials making decisions are the core of administrative justice. Their decisions will determine the impact on administrative justice. The emerging NWTs will not change the need for decisions, but will change the nature of the decisions being made. In order to ensure that NWTs promote administrative justice, it is important to consider a possible approach that maximises the benefits while reducing the risks.

The chapter has outlined the benefits and risks of NWTs. To summarise, the potential benefits include: reduced tax compliance gap, increased legal certainty and efficiency. The risks include: over-reliance on machines, poor data, lack of transparency and little oversight. Tax administrations are currently using NWTs *carte blanche*. Therefore, there is a danger that tax administrations could use NWTs with limited benefits and many negative effects that negatively impact tax justice. I suggest a three-fold approach:

(i) establish a regulatory body that could oversee the use of NWTs;[93]
(ii) develop a common framework that governs decision-making; and
(iii) establish a sandbox[94] that allows a place where new products, ideas and concepts are tested.[95]

A. Regulatory Body

The establishment of internal processes by tax administrations is unlikely to prevent potential abuses of NWTs as there is little transparency. At the same time, tax administrations cannot allow full access to taxpayers seeking to game the system. A regulatory body that has some oversight over how NWTs are implemented and developed could represent a reasonable compromise. Given that the risks of NWTs apply universally across government departments, the regulatory body should be considered across government departments.[96] Ongoing monitoring of the use of NWTs could aid accountability. Annual reports from the regulatory body outlining their activities, approving or denying proposed algorithms and maintaining a registry illustrate functional examples.

---

[93] Also suggested in Gavaghan et al (n 21) 76.

[94] M Fenwick, W Kaal and E Vermeulen, 'Regulation Tomorrow: What Happens When Technology is Faster than the Law?' (2017) 6(3) *American University Business Law Review* 25. A sandbox approach is also suggested in: A Veit, 'Swimming Upstream: Leveraging Data and Analytics for Taxpayer Engagement – an Australian and International Perspective' (2019) 16(3) *eJournal of Tax Research* 474, 496.

[95] This occurs mainly in Financial Technology areas.

[96] As suggested by Gavaghan et al (n 21).

B. Framework

In connection with the regulatory body, a framework that governs the use of NWTs is critical. Establishing a framework would require stakeholder input from the tax administration, regulatory body and other relevant actors. The concept of 'design thinking' is ideal for developing a framework. There is no concise definition of design thinking,[97] but the approach analyses the role of users of systems and developing testing of systems.[98] This approach has been adopted in various administrative contexts.[99] The key values of administrative justice could form over-arching principles: accuracy, fairness, cost-effectiveness and efficiency. A framework could govern the life cycle of a technology in five stages: idea, feasibility study, design and development, regulatory body approval, implementation and review. Each stage could include a series of tools to inform users of the potential benefits and risks. Various factors taken into account could include cost benefits, taxpayer impacts, accuracy of technology bias risks and transparency.[100] The framework should also include guidelines that ensure ethical standards for tax officials.[101]

Ensuring a coherent and accountable process should improve decision-making, rather than relying on tax administrations to develop internal processes. Furthermore, a framework reduces the risks for tax administrations of any potential technological disaster. It is important, however, that any framework accounts accurately for the benefits and risks of NWTs. A rubber-stamping exercise will not provide protection from potential abuses. At the same time, an onerous process will hinder the ability of tax administrations to improve.

C. Sandbox Approach

Several public authorities are taking a sandbox approach to develop new ideas in other fields.[102] A sandbox is a restricted zone that is used to create and test ideas. Common but difficult tax issues could also be tackled with NWTs. Tax administrations could adopt AI technology to quickly answer common tax questions in the form of a tax ruling. A tax ruling could be provided within seconds, rather

---

[97] See L Kimbell, 'Rethinking Design Thinking: Part I' (2011) 3 *Design and Culture* 285.

[98] Tomlinson (n 2) 64.

[99] A Clarke and J Craft, 'The Vestiges and Vanguards of Policy Design in a Digital Context' (2017) 60(4) *Canadian Public Administration* 476, 467–497.

[100] An illustrative example: New Zealand, 'The Privacy, Human Rights and Ethics (PHRaE) Framework', 1; available at https://www.msd.govt.nz/about-msd-and-our-work/work-programmes/initiatives/phrae/index.html (accessed 9 January 2020).

[101] Also suggested in: A Veit, 'Swimming Upstream: Leveraging Data and Analytics for Taxpayer Engagement – An Australian and International Perspective' (2019) 16(3) *eJournal of Tax Research* 474, 2.

[102] Australian Securities and Investment Commission (ASIC), Singapore's Monetary Authority (MAS) and Abu Dhabi's Financial Services Regulatory Authority (FSRA).

than months.[103] Alternatively, tax administrations could provide technology free to users via their website. Something akin to Blue J Legal could be offered for users to answer common tax questions or queries. This could dramatically decrease enforcement costs for the tax administration and enhance the tax morale of taxpayers. For example, persons unsure of their tax residency could go online and use an AI tool to assess their tax residency.

VI. Conclusion

The combination of big data, computer power and data analytics present an extremely powerful tool for organisations. Given the massive amounts of data held by tax administrations and their large economies of scale, they can unlock the value of their information. NWTs offer several potential benefits that contribute towards tax justice: reduction of taxpayer compliance gap, increased legal certainty and efficiency gains. These benefits could substantially improve public services to the least-advantaged within societies and improve overall tax systems. NWTs could significantly promote the administrative justice yardsticks of cost-effectiveness and efficiency. Tax administrations could do more with less.

NWTs also offer several risks, arising from over-reliance on machines, poor data, lack of transparency and little oversight. Use of NWTs should be carefully considered depending on the type of question asked by the tax administration. Data analytical tools should ensure repetitive trials to establish the viability of machine systems. NWTs could potentially hinder the administrative yardsticks of accuracy and fairness by relying too heavily on dubious data that could reinforce biases against certain groups. The institutional framework of tax administrations will ultimately decide whether NWTs are a net benefit for administrative justice. In this chapter, I have suggested a three-fold approach to increase the benefits of NWTs while reducing the risks, which could make a net positive contribution to tax justice. The future development of NWTs and their greater use in society will offer exciting research areas for scholars.

---

[103] Casey and Niblett (n 23).

INDEX

ability to pay:
  benefit principle and, 85, 126, 171–5, 178
  central value, 35
  distributive justice, 9, 157
  Hillen incentive and, 47, 51, 53, 56
  horizontal and vertical equity, 5, 10, 85–7,
     136–8, 151–2
  multinationals and, 61
  neoliberalism and, 95
  Nordic regime, 93
  principle, 9, 39–40
  tax competition and, 170
  UK tax regime, 89
  welfare law and, 126, 131
Addington, H, 242
Administrative Appeals Chamber, 254
administrative justice, 7, 245, 263–4, 278, 279,
    280
administrative tribunals *see* **Tax Chamber;**
    tribunals
age
  see also older people
  discrimination, 222, 238
Alarie, B, 268, 272
alcavala, 21, 26
Almunia, J, 68
Amazon, 57–8, 60, 61, 62, 66, 68, 72,
    75, 167
Anderson, E, 182
Apple, 57–8, 60, 62, 63, 66, 71, 72, 75, 167
Aristotle, 42
artificial intelligence *see* **New Wave**
    Technologies
Artificial Intelligence Tax Treaty Assistant,
    267–8
Asner, E, 83
asylum seekers, 117, 122, 134
austerity, 83, 94–5
Australia, 270
Austria, 89

Baker, P, 220
Belgium, 89
Bellamy, R, 123, 132

benefit principle:
  ability to pay and, 85, 126, 171–5, 178
  benefits for some, 178–85
  contract theory, 172
  developing countries and, 103
  meaning, 85
  non-residents and, 159
  Nordic regime and, 126
  rationale, 173
  Rawls on, 102
  tax competition and, 175–9
Benshalom, I, 161, 164
BEPS project:
  Action 12, 204, 210
  Action 13, 204
  Action 14, 204
  Action Plan, 203–6
  citizenship and, 118, 119
  digitalisation of the economy, 167
  fairness principle, 69
  Inclusive Framework, 8–9, 164–6, 193–4,
    196, 199–200, 220
  objectives, 66, 193, 204
  post-BEPS era, 205
  protection of taxpayers' rights and, 205
  rhetorical strategy, 195
  tax avoidance, 58
  tax competition and, 146
  tax justice and, 203–6
big data, 262, 264–5, 266
Bishopp, C, 247
Bismarck, O von, 89
Blue J Legal, 268, 280
Blum, WJ, 137
Brazil, 270–1, 272, 274
Broady, T, 226–7
Broekhuijsen, D, 4, 5, 7
Brundtland Report, 97
Buckingham, Duke of, 28
Burgess, G, 26

Canada, 96, 268
capital taxation, 92–4, 138–44
Caputi, P, 226–7

282   Index

Casey, AJ, 272
Centre for Tax Law (CTL), 11
certainty *see* legal certainty
Chan, A, 226–7
Charles I, 22, 23, 26–7
Charles II, 18, 32
Chartered Institute of Taxation (CIOT), 221, 222–3
China, 167, 270
Christian Aid, 65
Christians, A, 161, 164, 165
Citizens Advice, 236–7
citizenship:
  commodity, 172
  equality, 181–4
  EU rights, 122, 124, 130–1
  fiscal citizenship, 128–30, 131
  formal citizenship, 118
  gender and, 123
  informal citizenship, 118–19, 123–5, 127–8
  migrants and, 3, 117–21
  paying for, 146
  political citizenship, 130–1
  social citizenship, 125–8
  tax competition and, 177
  tax liability and, 119
  voting rights, 118, 121–3, 130–1
Cohen, J, 173
Coke, E, 27
continuation taxes, 140, 141–2, 148
contract: good faith, 59
controlled foreign corporations (CFCs), 144, 178
Cook, T, 62, 63
cooperation *see* information exchange
cosmopolitanism, 4, 161, 164, 168, 183
Crawford, BJ, 229
critical tax theory, 82, 136, 221–39
Cromwell, H, 18
Cromwell, O, 18, 21
Cvrlje, D, 225

Dagan, T, 3, 4, 163–4
Daly, S, 259
data analytics, 262, 265–6, 266
data protection: EU, 217–19
Dauber, N, 30
Davies, J, 22–6, 31
de Waal, F, 262
democracy:
  equality and, 42, 262
  global governance and, 196–7, 200

justice and, 191, 192
migration and, 121–3
proceduralist view, 193, 198
tax choices and, 185
Denmark, 89, 124
desert theory, 109, 111, 112
developing countries:
  BEPS agenda and, 165, 167, 193
  financing public goods, 107–8
  international tax justice and, 160–1, 164, 167, 187, 189–90
  OECD and, 3, 8–9, 188–9
  procedural v substantive justice, 193–7
  Rawls and, 162
  tax competition, 155–6
  technical education, 135, 148
Dicey, AV, 12
digital technology:
  access issues, 233–4, 275
  digital exclusion, 227–8
  NWT *see* New Wave Technologies
  older people and
    access issues, 233–4
    critical theory, 229
    double discrimination, 238
    empirical findings, 231–8
    previous scholarship, 223–8
    rectifying problems, 235–6
    research methods, 230
    scams, 236–7
    self-assessment methods, 234–5
    theoretical framework, 228–9
    United Kingdom, 4, 221–39
  UK skills, 225
disability discrimination, 222, 229, 238
discrimination *see* legal equality
disgrace, 7, 13, 101–2, 110–13, 114
Doyle-Price, J, 72
Dusarduijn, S, 7
Dworkin, R, 46, 101–2, 104, 113–14, 174

economic adjustment programs, 94–6
economic justice:
  concept, 36, 37–9
  contested concept, 39
  distributive justice, 37–8, 39, 45
  freedom and, 38
  Hillen incentive, 47, 51, 54
  objectives, 36, 37–8
Elliot, J, 27
endowment taxation, 162–3
equal sacrifice, 5, 9, 174

Index 283

Equal Treatment Bench Book, 255–6
equality *see* legal equality
Esping-Andersen, G, 89
estate taxes, 140–1
European Central Bank, 94
European Charter of Fundamental Rights,
    206, 211, 212, 213, 214, 216, 218
European Convention on Human Rights
    (ECHR):
  case law and EU, 212
  ECtHR jurisdiction, 206–7
  EU taxpayers' rights, 207
  fair trial, 214–15
  illegally obtained evidence, 213–14
  legal equality, 42
  private/family life, 212, 213, 214
  property rights, 42
  right to silence, 207–9
European Union:
  Action Plan for Fair and Efficient Corporate
    Taxation, 66, 70
  anti-avoidance package, 70, 118
  ATAD: fairness, 57, 59, 70–1, 72–3, 73–7
  citizenship rights, 122, 124, 130–1
  data protection, 217–19
  digitalisation of the economy, 167
  economic adjustment programs, 94
  exchange of tax information
    inter-continental exchanges, 217–19
    protection of taxpayer rights, 206–19
  Excise Duty Directive, 258
  fair taxation and, 96–9, 205
  free movement of goods, 257–8
  gender equality, 124
  good faith and, 59
  human rights, 206–7
  international tax justice and, 188
  list of non-cooperative tax jurisdictions, 191–2
  protection of taxpayer rights, 3
    exchange of information, 206–19
    illegally obtained information, 212–14
    right to silence, 207–12
    taxpayers' knowledge, 214–17
  state aids, 58, 66–9, 71, 73
  tax avoidance legislation, 58
  tax competition and, 68, 192
  Tax Transparency Package, 69
  VAT, 138
excise: 17th century:
  Britain, 18–34
  Davies on, 22–6, 31
  hearth money, 19, 20

Hobbes, 26–32
  natural justice, 17, 20–6, 30–2, 33
  Petty's case, 20–2, 32–4
  prerogative powers, 22, 24, 25, 26
  royal absolutist discourse, 17, 21, 22–33
  ship money, 27, 29, 30, 34

Facebook, 167, 218, 264–5, 273
fair trial, 207–9, 214–15
Finland: welfare state, 89
Forced Loan, 27, 30
foreign aid, 11
framework goods *see* public goods
France, 89, 274
Frecknall-Hughes, Jane, 4, 5, 9
free trade, 24
freedom: economic justice and, 38
Fuller, LL, 41, 43

G20, 58, 66, 69, 71, 72, 164, 165
Gavaghan, C, 268
gender:
  discrimination, 222
  neutrality, 5
    European Union, 124
    welfare provision, 124–5, 127
  reassignment, 222
  structural detaxation and, 95–6
  voting rights and, 123
General Commissioners of Income Tax, 241,
    242–3, 244, 249
Germany, 89, 213
global financial crisis, 64, 65, 82, 94
globalisation, 4, 117, 118, 122, 169–71, 174–85
golden visas, 118, 146
good faith: contract, 59, 76
Google, 57–8, 60, 61, 62, 63, 64, 72, 75, 167
Greece, 83, 90, 94–5
Gribnau, H, 7
Grotius, H, 24–5
growth:
  austerity and, 95
  OECD and, 91
  social justice and, 81–99
  sustainable development, 96–9
  tax base issue, 92–3
  tax neutrality and, 82, 90–1
Gunnarsson, Å, 3, 4, 5, 6, 9, 10

Haig-Simons income, 86, 87, 93
Hart, HLA, 72
Hayek, F, 90–1

Index

health care, 101, 110, 113
hearth money, 19, 20
Hewlett-Packard, 60
Hillen incentive:
  1st amendment, 50–2
  2nd amendment, 52–3
  3rd amendment, 53–4
  ability to pay and, 47
  abolition, 52–3
  conflicting values, 35, 36
  economic justice, 47, 51, 54
  legal certainty and, 53, 56
  legal justice and, 47–8, 54, 56
  objectives, 46–7
  relative justice, 7
  tax justice and, 46–55
  taxation of owner-occupation, 48–50
Hirschmann, A, 185
HJI Panayi, C, 2, 3, 4, 6–7
Hobbes, T, 22, 29–32, 33–4, 162
Hodge, M, 57, 60, 61, 63, 64, 72, 75
Hong Kong, 124
human rights:
  cooperation and, 190
  EU protection, 206–7
  exchange of information, 206–20
  international law, 205
  migration and, 148
  modernity and, 262
  NWT and, 269, 277
Hunt, E, 6

IMF, 94, 95
immigrants *see* **migrants**
India: caste system, 124
indirect taxation, 91, 92
Infanti, A, 161, 229, 239
information exchange:
  EU taxpayers' rights, 206–19
    covert methods, 215
    illegally obtained
      information, 212–14
    inter-continental exchanges, 217–19
    right to silence, 207–12
    taxpayers' knowledge and, 214–17
    uncertainties, 219–20
  international cooperation, 204–5
  remedies, 219–20
international cooperation *see* **information**
  exchange
International Covenant on Civil and Political
  Rights (ICCPR), 42

international tax justice:
  BEPS *see* BEPS project
  developing countries, 8–9, 187
  distributive justice, 158–62, 189–90
  information exchange *see* information
    exchange
  issues, 155–6
  justice problems, 189–90
  justice v legitimacy, 191–200
  legitimacy issues, 187–9
  legitimacy-justice fallacy, 197–200
  normative framework, 195–6
  path dependence, 189, 194–5
  political v substantive equity, 193–5
  pragmatism, 166–7
  procedural justice, 8–9, 162–6, 192–7
  sovereign duty, 161, 163–4
Ireland:
  17th century
    Catholic uprising, 27–8
    colonialism, 22–3, 33
    confiscated Catholic land, 3, 7, 18–19, 20
    excise, 17, 19, 34
  NWT use, 270
  state aids, 58, 66, 68, 71
  tax haven, 61
Italy, 90

James, S, 4
James I, 25
justice:
  categories, 263
  concepts, 36, 37–46, 155, 166, 263
  economic *see* economic justice
  fundamental concern, 262–3
  legal *see* legal justice
  procedural justice, 8–9, 162–6, 192–7
  Rawls, 157–8, 162
  tax *see* tax justice
Juxon, W, 28

Kalven, H, 137
Kaplow, L, 105–6
Kelsey, J, 95
Knott, A, 268
Kolm, S-C, 38
Krygier, M, 41
Kuźniacki, B, 267–8

Lahey, K, 95–6
Lang, J, 39–40
law merchant, 24–5

Index 285

legal certainty:
  clarity, 43–4
  constancy, 44
  Hillen incentive and, 53, 56
  legal justice and, 35, 36, 43–4
  NWT and, 271–2
  precision, 43
  principle, 41
legal equality:
  core principle, 35
  Hillen incentive and, 48, 56
  legal justice and, 42–3
  meaning, 222
legal justice:
  concept, 40–6
  Hillen incentive and, 47–8, 54
  legal certainty, 35, 36, 43–4
  legal equality, 42–3
  morality of law, 41
  objectives, 36
  principles, 42–5
  transparency and, 36, 44–5
legality principle, 40, 130
Leggatt Report (2001), 7, 244–5
Levin, CM, 61, 62, 64
liberalism, 84–5
Lind, Y, 3, 4, 9
Lindhal, L, 85
litigants in person:
  Equal Treatment Bench Book, 255–6
  General Commissioners and, 249
  Leggatt Report on, 245
  meaning, 248
  Tax Chamber, 3, 7, 241, 248
    case management, 250–1
    hearings, 251–4
    jurisdiction issues, 256–9
    previous system and, 256
    seizure of excise goods, 257–9
Locke, J, 162
Luhmann, N, 59
Luxembourg, 58, 65, 66, 68
LuxLeaks, 65

McCain, J, 60–1, 63, 70, 72, 74
McCarthy, T, 266
McCredie, B, 165
machine learning, 272
Maclaurin, J, 268
Malaysia, 165
Mariana, J de, 28
Marshall, TH, 123

maximin criterion, 157–8, 162
Maynwaring, R, 28
medical care, 101–2, 108, 110
Mehrorta, A, 172
Merula, P, 25
Microsoft, 60
migrants
  see also citizenship
  citizenship and, 3, 117–21
  commodifying immigration, 145–7
  democracy and, 121–3
  fiscal citizenship, 128–9
  fungible labour, 148–51
  globalised world, 175
  international tax justice and, 160
  investors, 145–7
  skilled emigrants, 148
  skilled immigrants, 147–8
  tax discrimination, 229
  tax fairness, 4, 136–8
  US policy, 133–52
  voting rights, 121–3
  wealth and capital, 138–44, 176
Mill, JS, 38
Miller, D, 37
Miller, D, 104
Mirrlees Review, 14
Monir, N, 4
Montesquieu, C de, 43, 274
morality of law, 41, 43, 52
Mosquera Valderrama, I, 165
multinationals:
  EU state aids, 66–9
  fairness discourse, 57–8
  international tax justice and, 161
  tax avoidance, 7, 73–6, 178
  US and UK tax hearings, 58, 59–65
  values, 73
Murphy, L, 12, 111–13, 172
Musgrave, RA and PB, 159, 160, 161

Nagel, T, 12, 111–13, 171, 172, 173
National Audit Office, 224–5
natural justice, 5, 17, 20–6, 30–2, 33
neoliberalism, 81–2, 91, 95
Netherlands:
  17th century excise, 21
  Hillen incentive *see* Hillen incentive
  right to silence, 208–9
  state aids, 58, 66, 68
  welfare state, 89
neural networks, 268, 270, 273–7

286　*Index*

neutral taxation:
　Europe and, 97–8
　growth and, 82, 90–1
　Nordic dual income tax paradox, 93–4
　tax base issue, 92–3
　utilitarianism and, 158
New Wave Technologies:
　AI interpretation of law, 267–8
　benefits, 262, 269–73
　biases, 275–6
　big data, 262, 264–5, 266
　components, 261–2, 264–7
　computing power, 262, 265, 266
　data analytics, 262, 265–6, 266
　efficiency, 272–3
　errors, 273–4
　lack of data, 276
　legal certainty and, 271–2
　over-reliance on machines, 273–4
　oversight issue, 277
　poor data and, 274–6
　regulating, 278–80
　　framework, 279
　　regulatory body, 278
　　sandbox approach, 279–80
　risks, 273–7
　tax administration application, 263–4, 273
　tax compliance gap and, 269–71
　taxpayers' rights and, 277
　transparency issue, 276–7
New Zealand:
　digitalisation of tax, 228
　NWT and tax, 270, 272–3, 277
　structural adjustment program, 95
NGOs, 160, 164
Niblett, A, 268, 272
Nordic tax systems, 89, 90, 93–4, 120, 124
Nuffield Foundation, 223

Occupy movement, 65
OECD:
　AI Tax Treaty Assistant and, 267
　BEPS project *see* BEPS project
　data analytics: definition, 265
　developing country representation, 3, 8–9,
　　188–9
　Going for Growth, 91
　international tax justice and, 156, 161, 164, 188
　legitimacy-justice fallacy, 199–200
　Model Tax Convention, 189–90, 217
　NAEC, 82
　opaque institutions, 165
　tax competition and, 65, 145–6, 193, 199

Office of National Statistics (ONS), 223–4, 225
Office of Tax Simplification (OTS), 224, 225,
　　227, 228
older people:
　critical tax theory, 4, 221–39
　digital technology and, 5, 222
　　previous scholarship, 223–8
　　rectifying problems, 235–6
　　scams, 236–7
　tax and
　　abandonment, 232–3
　　access issues, 233–4
　　critical theory, 229
　　double discrimination, 238
　　empirical findings, 231–8
　　errors, 233–4
　　forms, 236
　　lack of resources, 231–2
　　rectifying online problems, 235–6
　　research methods, 230
　　scams, 236–7
　　self-assessment methods, 234–5
　　tax codes, 232–3
　　theoretical framework, 228–9
　UK demography, 223–4
oligarchs, 138–9
optimal tax theory, 81–2, 90, 92–3, 97, 107, 158
Ordower, H, 3, 4, 10
Ormond, Duke of, 18–19, 20, 34
Oxfam, 65, 160
Ozai, I, 3, 8–9

Paris Agreement (2015), 97
Parker, H (Philo-Dicaeus), 32–3
path dependence, 189, 194–5
Paul, R, 62, 75
Peel, R, 243
Pendergast, WR, 164–5
Perrou, K, 3, 4, 7
Personal Tax Accounts (PTAs), 222, 227, 237
Petition of Right, 27
Petty, W:
　biography, 17–18
　Irish lands, 18
　natural law, 17, 20–1
　Treatise of Taxes and Contributions (1662), 17
　　assessment, 32–4
　　case for excise, 20–2
　　context, 18–20
Philippines, 165
Philo-Dicaeus (Henry Parker), 32–3
philosophical tropes, 6–7
Pistone, P, 220

Index 287

Pitt, W, 242
political discourse: fairness, 57–9, 71–3
Portugal: welfare state, 90
positivism, 74–5
prerogative powers, 22, 24, 25, 26
prisoners' dilemma, 194
private and family life, 212, 213, 214, 215
procedural justice, 8–9, 162–6, 192–7
property rights:
    Grotius, 24–5
    securing, 101, 102, 103, 105, 106
proportional taxation:
    core principle, 35, 56
    Rawls, 102, 106–7
public finance:
    disgrace, 101–2, 110–13, 114
    tax and, 4–5
    United States, 101–2
public goods:
    differences, 103–6
    disgrace, 7, 13, 101–2, 114
    financing, 105–10
        broken federal systems, 109–10
        developed countries, 108–10
        developing countries, 107–8
        disgrace, 110–13
        near-framework goods, 108
        tax aversion, 108–9
    framework goods, 101
    meaning, 103–6
Pym, J, 28

race discrimination, 222, 229, 275–6
race to the bottom, 92, 145, 151
Radbruch, G, 46
Rawls, J:
    Difference Principle, 104
    endowment taxation, 162–3
    international tax justice and, 162–3
    justice as fairness, 162
    maximin rule, 157–8, 162
    procedural theory, 8
    proportionate taxation, 102, 106–7
    reflective equilibrium, 163–4
    state approach, 71
redistributive justice, 12, 39–40, 51, 55, 82–3,
        87, 88, 91, 92, 97, 98, 159, 164
Reinhart, N, 21
relative justice, 6, 7
religious discrimination, 222
Rich, N, 27–8
Rosenzweig, A, 161
rule of law, 2, 9, 13, 40–1, 42, 43, 206, 218, 276

Sabel, C, 173
Sadiq, K, 165
Sawyer, A, 165, 228
scams, 236–7
Schantz-Haig-Simons income, 86, 87, 93
scholasticism, 21–2
Selden, J, 25
self-assessment, 222, 232–3, 234–6, 238, 243,
        253, 255
self-incrimination, privilege against, 207–12
Šemeta, A, 68
Sen, A, 7, 166
separation of powers, 274
sexual orientation, 222, 229
Shanske, D, 7, 13
ship money, 27, 29, 30, 34
silence, right to, 207–12
Singapore, 270
Smith, A, 6, 10, 84, 158, 166
Snape, J, 5
social contract theory, 3, 88–9, 162, 169,
        172–5, 180, 182–3
Social Development Goals, 97
Social Entitlement Chamber (SEC), 252, 254
social justice:
    fiscal cultures and, 83–4
    growth and, 81–99
    welfare state tax principles, 87–90
social network analysis (SNA), 271
solidarity, 40, 83, 126
Sommerville, J, 30
sovereignty see state sovereignty
Spain, 21, 26, 27–8, 90
Special Commissioners, 243–4
Starbucks, 57–8, 60, 61, 62, 63, 66, 68, 72, 75
state:
    coercive power, 171–4, 181
    loyalty-based/equality model, 171, 181, 184–5
    market/exit-based state, 171, 181–5
    promotion of justice, 169–70
    social contract theory, 3, 88–9, 162, 169,
        172–5, 180, 182–3
    sovereignty see state sovereignty
    state-centered approaches, 4
    utilitarian model, 170, 180–1
state aids, 58, 66–9, 71, 73
state sovereignty:
    17th century excise and, 21, 22–3, 33–4
    equality v markets, 170–1, 175–85
    EU taxation and, 72–3
    fragmented sovereignty, 176–8
    globalised world and, 169–71, 174–8
    international tax regime and, 159

288   *Index*

sovereign duty, 161, 163–4
tax competition and, 175–9, 184–5
taxation and, 171–5
statistical techniques, 266
Steuerle, E, 262
Strachan, V, 244
structural adjustment programs, 94–6
Suarez, F, 22, 28
subsidies, 35, 68, 91, 145
Summers, B, 4
Süssmilch, J, 266
sustainable development, 96–9
Swales, I, 64
Sweden:
1991 tax reform, 92, 93–4, 96
fiscal citizenship, 129, 131
gender neutrality, 124–5, 127
informal citizenship, 119, 124–5, 127–8
minorities, 124
municipal taxation, 130
tax bases, 92, 93–4
welfare state, 89, 124–8
Swift, A, 37
Switzerland, 207–8, 215

tax avoidance:
anti-avoidance rules, 43
BEPS mandate, 58, 204
effects, 13
EU and, 57, 58, 59, 70–1, 72–3, 73–6
legality, 75
multinationals, 7, 59–65, 178
tax justice mantra, 203
US taxes, 143–4
tax bases, 92–3
Tax Chamber:
case categorisation, 247–8
creation, 241, 245–6
litigants in person, 3, 7, 241, 248
case management, 250–1
Equal Treatment Bench Book, 255–6
hearings, 251–4
jurisdiction issues, 256–9
previous system and, 256
older people and, 235
previous system, 241–4
comparisons, 256
General Commissioners, 241, 242–3, 244, 249
litigants in person, 249, 256
Special Commissioners, 243–4
procedures, 246–7
public law jurisdiction, 257, 259

representatives, 246, 248
seizure of excise goods, 257–9
tax competition:
benefits for some, 175–85
developing countries, 155–6
EU and, 68, 77, 192
globalisation and, 170
investor immigrants, 145–7
non-sustainability, 98
OECD and, 65, 145–6, 193, 199
race to the bottom, 92, 151
tax compliance gap, 269–71
tax havens, 61, 177, 191–2
Tax Help for Older People, 221, 222–3, 224–5, 230–9
tax justice:
ability to pay *see* ability to pay
alternatives, 158
arguments, 2–5
binary debate, 1–2, 3
campaigning, 13–14
concepts, 1–2, 6–8, 39–40
balancing, 45–6
core principles, 35, 40–6
fair distribution, 36, 39
content, 8–13
contextualisation, 9–10
disciplinary background, 11
distributive justice, 156–62
early doctrines, 84–5
horizontal and vertical equity, 10, 85–7, 136–8, 151–2
national v cosmopolitan, 3–4
Nordic scholarship, 120
political positions, 11–13
procedural justice, 8–9, 162–6, 192–7
procedures and outcomes, 8–9
progressive/regressive, 136–8
relative justice, 6, 7
shared values, 13
state/taxpayer relationship, 2–3
Tax Justice (NGO), 160
tax neutrality *see* **neutral taxation**
tax subsidies, 35, 68, 91, 145
Tax Volunteers, 222
Taxman, 266
Teubner, G, 59, 75–6
Thailand, 165
Thomas, R, 3, 7
Thomson Reuters, 268
Tipke, K, 40
transparency:
EU Tax Transparency Package, 69

Index 289

legal justice and, 36, 44–5
New Wave Technologies and, 276–7
trust and, 44, 45
tribunals:
Administrative Appeals Chamber, 254
administrative tribunals, 7
law reform, 245
Leggatt Report, 244–5
previous tax tribunal system, 242–4
Social Entitlement Chamber, 252, 254
Tax Chamber *see* Tax Chamber
unified tribunal service, 245–7
structure of tax tribunals, 245–6
Trump, D, 134

United Kingdom:
conservative tax system, 14
demography, 223–4
digitalisation of tax, 228
Equality Act (2010), 222
excise *see* excise: 17th century
litigants in person *see* litigants in person
NWT and tax, 270, 277
PAC hearings, 57–8, 59–65, 66, 75
fairness debate, 63–5, 72
state/taxpayer relationship, 3
tax appeals *see* Tax Chamber
taxation of older people, 221–39
tribunals *see* tribunals
welfare state, 89
United Nations: global tax governance and, 196
United States:
data protection, 218
digitalisation of the economy, 167
federal system, 110
health care, 101, 110
immigration policy, 133–6
fungible labour, 149–51
skilled immigrants, 147–8
tax fairness, 136–8
unauthorised immigrants, 150–1
NWT and tax, 270
public finance disgrace, 101–2, 110–11, 114
Senate PSI hearings, 58, 59–65, 66, 74–5
fairness debate, 63–5, 72
social divisions and tax, 229
social provision, 13, 101
state aids and, 67, 71
Swiss agreement, 215
tax avoidance, 143–4
tax policy
basis of liability, 119

discrimination, 136
fungible immigrant labour, 149–51
immigrant investors, 145–7
negative income tax, 149–50
regressivity, 136–8
skilled immigrants, 147–8
wealth and capital, 138–44
worldwide jurisdiction, 146–7, 167
**Universal Declaration of Human Rights
(1948),** 205
utilitarianism, 84, 158, 159, 170, 179, 180–1

van Apeldoorn, L, 165
VAT, 92, 137–8, 140, 149, 270, 271, 276
veil of ignorance, 162, 163
Vestager, M, 67, 68, 69
Victor, 271
Vietnam, 165
von Groddeck, V, 73
Vording, H, 4, 5, 7

Wagshal, U, 89–90
Walker, B, 7
Ward, M, 3, 4, 5, 7, 10
wealth taxes, 87, 96, 97, 140–1
welfare programmes:
ability to pay and, 40, 87
deservingness, 5
disgrace, 7, 13, 101–2
fiscal culture and, 4, 82, 83–4
gender neutrality, 124–5
growth v social justice, 81–99
Nordic states, 125–8
redistributive justice, 3, 88
social citizenship, 125–8
social contract theory, 88–9
social justice tax principles, 87–90
structural detaxation and, 95–6
typology, 89–90
Welwood, W, 25
Wentworth, Lord, 28
Wicksell, K, 85, 102, 105–6
Williamson, J, 34
Winters, JA, 138–9
Wittgenstein, L, 103
World Bank, 95

Yoon, A, 268
York, Duke of, 34
YouTube, 273

Zelenak, L, 126, 129–30

Lightning Source UK Ltd.
Milton Keynes UK
UKHW020636140622
404400UK00004B/391